CRAZY

BY

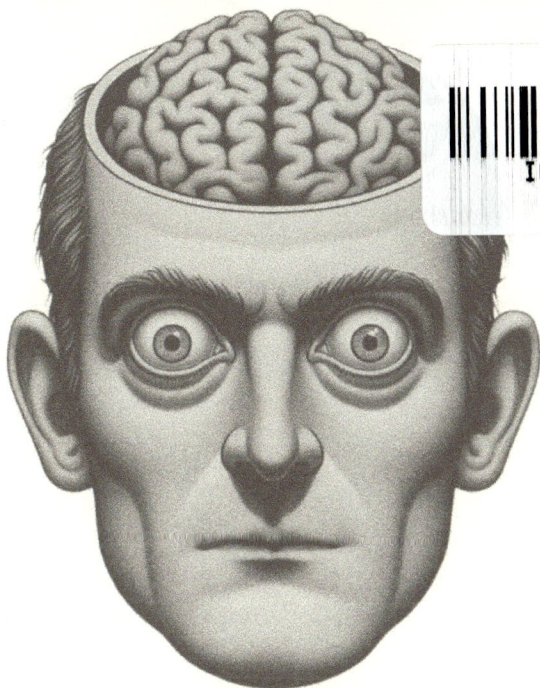

A NOVEL
BY

CHRIS
COOPER

CONSCIOUS

.

ISBN: 978-1-960882-16-5

Front cover image/interior design by:

ANXIETY DRIVEN GRAPHICS

AP

1. The Waste Land

The car crawls over the rumble strips along the highway, thumping on each rivet; gravel sprays, pecking against the undercarriage before it creeps to a stop on the shoulder. The reflective Exit 36 sign stands only a few feet down on the opposite side of the road, bedecked with large Starbucks and Panera logos, indicating that rich, overpriced, indulgent coffee and luxurious pigeon-portioned food are only a mile away. Dennis rolls down the windows, letting the mild spring air swim through the cabin and waft through his thinning hair. The warm, familiar breeze reminds him of being a guileless child with a full head of locks, playing with action figures outside in the same cool weather, a carefree existence, before the damage. He remembers the sunshine being much warmer, the colors more vibrant, and everything being so much brighter.

Sitting in the driver's seat, Dennis peers into the side mirror, his eyes lost in the reflection of the livid sky, searching for flashes of setting daylight amongst the sullen clouds. Intermittent amber rays pierce through the darkened nebula like glimmers of hope, diminishing with each passing moment, mirroring his fading optimism. Closing his eyes, taking in a slow, calculated breath, he recalls simpler times, like when he was five years old. The strands of his bowl-cut flapped in the wind as he slid down the slide of his miniature Mickey Mouse playhouse in the backyard. Uncompromised and full of vigor, content with just an imagination and pleasant weather; welcoming sunlight eliciting goosebumps as he pretended to be a vigilant pirate, soaring into imaginary foes with his dented plastic sword, waiting for his mom to bring him a peanut butter and jelly sandwich. His only concern being whether she remembered to cut the crusts off. He still remembers what it was like to be excited for endless possibilities and the future, being a grown-up, autonomous.

Reclining in the driver's seat, his breath stained with overtones of Jameson, his belly burning from the whiskey, a poignancy prodding his insides, he ponders the simplification of existence. Its process, likening life to a compacted metamorphosis: being born as fresh, malleable clay, easily impressionable, soft, and new; molds subjected to influences, numerous experiences, and life's vicissitudes. Each event pushing and pressing, affecting development and formation over time, shaping sediments and sentiments. Major life incidents and noteworthy moments, people coming and going, all carving impressions and leaving marks; casts sculpted and manipulated, affected by societal pressure and social impact, forged creations.

And eventually, the plaster ages and dries. It isn't as pliable, no matter how much force is applied. It's rigid and unwelcoming, an irrevocable shape. After a while, it's obvious: it's no longer unaffected clay. No, it's not what it used to be. It's hardened, hollowed with memories, tarnished by tribulations, calloused and cold, coarsened and old. And no dosage of sunlight can thaw the bitter; no amount of care can cure the cracks. Nothing seems to give anymore. Everything is heavy, because it's fucking stone.

"Did you hear? Mr. Clauden killed himself?" Dennis imagines the whispered question slipping from miniature mouths at school tomorrow, kids running rampant through the hallways of St. Vincent's, a private institution in an affluent part of northern New Jersey.

He ponders who they would get to replace him as an AP English teacher and if they'd fill his role immediately or whether they even could. Perhaps they'll cancel school in the wake of the tragedy. Flashing a wry smile and rolling his eyes in indifference, Dennis considers whether his suicide will truly be a tragedy or whether the bigger catastrophe is the way his life is turning out: a failed writer with a chasmic void who became a high school English teacher, teaching pompous, privileged white kids Shakespeare and the difference between "there," "they're," and "their." Yeah, he went from crafting gripping story arcs and developing characters with promising aspirations to taking attendance and advocating for the use of the fucking Oxford comma, obsessing over proper punctuation as a righteous cause.

Unhappy, or a "temporary stasis" is what the therapist called his disquietude before he stopped attending, realizing he didn't need to be analyzed by the hour, shelling out $180 a session to find out he was harboring resentment and dissatisfaction. Dennis knows he doesn't need to go broke to discover that his fiancée leaving him years ago is the catalyst for his perpetual dejection, an impetus for his thrownness and inability to adapt, mired in a perennial sense of sadness.

Grimacing, Dennis pictures his psychiatrist's fixated beady eyes, leering over with a perplexed look, probing with personal questions to elicit subconscious bullshit as the corpulent shill jots down copious notes, breathing heavily as he scribes. He hates how the incel fuck made a profit off his misery, dissecting his behaviors and proclivities like a lab rat, reducing his depersonalization to a clinical paragraph and a need for meditation along with a variety of overprescribed SSRIs.

And perhaps if he continued with treatment a little longer, maybe if he paid more out of pocket, he'd be able to deconstruct the new recurring dream he's been having. It's not the one where he's in grade school and someone's stolen his lunch, so he's probably going to starve. No, it's a new one where he's a personified sentence being chased by a possessed period brandishing a knife. Running through lines, dispersing words carelessly, he can't stop because the period persists, aggressively swiping at his back with a prodigious blade, trying to stab him. Fitfully, he'll turn back to gauge how far the period is, but it's always right on his tail, grinding its teeth in a rage with a manic facial expression; the animated punctuation mark slashing at the air, always just missing him. Yeah, he can't even imagine what's simmering in his unconscious mind; he wakes up every morning with a nervous vigor, but he reckons it's better than drinking coffee for that initial jolt of energy, a more holistic solution, instead of relying on the manipulation of neurotransmitters to eliminate his mental fatigue. Sometimes, a fluttering heartbeat is the only thing that reminds him that he's not dead.

Dennis hates how many years he spent in school, actually paying attention. He detests how many hours he spent devoted to reading, writing, and trying to perfect his writing prowess. He gets nauseous when he thinks about all the fatuous minutes dedicated to remembering newly learned vocabulary words, packing his mind with meaningless clusters of consonants. He loathes all the empowering TED talks packed with positive reinforcement he ingested in pursuit of nourishment for his blighted ego, the soliloquies about manifesting something positive. And he's convinced there's no such thing as karma. He knows he's just been conditioned to believe things happen for a reason, that people get what they put into the world, but he finally grasps the sentiment, how it's purely a placating platitude, quasi-fatalist nonsense recited by vacuous individuals to ease the sting of disappointment; the type of people that like their own posts on social media for self-validation.

Dennis likens life more to the *Fast & Furious* movies: a series that first brought exhilaration and enjoyment, a promising story that hooked with entertainment, memorable characters, a sequel to look forward to, until they just kept fucking coming. One after the other, evolving with new subtitles and identical personalities with just different names, each rendition worse than the previous, declining plots with tired, recycled storylines. And after ten installments, you've finally had enough. Vin Diesel is a soundboard of fraternity cliches, Paul Walker is still dead, and you just want it to fucking stop; you've seen enough. It's insipid, fucking mind-numbing, enough to make you go Oedipus Rex style on yourself, the gouging of eyes, not the having sex with your own mother part.

It's 8 P.M. exactly; the sky is clear from rolling opaque clouds, now blanketed with the sable hue of nightfall. The low-lit lamp posts line the sides of the highway, appearing six feet apart; their fuses warming as the dull lighting begins to spotlight portions of the street. Dennis finally steps out of the car, stretching out his arms like a relief pitcher being sent in to close the game, despite it being a losing effort. Rapid winds from fleeting vehicles brush against his face, forcing him to cower and brace, sending chills up his spine. He envisions being struck by an onward vessel, picturing his body clobbered, dense tissue smacking against the front of an oversized truck, packs of meat and flesh permanently embedded in its brilliant chrome grill.

Gazing across the broken white lines that run along the freeway, Dennis tries to muster up the temerity to launch himself onto the road. Glints from the distant oncoming headlights command his attention, but he resists, standing steadfast on the shoulder as he teeters, recalling the novel he's written, the 110,000-word manuscript he poured his heart into that was never going to be read. He wonders if maybe he should post one last story to his Instagram, even if he'll never get to see who viewed it.

His spirit is crushed, but it wasn't his fiancée Renee that quashed his optimism; no, it was the publishing industry that destroyed him, vanquished by the condescending pitching and selling process, the propositioning of literary agents, the posturing that went with solicitation. From drafting customized, ingratiating query letters to stroke agent egos, figurative fellatio in exchange for representation, each query letter chipped away at his spirit, cauterizing his sanity and aspirations. He's mulled over all the interminable time he put into researching each agent, studying interests and dislikes by inspecting their Twitter accounts, trying to establish common ground, and the innumerable hours spent drafting overzealous letters to spark intrigue.

And somewhere after fifty query rejections, Dennis realized the partiality of the industry, how his transgressive story stood no chance in a hyper-sensitive, progressive time. Marginalized for not being marginalized, he's even looked for loopholes in the patronizing calls for submissions that are ubiquitous on publishers' websites for "indigenous writers" and "underrepresented voices," thinking it might help that his 23andMe DNA test lists 5% African ancestry despite his low melanin levels. And maybe his disregard for those inner monologues suggesting he kill himself might constitute the silencing of a particular demographic, those seem to be suppressed, "underrepresented" voices, even if they're the ones inside his own head. He debated answering a call for "queer authors" by including an anecdote with his entry about how he once clicked on an ad about "local singles in his area wanting to fuck." It brought him to a gay porno website, and he wasn't entirely turned off.

But he knows he needs to compromise, comply with subjugation if he ever really wants a chance at being published. He'll need to revamp his narrative with trendy social conformities, changing his protagonist to a gender-fluid pansexual vegan with preferred pronouns in they/their Instagram bio and developing his plot with archetypal non-heterosexual supporting characters and interracial relationships. He'll need to weave in popular keywords, like systemic racism, equity, and climate change, and incorporate allusions to the pervasive patriarchy and the evils of capitalism to check all the buzzworthy boxes ingrained in the publishing industry's Manuscript Wish List.

It's not like he doesn't support any of the concepts either, absolutely not; he too hates how he has to sell himself every day, providing his academic services for compensation so he can survive. He once signed a circulating petition on Facebook to tax Jeff Bezos up to 70%, and he keeps his driving to a minimum to reduce carbon emissions. And most importantly, he even shared a black square on Instagram to defeat police brutality and/or white supremacy since he knows the only way to defeat the evils of racism and capitalism is to scold an entire population based on their skin color and monetize literature for profit.

But Dennis decided a long time ago he'd rather die than wash his story with vapid marketed wokeness, the commercial exploitation of social justice that serves no purpose in actually enhancing the story. And he's contrived a hundred reasons why he hasn't been published, all except for the possibility that he's not a good enough writer. Perhaps his writing skills are remedial, but he's not ready to admit his possible shortcomings. He could have considered self-publishing, accepting a participation trophy for temporary validation; he's pretty sure his Aunt Margaret would have written him a stellar review on Amazon, since she still sends him an electronic birthday card every year, but his problem has always been that he's intrinsically motivated.

"Fuck you, Kelly Watters," he shouts before flipping off an approaching car, recounting the name of the pasty, omniscient literary agent who declined his manuscript after reading the first three chapters.

The horn sounds several times as the SUV scurries by, rocking Dennis and his car with momentum. Discernible stick figure decals of a mom, dad, and two girls with purple bows are emblazoned in the lower right corner of the rear window as the vehicle hastens, accelerating as it passes. He hopes little Suzy asks mommy over the blaring Kidz Bop radio why there's a lunatic on the side of the road yelling and flourishing middle fingers.

An overbearing madness engulfs him like an incessant wave, shoving his head underwater as he struggles to breathe. It's a ceaseless battle he's convinced he just can't endure any longer, a tiresome war that exhausts him. He's been unraveling for some time now; the malicious voice in his head growing louder, more strident, and more audacious, flooding him with negativity and existential pessimism that obsesses over every little detail, finding faults in every nook.

"Kill yourself, you worthless piece of fucking shit," the deafening voice echoed on his way to school today as he considered letting the wheel take over.

He pictured himself veering off onto a better path, perhaps off a bridge, plunging into the silencing waters, inhaling undercurrents like Virginia Woolf. Dennis often romanticizes drowning, how there's something so serene about sinking into the currents, drifting off into a darkened abyss. It's a meditative descent until your body eventually convulses with autonomic gasps for breath, regardless of your desire to live or not. And it's really the only way to silence his internal critic, the voice that pokes, reminding him of his mistakes and inferiorities. He imagines he wouldn't hear much as he swallowed swells of water, overwhelming his lungs, depriving him of oxygen. He's even tried lashing out, arguing with strangers in the comment sections on social media, but that relief is only transitory, even when he constructs a cogent, compelling rebuttal to whatever topic.

Nothing seems to assuage his anxiety now that his girlfriend Christine is moving out and he has to move back home, since he can't afford to rent on his own. A barely solvent twelfth-grade English teacher who can't make enough money nor hold a healthy relationship, he's thirty-four years old, newly single, and living back home with his fucking parents. He never thought he'd ever have to move back in with his mom and dad, and he can't even fathom how crippling his living arrangements are going to be for his dating life, but none of that matters once you're dead, he tells himself.

Gaping directly across the lanes of the highway, Dennis focuses on the dark conifers that border the road, towering silhouettes that remind him of Bob Ross's happy trees. Burping up whiskey bubbles in between his smiles, he recalls watching *The Joy of Painting* on his couch when he was eight or nine. Tears roll from his eyes, falling like helpless raindrops; he remembers what life was like before the pressure of achieving goals and reaching milestones ate his soul away.

Unrelenting vehicles speed past as he marvels at their force, way above the designated sixty-five miles per hour speed limit, the impressive velocity and impact causing him to sway. He's not going to commit a Hemingway and put the barrel of a shotgun in his mouth, pulling the trigger to unleash the final flesh confetti; no, that's too crass, unbecoming. And he's not going to pull a Plath either and stick his head in the oven, building up carbon monoxide in his bloodstream, poisoning, depleting his body of red blood cells and oxygen; no, that's too banal, lackluster. No, he's going for a more understated ending, more dignified and ambiguous, like a great cliffhanger. He's going to make it look like he pulled over to fix his tire, and whether he slips, stumbles, or a driver loses sight of the road momentarily, Dennis will meet his demise from a careening mid-sized car, preferably one with a "Co-Exist" bumper sticker. It's the only respectable way to go since he decided that an accident would be a little softer on his family.

"These fragments I have shored against my ruins," he whispers.

A crisp draft dances along his forearms, the cold air becoming more perceptible with decreasing daylight. A shiver skips along his skin, evoking a deeper nostalgia, an imperceivable pain, the haunting of halcyon days when he'd sit with Renee, enjoying their morning coffee together on a random September morning. A heaviness encroaches his chest, creating a vacuum of breath. Dennis thinks of Christine and how he never apologized for wasting her time during the past few years of their relationship; an engraved memory of her sobbing as she cleaned out their apartment flashes before his eyes.

He pivots back to Renee, the reigning antagonist of his story, thinking how unfazed she's going to be by his death, imagining her sitting in a cozy breakfast nook adjacent to her bald husband, reading about his fatality in the newspaper. The portrayal elicits an embedded sorrow, a sensation where he can still feel the pieces of his broken heart, the burning of cutting shards still lodged, each sharp serrated edge stinging in his chest. And F. Scott Fitzgerald said, "There are no second acts in American lives," Dennis recalls, or some similar quote, a sentiment about there being no second chances or redos, attempting to convince himself to leap. A fleeting idea crawls into his mind, wondering if he should pray, maybe ask God for guidance, but he denies the suggestion since he hasn't talked to imaginary characters since he was a kid.

Ambling to the back of the car, present with each harrowing step against the pavement, Dennis sponges away at damp eyelashes with the back of his hands. The softening sole of his faux leather Oxfords buckles against the rigid road; it's that time of the year when he should reorder the same cognac Calvin Klein shoes from Amazon, returning the old, worn pair for a refund, a free renewal. But he's got a final task to complete instead, one that doesn't involve return theft, scamming retailers by taking advantage of their inattentive merchandise examination or their inability to notice a yearly customer's pattern of ordering and returning the same pair of shoes.

Dennis opens the trunk of his four-year-old matte black Infiniti, averting his eyes from the egregious seven-inch dent on his bumper from when he was high and backed up into a telephone pole in the abandoned parking lot of a Taco Bell months ago. He pushes his golf clubs aside to retrieve the concealed jack and spare tire; his TaylorMades are barely used. Exhaling an apprehensive breath, acquiescing to never breaking a ninety on eighteen, Dennis ambles back toward the front of the car with the jack in his hand. He doesn't even know how to change a flat tire or where to begin, but he doesn't think anyone will know he was incapable. He figures he'll need to remove at least one or two lug nuts to make it believable, at least make it look like he started changing the tire before he was hit. But he hasn't a fucking clue how to do it or what tool he even needs.

Dragging his feet with weighted reluctance, he catches the reflection of the streetlights on the side of his sleek sedan, a spiraling glow highlighting swirling scratches from frequent car washes. He realizes his next move is to puncture a hole in the car's tire for authenticity, otherwise his death may appear manufactured to investigators. And the car is so fucking expensive, he laments; he put $12,000 down to purchase it, and he's not sure if he can really bring himself to damage his tire. Listless, standing and staring at the left rear rim, Dennis holds the powder-coated jack in his hands across his body like an axe, unsure of the proper handling; a sundry of book reports sitting on his desk floats into his mind, the summer reading assignments still needing to be graded.

His stomach growls as he looks up, deflecting, noticing the gleaming green exit sign; the abstract emblem depicting a comforting woman, a maternal figure, reaching out with open arms to console him with hugs and pricey finger foods. Panera sounds delicious, and he's thinking killing himself on an empty stomach isn't a good way to go out. It may cause extra gastrointestinal issues and possibly ruin his organs since he's an organ donor. People on Death Row even have a last meal, cold-blooded killers, far worse individuals than himself, he thinks, dreaming about the "You Pick Two" option at Panera and how he always gets the butternut squash soup and turkey bravo sandwich. And although he always leaves hungry, he can't help but return once a week for partial satiation, racking up Panera reward points toward his next purchase.

"Fucking shit," he whispers, rubbing his chest with a soothing palm, holding the car jack like a back scratcher, dangling over his shoulder.

Wincing, a psychosomatic pain, Dennis has to do this, he reassures himself; there isn't any other way. And he isn't depressed with a "woe is me" perspective, the type of intellectually inferior despondency shared by confused young adults or attention-seeking lummoxes who can't bear to live life without a purpose or social acceptance; it's quite the contrary, he deduces. His condition is more of a dramatic awakeness, the excruciating pain of hyper self-awareness, understanding the absolute pointlessness of existence, the monotony of living similar days until the culmination of death, recognizing a race without a finish line. And maybe it's his nihilism or displaced existentialism, but he hasn't had a single memory in the past few years that hasn't escaped his hippocampus; he can already see how the rest of his life is going to play out: going to work, swiping on dating apps, and obsessing over the past, inflicted with the memory of his fiancée walking out on him. Eventually, he'll bury his parents, his brothers, and every other person he grew to love, a series of eulogies, living a muted reality, where days and weeks blend into one, a condition of recurring grey. And how can he continue existing in nebulosity, a permanent purgatory, when he's cognizant that the best days of his life have already been lived, he reaffirms.

He looks up again at the taunting exit sign, woozy from the booze, musing at the Medusa-esque Starbucks icon; a caramel macchiato from Starbucks would really hit the spot too, he surmises, imagining sipping on sweet notes of vanilla syrup, wiping the rich, creamy foam away from his top lip. He could probably snag a mobile order from the countertop too, a small one just sitting around; it's not like any of the baristas verify when people pick them up; he might even get lucky and snatch a freshly made pumpkin spice latte. Turning, glimpsing back down the highway as the approaching car beams mesmerize him once again, paralyzing him momentarily, a starry gaze; he considers his aging parents, the impact his death would have on them, forcing them to bury a child. He thinks of his selfless father's tired face, the man working his entire life to provide for his children, only to repay him with a tarnished legacy, the premature death of a son.

Trembling with sorrow, he continues staring at the lustrous sign. Saturated tears distort his view as he recalls a similar vision from when he fell off his bicycle as a child, reluctant to ride without training wheels, his father running behind him to supervise, scooping in, lifting him off the ground every time he fell.

"You can do this," he whispered to Dennis, positioning him back on the bike.

"I don't think I can anymore," Dennis exhales.

"But I won't do this to you."

And perhaps imbibing ample Jameson beforehand is to blame for the maudlin pantomime on the side of the road, he knows; he's always had an affinity for theatrics, dressing up as Batman's nemeses as a kid for the longest time. A penchant for impropriety, Dennis was always drawn to the villains, never donning a superhero's garb, identifying with darkness at an early age. Perhaps he always possessed an inherent sense of self-loathing, or maybe he recognized he wasn't one of the good guys.

But subconsciously, he knows he was never going to commit suicide, especially since he forgot to clear his browser history. No, he's just drunk on the theory of death, sentimentalizing about the end and how serenity, eternal bliss, is always just a step away, an opportunity to stop the sting of rumination and dread. He appreciates the sensory feeling it produces, his nerves rattling as he envisions his mangled body on the pavement like roadkill. It's a giggly intoxication elicited by flirtation with mortality, the nervous energy that swarms his heart; it makes him feel alive.

Sitting at the table in Panera, sleepily gazing at his exorbitant sandwich and toddler-sized bowl of soup, Dennis grasps his phone to see if he has any messages, pretending there's a possibility that someone wants to talk to him. Noticing it's only 8:45 P.M. on a Friday night, he wonders if this is how weekends are going to be from now on without Christine.

Hastily opening Instagram to check who has viewed his story, Dennis indulges in quick dopamine boosts from social media, the pursuit of notifications, hopefully anticipating a message, a like, or some sort of transient alert. He uploaded some stupid picture of the sky earlier at work as if he were profound or an artistic photographer. Fifty-five people have viewed it so far, but Christine isn't one of them. It's mostly strangers, digital acquaintances he's met through arbitrary follows and dating apps, random people, mostly girls that he follows who selected to follow him back. It's only been seven days since their breakup, so he imagines she's going to carry resentment for some time. She'll probably unfollow him on Instagram and remove him on Facebook eventually, just like Renee did.

His Instagram account features mostly thought-provoking pictures of scenery or photos of his food, with the occasional motivational quote to spark intrigue. Dennis debates snapping one of his lavish sandwich, using portrait mode to zoom in on the melted cheese and maybe incorporating a humorous hashtag to go with it, like #itainteasybeingcheesy or #saycheese, but he's not sure he can resist any longer. His stomach grumbles louder than before, demanding to be fed. Despondent inside the dull, desolate Panera atmosphere, Dennis is relieved he doesn't reside anywhere near St. Vincent's; the prospect of running into any of his students makes him queasy.

Sitting at a hexagonal table amidst scattered geometric furniture, an ambiance of fitting shapes, Dennis faces the window to people watch. He wants to get another food item, since his appetite has been insatiable lately, and he knows he'll still be hungry once he leaves, but that looming moment when the cashier spins the tablet around, preloaded with tip options starting at 20%, is enough to make him sick. And he knows he'll give in, forfeiting a dollar, but it sure as hell

18

won't be anywhere near fucking 20% for just taking his order. Still, oppressive tip culture is enough to kill his hunger.

Pushing his feet back and forth against the floor, rubbing his shoes against the low pile commercial carpet, he sinks his teeth into his savory sandwich; the worn leather seat squeaks of his upright chair with each maneuver of his body, the unstable legs chattering every time he leans back. The vacant Panera provides dismal excitement, just an aroma of burnt coffee beans and the strumming of a dull acoustic guitar from the overhead speakers, possibly an old Jack Johnson song. Dennis deduces it's not too popular of a hangout on a Friday night, imagining recently single guys his age should be at boisterous bars or clubs in the city with guy friends, but that isn't him; he's pretty much ruined every single friendship and relationship he ever had.

All the people he ever hung out with were Christine's friends, and before that, it was Renee's friends, since he doesn't have any companions of his own; he's not much of an extrovert, more of an over-thinker. And you would think he'd learn after a while that the friends acquired during a relationship were only temporary, that the drunken conversations and heart-to-hearts shared over an abundance of beers were simply hollow, placatory surface dialogue. But he's always been a sucker for connection, especially since both his brothers are married, rendering them inaccessible to any sort of good-time or reciprocating friendship.

He quickly opens his Tinder app, swiping left and right with an impetuous urge, hoping to ephemerally fill the void of loneliness, abate his current awkward isolation, needing to feel engaged. It's just what he needs to feel better, he decides, reading desperate bios about chasing love and being "ready to settle," knowing that he could potentially meet someone new is just the solace he needs, a short-term mitigation of possibilities, palliative treatment. He wonders how he could have gone from almost getting married to now being on a dating app, how he went

19

from co-owning a home years ago to now moving back in with his parents. Like a classic Greek tragedy, Dennis routinely mulls over his fall from grace.

Gawking blankly into each girl's eyes as they appear across the screen, he needs to find a pair to get lost in. Continuing to swipe like strings on a guitar, as if he is looking for something specific, playing a desperate song, a quest for dark features and a brunette archetype. Deep down he knows exactly what he's really looking for; he's hoping to come across the piercing brown eyes that filled his life years ago. The same distinguished face he had gazed into deeply and repeatedly, longing for the familiar pupils he had looked into when he asked her to spend eternity with him; the ones that linger in his dreams, the same duplicitous eyes and diabolical soul that ruined him.

Unraveling the other half of his sandwich, biting into the crunchy crust, relishing the toasty bread and costly bacon strips that layer the inside, the thought of purchasing a creamy macchiato lingers since Starbucks is probably closing soon. Spicy mustard drips from the corner of his mouth, but Dennis proceeds, consuming his food with primitive etiquette, chewing, stuffing his face with additional bites before swallowing. Shoveling soup into his beak, Dennis slurps from his spoon, never letting his palate become unsatisfied, even at the liquid's piping hot temperature.

It's been over forty months since his last interaction with Renee, when they spotted each other from afar at a golfing range. He's been keeping track, and they stared at each other for at least a minute as Renee shook her head with an anxious smile before Dennis turned away. It was an uninterpretable encounter with no real outcome. Pretending she didn't exist once again, he adopted the Ostrich Syndrome instead of conjuring up the repressed trauma and queries, like when the hell did she take up golf?

And he's been wondering ever since if he's going to come across her again, if they'll ever be in proximity, if they might inadvertently swipe right for each other on one of the inane dating apps. He often debates if she'd talk to him, but he knows she'd never be on a dating app; she'd deem it beneath her, too inorganic, he presumes. But Dennis still finds himself involuntarily fantasizing about her being single even though he's aware she's been married to Carl for a couple of years now. Angina ensues every time he thinks of her with him, the odious troll; his neck constricts, quelling his lungs temporarily, provoking full-blown panic and disgust when he ponders over the reality that she chose a guy named fucking Carl over him, a gross banal name that sounds like a mild stroke every time it's enunciated. Like who really looks at a fucking baby and names it "Carl," he obsesses, shoving the rest of his sandwich into his mouth, devouring his feelings.

Glancing up from his phone, he notices a buxom female collecting trash from a table as she hums a low melody. Shaking his reverie, Dennis smiles automatically; her green apron and coordinating visor command attention, a clear indication she's an employee. She returns the tray to the waste station and ventures by, still thrumming her tune, flashing a warm, inviting smile. Her eyes, a light shade of brown, like pools of honey, light up her face completely; her countenance flushed with a soft pinkish hue, a youthful complexion. He wonders if she is single, contemplating whether he should strike up a conversation, but he finds comfort in his passiveness, lack of action, since social interactions have become too cumbersome for him.

Vibrating on the tabletop, bouncing around, his phone lights up; it's his mother calling. Waves of anxiety flood, currents of concern sinking his heart, conditioned to always imagining an emergency whenever she calls. But she's the last person he really wants to talk to right now, so he quickly hits ignore before returning to his sumptuous sandwich and soup, beset with guilt for not answering.

Opening his Tinder app once again, Dennis reconvenes his insatiable pursuit, swiping for comforting stimulation, numbness, like a pain-stricken patient pressing for more morphine. Fervently swiping on pictures of girls that resemble Renee, Dennis grins with amusement as if he's window shopping. Swiping left and right but mostly right; it's weird not having to hide his phone anymore, still uneasy, as if his breakup with Christine hasn't sunk in yet. Dennis had downloaded both Tinder and Bumble during the last six months of his relationship with Christine, reveling in clandestine interactions with suitors, and although he never slept with anyone, he entertained it. Like a retired athlete, he sought validation in knowing he could still perform, attract a mate, practicing banter, reaffirming he was still capable, which became corroboration he needed to break things off with Christine.

As the caliber of bachelorettes wanes with progressing swipes, Dennis decides it's time to open the Bumble app, which he determines is best used for searching for new long-term relationships, since the quality of girls on Bumble seems to be drastically higher than on Tinder. He wonders how long it will be until these types of apps are shut down for misogyny, since they promote shopping for women like commodities, but he just can't resist. He frequents eCommerce websites all the time, browsing Amazon and adding items to his cart with the click of a button, so he considers the digital dating realm just another form of commerce but with people; each match notification akin to a "proceed to checkout" prompt. And he knows he should probably do some major work on himself before he starts dating again, since he thinks deep down he's incapable of loving, but it's all he's ever known and done, seek intimacy, streams of oxytocin.

"Excuse me, sir, are you finished here?" the budding girl grins, flaunting her delicate features; glistening gentle eyes and florid cheeks brighten her symmetrical face, teased curly locks nestled on her shoulders.

The innate masculine urge to pursue any attractive, friendly female sets in, turning Dennis into a veritable stereotype, as he debates whether this is a good chance to chat her up, but there's only bland small talk floating in his frontal lobe at the moment. She's carrying several trays that she's retrieved from other tables, balancing bowls and silverware.

"Yes. Thank you," he replies, smiling ostentatiously, trying to convey interest with enthusiasm.

He's not sure if he should assist her or just let her do her job. She smiles again, shifting her load to her left arm, flipping her hair with the flick of her free hand; she collects his sandwich wrapper and attempts to stack his utensils in the soup bowl. Glimmers from small ear piercings in her right cartilage catch Dennis's attention; he surveys, perhaps for a tattoo behind her ear, positing she's a wild child. He can't tell if her hybrid legging/slacks are part of her uniform or just a personal choice of style.

"Let me help you take this," Dennis insists as he stands up, aware that she won't be able to carry additional dining items.

"Ugh. Thank you," she replies with a reluctant sigh, like she's disappointed she couldn't do it by herself.

Lurking by her side to the disposal stations, carrying his tray, unable to think of a single thing to say, he can't remember the last time he's even tried to pick up a woman in person. All he's been doing the past few weeks is binge watching Netflix and exchanging frivolous witticisms with women on his apps; his melancholic disposition certainly isn't going to win any dates, he infers. He's not sure if he should ask for her phone number or maybe her Instagram handle, but he can't tell if it's too soon; romantic comedies always make it seem so easy to meet someone in public, two people smiling at each other as if it's some instant calling card for romance, effortlessly exchanging numbers. And maybe that's the implicit part of the comedy, how fucking absurd it is, the way they portray strangers connecting so effortlessly in public.

"So, how long have you been working here?" Dennis inquires, defaulting to interrogation.

He wonders if he should give her a tip, maybe a few dollars, but he realizes he never carries cash, since he's a typical millennial; he debates asking for her Venmo.

"I've never seen you here before."

It's not like he's been to Panera on a Friday before, but he figures it might conceal his attraction.

"Um, like six months now," she replies, smirking, avoiding eye contact as she sorts ceramic bowls and flatware.

Handing her his tray, Dennis loiters, inspecting her peculiarity, perplexed by the lack of transparency. She's vague, equivocal, and he can't decide whether she's immature or completely disinterested. Why isn't there some fucking clear-cut sign, he ponders. He thinks back to psychology class and remembers the most memorable lecture, the one that examined the behaviors of women with attraction and how they usually displayed subconscious signals of interest, like subtle body positioning, directing their feet at a point of interest or an exposure of the wrist, none of which she currently exhibits.

"So um..." Dennis mumbles before a paunchy employee wearing a snug visor and tight apron waddles forward.

"Kirsten, your dad is here to pick you up."

Dennis looks over to the front counter, noticing an older gentleman holding up a pink backpack. Sporting a striped tie and a gray pea coat, the man glances at his phone while dangling the pack by its shoulder straps; he looks like he just got out of work, perhaps still preoccupied with emails. Dennis realizes her dad isn't even that much older than him.

"Hey, Dad. I'll be right there," Kirsten peeps, tossing the remaining garbage before scampering away, halting any further conversation.

Perspiration leaks from Dennis's brow, shaking his head in disbelief; the girl must be younger than seventeen since she can't drive.

"Jesus Christ," Dennis whispers, reproaching, picturing Chris Hansen popping out at any moment, commanding him to "take a seat."

"Sir, we are closing. Are you finished?" the troll pries with an aggressive tone, hanging over the checkout counter.

Sauntering outside, Dennis observes the pert Kirsten hopping into the car with her dad; his black Escalade hums as billows of smoke pour from the exhaust, possibly releasing more carbon emissions than a street in China. Shocked and disturbed, Dennis can't fathom that he's been enticed by a youth and almost attempted to vamp a kid.

Embarrassed, disgusted, and speechless, Dennis idles, realizing he's going to be in for a rude awakening if he's going to ever start dating again. How the fuck is he supposed to know how old girls are; he wonders if there is an app for that, like some sort of face scan; he ponders if it will be appropriate to ask for identification before proceeding with each new interaction.

Dennis's phone vibrates inside his pocket. Retrieving it with apathy, exhaling as he yanks it from his pocket, like it's a fucking pest leaching on him, the host. He proceeds to leer at the Escalade as it pulls out of the parking lot, the $90,000 monstrosity rolling into the road.

"Hello," Dennis utters, his eyes fixated on the exhaust pipes of the luxury utility vehicle, emitting fume lines as it accelerates down the street.

The shrills of his niece and nephew echo as he holds the phone to his ear.

"What's going on, Den?" his brother John mutters.

"Just getting something to eat," Dennis replies, fighting the itching urge to open one of his apps; he debates putting his brother on speakerphone so he can peruse pretty women or check his Instagram story, since reality seems to lose its luster rather fast.

"I'm bringing the kids home from practice, and then I'm taking Reese to a sleepover at her friend's," John murmurs, breathy as if he's in the middle of jumping jacks.

"Do you know what time the dinner for Dad is tomorrow night?" John huffs, exhaling with a frustrated pitch, sounding occupied.

"Did you say you were working out?"

"No, I'm just pulling in the driveway with the kids," the children clearly clamoring in the background, the perceived sounds of Reese singing a familiar Taylor Swift song, the one about never getting back together.

"Then why does it sound like you're fucking jumping rope?" Dennis quips.

"Daddy, I want Frozen," his nephew Jake's voice resounds, followed by a whine that resembles a parakeet being tortured.

"Hey, Reese and Jake, cut it out!" John sneers with a dampened, distant voice, which Dennis attributes to John pulling the phone away from his mouth to turn around and shout at the kids in the backseat.

John isn't the most technologically savvy at forty-four years old, so there is little chance he knows how to set up his phone through the car's Bluetooth capability, Dennis asserts. Their father's birthday weekend is coming up, which is probably why his mother called him earlier; Dennis remembers his mother told him about having a family dinner to celebrate Dad's big day when he dropped off the last of his things at the house. He had turned his key in from the apartment to the landlord earlier that day.

"I think the dinner is at seven," Dennis replies with an interrogative pitch, hoping his brother has also been told the time but just needs a reminder for confirmation.

"Seven o'clock? Jesus, I have to start getting the kids ready for bed by eight," John sighs, the ticking of his blinker sounding.

"I can't really hear you," Dennis exclaims, pulling the phone from his ear, staring at it with contempt, shaking his head.

His older brother is flustered with fatherhood, juggling the kids' extracurricular activities as his illustrious wife works overtime at a multinational investment bank; she's been the bread winner for a few years now, swapping the gender roles of marriage while advancing up the corporate ladder.

"Yeah. I'll be there," Dennis rebuts, gazing up at the tempting Starbucks emblem; a letter board hanging below reads, "Open til 10 P.M." in black italicized letters, eliciting subtle joy.

He shrugs his shoulders, pondering whether getting a latte this late will keep him up to 3 A.M, but then he considers that maybe superfluous caffeine is just what he needs, a deception of adenosine receptors to fool him with the illusion of ambition so he can write. But in actuality, Dennis knows he has a better chance of committing suicide before he tries to write another novel.

"Ok, man. I'll see you there," John bellows before hanging up.

2. Nothing Gold Can Stay

Scampering through the parking lot of the strip mall, Dennis and Renee made their way from the car to the restaurant, fighting the frigid February gusts. The faint aroma of burning wood lingering in the air meant snow was on the horizon. Hunching over, wrapped in their matching scarves and winter coats, they pushed through the unrelenting gale with arms intertwined, clutching each other close to keep warm.

Dennis's nervousness for the night ensued. A fluttering heartbeat persisted with each step, trapping him in his head; perhaps he had messed up some minor detail, like the embossed monogrammed napkins having the wrong initials, even though he checked them 106 times. Or maybe he folded them wrong, he thought to himself. Maybe he forgot to inform the chef about her Aunt Laura's shellfish allergy, and she was going to keel over and die before he could even propose. Her face falling flat into the platter; his negligence completely derailing the evening, turning the night into a family tragedy.

Bunching her face with an adorable expression, scrunched like a cabbage patch doll, Renee scurried along, hugging Dennis's arm tightly, squinting as if a wrinkled visage would shield exposed skin from the blistering winds. Approaching the entrance, they broke from each other's grasp. Dennis held the door open, fixated on Renee's face, anticipating her reaction as she entered the room, a collection of people waiting on her arrival.

"Surprise!" everyone erupted, tossing confetti in the air, arms splaying out with excitement as party horns tootled.

Adorned in a purple cardigan, Renee's mother approached from the audience, filming the arrival on her phone with an elated smile. Kirsten, Renee's best friend from college, who Dennis had flown up from South Carolina to attend, leaped forward in a paisley dress, holding up a medium-sized cut-out sign composed of black block letters spelling "Surprise;" each bold letter spangled with glinting polka dots, identical to the "Thrive" tabletop sitter they had on their bedroom dresser.

The flickering of cameras and hooting filled the room like a red-carpet event, dazing Renee as she covered her mouth in shock, fluttering her eyelashes in disbelief. Her face flushed like a jovial Christmas decoration, her eyes widened with bewilderment, glistening in the light from the sparkling chandeliers overhead. Renee surveyed the room, taking in the droves of familiar faces in attendance. From coworkers to distant cousins, the front of the restaurant was packed with people waiting to surprise her; chairs and tables festooned with balloons and streamers; confetti scattered on the floor as if Tinker Bell had been gutted and following the trail of glimmering paper would lead to her carcass, an appropriate décor addition since Disney was Renee's favorite.

Everyone stood and applauded as a speechless Renee curled, her hands on her hips, laughing as she gathered it in, astounded by the presence of almost everyone she knew. Dennis had been planning her surprise thirtieth birthday party for over eight months, conferring with her parents and friends about how to pair the proposal with the party, since she often remarked how she needed to be engaged before she turned thirty. The pain of missing a societal milestone by the end of early adult age was too much for a quintessential millennial to bear.

He had spared no expense either, working extra hours as an editor so he could incorporate every detail, tailoring the party to Renee's exact style. Providing a coral and taupe color scheme with white and golden hues, an open posh ambiance with lavender-scented plug-ins, reminiscent of the candle they had in their living room. He had checked off every nicety he could think of, since he knew her so well.

"You did this?" Renee exhaled, trying to decipher the entirety of the moment.

Her mouth ajar, her protuberant orbs flittering, an ambiguous gesture, and Dennis couldn't tell whether she was filled with sadness or joy as discernible tears began pooling in the corners of her eyes.

Nodding as he smiled, Renee pulled him close, meeting his lips; her hands rubbing the back of his head while she twisted her fervent tongue into his mouth, melting in his arms with passionate affection. Her duffle coat pressing against him as the kiss continued, the soft fur from her hood brushing against his hands behind her back. Breaking from the intimate display, Renee turned, beaming a pleasantly surprised smile, peering around the room again as if she thought she had been hallucinating before.

"Let me take your coat," Dennis instructed, laughing at her astonishment; he crushed it, he thought to himself.

Removing her jacket, she flashed an adoring stare with sparkling orbs, silent with an unrestrained gaze and surrender, an affirmation that she was his. Washing away all the built-up anxiety he had been harboring while trying to plan the perfect surprise, it was apparent to all that Dennis had done good.

Cradling his chin and gnawing at his bottom lip, Renee returned to kiss him once more with effusive warmth, relinquishing her kiss after a slight bite, a pull of his bottom lip, animalistic desire. She then parted, venturing off to greet everyone individually, hugging and kissing each person on the cheek, exchanging pleasantries; her kiss still lingering on Dennis's lips; he couldn't wait to propose.

"Nice job," her brother Mark remarked, creeping up out from Dennis's periphery.

Mark reached out to address him with a high-shake, a term Dennis coined for the handshakes that started out as high-fives but transitioned into full handshakes mid squeeze. The type of gestures usually exchanged between good friends, so Dennis felt even more secure with his relationship with Mark.

Renee's older brother Mark was thirty-eight and had been married to his wife for seven years. Ennis, their child, was a real cutie, often picking his boogers and eating them with an inane smile but still a well-mannered munchkin. Mark and Dennis had become much closer ever since Dennis disclosed he was planning on proposing after two years of being together with Renee. They'd get together to watch football on Sundays in Mark's basement and drink a couple of beers; Mark would root for the Eagles and Dennis would cheer on the Giants, flippantly antagonizing each other whenever an opposing team scored. They'd exchange witticisms and diatribes, often referring to the presumed inadequate size of each other's peckers, real masculine camaraderie, fraternity shenanigans like they were in college. Dennis was pretty sure he was going to ask him to be his best man too, a question he would never get to pose.

"She was really surprised, you made her night, bud," Mark smiled, handing Dennis a Bud Light, a gesture of appreciation; his sleeves rolled up and his forearms damp, as if he had retrieved the beer from a cooler.

"Think she has any idea what's coming next?"

He shook his head and chuckled, his five o'clock shadow neatened for the evening.

"No way, man."

Dennis's gaze drifted back to Renee, who moved through the room, greeting each person warmly, like a procession of endearment. His eyes followed her curvy figure, outlined by sleek dark slacks, her face glowing with excitement, her radiant smile reaching him from across the room.

"Well done, Dennis," her parents cheered, approaching with open arms; her mom leaning in close, kissing Dennis on the cheek, avoiding too close of contact to avoid makeup rubbing off on his white button-down shirt.

"You got her good, honey," she smiled, rubbing his shoulder; her pink glasses pressed against her stout face.

Her father, Rich, a dour businessman who always wore a grave expression, extended his arms and gave Dennis a big hug; his hair was slicked back like a salesman's.

"You really pulled it off, Den," he chuckled, patting Dennis on the back for a job well done, an overly friendly greeting.

Dennis couldn't recall ever being hugged by Renee's father before, let alone welcomed with so much warmth, so the sentiment resonated. The grandkids would call him "Pop" or "Doc" or maybe "Pa," he speculated, something terse and direct to match her father's stern demeanor; perhaps the future was a golden bricked layered road with wealthy, loving in-laws guiding them to a marriage of happiness, a real terrific life, he envisioned.

"Thank God, the past few months have been crazy. I'm pretty sure I almost slipped up and told her on a couple of occasions," Dennis blurted, shedding a timid smile, turning back once again to look for Renee, always searching for her.

"Well, you really pulled it off, honey," Mary, his mom chimed in, emerging from the crowd with his father Russ, strands of her short blonde hair hanging over her round spectacles.

"I think I did," Dennis chuckled, kissing his mom on the cheek before hugging his father; his dad sporting an abalone bowtie, a real dashing attire with an open navy blazer.

"You look sharp, Dad," Dennis smiled, clutching his elbow to admire his outfit.

"Had to look good for my son's big night," he grinned before greeting Renee's parents; Russ and her dad both worked in the grocery industry as food brokers, a common topic of conversation whenever the families were together, comfortable commonality.

But the relief was only transient as his anxiety sprawled, pooling sweat developing in Dennis's armpits, growing even more nervous with each passing minute, the looming proposal, its severity. He needed to execute but knew he had to wait until the birthday cake was served. That's what Jillian, her BFFL and he decided would be best, visualizing the clandestine text messages he hid from Renee for more than half a year, before jealously checking his phone became a regular occurrence.

After the Carvel ice cream cake was devoured, Renee's absolute favorite dessert, everyone began circling around the pair just as Dennis had planned with the families. The two had just bought their first home together, just three weeks prior, which added to the craziness of planning the surprise party. And Renee, two years older than Dennis, carried a steady confidence that had always fascinated him. But it was over those few weeks that Dennis became even more convinced that she was the one for him. There was something profound about moving in with someone, packing belongings together, navigating each other's tendencies, and sharing the rhythms of daily life that revealed their truest selves, foibles and all. But as Dennis adjusted to this new reality, he realized he absolutely adored and cherished Renee. While the stress of merging two lives might drive some couples apart, Dennis found that living with Renee only deepened his love for her. Each day, he fell a little more in love, captivated by her subtle mannerisms and unconscious behaviors, like the way she always gazed out the window on sunny mornings, humming a show tune.

They had found their dream home, embarked on several DIY projects together after viewing YouTube videos, picked out color schemes and furniture accents, and the rest just fell into place, along with appreciation Facebook posts and late-night conversations about their future together under cozy Sherpa blankets and all. They were moving through life's milestones with grace. The few weeks of compromising on furniture pieces, color palettes, and spending Saturdays at Home Depot were some of the best times of his life. Donning comfy sweatpants and worn shirts, duster clothes, even doing the most mundane things with Renee seemed to bring joy, the true testament of a soulmate.

After they finished singing "Happy Birthday" and Renee blew out her candles, Dennis descended to his knee, his heart a spastic drumbeat, turning to Renee as he retrieved a flat jewelry box from his back pocket, purposely sized to not be noticeable. Radiating with restlessness and anticipatory nerves, Dennis held out the opened ring box with the oval diamond, flashing a vulnerable smile. Rising from her seat, glowing with effervescent eyes, Renee placed her hands on top of her head, her mouth agape as she realized what was materializing.

"Renee, will you marry me?" Dennis supplicated, looking up at a trembling Renee; her hands flexed, placed on the sides of her cheeks, a silent scream pose.

Her lips quivering as tears began to fall, she gazed at Dennis with pure affection; her beautiful white smile paired with brilliant dark eyes contrasted perfectly against her gray cable knit sweater; her brown locks lay twisted, carelessly adorned on her shoulders, uncoiling from the night's thrill, and Dennis couldn't help but stare at her with fire, devotion, and complete unconditional love.

Genuflected, completely exposed and vulnerable, time seemed to stand still for Dennis as he slipped in and out of dreaminess, partially tapping into their future together and its beautiful possibilities. Envisioning adopting a dog together, having children, and living their lives enthralled with each other. Beaming with exhilaration, his eyes moistened with joyful tears; there wasn't a single thing about her that he didn't love: from her gentle touch to her frizzy hair in the morning to way she refused to put her clean laundry away until the weekend, every single aspect of her was perfection to him. She was the one he was going to be with for the rest of his life; she was going to be his wife.

"Yes," she shuddered, fighting back an onslaught of overwhelming emotions as the ovation sounded, a real Hallmark moment.

Rising from the ground as knotted future spouses, the crowd clapped as the couple kissed each other deeply, the reception echoing even louder in the capacious venue, an enchanting moment. The jubilation from the applause and whistles boomed throughout the restaurant while they embraced, cradling each other's faces as they kissed. The room imbued with vitality as if love leaked from every nook and crevice.

They kissed passionately, slowly in a transcendent epoch as the flickers from everyone's Smartphone lights captured their engagement, footage he would have to rehash via Facebook memories every February 24th for years to come. The electricity from her touch lingered on Dennis's skin, eliciting goosebumps up and down his arms and neck. Clasping hands together, she pulled Dennis close once more; their chests pressed together as they hugged, whispering in each other's ears.

"I want forever with you," she whispered, leaving a warm, remarkable sensation on the edge of his ear, a lingering confession and promise that nestled into the center of his heart.

Her pithy statement, soothing the darkest of insecurities as a sense of resignation overcame him; sinking into her arms, Dennis felt loved entirely, fully seen, and secure. It was the most magical moment he ever experienced, a core memory for certain, an unprecedented occasion that would replay over and over in his mind for years to come, especially at his darkest hours. An effable warmth radiated from within, defrosting even the coldest of thoughts, a settling of his soul. Completely sober, it was the first time in his entire life that he felt utterly content. There wasn't a single stress, rumination, or poignancy that came to him. Not a single regret entered his brain nor permutation because every decision he had ever made had ultimately led him to that night; every interpreted failure or misstep was justified because it guided him to Renee. His heart and mind were stable and calm, a conviction that life was just beginning.

He wasn't ever entirely sure what genuine happiness felt like or if he had ever truly grasped it before, but he decided the fulfillment, the elation he experienced that night was the closest he'd ever come to pure genuine bliss. It was a defining moment, a memory he'd forever try to revisit, a feeling he'd forever try to recapture. It was the pinnacle of his happiness and the beginning of the end, the peak before the fateful plunge.

####

Storming through the classroom door, Dennis's messenger bag dangles precariously by a worn strap, the aged leather marred with scuffs from years of use. He glances at his watch as he dumps the bag onto his desk, sending stacks of papers, pens, folders, and other office supplies tumbling over. The abrupt clatter startles the class, causing slouching teenagers to sit up straight in unison. The room falls silent as they watch him frantically rummage through the spilled items, fumbling with folders in a haphazard attempt to clean up; he's too stoned.

He's been late and high every day this week, even though he arrives at school two hours early. For a few weeks, he slipped into the computer annex to work on a short story, a new project since his manuscript apparently sucks. He found solace in the semi-silence, comfort in the soft buzzing of running desktops, enough to punch out some consonants and a work in progress. But that was only temporary.

Recently, he doesn't even make it out of the parking lot, let alone his car. Instead, he ventures into the vortex, getting lost in a social media sinkhole. He spends over an hour scrolling through Instagram reels, liking content, and flowing down algorithms like white rapids until he reaches the sewage of digital media. And it's a slow descent too, starting with oddly satisfying clips that, oddly enough, aren't satisfying, people cutting soap bars or trimming grass. He'll browse aimlessly, drifting into ASMR content, breathy influencers whispering into their sensitive microphones, tapping sounds and spray bottles spritzing. Then, it's a series of swipes and hearts that sends him swirling into the abyss: videos of toothless crackheads performing synchronized dance routines, midget strippers with visible facial deformities singing '90s pop songs, and even beheading videos from Morocco or Pakistan seep their way into the feed from time to time, desensitizing him to brutality.

And he really needs the distraction, otherwise he'd get lost in cogitation, revisiting vignettes and evocations, rehashing dialogue he had with Renee. He's even recapped tenth grade baseball tryouts when he got cut from the team and reexamined anomalous instances from years ago, like the time a hostile old man with a haggard ponytail hung out the driver's side window at a stop light, haranguing about the dangers of tailgating, screaming at the top of his lungs over Dennis's car's proximity.

Dennis spends most of his life in his head, spiraling down his hippocampus, obsessing over past decisions, even the most trivial of occurrences, imagining how things could have been different. He thinks about how he could have told his grandmother, before she passed, how much he appreciated her cooking and warmth, instead of just nodding along absent-mindedly to her stories. He regrets ghosting the girl from his freshman psychology class after their drunken hookup; she had shown genuine interest in seeing him again. He still feels guilt over how he treated his college roommate, Ralphie, the closest thing he ever had to a best friend. But Dennis was never good at handling emotions, especially while fueled by illicit stimulants. He remembers snorting copious amounts of cocaine and starting fights, like the time he threw one of Ralphie's high school friends down a flight of stairs after losing a beer pong game during homecoming weekend. And maybe all those selfish, reckless moments were the catalysts for his current situation. Maybe this is his comeuppance, he thinks, and he's stuck on a path to a damned destination. He's not the protagonist, he gets it; he's just struggling to figure out what his role is.

The marijuana alone certainly isn't helping, and his conscience won't let him smoke weed while occupying a bedroom in the basement at his parents' home for the fear he'd fulfill a stereotype, rendering himself a verified failure. So Dennis partakes in a delightful concoction on his ride to work, a partnership of weed and coffee. It's an upper paired with a downer to help slow the mind or at least deter it from heading in a different, darker direction, a tonic of vigor coupled with apathy seems to keep him in the present moment instead of the past. The caffeine modulating, manipulating neurotransmitters, mimicking adenosine, deceiving his brain with induced ambition and reduced existential dread; it creates a forcefield for his mind, an illusion of hope, he thinks, where the negativity can't infiltrate.

Collecting himself, Dennis reorganizes his thoughts, letting out frustrated huffs and sighs; the class whispers, coughs and faint chattering reverberate throughout the stuffy box of adolescents. A light beams from his desk, catching his eyes, his phone glows with a banner flashed across the screen; he remembers he has to stop by to pick up the last of his things from the apartment. He's also planned to give Christine a check for $2000; he figures it might help her buy some things for her new residence, and maybe compensation for collateral damage would make his gnawing guilt go away.

"I've left the rest of your stuff in the box by the front door," a text from an aloof Christine reads, a stark contrast from the affectionate messages he used to receive.

Dennis leans over the desk to glance at his phone momentarily, defeated, looking up to notice curious faces gazing; he wonders if they know he's blitzed. He ponders opening his Instagram app for a quick fix of dopamine to abate the paranoia; maybe one of his new digital acquaintances liked the Ernest Hemmingway quote he shared earlier: "Happiness in intelligent people is the rarest thing I know," and he loves this quote because it means maybe he's just too smart for his own good, and he's just a genius, actually.

Glimpsing up again from his desk, cognizant of the countless watchful eyes fixated on his abnormal episode, waves of anxiety ensue, a dreadful caprice. A preponderance of heavy stares leer upon him; kids are judging, forming opinions, he just knows it. And he needs to shift back to teacher mode; he needs to reestablish authority, he tells himself.

"Robert Frost," he announces after an apoplectic harrumph, making sure to really hock up some phlegm in the process, determined to dominate the energy dynamic.

Sweat pours from his armpits as Dennis moves his arms, feeling the uncomfortable moisture in his pits; his eyelids weigh as the onslaught of cotton mouth begins. Turning his back to the class, snatching the Virginia Tech mug of tepid coffee from his desk, Dennis gulps down the remaining cold java in pursuit of positivity. Yesterday's coffee trickles, leaking out the sides of his mouth as he swallows.

"Now," Dennis declares.

Approaching the whiteboard, removing the cap off a red marker, he writes "Robert Frost" in large letters, underlining the iconic name for emphasis.

"Is anyone familiar with Robert Frost?" Dennis trumpets, oscillating back, walking forward like an intrepid sailor.

Heading into the sea of fledglings, he wipes coffee residue from his mouth as his dry eyes burn. Scanning the room with the hope that one of the intellectually premature fetuses might engage him in dialogue, Dennis searches for curiosity, a cocked eye. It's been a while since he really talked to anyone. Surveying the room for a raised hand, scouring for any infantile shitbag with a phone out, detesting the generation of over-stimulation and pervasive ADD. Aware of his projection, Dennis peruses the aisles with a Draconian demeanor, sliding obstructing backpacks laying in his path to the side with his foot, as if he were clearing a walkway to somewhere significant, somewhere better, maybe off a tall edifice, the final fall. Peering around for eye contact from anyone slightly intrigued, holding his hands behind his back, exuding confidence; he's disappointedly met with the omnipresent gaze of boredom and the presence of adolescent indifference.

Suddenly, an ungainly arm lofts into the air from the back of the classroom, a frivolous hand with long skinny fingers from the sleeve of an oversized blazer; it's Jonathan, the impudent kid Dennis sent to the Dean's office a week ago for texting during class. It's only early October, five weeks into the school year, but already Jonathan has found a way to agitate Dennis. There was nothing worse than inattentiveness, a lack of respect for classic literature; he was a fucking Philistine, a complete wastrel, Dennis had decided, already envisioning failing Jonathan once the school year ended. Perhaps it was Jonathan's carelessness with his first paper in which he referred to the protagonist in "The Minister's Black Veil" as Mr.

Cooper instead of Mr. Hooper, or maybe it was how he always had a witty intonation whenever he posed a question or statement, as if he were making a mockery, looking to rouse the class and garner a reaction. Dennis wasn't entirely sure if Jonathan was the quintessential wise guy or just a complete dumbass, but either way, he shouldn't be in his AP English class; his daddy had to be a school donor, Dennis postulates.

He points to Jonathan, the long teenager coiling up in his chair like a snake.

"He wrote 'The Road Less Traveled'?" Jonathan blurts, leaning back with a sly smile as if he's an advanced reader, marveling in vast knowledge, an attitude like he just nailed the final question in *Jeopardy!*

He's referring to the "The Road Not Taken," a poem Dennis fucking hates; its concluding lines reduced to a contemporary cliché. He despises the narrative with a passion and not because of the content but because of how people misinterpreted the prose. Prevalent in all graduation speeches, motivational monologues, perorations, and other momentous events, the trite words of Frost's quest are recited to evoke inspiration and celebrate the rewards for forging one's own path. And just like Jonathan, most people refer to the revered poem as "The Road Less Traveled," instead of "The Road Not Taken" because taking a road less traveled requires bravery and resonates more than referencing a road that wasn't even taken. It takes courage to choose a road less traveled; it's empowering, a proclamation of confidence in decision making and positivity, but that's not the sentiment Frost intended.

Most people gloss over the opening stanzas, where the protagonist admits both roads were unequivocally traveled on the same, admitting there wasn't some major decision made to select the path but rather it was just an arbitrary choice, a thoughtless chance decision. And while most people recognize the poem as a reward for those who take chances and metaphorically take roads less traveled, it's clear by the end of the poem the protagonist is more concerned and left wondering about the road he didn't take than the road that he did. The story is called, "The Road Not Taken," and not "The Road Less Traveled" because the decision of not taking that other road is still something the protagonist wonders about. It's a decision that perhaps still haunts the traveler, still thinking about the road not taken, not the road less traveled.

And Dennis is all too familiar with second guessing and roads not taken; he's not sure about the road he's on, questioning everything he's doing lately. He's thinking this road is going to lead to somewhere not too nice, maybe a dark alley where he'll be bludgeoned with regret and nostalgia. Christine had been such a positive influence on his life, bringing giddiness to his monotony, vivacity to his weariness; she'd slap the toothbrush out of his mouth while he sleepily brushed his teeth in the morning, just to get a rise out of him. She seemed to mitigate Dennis's overthinking over the years, a holistic remedy for obsessive contemplation, reminding him to not take life too seriously. Sundays she'd make pancakes and prepare lunch for the two of them for the week. Maybe he's going to starve, he thinks. She seemed to stop the hurt from settling inside too long, so maybe now he's just going to bleed out.

Dennis considers humiliating Jonathan with a snarky comment to mask his own pain; maybe something about the kid's hairless legs he saw during gym class, trotting through the parking lot like a helpless baby bird waiting for its mother to chew up food and spit it into its mouth. But he decides against it; maybe the kid is trying, Dennis hopes. Despite loathing the obtuse embryo, it's not for lack of effort. It might have more to do with Jonathan always forgetting to underline the titles of novels in his assignments, something Dennis has emphasized a thousand fucking times, an inherent dolt.

But Dennis's disdain for Jonathan runs deeper, and it's not just that he knows he's clearly using ChatGPT for all his writing assignments, as evidenced by his

43

overuse of the verb "delve." No, it's the brand-new BMW Jonathan drives, courtesy of his wealthy parents and that he will never truly struggle, always cushioned by his family's prosperity. He'll never know the pain of falling because someone is always there to catch him. And worst of all, he'll believe he deserves it, living a supercilious life enabled by his parents.

Dennis vividly remembers being the future fraternity brother's same age, driving a fucking Toyota. His father made him work summer maintenance jobs to pay for most of it, instilling the value of money. Jonathan wouldn't be seen driving a Toyota; he'll never learn to respect hard work and appreciate the process of putting in the time to attain a goal. The kid smirked after everything he said, feigned with sincerity and hemmed with the sense that he was superior to his peers, a cynosure worthy of praise. He was going to grow up and be that asshole who never returns his shopping cart to the collection station in the parking lot but rather leaves it by the curb for someone else to return, if it doesn't eventually coast into the side of somebody's car. He'll grow into the dickhead who blows through yield signs and then flips the finger to other drivers who honked because the world clearly revolves around him. He'll become the shit-stain that doesn't say "thank you," when someone holds the door open for him, all because it was expected. And more troublingly, he'll morph into a wannabe philanderer who never takes "no" for an answer when he makes advances on a girl. His super ego is instilled with entitlement, coddled by privilege, paving the way for a life of prerogatives and no real accountability.

"'The Road Not Taken,' but close enough, Jon," Dennis flashes a wry smile, trying to shake the visions of backhanding him, the pop of flesh, smacking into the back of his palm.

"But we aren't discussing that today," Dennis remarks, clearing his throat while unwittingly licking his lips to abate the dryness.

Leering around the class once again, he adjusts his skinny cornflower blue tie, aware of his side pant pockets as he slips his hands inside. He's pulled into a reverie, detaching from the lecture; he didn't sleep last night because somewhere festering in the back of his mind, Dennis is cognizant of today, the date from five years ago that he was supposed to marry Renee. And he knows if he goes on Facebook today, he'll be ruffled by a memory, a photo pinned to the top of his feed, showing them outside their venue six years ago, toasting with champagne after booking the day.

Turning his back, shunning the class, he proceeds to the whiteboard once again to write the date on the board "October 10th " with a trembling hand. His heart tremors, triggering a fitful wave of anxiety; it still feels like only yesterday they used to sleep in the same bed, holding hands as they drifted off. His stomach churns as palpitations persist, and he debates reaching for the trash can, just in case he might throw up as dread drains into his gut.

"Nothing Gold Can Stay," Dennis inscribes on the board in big loopy letters, meticulously retracing each vowel, trying to impede the flood of memories and thwart welling emotions; his lecture is already a mess.

He briefly recalls grade school and how teachers hounded students about learning to write in script. "You know, when you get older, you will have to write everything in script," he remembers being berated, especially because he could never make a legible "Z" in cursive. Twenty-five years later, and the only thing he ever writes in script is his signature and the names of works he discusses with the class for the day on the whiteboard.

"Open your textbooks to page thirty-four," he announces, evading further thought tangents, picking up his book and setting it on the lectern.

He really feels like maybe he could puke, but maybe that's just what he needs: a visceral cleanse to kill his cancerous internal monologues. So, he pulls

45

the trash can close to his side, looking down into the fresh pink plastic garbage bag.

He grasps the sides of the wooden stand with a firm hold, hoping it will keep him grounded, focused; he feels the impulse to check his Instagram, perhaps Renee also remembered the significance of the day and finally decided to reconnect.

"Nothing Gold Can Stay," Dennis repeats loudly, looking around the class, deciding on which student should read.

He figures he'll start with Julia, since she's always energetic in the morning and a solid reader with clear articulation.

"Julia," Dennis calls, catching her timid eye contact as her head remains hanging over her book.

He nods to confirm his choice of reader, which is met with a quick smile before she begins.

"Nature's first green is gold, her hardest hue to hold," she articulates with a chipper cadence.

"Her early leaf's a flower; but only so an hour," she annunciates, gawking up at Dennis after each word like a docile worker seeking validation for a job well done.

"Go on, keep reading," he remarks.

Julia is plumpish with wild eyebrows, a clear indicator she isn't invested in her appearance yet, still possessing naivety from childhood, something Dennis admires.

"Then leaf subsides to leaf. So Eden sank to grief, So dawn goes down to day. Nothing gold can stay," Julia concludes, looking up at Dennis, anticipating further direction.

Her over-enunciation of multi-syllable words is apparent, as she blinks her eyes excessively, a distinguishable try-hard and over-achiever

"Who wants to interpret this poem?" Dennis poses, perambulating down the first row of desks, calculating steps as he processes his current mental state, reaffirming his control.

Like a vulture circling its prey, creeping around the room, he catches a whiff of weed, not entirely sure if it's from one of the kids or if it's his own aroma. Perhaps wisps of cannabis seeped into his shirt as he sparked his bowl earlier; maybe he should panic and charge out of the classroom, he ponders; maybe even pull the fire alarm.

"Well?" he inquires, holding his hands behind his back.

"Nature's first green is gold, her hardest hue to hold," Dennis asserts; he doesn't need the book, the poem is written all over his heart.

Nobody makes eye contact, just blank stares at their textbooks as he continues his circling, swiveling his head to identify any participants.

He's captivated by a lithe wrist that rises in the air, a twisting hand, embellished with a quaint gilded bracelet.

It's the new girl Megan with pursed lips and an adamant hand held high, a slight wave from side to side; her keenness apparent, a sunflower in a field of dandelions.

"Go ahead," Dennis allows.

"Well, hue is referring to color, right?" Megan queries with furrowed brows.

She's a polite, pretty girl, soft features with a symmetrical face; she seldom interacts, so Dennis hasn't paid much attention to her. From what he recalls, she's gotten two As and a B+ on her first three assignments. Her notes say she transferred from a public school to finish her general education. He wonders why her parents sent her to finish her senior year at a private institution, considering whether she had done something bad, and this was her punishment.

"Yes, go on," he nods.

Megan's smile brightens her entire face; her bow-shaped lips outlined with a dark lip liner, emphasizing fullness.

"So, he's saying that nature's green is gold and it's the hardest to keep?" she asks nervously, her intonation tapering off toward the end of her question.

She leans forward in her desk, perhaps to focus better; her curly brown hair falling flush on her shoulders. The top two buttons of her sweater are unbuttoned, revealing the top of a lower cut yellow T-shirt; her innocence beams with each frantic blink and awkward, timorous smile, catching Dennis's undivided attention.

"Keep going," he encourages, adopting a softer pitch, continuing his examination.

"Her early leaf is a flower, but only so an hour," she drawls, glancing up at the ceiling as if she is seeking a clearer interpretation from a higher power, her hazel eyes vivid in the morning sunlight.

"I think this means that flowers are only around for a short time?" she asks, raising her eyebrows as she crosses her legs, shifting her left thigh atop her right, bringing attention to her defined quads and pleated school skirt.

She folds her arms, gazing back at her book, a slight smirk on her face.

48

"Keep going, let's hear your full interpretation," Dennis replies for positive reinforcement.

She smiles warmly, flashing straight beaming teeth before she continues reading; Dennis returns the smile, surmising she must have had braces to achieve such aligned dentition; he's still super high.

"Then leaf subsides to leaf. So Eden sank to grief."

"Hmm," she says, sitting up as she glances at her book; her long eyelashes fluttering as she thinks, her vibrant eyes outlined with dark eyeliner.

Dennis adores her desire to decipher, provoking salacious thoughts in his head; the fact that she looks like every single teacher/teen schoolgirl porno he'd ever seen also contributes to his erotic daydream. His rampant pornography addiction has dulled all sensibility, contaminating his taste and sexual expectations, destroying any chance at experiencing healthy intimacy. It's not his fault though, he reasons. The technology is just too advanced, making explicit pleasurable content easily accessible at his fingertips, the biggest breakthrough for the male species in the past fifty years: catalogues of erotic material, from bawdy to hardcore, searchable by fetishes, duration, and ratings with high-speed internet, endless mature content for a boundless, insatiable need. Recalling being fifteen years old, he still remembers having to search for adult videos on Kazzaa, selecting options based solely on the file name without a thumbnail, and he'd wait for three days for it to fully download before he could watch it, delaying his gratification.

"I'm thinking Eden is referring to Adam and Eve and how Eve sinned?" she says.

"So dawn goes to day, nothing gold can stay."

"So I think this poem is about how time goes by super-fast," she adds, offering an apprehensive smile, placing her elbow on the desktop, holding her chin with a closed palm, a thinker's pose.

"Does everyone agree?" Dennis asks the class, surveying the room, invoking a period of silence as he attempts to deflect the raid of obscene thoughts.

"I think it's about how twisted this world is actually," Jonathan remarks, prompting all the students to turn toward the sound of his voice.

Dennis shakes his head, realizing who is interjecting; the kid never raises his fucking hand.

"Raise your hand," Dennis scorns, glaring at the juvenile interrupter; he is ruining his high and discussion.

Jonathan deflates into his seat; his wrinkled neon green polka dot tie hangs too low from his neck, indicative of his inability to properly tie a knot. Long frowsy hair sits on his oversized head like a nested animal, and the faint remnants of facial hair gathering around his mouth make Dennis think he's addressing an untrimmed prepubescent vagina; he debates whether he should give him a demerit for his facial hair.

"I think this poem is about how sick this world is. Like when you start out as a child, you're so vulnerable. And over time, this shitty world just destroys you," his raspy voice remarks like the scrappy lead singer of a fucking Emo band from the early 2000s.

Smiling reluctantly, Dennis breathes through his escalating anger, desperately searching for a parasympathetic state. He looks up at the ceiling, trying to steady himself, exhaling slowly as he attempts to summon patience. Jonathan thinks he's edgy and cool, but what does he really know about the world, Dennis wonders. He's a fucking fetus in a blazer, unbruised by life and probably still smelling like baby lotion. He hasn't even felt the full dick of the world, just the tip.

"Sorry I cursed, Mr. Clauden," Jonathan frowns in a disarming attempt, folding his hands.

Rolling his head around his neck in a counterclockwise motion to release tension, Dennis catches a discernible coffee stain on his pants, a brown blemish on his modern fit from the earlier chug, and it pisses him off, even if it resembles a happy face.

"What does gold signify to you, Jon?" Dennis poses with a poised demeanor, staring down at the floor, fixating on a dented linoleum tile, which has probably been there for fifty plus years.

He contemplates on how many hapless, washed-up writers who became English teachers prowled the same floor over the years, engaging in similar dialogues.

"Um, what do you mean?" he asks, scratching his furry chin.

"When you think of gold, what certain things come to mind?" Dennis asks, wetting his fingertips, dabbing at his pants' stain; the muddy mark goading him, taunting with its presence, knowing he'll have to spend extra care later on, spraying it profusely with Shout to ensure it comes out in the wash.

"Like in my head?"

"No, in your kneecap, dude," Dennis shouts, shaking his head as he flips his thumbs through his tie.

The class lets out a soft collective chuckle.

"Oh, Mr. Clauden?" Megan squeaks, raising an ardent hand once again, only this time

Dennis thinks he notices faint cuts along her left wrist.

"Yes, Megan," Dennis tweets with an affable tone, lingering forward to get a better look at her exposed wrist, further piquing his curiosity.

"When I think of gold, I think of expensive jewelry," she answers with a soft, sincere voice, retrieving her hand from the air and placing it back down by her waist, out of sight for further inspection.

She leans forward, expressing interest in the conversation, pushing her hair back behind her ears, revealing a small obscure tattoo on her upper neck, underneath her earlobe.

Folding his arms, Dennis turns back to the front of the room and sits on the edge of his large rectangular desk, dangling an outstretched foot from the floor.

"And what is jewelry? What does expensive jewelry symbolize?" he digs, his arms folded as he speaks with an inquisitive pitch.

Megan squints her eyes, puckering her lips in thought; Dennis slips off into another reverie, speculating on whether she is seventeen or eighteen, glowing with admiration for her zealous participation. It's evident she cares about literature and learning, not to mention she's attractive. She gets it, a future influencer with 100k followers, he speculates.

"Valuable stuff?" she chirps, flipping her hair with a half-smile, nervous, as if maybe she's second guessing her answer.

Dennis stares, searching her artless eyes for a spark, a steady look, assessing if there's a mutual interest.

"Precisely," he belts, rising from the desk with an emphatic finger in the air, trying to select his words carefully so the class fully comprehends the lesson.

"Nothing that is of value will ever truly stay in your life."

Glancing up at the ceiling, Dennis combs his tie with an open hand, a soothing tick to mitigate the looming emotions. He stands tall, resolute, and melancholy, as if the words he's about to articulate are meant for no one else but himself.

"Anything that's ever good in your life. Whether it's family, money, significant others, good times, or even just life itself, it's all temporary, impermanent," he begins, his voice strong and commanding yet tinged with a deep, underlying sorrow.

He pauses for a moment, letting the weight of his words settle in the room. His eyes flicker across the faces of his students, who are now completely captivated.

"Those late-night conversations with your crush, falling asleep while still talking, the phone pressed between your shoulder and your face, your ear tingling from whispered words, your mind bubbling with oxytocin. Those nighttime drives with your closest friends, the shared silence and laughter," Dennis continues, each sentence delivered with austere precision.

Megan's gaze is fixed on him, her fingers absentmindedly playing with her skinny necklace, twirling it as she listens. Dennis notices but doesn't break his rhythm.

"Those magical life moments with laughing friends, surrounded by the ones you care about, giggling until your insides hurt from jokes and banter. Those precious times with your parents and relatives, annual holiday gatherings around bountiful tables and familiar smiles," he expounds, his tone unwavering as he locks eyes with each student, his gaze piercing.

His eyes, now almost bestial, radiate a cold intensity as he surveys his students like helpless sheep, their mouths slightly ajar, the room weighed down by the gravity of his words.

"None of it lasts forever. Everything you love will eventually go away, in time. Everything that you come to cherish in your life will end. Nothing gold will ever stay," he concludes, the finality of his words hanging in the air, leaving a heavy silence in their wake.

3. Through the Looking-Glass

"You two are just going to love this home," the voluble realtor announced as they strolled toward the front of the home.

Dennis flashed a tepid smile, pondering how many times she repeated that same sentiment with feigned enthusiasm over the past years and how many couples had been allured by her bloviating. He imagined the same exhibition was performed for numerous pairs and newlyweds, complete with similar shrilling intonations and disarming, animated facial expressions to elicit intrigue and zeal.

"The neighborhood is amazing, and you are literally within walking distance of the cute town," she added, waving her arms ardently, bubbling with her peppy quirkiness, an attempt to charm.

She was in her late forties with a Teletubby-like stature, Dennis deduced. Her make-up caked on, her raggedy skirt frayed with loose hems, a tacit implication it was the only professional wear she owned. Dennis pictured her real estate career materialized after years of being a stay-at-home mom to assuage boredom and revivify her self-worth, struggling with resurfacing identity issues after the radiance from marriage and raising kids wore off.

She continued her script, chirping on about all the amenities, prattling to Christine, pretending to be interested in their lives. She asked constant questions, conveying curiosity and conviviality, smiling profusely after disclosing a personal fact, anything to seal that 6% commission.

"Super close to all major highways too," she smirked, turning to gaze at the two; her poorly applied lipstick seeped onto the front of her teeth, another indication she was older with fading dexterity and diminishing eyesight.

Dennis imagined her fighting a tottering hand as she applied her makeup in the morning, squinting into her compact vanity mirror.

It was a house with three bedrooms and two bathrooms located just off 287 North, offered at a decent price; Dennis assumed it had to do with the adjacent road being a double yellow. The front yard was barren from the winter, remnants of leaves crunched under each of their steps. A fire pit sat at the end of the driveway, the air still lingering with the redolence of burning wood. The coldness of winter crawled, creeping on fingertips and exposed skin, forcing partners to cling to each other closely.

Ambling to the front door, Christine pointed out the Adirondack chairs arranged on the lawn, sitting next to each other, the two weathered wooden seats waiting for lovers to return. Christine turned and smiled at Dennis, grasping his hand with an eagerness, pulling him with excitement as they entered the home; her curly brown locks pushed back, taut against her head as if she wanted to avoid any distractions while she inspected the house. Her face perked, the whites of her eyes sparkling in the Sunday sun. She had talked about coming to see the house all week long, texting Dennis while she was on her lunch break at school, sending him additional photos as they became available.

"Built in 1953, this charming colonial has undergone a complete renovation in the past two years," the realtor recited, holding up pointed fingers as she spoke, gesticulating.

She had given Dennis her card and told him her name earlier that morning, but it easily slipped out of his mind, just like the elucidation he had at Weichert realtors while he was checking to see if he had been approved for the mortgage.

Critical plot ideas came to him while he was conversing with the advisor and signing papers, but he was too occupied to jot down the details. He didn't know how he was going to end the book he'd been brainstorming about, but he knew he wanted the protagonist to be shot and killed, something real fucking twisted.

Dennis nodded, replying with consistent affirmations. "Right," he'd respond to the esoteric financial language about interest rates and closing costs, something about points; the willowy advisor venturing off on a tangent about his family after every few pages they reviewed, frequently describing his littlest daughter as a "delightful devil," a term Dennis thinks he heard used in an old Geico commercial.

He pondered how deep one's banality must be if alliterative nicknames from insurance commercials made lasting impressions on a person's diction, even inspiring nicknames for the offspring. But Dennis was going to buy a home, finally; he really needed to. Renee had moved in with Carl, apparently, from what Dennis had accidentally discovered on Facebook, so he was going to fucking buy anything, and whatever the towering advisor said didn't really matter.

The entrance of the home led to a compact living room with dusky gray walls, amplifying its lack of capacity. Wisps of vanilla scent suffused the air; the rustic hardwood floors had been recently refinished. The sweet, subtle fragrance and the hand-scraped wooden detail provided a warm, inviting ambiance, like a cozy forest cabin a family of four would spend inside, huddled around one another, playing board games by the fireplace.

A brick hearth was the focal point of the room, exuding a homely feel. It was a charming dwelling, infused with affection from the residing loving couple; intimate pictures adorned the walls in array of Pinterest-inspired configurations. Folded plush blankets sat on the neutral-colored couch; a large flat screen hung on the opposite side wall with a slideshow of wedding and birthday photos playing, complementing the loving nucleus. Dennis pictured the newlyweds, maybe with their newborn or older dog, gathering on the couch, watching a family movie; they'd enjoy wholesome animated flicks, simple, silly storylines they could laugh at, he imagined. The den was tidy, radiating with pride and consideration, admiration for their home; the owners cared about preserving their nest.

Christine galloped over to the fireplace, emulating a cowboy riding a horse; she turned and looked back at Dennis with a coltish smile, locking eyes as if she were trying to make him laugh.

"Wow," Christine smiled, crouching down to check out the footing, inspecting the corbels that supported the mantel shelf that ran diagonally across the layered bricks.

She looked back at Dennis, her mouth primmed, her inquisitive eyes staring as she tried to interpret his opinion of the place.

After five seasons of Chip & Joanna, Christine had propagated her wish to have a quaint fireplace with a shiplap mantelpiece where she'd display pictures of the family and decorate with curios. They had conversed about how pleasant it would be to return home after a long day, unwinding with each other, burrowing under blankets while a warm fire flickered nearby. Running her hands across the mantel with a glaring grin, Christine advanced swiftly to the next wall, continuing her pensive inspection; Dennis could tell she adored the home by her absorption.

Proceeding with the tour of the home, they ventured upstairs with the insufferable realtor and her accompanying affectations, regaling Christine with selling features and chit-chat.

"The bathrooms were both updated this past year with meticulous care," Danielle boasted with her strident voice, her crimped hair and spray tan pairing perfectly, rendering her a relic from the '80s.

Dennis couldn't imagine what aspect of her life from that era she so desperately wanted to hold onto; perhaps it was the last time in her life she was happy.

Peeking into each bathroom, Dennis noticed the newly added subway tile, which was something Christine constantly brayed about having in her ideal home. It was the classic clean modern update, lauded for its versatility by Joanna as it could be used as a backsplash, flooring, and more.

Skulking around the corner, Dennis uncovered a spacious spare bedroom with a window view into the backyard, envisioning transforming it into an office, a place he could escape to, cloistering inside to read, work, or possibly draft another manuscript. He stood in front of the room with a blank expression, devising, pinpointing where he would place his desk, a television, couch, and so forth. He really wanted to place a brown leather couch with nailhead trim along the back wall, one of those classic library accents that exuded sophistication. Maybe he'd hang a thought-provoking painting above it, perhaps an abstract piece to imbue creativity, he pondered. He closed his eyes, picturing grading papers, perched in front of the bedroom window, the best spot for an industrial desk.

"And over here is the master bedroom with skyline windows above," Dolores echoed in the hallway, each of her sentences tapering off with a lofty inflection; Dennis still couldn't remember what her name was.

Creeping out of the room, Dennis met Christine in the hall with her wide smile; her excitable energy catching his attention, grabbing him by the hand once again, pulling him to the master bedroom. The endearing sunlight peered in from the window, shining directly over the bed. The space illuminated with an intimate brightness, a transparent radiance that spotlighted the bed, a shine that reveals every inch of one's body, highlighting skin blemishes, wrinkles, self-conscious skin folds, putting vulnerability on full display. Dennis stood in the bedroom, visualizing close morning encounters with the amatory light, bodies entangled, exploring the crevices of each other, irradiated, and enclosed by resplendent pillows and sheets. They'd hug and kiss, cuddle, and laze before they'd finally get out of bed.

"What do you think, babe?" Christine asked with a soft, insecure cadence; her bottom lip always curling whenever she was unsure.

Crossing his arms, standing in the bedroom, he tried to conjure up a verdict, struggling to reach a ruling. Gazing over toward an elated, eager Christine, her eyes gleaming with joy; her fit physique, her trim waist and small stature, always commanding Dennis's affection. He loved to hug her and pull her close, like a plush stuffed animal. An overwhelming sense of nothingness obscured his mind, emptying the wind from his chest, a listless haze, like he were frozen in time, just watching his life pass by.

Maybe he was dead, Dennis pondered, and this was just the remnants of his brain synapses firing off the last of his cerebral activity; perhaps it was all a dream. He contemplated picking up the lighter next to the Pumpkin Spice Home Goods candle and scorching his hand; maybe then he'd feel something

"Oh and just wait until you get a look at the divine kitchen," Diane exclaimed, clapping her hands once before clasping them together, placing them against her stomach, smiling like a schoolteacher about to unveil a big surprise to the kids.

Journeying back down the stairs toward the kitchen, the round realtor persisted, spewing more seller facts, highlighting the acclaimed school system, low property taxes, and a new septic tank. The kitchen was spacious and featured a rustic motif with alluring lines, wooden gradations, earth tone hues, and chic lighting. A dark caged chandelier with Edison bulbs dangled above the farmhouse sink; Christine's face beamed with awe.

"All previous owners prided themselves on keeping this home immaculate. Not only is this place completely renovated, but all the appliances are brand new," she continued, performing her proclamations.

Dennis glanced at Christine, her adorable, beatific gaze meeting his eyes momentarily as she marveled at the kitchen, swaying her hips and pumping her arms like a cheerleader, celebrating its magnificence.

"I love it," she uttered with a rhapsodic lilt, picturing their lives together in the home, memories made in their first official house.

Dennis recognized her rapture; he longed to share the same sentiment, that heart-fluttering excitement for the future; he searched for a response, but he couldn't find the words. Instead, he was still, stoic, captured by the red and white zig-zag rug that lay on the floor; Renee loved chevron rugs, he remembered.

"The Auburn tattered oak beams of the floor really command your attention," the realtor babbled; her glib words muddled like white noise to Dennis.

Peering around the kitchen, Dennis immediately noticed the large window above the sink, with sunlight fluorescing through. He slowly followed the rays through the black-framed window, gazing out into the backyard as he held onto the edge of the porcelain sink, slipping into a wistful reverie. He could hear Christine and the realtor conferring, and then it dawned on him: the realtor's name was actually Mirana, the furthest thing from Dolores or Diane. And he thought maybe he had mistaken her for Dolores because she bore a striking resemblance to his second-grade teacher, Miss Dolores, the grammar queen who attacked his pop quizzes with an overzealous red pen. But she became a friend years later, well, a Facebook friend, and her once-austere critiques were replaced by cheerful birthday wishes on his wall each year.

Turning toward the window, magnetized to the backyard, he visualized Christine and their first-born child playing on a cool summer's day. A full swing-set stood in the middle of the grassy pasture as Christine pushed the baby on the little swing; the little one cackling and cooing with each back-and-forth motion.

"Den?" Christine whispered, startling Dennis; he noticed Mirana and Christine staring as if expecting an answer.

"Sorry, what?" Dennis asked, vexed by some unidentifiable impetus.

"We're going to take a look in the garage, are you coming?" Christine glared with one eyebrow raised, confused with his behavior.

"Yes, I'll be right there," he replied before turning back to the window, peeking through the looking glass once more, trying to recapture the scene he was living.

Only this time, he noticed it wasn't Christine pushing the baby in the swing. No, it was a different brunette with a curvaceous figure; it was Renee. Looking up from pushing the baby, she smiled at Dennis.

"I want forever with you," she mouthed.

Shaking his head with angst, sensing the looming pathos, he turned toward the side door and made his way to the garage. As he passed, a miniature chalkboard hanging on the wall caught his eye: "I love my family" with a big heart next to "family." The "a" in "family" was replaced with a smiley face, and three stick figures were drawn in the lower left corner, holding hands and wearing broad smiles. The smallest figure appeared to be holding a dog on a leash.

A sharp, sudden ache prodded his chest, a nervous sensation, like the drop of a rollercoaster. The tension radiated inward with impact, like a powerful punch or a figurative defibrillation; he wondered if it was a panic attack. He hadn't had one of those in years.

Nothing felt right, Dennis decided. He had been covering his wounds with tenuous bandages of diversion for the past few years, hovering above himself, passively living his life. He existed in a haze of idleness and enervation, hoping Renee would resurface so they could resume their life together. But it was becoming increasingly clear, a sober realization, that he would now have to start making real choices, momentous ones, not the trivial decisions like updating his relationship status on Facebook or posting a picture of Christine on Valentine's Day on Instagram. These new decisions were more consequential, more poignant, and they were going to send him on a new path, in a completely different direction in life, further away from Renee, wherever the fuck she was.

And like a slim icepick slipping into his heart, Dennis painfully realized the only real home he knew or wanted was with Renee, and buying a home with Christine meant Renee could never come back, even if she wanted to.

"Babe, come outside, there's a rainbow," Christine rejoiced, bursting through the door, holding it open, flashing her charmingly rounded Chiclets of white teeth.

Dennis surrendered and walked toward the door; Christine leaned in, kissing him on the cheek.

"I think that rainbow is a good sign," she said.

63

Dennis opens the top cabinet to access the dishes, taking down crockery from the highest shelf, extending to his tippy toes. It's his father Russ's birthday, so naturally his dad is toiling away at the stove, cooking dinner for the family. He isn't one for restaurants or making reservations, dining out for a costly bill when preparing homemade Italian food would suffice, even if it's for a special occasion. But his father doesn't think his birthday is worth celebrating; he's not too thrilled with turning eighty this year.

Bouncing back and forth between burners, breading chicken cutlets and sampling the sauce, his father conducts himself in a fervid fashion, like a culinary commander, never forgetting to stop, stir, and taste everything that's cooking on the stovetop, seasoning as needed, commentating on the process.

Dennis deals out dinnerware to the table, placing each square earthenware plate with a coordinating bowl to create a compact place setting, a small salad bowl on top of the bigger plate. He can't remember which side the utensils go on, and he's torn on whether the fork goes on the inside or the outside of the spoon; he's thinking maybe the spoon might just sit in the bowl like an instructive hint.

"Alexa," Dennis commands.

"How do you set a table with silverware?"

"Sorry, I don't know that," the automated female voice replies.

"I'm telling you, we have the dumbest Alexa," his mother sneers and chuckles, an ambivalent combination.

It's a tone that Dennis recalls her using many times during his life, usually indicating it was his fault to some extent, and she's expecting Dennis to take action, solve the problem, rectify, perhaps even reprogram the Alexa or return it, he contemplates.

"Alexa, does the knife go on the left side or right side of a place setting?"

"Here is something I found on the web," Alexa answers without providing a further explanation.

His mother smirks and paces the kitchen, setting down freshly washed and folded towels on a barstool by the kitchen island.

Dennis's parents live in a two-story, three-bedroom townhome with a large basement that includes a spacious bedroom adjacent to a smaller one. They prefer the upstairs bedroom, avoiding the flight of stairs, which leaves Dennis with the larger space downstairs. The only time his mother ventures down is to use his bathroom, as it's the only one with a tub. And Dennis has lost track of how many times he's nearly cracked his head open by slipping on the leftover pools of baby oil on the tub floor. His mother soaks in baby oil as if it's a cure for calloused skin, always forgetting to wipe it down afterward, no matter how many times he reminds her. He figures it's a small plight worth enduring, considering he's not paying rent.

"I'll help you, honey," his mother Mary smiles with a rueful closed-lip grin, a maternal pity for his inability to set a proper table setting.

Her perfectionism, the real motive for her desire to help. But he's happy to oblige, if it makes her feel better.

"All those years growing up, and you never paid attention?"

His mother must have shown him a thousand times when he was younger, he recalls, debating whether he should just wing it. But he doesn't have an ounce of confidence left to execute; he can't even fake it.

"Remember, you always set the utensils in the order they'll be used. Forks go on the left, with the salad fork on the outside, and knives and spoons go on the

65

right. Soup spoons go on the outside," she says with a smile, placing each item down precisely, ensuring everything is orderly and impeccably presented.

Mary moves from place setting to place setting, bowing as she studies her reflection in the stainless-steel surfaces, making sure no blemishes or food residue escaped the dishwasher cycle. Dennis notices her deteriorating posture, her physicality dwindling with age. He quietly steps beside her, lightly pressing his hands on her shoulders, gently pushing her shoulder blades back.

"You're hunching again," Dennis remarks softly, intending concern, not criticism.

Her short blonde hair sits behind her ears, the only hairstyle Dennis ever recalls her having, the quintessential '90s-inspired cut every mom gets after being married and having several kids.

"I know," she sighs with a wry squint, shoving her shoulders back to compensate.

Reaching over, picking up the utensils, heedfully setting each plate with an accompanying salad fork, Dennis relishes carrying out tasks and chores for his parents. It's the only thing that seems to relieve his disconcertment; he still seeks their approval, even more than when he was a kid.

The guilt is eating him again, devouring his insides, feasting on his dejection and regressing mindset, consuming even periodic sanguine moments like a parasite. Renee is festering in his mind again, a dormant tumor resurfacing. Memories and missed opportunities to reconcile beleaguer most of his waking moments; perhaps he could have done something drastic, maybe he should have fought harder for her to come back, sending her one more text; he can only imagine her annotations on his current living arrangements.

He's even had a conversation with ChatGPT about it, seeking guidance from artificial intelligence. Prompting it with philosophical questions like "How do you know if someone was meant to be your soulmate?" and "Is there more to love than just surges of oxytocin, serotonin, and dopamine, creating feelings of lust, familiarity, and comfort?" He's even asked it to rate his new living situation on a scale from one to ten in terms of desirability, only realizing shortly after that ChatGPT seems to rate almost anything an eight, regardless of context. But his line of questioning seemed to elicit only trite responses, compilations lifted from self-help blogs about mindfulness and self-care, until eventually he ran out of prompts, since that's all he could get from his free subscription.

"Alexis, when will the timer be over?" Russ shouts, but the room remains silent.

"Alexis?" he repeats, staring confusedly at the small device perched on the secretary desk in the corner.

"Dad, it's Alexa," Dennis chimes in, grinning with amusement.

"Huh?"

"Here, watch. Alexa, how much time is left on the timer?"

"There are no timers set," the robotic voice replies.

"Jesus Christ," Russ mutters, tossing ravioli into the strainer.

"Guess I'm winging it like usual."

"What time are the kids coming?" Russ asks, pivoting, steam rising around him.

The ravioli is for John's kids since they hardly eat anything else. Dennis's niece and nephew, five and eight years old, are hooked on simple carbohydrates, rarely venturing beyond mac & cheese or some kind of pasta.

"I think Natalie texted me earlier and said they'd be here around 6 P.M.," his mother sighs as she pairs the larger dinner plates with the decorative charger plates she added, reorganizing the place settings.

She proceeds to undo the napkins Dennis had placed beside each plate, refolding them to her liking.

"We told them 5:30," Russ huffs as he pulls out a big salad bowl from the cabinet beside the stove, letting the door slam.

"I know, but you know they're never here on time," Mary shakes her head, exhaling with each refolding; Dennis can't decipher if she's aggravated at his poor napkin folding or whether it's directed at his brother and inconsiderate sister-in-law.

Natalie, his sister-in-law, hasn't really given a shit about the family since she and his brother got married. Her focus has always been on her own family, prioritizing visits with them on holidays and neglecting to communicate clearly with John's family. She rarely thinks to include his parents in spontaneous get-togethers.

"Maybe if he grew a set of balls," Russ murmurs under his breath, tossing lettuce into the bowl, spreading olive oil liberally.

"Ok, so I need to get some more olive oil," he whispers to himself, the newest manifestation of his old age.

Aside from the abundance of gray hair, other signs of aging are becoming more apparent to Dennis. But at least his father can converse with himself amicably; Dennis can't remember the last time he's had a productive internal dialogue without suggesting self-harming.

"I'll go get it, Dad," Dennis volunteers.

"Huh?" his father replies, scanning his face for a reference.

"Didn't you say you needed more olive oil?"

His father's eyes dart back and forth in deliberation, as if trying to comprehend how Dennis can read his mind. His withered face, now marked by more liver spots than just a month ago, resembles a bruised boxer, staring back at Dennis with a blank expression. His senescence stings, a solemn reminder that one day Dennis will pick up his phone with a heavy heart, desperate to talk to his father, but he'll be long gone.

"Oh yeah," Russ replies, nonchalantly as he returns to his laborious endeavor, committing to perfecting his grandmother's sauce.

"You're going to come with us next weekend to Chloe's communion, right?" his mother questions with an assertive tone, lips pursed as if she's expecting a response immediately and prepared to admonish for an unacceptable answer.

"Yes. I told you I bought the plane ticket a couple of weeks ago, remember?" Dennis remarks, glancing over his shoulder as he makes his way into the garage.

Since he could remember, his father had designated the garage as the second pantry, a repository for supplies, like a miniature Target.

Russ hasn't retired yet; he's approaching his fiftieth year as a food broker, which means he always has an abundance of assorted food items. He hasn't parked his car in the garage in years, having set up multiple racks and shelves to store his reserves. Like a credulous conspiracy theorist, he always keeps a surplus of essentials, enough to last two years, just in case the apocalypse ensues.

"Ok, just making sure. It's important to be there for Tommy and his daughter. It's important to maintain relationships, Den," Mary lectures, softening her tone to ease any perceived antagonism.

The only real communication Dennis has with his older brother Tommy, outside of the obligatory happy birthday and holiday texts, is through Facebook. This digital realm is where Tommy lives vicariously through his online persona, uploading workout videos, showing off his tattoos and new additions to his gun collection, and periodically posing in Punisher T-shirts while holding various shotguns. He loves to share selfies of himself drinking locally brewed beers with terse captions like "Beer me," always posing with IPAs and a thumbs up. He routinely shares footage of himself shooting beer cans in his backyard to show off his marksmanship, often accompanied by a "Fuck around and find out," or a "Don't tread on me" caption, a real patriot. His feed is also filled with posts about how happy he is down in Louisiana, lauding his wife with an uxorious demeanor, explicitly commenting "Sexy" with eggplant emojis on her photos for all to see. But it's not Tommy's self-aggrandizing digital presence that perturbs Dennis; it's the yearly birthday posts in all caps that get under his skin, complete with terrible grammar, remedial punctuation errors, and condescending felicitations, each one belittling him with an indirect insult:

HAPPY BIRTHDAY TO MY BABY BROTHER. YOUR STILL A BABY AND HAVEN'T REALLY GROWN UP YET. MAYBE YOULL GET A GIRLFRIEND THIS YEAR, LETS HOPE.

"I know, Mom. That's why I'm going," Dennis exclaims, twisting the top off the new bottle of olive oil, setting it down on the kitchen counter.

He sits down at the kitchen island, observing his father scrupulously patting down chicken cutlets, dabbing each with a paper towel, occasionally tossing one back and forth in his hands, emulating the technique of a pizzaiolo to absorb the moisture. Dennis contemplates if all Italian meals are made with the hands, gripping and shaping, lobbing for preparation.

"This is how you keep them flavorful without all the grease," Russ declares, smiling at each one like a masterful creation, admiring his culinary artistry.

The impulse to pull out his phone hits Dennis like a diabetic experiencing a drop in blood sugar, his heartbeat quickens, gripping him until he complies. He's immediately disappointed by the lack of notifications. He unlocks his phone to dig deeper, hoping for a like on the Instagram photo he just shared: *One Flew Over the Cuckoo's Nest,* with its patina cover and '70s vibe lettering, a book that exudes a subversive edge, the kind of book, Dennis decides, an eligible, philosophical bachelor might read. Maybe there's an email from a literary agent offering representation; it's been three months since his last rejection letter, but he still holds onto a shred of hope, thinking a few more responses might trickle in, residual optimism, circling the drain.

He looks up and sees his father, still marveling at his finished meal. His father is ecstatic, and Dennis adores his liveliness, acutely aware of the transient nature of the moment. He knows that in fifteen years or so, he'll look back on this night, remembering his father and how much he loved him.

"I can't wait for dinner, it smells so good," Dennis says loudly enough, just in case his father can't hear him.

He puts his phone away, vowing to keep it out of sight until the night is over, no matter how much withdrawal he experiences.

"Well, if your brother ever gets here, we can start eating," Russ howls, swiftly transitioning from joy to annoyance, agitated at John's tardiness.

"We don't have to wait for him. We told him what time to get here," Dennis replies eagerly, placing his hand on his father's shoulder in an attempt to ease his tension.

But his father persists, wiping down the dirty sink and running hot water over the messy pots and pans. Dennis realizes he's trying to delay dinner as long as possible, hoping that John, his wife, and the kids will arrive by the time he's finished cleaning up.

"Come on guys, let's eat one of the tomato and mozzarella spreads," Mary suggests, lifting the small recently prepared platter from the center island, bringing it over to the kitchen table.

She pulls out a dining chair and takes a seat, smiling at Dennis conspicuously as if she's trying to convey something more. She continues her glance while biting into the appetizer, slices of tomato layered with mozzarella, basil, and balsamic vinegar, one of his father's best dishes.

"Here, take a seat," she says with a weary smile, struggling to pull out a chair for Dennis.

"Alexa, play my favorite song," Mary requests, turning toward the small speaker on the countertop with an earnest anticipation, her tone elevated to ensure Alexa hears her command.

"Sorry, I can't do that right now," Alexa responds, causing Mary's shoulders to droop and her face to frown simultaneously; it's a pout Dennis can't help but recognize as a similar reaction he has when he's disappointed.

"What's your favorite song?" Dennis asks his mother.

"Rhythm of the Rain."

"Alexa, play 'Rhythm of the Rain,'" Dennis instructs with an authoritative tone, an ardent determination in his voice, resolute, as if he won't accept "no" for an answer.

The trickle of falling raindrops plays, followed by the reverberating chords of a celesta.

"Listen to the rhythm of the falling rain, telling me just what a fool I've been," the smooth, mellow voice sings.

Dennis's mother smiles, lost in the melodic tones, humming to herself and swaying with the beat, enjoying the music, unabashed by his presence. He sits and reflects on a future day, when he is an old man and his family has all passed. He imagines hearing this same tune on one of his Sirius XM channels, perhaps the '60s on 6, and instantly recognizing the harmonizing hook, the distinct tempo, and the melancholic lyrics. In that moment, he'll be transported back to this very day, back home with his mother. The realization fills him with gratitude for the present and reluctance for the future, a moment that's both a blessing and a curse.

"The only girl I care about has gone away, looking for a brand-new start," the solemn words resonate over the celesta chimes.

"But little does she know that when she left that day, along with her she took my heart," the hook concludes atop a soft drum patter.

His mother has been on edge for a few weeks now, spending three nights a week at his brother John's house to help watch the kids, a commitment Dennis believes is draining the life out of her. Natalie has been working late, leaving John to manage the kids alone. Mary forces herself over there every night to make sure dinner is made and the kids are taken care of, and John never denies her insistence to help, whether he needs it or not.

"What do you guys want to drink?" his father asks, opening the refrigerator, fidgeting, grasping the handle with nervous energy.

He's disappointed in John, deflecting as he's running out of tasks to delay dinner.

"Water," Dennis replies.

"I'm okay, hon," his mother answers, huddling over her tomato and mozzarella, picking pieces off to nibble on.

Russ retrieves a water and a Coca-Cola, placing the soda by Dennis's table setting and the water by Mary's.

"I think things are getting worse between your brother and Natalie," Russ comments with a somber lilt, fumbling with the utensils for no particular reason, his spectacles sliding off his nose.

He's fixated on something, brooding; his distressed expression conveys both worry and pessimism.

"Every marriage has its ups and downs," Dennis blurts in desperation to lift his spirits and imbue positivity, like an inspirational quote shared by a battered housewife on Facebook.

John's been married for a decade now, blessed with two healthy kids, but Dennis can never quite tell if he's happy. Their conversations never seem to go beyond surface-level topics; there's a lack of depth and personal sharing between them. It feels more like an acquaintance-level relationship, where they exchange quips, discuss sports, and recommend Netflix shows. With John being ten years older, he has always seen Dennis, the youngest of the three brothers, as just a child, or at least that's how Dennis has always felt.

"Poppa, Mom-Mom?" dulcet echoes project from the entryway, accompanied by the sound of little feet drumming against the floor.

"Oh no, is that Reese?" Mary exclaims, rising from her chair to greet the company.

Behind Reese, John ambles into the kitchen. Reese sports a puffy winter jacket and shorts, a strange combination of conflicting seasonal wear, especially for October.

Quickly unzipping her jacket, Reese tosses it onto the floor before journeying downstairs to play with the engaging games and little knickknacks Mary had picked up to keep the kids entertained, anything to keep them off their tablets.

"Sorry we're late," John mutters, immediately opening the refrigerator to grab a soda, stooping without the need to; his hair tousled as if he's just woken up or fought a large mammal in a forest.

"I told you 5:30," Russ bellows, throwing infuriated hands up in the air, emphasizing his annoyance; he stands behind the kitchen counter with the multiple meals sprawled, ready to be served.

Drinking his soda, gulping indulgently, John tosses his head back with each guzzle, avoiding eye contact. His face is sullen, sunken like that of an aged boxer. Dennis glares at his gaunt brother, speculating on whether he's going to respond to his father.

"Weren't you guys supposed to be here at 5:30?" Dennis barks, furrowing his brows and crossing his arms in agitation.

It's their father's birthday, for fuck's sake, the least John could do was be on time, Dennis boils.

"Yes, Jesus, we were running late. We're always running late," John sighs, slurping his soda as he slouches, his dreary eyes glaring off into the distance.

Dennis notices the faint outlines of John's rib cage through his long-sleeve waffle shirt; he resembles a zombie that's clearly not getting enough nutrition from human flesh.

"Where's Natalie?" Russ interrogates, more stolid, concerned with a stern voice.

Russ lifts the plate of chicken cutlets and delivers them to the kitchen table.

"She's got to..." John maunders, wandering over to the TV in the next room, sitting down on the couch.

John turns the TV on and flips through channels with immediacy, trying to locate whatever sports game is on.

"Jesus, they're losing," he announces, lashing his fist in the air.

Russ sits at the dining room table, waiting, listening for John to answer his inquiry about Natalie. He leans in John's direction with anticipation. Dennis watches, growing indignant with each unanswered passing minute.

"Dad is talking to you," Dennis says, trying not to exacerbate the situation.

"She has something with work, but she's stopping by later," he mutters with a glossy stare.

Dennis can't ascertain if John's annoyed with Natalie for not being there or with them for asking where she is.

Dennis recognizes John's defeated disposition, the hurt written all over his face. It's as if his conversations with his wife have been giving way to constant disagreements; there must be something going on with him, Dennis decides.

"Where's Natalie?" their mother probes, beetling over to get closer to him.

"Where's Jake?" she continues with her inquisition.

John alights from the couch seemingly out of discomfort or disinterest; he shuffles over to the dining table and sits down, helping himself to a salad portion.

"I don't know, she's got a conference call or something. Jake is at home, playing PS5 online with his friends," John mumbles before shoveling salad into his mouth, gorging like he's filling a void; Dennis can't tell if he's lying or if he just doesn't really know.

Mary rolls her eyes, placing her hands on her hips like an angry teacup, scampering over to the dining table. She huffs and hisses, pointing an austere finger at John, a recognizable sequence Dennis recalls his mother conducting right before she's about to lecture.

"Let me tell you, John. Your wife is a bitch," she articulates, hurling with frustration; her finger pointed, drawn like a dagger.

"Reese, it's time to eat!" Russ declares, shouting from the top of the basement steps; her feet rattling as she ventures upstairs.

John gobbles his food, letting out an abrupt chuckle at his mother's comment; he continues chewing without providing a further explanation, deflecting without discourse.

"She doesn't care about this family. It's your father's birthday," Mary continues in a lowered tone, trying to make eye contact with John.

"Mom-Mom, what did you say about family?" Reese questions, catching the last bits of the conversation.

She proceeds, stepping forward with cautious curiosity, her blue eyes as lucid as the ocean, her cherubic face, angelic and smooth. Reese possesses a childish naiveté, slower to develop compared to most children her age.

"I said family is most important," Mary replies sternly, glancing over at John before turning back to Reese with an impassioned smile.

She bows down, gazing at Reese with love. Reese reaches out with her tiny arms, wrapping them tightly around Mary's legs.

"Well, I love my family," she cheers with a cheesy grin, burying her face in Mary's lap.

4. The Cask of Amontillado

Approaching Dennis with a feverish tenacity, Renee lured him to the bedroom, tugging at his belt buckle, beguiling with an impeccable smile. Her soft, sensual lips and hands fondling, provoking his loins, impelling as she pulled at the waistband of his jeans, slipping her tongue in his mouth as she slid her hands down his pants. Throbbing from anticipation and still strung-out from slinging passive-aggressive insults, they finally blitzed each other like two seething gladiators, charging with ferocity, colliding onto the bed. They tore at each other's clothes like desperate scavengers in the pursuit of flesh, feasting on each other's exposed skin. Dennis's hand softly clutched Renee's mouth, sinking his teeth into her neck, kissing with a lingering bite. Wrapping her legs around him tightly, she dug her fingers into his back with determined claws, piercing through him with passion. They had argued the entire week, the tension and irritability galvanizing their concupiscence.

"I want you inside me," she whispered, blowing gently in his ear, reaching down to grab him.

Gyrating with each exhale, she beamed an erotic gaze, grinding teeth, biting the bottom of her lip. Her palms retrieved his cock, caressing his elongated shaft with a twisting motion; her right wrist always rotating before reaching the head, sliding her hand down the base with a grasping pull; her left hand cupping his sack, manipulating her fingertips into the wrinkles of the smooth skin, massaging dutifully.

Dennis closed his eyes, surrendering himself to her pleasurable clench, trying to forget about the torrents of slights they exchanged in their last argument and the back-and-forth direct messages he had uncovered on her Instagram the night before. Some digital stranger named Carl and she had been exchanging witty banter in her DMs for a few weeks, liking each other's posts and commenting heart eyes on pictures.

"He's just a nice, friendly guy," she told him with an irreproachable sigh, trivializing the confab and Dennis's concern.

They were engaged, so the possible infidelity stung, crippling, carrying all the way down to his stomach, eliciting a painful nausea and paralyzing headache. But Dennis hadn't noticed nudes or anything too provocative, he reasoned, so he decided he was going to ignore it like a fresh cut that wasn't deep enough to penetrate or cause any damage, avoiding the scab until eventually it healed itself. Unfortunately, he didn't take the discovery well, losing his temper, calling her a "sullied cunt," adding a vocab word to the harsh expletive in an attempt to dull the impact. But his comment proved to be incendiary, igniting, leading to a house fire of assaults, transforming their bedroom into an oven as they scorched each other, burning with personal foibles and scathing comments about inferiorities.

They had never been cruel to each other before, Dennis thought to himself as he slammed the bedroom door, retreating downstairs after she called him a "shitty fucking writer." They were growing distant, the bitterness becoming palpable. It had started with petty remarks based on observations, like the way Dennis left crumbs on the kitchen counter after snacking or how he didn't listen to Renee, failing to retain information from their conversations, losing focus after the first few words, forgetting to text her relatives on their birthdays and making weekend plans without confirming.

He was occupied, immersed in his words and thoughts, trying to finish the manuscript. It required all his attention and effort, leaving no motivation to achieve his master's degree in education like they talked about so he could become an English professor. And he knew being a freelancer without steady benefits wasn't the most auspicious or secure way to make a living, but he wasn't sure if teaching was going to be for him. A career cultivating young minds seemed cumbersome, like an obligation with major responsibility, a sure way to extinguish any creativity. Renee nagged him for a while before she became distant and laconic, keeping all communication terse; their strife exacerbated by Dennis unlocking her phone one night out of suspicion, digging through her DMs and emails to find a compromising conversation.

"How do you want it?" Dennis yanked her close, unleashing pent-up aggression, leering at her with a salacious look, his forehead pressed against hers.

The toxicity of their hurtful words still echoing in Dennis's head, heightening his hard-on; her malice still rattling his mind and stimulating his libido.

"I want to be on top," she declared, rising and pushing him down on the bed; her eyes fixated on his, advancing forward, climbing with a swift, gainly turn and mount, pressing her hands on his wrists, an intertwinement of intimacy.

Her devilish eyes glowed with licentious intent, an evocative gaze, piercing right through him; Dennis remembered thinking he wasn't going to last more than ten seconds with all the rising tension.

Dennis entered her, nestling inside, reveling in the moist warmth, the friction of smooth flesh, a transcendence of pleasure, unleashing a heated wave of euphoria, his body rewarded with remarkable sensations. Sex was always incredible before, but this encounter was extraordinary; the contrast of hurt and desire, the dichotomy of lust and love, an intoxicating amalgamation, was the ultimate aphrodisiac, an amplified release of emotion. And just as she inflicted pain before with her words, she now treated him with her body; every inch provided an incredible stimulation of feeling, a climbing ecstasy that was amplified with every gasp and moan, a purification of touch.

Penetrating with purpose, each thrust pushing Renee's legs open wide; her arm extended behind her back, reaching underneath, burrowing into his taint, applying pressure every time he reentered her. Without breaking her ogle, she continued riding him, absorbing each prod with delight, sharing a lascivious smile. Letting his head fall back onto the pillow, Dennis lost himself in her stare, relaxing his body and allowing his mind to rest, living in the moment and rejoicing in the pleasure alone, a satiation of primal urges, a surge of oxytocin. She was fixated on pleasing him, and Dennis could feel it building as he neared climax.

"Just come in me," she breathed, lying on top, her dampened breasts pressing against his chest as she bounced on his lap.

"What?"

"Do it. Let's come together," she implored with eagerness, her body radiating with humidity, an obsequious look that amplified his orgasm.

"I'm coming," he shouted, kissing her passionately.

Their bodies quivered, pulsating as they discharged. Their sweat wicking together, fluids mingling as their bodies entangled; it was a magical moment made everlasting, as if they both entered a different dimension together, letting the world fall behind. Their impressions still abiding on each other's bodies long after they finished, glowing, welded with warmth.

They lay on top of each other for a while after, chests pinned together, breathing in unison, circulation restoring and hormones balancing. Dennis wrapped his arms around her, rubbing his hand against her back, gently scratching with the faint pass of his fingertips. He pictured their wedding, it was less than a year away. He smiled, concluding by then, this would all just be a distant memory and they'd be honeymooning for a few weeks and Carl would be just an afterthought. Drifting off to sleep, he held her hand as she snoozed on top of him. Peacefully they slumbered, as if all the malevolence had been extinguished, the thrown dirt cleansed; it was the first time in two weeks that they occupied the same space, instead of opposing positions on the edges of their bed. The morning was going to be the first day of starting anew, Dennis delighted, triumphant. Gaping at Renee sleeping peacefully, his eyelids grew heavy, his nose swathed with her soothing scent; Dennis felt himself falling deeper in love with her, as if it were even possible.

He should have known better when she took charge, since she never initiated sex before; he should have sensed there was something awry, but he was too consumed with her, blinded and exposed. And while he was falling deeper in love, she was, unbeknownst to him, saying goodbye.

####

Trampling feet fill the hallways while the abrasive school bell rings, whistling as kids pour out of the cafeteria. Dennis jolts from the startling cacophony ringing through his ears, launching himself back into his chair; he's fallen asleep again at his desk during lunch time. He's been eating lunch in his classroom for the past two weeks, ever since he settled in with his parents. With no intentions of socializing with colleagues, he's wondering if maybe he'll regress to a primal being, more visceral, like he was back in college, solely motivated by narcotics and female genitalia.

He feels himself becoming more reclusive, especially since the only person he hung out with for the past four years was Christine. His tolerance for small talk is dissipating; his ambition to engage in trite interactions is non-existent, and if the biology teacher tells him one more pun joke in passing, referencing the periodic table of elements, he's going to call in a bomb threat to the Special Olympics and possibly light himself on fire or at least that's what he tells himself. His capacity for external dialogue is diminishing; his internal monologues are deafening; he can't even focus on a thirty-minute episode of *Californication*. He knows each episode is going to feature the charming protagonist engaging in philandering, fornicating with any girl that appears on the screen for more than two minutes and that the three minutes David Duchovny spends writing is going to materialize into a brilliant manuscript. But Dennis just can't even pretend anymore that life's some big Showtime comedy; he can't fake it, no matter how hard he tries.

He took a Benzo earlier, he thinks, or maybe he's just too tired; he's not sure, he can't remember. But he hasn't been sleeping much, and it's not because he's been sucked into the vapid expanse of new age narcissism, late-night trauma reels on Instagram, where people set up tripods to film themselves crying over some cataclysmic event, like a breakup or a death, drawing him in like a passerby rubbernecking a car wreck. No, it's because he's haunted, he thinks, visited by dark, devious eyes that urge him to come back home, crawl into bed, and send her a friend request on Facebook.

It's been years since he took any of his antidepressants, even before Renee, but he's convinced it might help assuage some of his psychosis, compelling nightly doses and hearty breakfasts. The medication he found had been in his toiletry bag for almost ten years; the first psychiatrist he ever saw prescribed him a profusion of psychiatric pills after a single session. Dennis deduces it was a facet of the doctor's ploy: drug and treat like a feral animal, establishing a repeat customer with a subservience to expose for profit. So, he's hoping expired drugs might provoke peace, maybe quiet his conscious, even it's for a little bit. He needs a break from his duality. He likes the way it makes him feel, the drugs, like he's floating, featherweight, and if he falls or crashes, maybe he won't feel it. This time, maybe it won't hurt.

Like a thick liquid, kids flood into his classroom, dropping backpacks and pulling rusted chairs against screeching floors. Reeling in his hypersensitivity, he shoots up out of his chair, widening his eyes as he gauges the class, blighted by his insobriety. He wonders if he has enough focus and composure to teach; he's not sure if he can even formulate a sentence; there's discernible drool all over his tie, fresh bubbles from his snooze. Dennis turns to the whiteboard as the class quiets, shielding himself, removing the cap from a green marker; it's the one he uses on Wednesdays, color coordinating his markers with days of the week. He writes the date in big bubble letters, trying to keep the inscriptions level, allowing space after the date before writing the day's topic: "The Cask of Amontillado."

An intrusive chuckle catches his ear.

"Mr. Clauden today is Monday the twenty-sixth," a tenor voice proclaims, announcing from the back of the classroom.

Dennis whips his head over his shoulder, looking back, his body facing the whiteboard as if he's guarding himself from further scrutiny.

"Thanks," he replies, realizing his oversight.

Waves of nervousness crack his consciousness, evincing susceptibility and insecurity. He's timid, wondering if he's too high to continue the lesson; perhaps he should just take a day or call 911 because maybe he's dying; maybe he should ask the assistant Dean to watch the kids and play a movie for the last two periods of the afternoon. He has a DVD of *Romeo and Juliet* starring Leonardo DiCaprio in his desk as a back-up lesson designated for a substitute's sick day coverage.

"Edgar Allan Poe," Dennis declares, clenching his fists, determined to battle his crippling faculties.

He wiggles his finger as he swings his arms back and forth across his body, resiling, like a basketball player getting ready to shoot a free throw at the foul line. He knows if he can establish control of his limbs, his mind will follow. He gave the kids a full week to read the six-page short story along with Poe's biography, emphasizing the need for diligence since there was going to be an intensive class discussion.

"Who could tell me a little bit about him?" Dennis asks, surveying the room, trying to decide who to call on, a deadly sniper focusing on a helpless target.

"Grace," he chooses, smiling toward the lengthy blonde with the conspicuous clenched chin; she's the semi-present scholar, the one who did just enough work to get a decent grade.

She uses the phrase "as a matter of fact" in every other paragraph in her essays. Grace is a pleasant girl though, really, Dennis decides; she always asks for permission to use the bathroom properly instead of using "can," which inquires whether she has the ability to perform such an action.

"May I use the restroom?" she'd ask.

And shallow exchanges are all Dennis can tolerate with Grace because her contributions are obtuse, expounding on literary analyses during class, using crutch words like "um" and "like" liberally, always postulating about love motifs in every story by suggesting ridiculous symbolic correlations. But she always replies with an appreciative, "Thank you," after being granted permission to use the lavatory; and gratitude is something Dennis admires, courtesy, a quality that separates the decent from the deplorable.

"Um, he was orphaned as a baby and didn't he like become an alcoholic and a drug addict?" Grace fuses a declarative statement with a question, a tactic that seeks positive reinforcement.

Dennis obliges, flashing a perfunctory nod and smile, folding his arms tightly against his body; he takes a deep breath before raising his hands to scratch his neck, resisting a compulsion to strangle himself. He wonders how much force and pressure he could actually self-administer until he would pass out or if he would even be able to choke himself for long enough to black out.

"Those certainly aren't the best things to be remembered as. And although he was an alcoholic, it was Rufus Griswold, Poe's nemesis, that fabricated the stories of Poe being a drug addict."

"But it definitely helped people become interested in him."

"How about some of his accomplishments?" Dennis poses, scanning for a new participant; Grace has a string of asparagus stuck in her front teeth, probably from a breakfast omelet, dark vestigial vegetable lodged between incisors, commanding too much attention.

"He married his ten-year-old cousin. Didn't he?" a projecting voice suggests, a vociferous tone as if it's intended to disrupt the discussion.

The class chuckles, and Dennis turns to notice Block Face hunched over in his desk, trying to dodge behind the shoulders of the student sitting in front of him. The class continues their lull, bleating like drugged sheep. Block Face's name is either Andrew or Anthony, but his rectangular head reminds Dennis of a particular Lego piece he used to build with when he was a kid, and Dennis doesn't have any more cerebral storage to retain names. He's too busy trying to learn two new vocabulary words a day, starving himself from dinner if he can't recall a precise definition the next morning. He thinks it's a good way to build character though, suffering for shortcomings like Nietzsche. Maybe he's a masochist; Dennis doesn't know, but he thinks he deserves it.

"She was thirteen, but either way, I wouldn't call that an accomplishment," Dennis defuses the provocation, ignoring the bait.

"Mr. Clauden, what do you mean by people only being interested in Poe because he was a drug addict?" Megan questions with one eyebrow raised, her tone stern but yielding, inviting deeper conversation.

Megan is a name he remembers and a face he hasn't forgotten. She's the only thing he's been looking forward to at work lately, the possibility that she's not as vacuous as the rest of her cohorts.

"Sorry, I should have raised my hand," Megan quickly retreats, sinking back into her seat; her shoulders drooping like a wilted orchid, her emerald eyes mesmerizing.

"That's ok," Dennis smiles.

"But it is true, if you really think about it," Dennis says, moseying toward her, maintaining eye contact.

Gazing back with a bemused expression, Megan twists her puckered lips and crosses her arms as Dennis approaches, a defensive pose, like she feels vulnerable or uncomfortable.

"Well, think of all the songs you listen to today. Your trap music with rappers all talking about getting high and snorting whatever, popping pills," he explicates, pausing his exposition as he looks around the room.

"It makes them cool, right?"

"Bro, I think what you're trying to say is it gives them mad clout," Jonathan pipes with a forceful voice, holding his open palm to the side of his mouth, emulating a megaphone.

"Yes, thank you for translating into modern terms for me," Dennis replies with haste, preventing the intrusion from derailing his thought process and the class's focus.

He debates scolding; he knows he can verbally eviscerate Jonathan, but he knows Jonathan is just a dense occupation of adolescent clay, not worth the aggravation in his current state. He's already borderline freaking the fuck out; he feels the disconnect resurfacing, the worry returning associated with tingles nipping down his elbows, trickling down to his fingertips. He doesn't know how many milligrams of downers he's digested, but he can't become defensive; he can't give in to the conspiracy or it will escalate his nerves. He knows he needs to remain resolute in his lecture, letting his subconscious take control, like a captain relinquishing the wheel to the chief mate.

"I guess you could say that's where it originated from. The more provocative and notorious you were, the more appealing."

"So even though he was slandered by Griswold, it actually worked for Poe's benefit," Dennis declares, waiting for more goading from the emboldened embryo.

Sauntering with arms crossed, Dennis peers, examining each teenager's face, inspecting for intellectual interest. He journeys toward the back, noticing a quaking Tim, anxiously raising his hand; there's a good chance he's dreaming, he thinks.

"What's the story about Griswold all about, Mr. Clauden?" he asks with an excitable demeanor, overflowing with eagerness, positioning his hands as if he's covering something precious that he doesn't want anyone else to see.

Dennis realizes Tim is attempting to conceal his unpreparedness, pretending he's in possession of the printout all the other kids are reading from, hiding the empty desk surface with his hands, a failed deception.

"I'll tell you all about it as soon as we finish today's lesson, but first, could you read for us, Tim?" Dennis inquires, squinting his eyes as he stands directly over his desk, leering with a predatorial stare, watching as if Tim is a mouse mired in a glue trap.

"Uh," Tim snivels, lifting his backpack from the floor with a nervous swiftness, frantically sifting through the contents of the interior pockets.

He pulls out papers, dropping them on his desk as if he's searching for a desperate lifeline, a raft to prevent him from sinking and being subjected to a circling shark.

"I can't seem to find it," Tim whispers, continuing his rummage, reaching into his backpack to continue his diversion.

Dennis recalls Tim Drury's current grade and the email his mother sent after he received a "D" on his essay, asking if there was an opportunity for extra credit to revise the grade. Poor Timmy broke up with his girlfriend recently and has been preoccupied, his mother disclosed.

Timmy finally glances up at Dennis, placid and indifferent, a complete transformation as if he's expecting a pass. An inexplicable rage captures Dennis, emanating from his chest, a heated centrifugal force that irritates his skin, like a nagging itch just out of reach.

"Well then, go to the Dean's office," Dennis exclaims, pointing to the door, perturbed.

"Oh bro, Mr. Clauden. I promise I read the story. I just don't have it with me," Tim pleads, pushing his hair back, tucking strands behind his ears before closing his hands, holding up his clutched palms together as he begs.

His nonchalant attempt at establishing some sort of familiarization with Dennis, as if they're pals and play pick-up basketball games together at recess enrages Dennis even further. Tim is bound to become a future barista, Dennis infers, capping out his career path at crafting coffees while wearing an apron that's ornamented with social justice issue pins. He imagines Tim's parents push him toward thinking independently while he consistently chooses to do nothing with his freedom except expect sympathy and lenience, the ethos of the modern progressive age.

"This is advanced English, and you're continually unprepared. If you want to waste your education at the expense of Mommy and Daddy's money, that's fine. But you will not be a part of this class while you do nothing," Dennis castigates with deep contempt, releasing building vitriol.

Tim gawks at Dennis; his raggedy long hair reminds him of the classic kid from college that cuts his coke up with caffeine and creatine, mixing similar white powders, camouflaging for profit. He'd charge ninety dollars for a gram, and you'd know it was caffeine not only because of the burning sensation but the persisting sweat; good coke raised your heartbeat, not your body temperature.

Tim remains seated. Sighing with frustration, he avoids eye contact, hoping it might diminish the conflict. But his reluctance to leave with each passing second and his fucking dumbfounded expression exacerbates Dennis's anger, like the quintessential college kid that hangs around for way too long following a smoke session.

"If I have to tell you one more time to leave, Tim, we will seriously have issues," Dennis snarls, partly wondering why he's become so aggressive and hostile with misplaced anger.

Luckily, Tim capitulates, standing up from his desk with a meek disposition, stooping as he vacates the classroom, like a captured soldier being led to his execution. But Dennis could have been a bigger dick if he really wanted to. He could have written him up for his stupid fucking vape pen he keeps tucked into the front of his backpack, displaying it with hubris as if teachers didn't know the different between a Juul and a flash drive.

"Now class, please turn to page one, and let's see... Megan will you begin reading?" Dennis unsurprisingly instructs.

Megan is quickly turning into Dennis's favorite student, and he seldom takes a liking to any anthropoid, let alone a student. She looks up toward Dennis and smiles, scooching up in her seat as she glances down at her book; her face flush and perk as she flips her hair back, revealing black gauge earrings, eye-catching accents.

"The thousand injuries of Fortunato I had borne as I best could, but when he ventured upon insult I vowed revenge," she reads.

"So, what does this tell you?" Dennis interrupts, canceling out the audience, focusing in on Megan solely.

Megan engages with zeal, sitting upright, glimpsing upwards to the corner of the ceiling as if she's in deep contemplation, a behavior Dennis recognizes as her default thinking display.

"That out of all of the things Fortunato did to him, it was the insult that made him want to get revenge?" she asks; her eyes widening as her moistened lips glisten in the sunlight.

"Correct," Dennis beams back at her; he's enthralled.

"Please, resume reading."

Megan reads loudly, poised, careful with her pronunciations, pausing after each line break. She's confident in her delivery, as if she knows she's in the good graces of a monarch. Dennis studies her closely, like a newly hatched nestling; her lips pursing dramatically whenever she enunciates words; her recently straightened hair sits, perched on her shoulders as she sits with her legs crossed. She reads with enthusiasm, enunciating words like "point," "precluded" and "punish" with precision. Her high cheekbones elevate her appearance, complementing her delicate hazel eyes and petite nose. She articulates, "Fortunato" and "Montresor," perfectly as if she's read the story several times before. Her plaid skirt lays just above her knees; her lips move gracefully, sparkling with each word she speaks. Dennis is captivated with her soft yet assertive, angelic voice; her seamless speech and reading speed is arousing, admiring her oral abilities. He wonders how many followers she has on Instagram, what her follower-to-following ratio might be, or if she's even aware of the vanity metrics involved in curating a social media persona, the careful posturing of self-presentation with few posts and a higher follower count than following.

As the story approaches its midpoint, Dennis realizes he needs to have at least another student read aloud like he usually does, but he can't stop the recitation; he's lost in Megan's narration, catching eye contact with her every time she looks up, lost in her studious face. She's not wearing glasses like she usually does, Dennis realizes. Her eyelashes seem longer, more arresting with each flicker; her dark liner applied precisely to bold burgundy lips. He needs to be less obvious and stop lechering, but he can't help it.

Dennis turns and notices Jonathan slouching in his seat, slowly descending as he tries to hide his cell phone. He's clearly texting; the discernible blue glow from the device reflecting off the desk's surface.

"Jonathan," Dennis shouts, startling him as he perks up with frightened, starry eyes, dropping his phone on the backpack beneath his legs, a clever attempt to divert attention away from his texting.

"Yes?" he replies.

"Please pick up where Megan left off."

Jonathan shuffles a few pages, swapping sheets, turning one over and flipping it back again; he has no idea what page they're reading from.

"Uh, what page?"

"Page four, my conspicuous text messenger," Dennis instructs as his stomach grows; it dawns on him that he forgot to eat lunch again.

"Uh ok, at the top?" Jonathan asks.

"That's a good start. Pick it up at he repeated the movement."

"He repeated the movement- a grotesque one. You do not comprehend, he said. Not I, I replied. Then you are not of the brotherhood," Jonathan reads, stammering his words, struggling to pronounce "grotesque," articulating it as "groo-tesk."

"Now why is this part important, Jonathan?"

"Why is this a crucial moment for our protagonist and antagonist?" Dennis adds, his hangry state increasing with each rumble of his belly.

Jonathan raises both eyebrows and leans forward; he puts the pages down, lowering his face to examine it, placing his palm on the side of his head, pondering blindly.

"Like important just in general?" he asks.

"Sure, tell us," Dennis directs with a sarcastic cadence, a sharp delivery.

"Well, they seem friendly?" Jonathan asks rhetorically, his sentence heightening in pitch toward the end, posing a question.

"Try again," Dennis snaps, placing folded hands behind his back; cognizant of his slouching, he stands up straight, hyperextending his neck and contorting it swiftly, stretching facet joints, popping, a mannerism he executes when he's incensed.

He's already sent a kid to the Dean's office, so he's going to have to deal with Jonathan differently, as another one might look like ineptitude as a teacher, an amateur without control.

"I just don't really know," Jonathan replies, surrendering with a somber tone.

"Well, take your phone out. And open a text message," Dennis commands, raising his voice in austerity.

"You want me to take my cell phone out?" Jonathan inquires with a befuddled look, his jowls retracted, expressing confusion, as if he's being falsely accused.

"Yes, reach down and grab it from your backpack."

Smiling students stare, amused with the escalating encounter.

"Open up a blank text message, and jot this down," Dennis orders, venturing over to his desk; Dennis's arms still placed behind his back; his chin jutting out, as if he's bracing for a blow to the face.

"Jot what down?" Jonathan asks, alarmed, maneuvering his backpack with frantic feet, maintaining eye contact.

Dennis notices the addition of several edgy black bracelets to Jonathan's wrist, dangling as he frets, gesticulating, adding to the pantomime; a visible "Black Lives Matter" band is entangled around the other solid ones, a blatant violation of the school's non-political messaging policy. And Dennis isn't agitated at the message itself; no, it's the social justice fashion statement, the virtue signaling, Jonathan parading as some self-appointed white savior that pisses him off.

"Jot down what I'm about to tell you."

"I figure you can't go ten minutes without looking at your phone, so maybe if we put it in a text message, it'll resonate with you."

Students look on, glued to the intensifying interaction, watching with nervousness, the room filling with pressure, a heaviness, perceivable tension. The class grows silent, and Dennis notices grins on kids he's never seen before; he wonders if he's hallucinating as he now realizes he's taken at least ten milligrams of lorazepam, about four times more than the recommended dosage, which might explain why he can't feel his heartbeat or why he's experiencing real time on a five-second delay, with words escaping his mouth before he actually processes them. But like a determined pilot experiencing turbulence, Dennis is staunch on landing this flight or possibly crashing it into Jonathan.

Jonathan flashes a tentative smirk, glancing around the class to gauge the reactions of others to decide whether Dennis is kidding or not. He retreats into his seat, sinking as he realizes the severity of the situation.

"I'm serious, take your phone out and open a new text message," Dennis demands.

Huffing and puffing, Jonathan rubs his eyes with the back of his hands, sticking his tongue out to dampen his lips, a nervous tick, Dennis speculates. Jonathan reaches down to retrieve his phone; his bright yellow pineapple socks peek out from underneath his wrinkled teal khakis; he's already begun his transformation into the typical frat tool bag, peacocking.

Dennis stands directly in front of Jonathan's seat, scrutinizing, squeezing his crossed arms against his body, his sleeves rolled up, emphasizing his bulging forearms.

"Now, begin texting," Dennis announces as Jonathan looks up with beady eyes.

Jonathan's skinny face exhibits a grudging expression with whimpering lips and panting pupils, as he places his hands on the phone to prepare his text.

"Hi Mom. First and foremost, I would like to thank you for spending your hard-earned money on sending me to such a wonderfully prestigious high school."

Staring forward with an aloof daze, Jonathan clicks on his smartphone; his fingers moving swiftly across the miniature digital keyboard on his screen. If only his dexterity for sending text messages could translate into something worthwhile besides quick, flat communication, he might be worth something, Dennis postulates.

"Today, we learned about the 'Cask of Amontillado.' And while I was unprepared for class, I still learned about one of the most crucial moments of the story," Dennis continues his monologue.

"I'm going to look over this text once we're done, and if it's not completely word for word, you will get a zero for today," he remarks, wrapping his right arm across his body, clutching his left elbow, unwavering as he remains in front of a timorous Jonathan.

Dennis caresses the bottom of his neatly trimmed beard with his index finger and thumb, like a modern, animated philosopher, considering his words carefully.

"One of the most defining moments of this story is when Fortunato asks Montresor why he doesn't understand the symbolic gesture of the masons. Fortunato implies that because Montresor doesn't comprehend his grotesque movement, then he must not be of the brotherhood, the masons."

Jonathan's face writhes in frustration as he continues texting; Dennis already pictures the long overdramatic Facebook post Jonathan will share tonight, grumbling about it later with indignance: "Mr. Clauden is such a dick, blah blah."

"Are you getting all of this?" Dennis queries, placing his hands on his hips.

"I don't want to see a single typo."

Jonathan nods as he continues punching away at his tiny keyboard; his eyes racing back and forth like a rambunctious typewriter ribbon.

"Fortunato is right and had he continued pressing Montresor, he would eventually realize he was not a mason after all. This is the only instance and quite literally the most critical element where Fortunato has almost figured out he is being tricked."

"Got it, Jonathan?" Dennis asks, leaning forward, trying to detect any instance of resentment; Dennis scans for a scintilla of attitude in his demeanor; just a wisp of defiance and he'll be marking Jonathan with a zero.

"Yes," Jonathan mumbles.

"Great," Dennis replies, snatching the phone from him, making sure the text is addressed to his mother and not just another friend before pressing send.

"Let's add 'I love you' at the end for extra affection because who doesn't love their mommy?" Dennis delights, adding to the text before sending.

The class cackles, and Dennis places the phone back on Jonathan's desk before strolling back toward the front of the classroom; his peers continue their trance, staring at Jonathan as if he's just been pantsed and pushed over in complete humiliation. Dennis turns back to the class, noting Jonathan's scrunched, disgruntled face.

"Now how might this story pertain to contemporary society, you might be wondering?" Dennis poses.

And he's no longer feeling like a pilot; Dennis is feeling more like a passenger actually, ready to jump from the plane without a parachute. He's feeling a stirring from within, a visceral venom from the bottom bubbling, sneaking up his esophagus as he stands in front of the class. He considers delivering an optimistic epilogue, but he decides against it; it's not authentic, and he's not a pilot anymore. He's a doctor, he decides, and it's time to rip some bandages off, even if it's premature.

"While social media has us happily connected with our disconnect, thinking we have everyone figured out by what they project to the world, do we really know people as much as we think we do?" Dennis poses.

"As many of you head off to college next year, you'll be faced with many situations that require you to make important decisions. Judicious assessments."

"You'll be tried and tested to see who you can trust. You'll go to a party, or you'll be pledging Alpha Sigma Theta loafer shoes and you'll most likely be under the influence," Dennis postulates as he roves, lingering down the first row of seats, glancing at every other student, noting a singular differentia on each kid as he continues his walk.

"Will you be confident in your decision making while you're wasted?"

"Will you know who you can trust?" Dennis canvasses with slight condescension, rambling, stopping after each sentence to catch distracted faces or blather in the back of the class.

"Will you know who is trying to take advantage of you?" he asks as he reaches Megan's seat, catching eyes for an extended moment before resuming his rhetorical questions.

Renee's dubious eyes flash before him, catching Dennis off balance; he wonders how much more stimulating a college class discussion would be; he likens his classes dialogues to YouTube comments, word regurgitation from assorted beings that feel the need to talk, even when they have nothing of value to say.

"Will you be just as foolish as Fortunato and ignore all the warning signs?" he theorizes, fighting off the face of his ex-fiancée and permutations of an accomplished career as a professor at an esteemed college.

"Will you be fooled and fall asleep with your shoes on while the entire party draws dicks on your forehead in magic marker?" he suggests as several discernible students flash widened eyes and surprised expressions.

"Will you be too hammered and fall into the trap of a predator, who could potentially molest you? Maybe filming the intercourse to relive the moment."

"Will you be too annihilated and walk into oncoming traffic or fall off the roof of some frat house? Perhaps severing your cervical vertebra, rendering you a paraplegic, confined to an existence in a wheelchair and requiring assistance to use the bathroom."

Dennis reaches the front of the classroom unscathed, completing his conquest through the sea of desks and personalities around the room. He notices a preponderance of somber faces gazing back, disturbed by his lecture. Uncertain looks and uncomfortable stares, it's evident the class isn't sure whether to be afraid or intrigued. Dennis crosses his arms and stares up at the ceiling, noticing the tinges of water spots, an accumulation of blemishes from over the years on the mineral fiber tiles. The misty, textured white boards with weathered brown swirls and spots resembling a spoiled crumb cake, a metaphor for the day's bittersweet lesson. Clearing his throat, Dennis pauses before propagating, heeding the bewildered faces that gaze back at him as if he's about to disclose a terrible secret. He's losing it, he knows, his future looks bleak, but for now, he's ready to deliver a resonating peroration, one that rattles and inflicts, exposing vulnerabilities.

"Chances are none of you have really even thought about any of this, and you're not going to get walled in like Fortunato, but rest assured, you'll probably be deceived and possibly exploited to some capacity, most likely by someone you trust, maybe even someone you love. Most of you will make terribly stupid decisions at college while under the influence of some sort of drug that results in awful occurrences, imbroglios, and other trauma-inducing, life-shaping events."

"And there's always the reality that one or two of you will never recover from it; it'll be what spoils you, destroying the rest of your life," his disquisition sends shockwaves through the room, rendering the class a morgue, discernible tears forming in the eyes of several students.

"And then there's always the grim possibility that one of you will be dead before you even graduate college, suffering a harrowing fate, leaving your parents with a lifetime of unbearable sorrow and grief."

5. Notes from Underground

The gossiping of rich housewives resounded in the background, a white noise, as Dennis sat across from the TV, correcting a pile of midterm papers in his lap; the pooch nestled beside him, digging itchy ears into the side of his leg, snorting, play-sneezing with a lively demeanor. Corpse-like creatures with bleached hair and paralyzed facial muscles opined on the big screen, complaining about other cast members, supposed friends, and their super stressful, luxurious lives.

Dennis and Christine had watched the first season earlier that week while he graded tests, each episode depicting cringeworthy encounters of spry drunk ladies fighting, crying, and laughing, sequentially. And Dennis could easily cancel out the cliché dialogues and empty plot lines to focus on his work, but the cutaway interviews always caught Dennis's attention; he had to listen to them talk, pontificate, watching with fascination, bewildered by their lack of depth, distracted by their expressionless countenances, bloated facial features, and noxious personalities. He wondered how such fucking hollow individuals could be so wealthy. Vacant, ignorant, and incredibly emotional, as if the years of Botox slipped into every aspect of their existence, poisoning brain cells, altering amygdala, and numbing cognitive functioning. Too rich to have any real problems, so they created their own drama, magnifying trivial matters, and wallowing in self-pity. Reality TV provided a platform for narcissism, elevating insipid individuals to super stardom, he theorized.

Christine loved the Bravo channel and every one of its fatuous reality TV shows, entertainment for people who wanted to turn their brains off and check out, indicative of what contemporary society desired, not having to think. She'd come home after work, sink into the couch, and drift off to sleep with *The Real Housewives* playing in the background. She could watch them for days, but she wouldn't really be engaged; she'd be on her phone most of the time, Instagramming, trying out a filter, looking up a recipe, or filling out a Pinterest board. Christine could watch any series, as long as it offered predictability and simplicity, so she could follow along without much effort.

Dennis turned the TV on anyway, out of habit, even though Christine wasn't home, resuming the episode they hadn't finished from the night before. He sat on the chaise lounge with his headphones on, partially covering ears, positioned perfectly to drown out the shrills of elder hyenas with revered symphonies, lighter homophonic melodies and chordal accompaniments. He had read online that listening to classical music was good for focus, like rhythmic Adderall, captivating reverberations. Eventually, he looked up to notice the nonsense portrayed on the broadcast, pushing off his earphones to listen, paying attention for a little while, until one of the ballooned caricatures recited some platitude or trite statement about life. It was always something along the sentiment of "Live, Laugh, Love," and then he'd have to immerse himself back into the papers, turning his music up louder to cancel out any vapidity from possibly leaking into his head, afraid he might actually become dumber from watching. The grading helped, affirming his intellect and validating his confidence in his competence. He circled errors erratically and aggressively with his red pen, carving loops around misspellings and typos. And after only two essays, it became apparent most topics were picked out of procrastination, failing to give any thesis considerable thought or conduct research. After eight papers, Dennis noticed arbitrary punctuation littering almost every page, realizing almost all the students had no clue how to properly use commas; a lesson in basic punctuation was definitely something he needed to cover in the next unit, he noted.

"My thesis statement is that Edgar Allan Poe was a manic depressant," Dana Killefer's first line read.

Cringing with clenched fists, he ground his teeth with antipathy; Dennis had instructed on multiple occasions not to make thesis statements blatantly obvious:

"Do not announce your thesis," he wrote emphatically on the whiteboard in large letters, underlining for importance.

Sighing, defeated, he circled the glaring statement several times in red ink, emphasizing the negligence.

"I told you not to do this," he wrote along the margin, adding a punctuation mark at the end.

Lifting the next packet of stiffly stapled papers, Dennis sipped his coffee, seeking superficial vigor and motivation, searching for the tolerance and drive to read rubbish, more pages of non sequiturs and insignificant theories on literature, laced with grammatical abortions and butchered sentences. Paragraphs packed with typos: "Seldomly" instead of "Seldom," "Irregardless" instead of "Regardless," and several other enervating malapropisms and terrible syntax structures. Paper after paper awaited, more myopic thesis statements and run-on sentences strategically placed to extend just enough past the 3000-word count requirement and reach the required eight-page length.

And Dennis had been painfully aware that "irregardless" had achieved "official" status, courtesy of Merriam-Webster's latest inclusivity directive, promoting even more shitty writing. He'd seen the news headline on Yahoo, right after the super compelling "Being on Time is Linked to White Supremacy" thought piece penned by a white professor from Duke. But he was never going to cave, no matter how many likes or shares the bullshit neologism amassed. And he'd almost rather have encouraged his students to use ChatGPT if it meant sparing him from reading rudimentary prose written by underdeveloped brains.

Before picking up the next paper, Dennis debated whether to lacerate his wrists with a dull blade he kept in the bathroom or open Instagram, pulling up a political post to argue with a stranger in the comment section, calling the anonymous interlocutor a "feckless cunt" or maybe a "myopic catamite;" he had read about pederasty in ancient Greece from a recommended book pop-up ad and how young boys were kept for homosexual practices. But he decided to open his laptop instead, pet the snoozing pup curled up next to him, and venture onto Facebook. He hadn't logged on in months, fighting urges of empty stimulation, realizing the absurdity of the platform: the people projecting the lives they wanted others to believe they were living via miniature profiles, conveying happiness at all costs, posting delighted pictures and sharing helpful articles to convey their virtue and maturity.

But something was really poking at Dennis, an itching impulse and nagging curiosity, like maybe some dire message was in his inbox, just waiting to be read, or maybe a friend request from somebody important was waiting. Maybe from someone he used to know. He didn't want to get too engulfed in a Facebook visit though, he just wanted to check his notifications; he knew that if he stayed on for more than ten minutes, he was going to be compelled to search and journey down a rabbit hole of his past, clicking through photos and memories, possibly looking up ex-girlfriends from over the years.

His feed loaded, and a familiar face appeared: a mature redhead holding a toddler in her arms.

"Susanna Murphy uploaded 16 photos to the fall album," the first header read.

Susanna is a woman he hadn't thought about in a very long time, since he was much younger; her weathered appearance conveying depreciating age, a stark contrast to the smooth contoured face he used to kiss with vigorous lust and desire as a budding teenager. He already regretted logging into Facebook, cognizant of his mind drifting to the past. She was married, a new last name, and the little one must have been her kid, he surmised.

Before he could log off, a little red flag in the top right corner popped up, eliciting a jolt of dopamine, signaling a surprise; he had ten notifications, enticing him to engage, releasing his restraint. He clicked with interest, excitement, giddy at the possibilities. But they were mostly invitations from people he went to high school with who he hadn't seen or talked to in over ten years, asking to like some Facebook page or join a promising pyramid scheme, some ploy to work from home for $500 a day or lose thirty pounds in thirty days by rubbing some hundred-dollar cream on common areas of the body where fat is stored. One notification was a "memory" from ten years ago; it was from Jeremy, a friend from college he hadn't spoken with since 2015, a couple years after they graduated. Clicking the link with reluctance, anticipating looming nostalgia, Dennis wondered which evocation he was going to visit and relive temporarily; it was a picture of them playing beer pong their junior year of college at Virginia Tech; Jeremy had uploaded it on his birthday that year with accompanying banter:

"Happy Birthday, BITCH. Love, your beer pong partner who always carries you."

Transported to his off-campus apartments on Bradley Drive, Dennis could still hear TI's "You could have whatever you like" booming in the background as the robust Bose speakers rattled the makeshift beer pong table they had set up across several barstools. The redolence of weed smoke still lingering in his nostrils. They had found a slender piece of plywood outside their place by the dumpster, which they used as their go-to beer pong surface, propping it up outside before football pre-games on warm days. The four-foot by eight-foot board became a canvas for graffiti over the year, a time stamp, inscribed with doodles and messages from girls they were pursuing, along with classic penis references to varying degrees, ranging from "I Love Cock" in black letters to a full-blown depiction of a ball sack, detailed with precise pubic hairs and wrinkles running across the scrotum.

Halcyon days, Dennis recalled. He had truly believed they'd be friends for life, often discussing the ridiculous "Best Man" speeches they'd give at each other's weddings someday. But Dennis knew it was his fault their friendship faded, failing to return phone calls and reciprocate text messages, forgetting to post birthday messages each year on his wall. Jeremy still lived in Virginia, so the only way they could communicate was digital; it wasn't like they could just walk outside into the hallway of their apartment to chat anymore, their friendship required consistency, effort, something Dennis was never good at.

"Handsome guys," a comment read underneath it from a Renee Trivella, posted a few years ago, an unrecognizable name in bold letters without a clickable option to visit the profile, which meant it was a blocked user.

Dennis blanked, wondering who the inaccessible person was, poring over the profusion of women he dated or fornicated with over the years that would have posted such an endearing message. And then it came to him, a sobering realization: Renee had married Carl.

Frozen, he slipped into a sinkhole of thought, pausing time for what seemed like was eternity; shrouded in an ineffable haze, Dennis stared, detaching, his vision darkening everything around him except for the silhouette of the laptop monitor. He quickly searched for "Carl Trivella," since he knew his profile was public from stalking him years ago. His heart pounding with panic as he sifted through uploaded photos, each click coinciding with a thunderous heartbeat. His palms sodden with nervous moisture, the laptop mouse dampened with sweat. The cold wetness intensifying as a picture of Renee and Carl appeared from their wedding day, sending a surge of dread to his stomach, eliciting a terrible nausea.

He clicked, viewing images from their magical day, never allowing himself to fully focus, a defensive approach to prevent his heart from fully degrading, possibly incurring more damage, an attempt to dull the sting. A manifold of thoughts ran through his head, but not a single perception fully processed, not a sole sensation fully felt, deadened, debilitated, her fading smile glimmering in the undercurrent of his memory. Gazing off into the distance of their apartment, he had seen enough; he struggled to absorb the newly discovered information, fighting off the compulsion to punch his desk or cry uncontrollably as flashes of heat and goosebumps stippled along his arms. They had only broken up four years ago, there's no way she could be married already, he dredged.

Maybe he should have done something over the past years, he ruminated; perhaps he should have reached out to her or fought harder for her. Staring off into the corner of the living space as the afternoon sunlight faded, illuminating the floor, revealing specks of dust and dog dander floating in the air, he journeyed back to a random Sunday with Renee that featured a similar sunlight, warming their backs as they cuddled on the couch. That familiar afternoon glow and mild breeze he associated with her for the longest time was no longer theirs to share, he realized.

He felt hollow, embarrassed by the false hope he had been harboring for years like a desperate climber dangling from the edge of a cliff, grasping with his last ounce of strength, holding out for a rescue, a possible reconciliation. Dennis hung his head, hunching over the keyboard, fighting back against the vomit stirring; they had been living separate but parallel lives, he proselytized, and despite going their separate ways, traveling on different paths, there was always a chance they might cross paths again, astray, but never too far out of reach, Dennis believed. The possibility of finding each other again was always there, like a life raft, whenever he felt at his lowest and sinking. But her journey was now complete; she had chosen her life partner, and it wasn't Dennis.

And he had envisaged all types of happy rekindlings: outside in the rain with coordinating black umbrellas at 2 A.M. with The Script playing in the background, extemporaneously meeting outside the bar they had their first date, hugging each other in dramatic fashion as they'd drop their umbrellas in the heat of the moment, soaking each other up in the downpour. Or perhaps it'd be the postcards they would write each other in ten years, serendipitously delivered to each other at the same time. Their pen-paling eventually escalating into a courageous phone call and dinner date, where they would have mind-blowing sex afterward, just like they did the last time, picking the passion up right where they left off. But it wasn't going to happen; there were no more possibilities. He was just a blemish, reduced to the other guy, a slight detour, a supporting actor in the love story of Renee and Carl, and he was stained, expendable; he was the throw-away.

His mind flooded with stored moments he refused to let go of. They were precious memories they shared and kept protected in a capsule, as if some day they'd sit side by side and open it, reminiscing: the long car drives out to see her parents or the time they stole the free shots from the couple who was fighting at the bar. Or the night they got thrown out of the diner for singing Black Eyed Peas too loud and the profound early morning chats they had about getting older, wondering where they'd be in a certain years' time, conjecturing about what their kids would be like. Dennis revealed himself to Renee, shown her exactly who he was inside, unveiling vulnerabilities and the debilitating fear of being alone, wondering if his soul was too tattered to be saved.

"You're not defined by your thoughts. It's your actions that determine your character," she had told him, gently squeezing his hand as they lay enmeshed under toasty covers, warmed by their exposed bodies, the smoke still lingering from the joint they had shared.

He had opened himself to her, stripped away his ego, uncovered and susceptible, disclosing all his inner workings, intricacies and quirks, habits and foibles; she knew the real him. And Dennis had always believed deep down that at the root of their separation was a fear of commitment, speculating Renee had manifested some subconscious obstruction, a pathology, influenced by the brief affair her father had with a local woman he'd met at the grocery store when Renee was young. But Dennis now knew it was all bullshit; she knew exactly who Dennis was, and she wasn't afraid of commitment; she just didn't want to commit to him.

Processing the finiteness of his finding, Dennis pondered the influence of timing; maybe they just weren't meant to be, they had met too young; perhaps meeting a year later would have ensured the stars aligned, their glue stayed sticky. But no, and there was no reason; there was no lesson to be learned, no message to be deciphered or whatever platitudinal explanation the mind could conjure up to comfort or rationalize. They weren't "cubs" like they used to call each other affectionately in baby talk, no, they were just two arbitrary primates that shared a brief stint of cohabitating and fornicating in the 21st century. And just like the leftover crumbs on the kitchen counter and the aspirations they once shared for a future together, nothing mattered anymore. Gazing around the apartment he shared with Christine, he could feel a draft pass through him, exposing the schism from within. Cognizant of his emptiness, he hated himself for feeling this way; pulverized and beaten, he hated how his heart hurt when it should have felt full and comforted from Christine.

Transfixed on the floor, bowed from his discovery, he gaped with a vacant, melancholic stare, gazing into the abyss; his peripherals detecting the dog licking his arm, repetitive passes of moistened sand-like friction grazing his arms, sensing his agitation and turmoil, but Dennis shoved Cooper away, brushing his thick curly Collie hairs off. The dog retreated on the couch, squatted on his hind legs, and then jumped off, leaving behind a puddle of piss that would soak into the fabric, creating a permanent stain Dennis could never remove.

####

"And what name do you give your daughter?" the priest asks, raising an overhand palm over the little one's head, motioning with his hand as he poses his question.

"Faith," his brother's wife replies, her face smirking with a charming smile, scrunching her button nose; she's a petite southern woman ten years his elder, adorned in a quaint sun dress, a lace bottom accentuating her garb.

Dennis's brother Tommy holds his four-year-old daughter in his arms awkwardly, like an outstretched turkey about to be placed into the oven; he grins oddly, rocking back and forth, flashing a childlike smile at his wife. The overhead pendant lights casting an illuminating glow; his bald head glistening with sweat, reflecting a polished surface; Tommy shaves his head with a razor now. Dennis ponders the possibility of Tommy being drunk or high, indulging in an Irish breakfast or stimulant, snorting some sort of powdery residue since he was always hopped up on something to "take the edge off."

Dennis wonders if Tommy really buys into the non-secular bullshit or if he's just placating himself and his recently wedded wife, attempting to rectify, making himself feel better about leaving his first wife while she was pregnant for his married secretary.

"You have asked to have your child baptized. In doing so you are accepting the responsibility of training her in the practice of the faith, by loving God and our neighbor," the priest proclaims with a sonorous voice, gesticulating with each proclamation; his beige cassock draped over his bony shoulders, his hair slicked back with rectangular specs perched on his hooked nose.

Dennis contemplates if Tommy and his wife are truly absorbing the priest's esoteric monologue, comprehending the message to any capacity, as the clergyman inquires on "training her in the practice of faith," showing her the way of "God." Teaching her principles, guiding her with values, instilling morality, virtue. The ethics outlined by God, the principals and morals taught by Christ. Dennis wonders if that's why they waited and didn't have their daughter baptized right away; he assumes they needed to feel better about their standing with God first, cleanse themselves from their transgressions before including sinful offspring.

The whole ordeal is a complete farce, blatant hypocrisy, Dennis decides, which is why he can't take any of it seriously; his brother and his wife Haleigh forming a pious family after committing adulteries, cardinal sins to be with each other, carrying out a clandestine love affair and covert office trysts. After two months of surreptitious encounters, they both left their spouses. They had broken several commandments, indulged in sin: coveting thy neighbor's home and wife, and now they are propitiating for their debaucheries, attempting to vanquish suppressed shame by attending church every Sunday since, repenting for their vices. But they've been together for four years now, so Dennis thinks maybe he's being too cynical, recognizing his possible projection that's jutting from his own internal conflict; he misses being in love.

Dennis sits in the aisle next to his father and mother, which is necessary since they never know when to release the kneeler down to pray and can no longer follow directions accurately. Russ is perched next to Dennis, smiling adoringly as he listens.

"I really hope I'm here to see your child be baptized one day," he leans over to Dennis, whispering his wish, smiling but keeping his eyes fixed on the altar.

His words strike like a sledgehammer to Dennis's chest, paralyzing him momentarily, eliciting a deep sense of anxiety, unsettling cogitation; his eyes fill like tiny hopeless rivers, causing his nose to itch, so he digs his face into his sleeve to avoid a possible sneeze and a major breakdown.

Dennis wonders if his father will still be around by the time he has kids or even gets married; he's mired by the inevitable, the future, the unknown, an existence where everyone he has ever loved is dead; he can't imagine being lonelier than he is now. He considers how much time he has left with his father, pondering the chances of reaching his mid-forties with him still around. Mathematically, he's destined to live the second half of his life without him, his best friend by default, his only friend. And this is all new to Dennis, this constant foreboding and poignancy, and he's never been more terrified; he's starting to realize the world is bleaker without Christine around.

He glances over at Russ, watching his mannerisms, admiring his interest; his father sits up straight, hyperextended, moving his head back and forth like a sprinkler head, trying to get a better view of the ceremony, afraid he might miss a wholesome moment. Dennis wants to say something, but he can't find the words; he wants to respond with something encouraging, something reassuring, but he's got nothing. His father is reciting the priest's soliloquy under his breath, clearly not giving his comment any more consideration, whispering to himself. And Dennis knows he'll rehash the conversation with his father later while he's alone in the shower, trying out different responses as the water cascades onto his hanging head. Maybe this time he'll think of something to say, something that could have bridged the silence between them. But it won't matter; it'll still be too late.

"Show us, O Lord, your kindness, and grant us your salvation," the priest drawls, holding his right arm out, signaling the sign of the cross.

Sunlight peers through the stained-glass windows above; jigsaw cuts with overlapping monochromatic hues brighten the interior, luminous rays illuminating the pews with translucent beauty. The tinted glass composite depicts vivid scenes of angels, nobles, and animals, aureoles gleaming with extra emphasis as Dennis tries to decipher the parable depictions emblazoned above. The kaleidoscopic portrayal and lucid colors propel Dennis into a stupor of speculation, deliberating on a synopsis of religion.

He recalls Camus's description of religion as philosophical suicide, a forfeit of deeper thought, attributing the marvels of existence to the creation of some guy in the sky who everyone lives with after they die if they're good, like a big gleeful family. But it's more, he decides, reducing religion to a crutch for the desperate, a pillow for the uncomfortable, philosophical floaties for those too afraid to swim in the intellectual deep end, the formidable abyss of living without their hands being held. Religion is for those that need to navigate with supervision, like riding with training wheels, accepting dogmas and absolutes, never questioning the questionable.

And Dennis recognizes the allure of salvation, a remedy for the hurting and solace for the old, the comfort it brings, attributing all of life's vicissitudes to God's plan. Every instance a lesson or a blessing, a safety net for those afraid of failing. Believing that death is never the end and existence never really ceases, the promise of everlasting life, attracting people toward the end like flies magnetized to a brilliant lightbulb. Because it's too harrowing to fathom the possibility that we're insignificant, replaceable; it's too daunting to accept the probability that life has no inherent meaning, that there is no mystical guardian watching after us, providing guidance when needed, directing us to a fucking happily ever after, but we aren't that special. No, the fact that existence is evanescent and there is no destination is terrifying; it means our actions are consequential, requiring personal accountability and that's too heavy of a burden to carry for most people. No one wants to lug weight around, that's exhausting, but Dennis dissents; he knows if he stares into the abyss long enough, eventually, the abyss will stare back.

Dennis is feeling it, he's heading into a tornado of thought, a fall into the recent manifestation of irritable energy that forays his nerves, antagonizing his mind, like he's crawling out of his fucking skin. He thinks they're subtle panic attacks festering beneath the surface that his subconscious can manage, so he thinks it's best to just endure, placing newspaper over the spilled milk.

He glares up at the image of a vibrant Jesus, the personification of good, the protagonist of the Bible. He's the most charismatic megalomaniac in history, cobbling a family of followers like Charles Manson but with a more altruistic objective, Dennis deduces. Perhaps Jesus was just a schizo with a vision, like any lunatic with a penchant for prostitutes, proselytizing with eloquent rhetoric, converting, and claiming to be the son of God like many others. At the age of forty-seven, Jim Jones led a mass suicide of almost 1,000 followers for salvation, convincing them the only circumnavigation for damnation was drinking a tall glass of cyanide. And who really knows what would have happened to Jesus had he evaded Judas and the Romans, living past the age of thirty-three; maybe he'd have had a couple of kids and divorced Mary Magdalene, Dennis considers. Maybe Jesus would have become an addict, eventually becoming drunk on his own power and influence, evolving into a more vindictive character, feeding off attention and vulnerability, adding to his family until it became an army, conquering for deliverance.

Dennis glimpses over and notices his brother John struggling to keep his two kids under control; Jake is flapping his arms around, begging for his tablet while Reese giggles, glancing at the mesmeric performance of the older lady a few rows ahead; her hands in the air as she wobbles in empathic prayer. Natalie sits next to him, flagrantly glaring at her phone with an empty smirk, her default on display as her husband is besieged.

"It will be your duty to bring her up to keep God's commandments as Christ taught us, by loving God and our neighbor," the priest instructs, holding his hand in the air as if he's directing an apparition, closing his eyes with each utterance.

Dennis looks over at his mother; Mary sits attentively, her hands folded on her lap, nodding, listening to the priest's words as if she's trying to detect any violated stipulations that pertain to Tommy and Haleigh's unique situation. She's been confused on how to feel about her son's dalliance and newly formed family for a few years now; she's not sure how to feel about her son's infidelity, still struggling to invoke optimism and embrace her new daughter-in-law, but she's ready to try.

"Do you clearly understand what you are undertaking?" the priest asks the couple with solemn annunciation, pausing after each word, nodding his head for reinforcement.

They turn and look at each other; Tommy rocking the little one with a soft sway and gentle bounce; Haleigh placing her arm on his elbow, brushing her shoulder up against him, turning to face the priest as if they are posing for a portrait.

"We do," they answer simultaneously.

The priest proceeds down the queue of parents with their original sin-stricken children, stopping to acknowledge each couple with a touch of the arm or shoulder. Exchanging smiles and greetings, the priest continues, turning to each cooing cherub, clutching miniature arms gently before manipulating the sign of the cross on each child's forehead. Partners stand with their precious bundles, offerings for the oracle.

Dennis notices a busty blonde clutching her newborn close; her gawky husband dangles a restless arm with an anxious vigor, using his free hand to scratch his ear every so often, a nervous tick. His left hand buries in his side pocket, seeking comfort from being observed. The blonde ovals her mouth, pursing, making faint bubble noises at her little one. Her moistened lips rounded, creating a cavernous opening, surrounded by a wettened mucous membrane, a sensual orifice that Dennis fixates on; unseemly thoughts pervade his mind, like maybe she likes her nipples sucked hard while she's being ravaged, her legs straddled, her back arched, making it easier for her tits to reach his lips. His visceral urges are surfacing; the id poking at his loins, demanding to be satiated. He's aware that his lack of physical contact is wreaking havoc on his brain chemistry, thirsting for oxytocin and dopamine relief; he's not sure how much longer he can placate his needs.

As the mass concludes, the families pile out, congregating by the entrance. They gather in little circles, all facing one another, directing for pictures, hoping to get a shot by the oversized wooden cross propped up against the wall.

"It's so good to see you guys," Mary greets, kissing Tommy on the cheek.

Her ambivalence transmutes into enthusiasm, a need to make the occasion as comfortable as possible for everyone. Tommy welcomes her with a stale hug; they were never really affectionate growing up, Dennis remembers. But Tommy is still holding a grudge from when his mother admonished him for leaving his pregnant wife years ago, when she delivered a myriad of diatribes over the phone.

Mary wasn't sure how else to respond after discovering her son had abandoned his pregnant wife for another woman and was now expecting a child with her.

Tommy hugs his dad, offering some witticism about his old age. He turns to Dennis.

"My baby brother," he chirps, slithering his hand out for a handshake, which transitions into a grip shake; their hands gripping and pulling off each other, like some intrinsic ritual, a sign they're from the same tribe despite their differences.

"At least you guys aren't ever alone now that Den is living back home," he chuckles, giving a thumbs up with a wry smile as he steps back.

Slighting is Tommy's standard vernacular, it's his only form of communication once he reaches past surface talk, always condescending to build himself up, a defense mechanism for underlying insecurity, Dennis diagnoses.

"You're never as real as you are when you're about to die," Dennis deadpans.

"What?" Tommy asks with a startled expression, squinting his eyebrows.

"You look older than Dad," Dennis revises, pivoting from his dark disposition into something more basic, more Tommy's speed.

"You guyssss," Russ giggles, grinning as he pats Tommy on the back.

"You two are always busting each other's balls."

Dennis can't decide if his father is trying to include himself in the humor or if he's just trying to diffuse the situation.

"We're having food back at the house," Haleigh publicizes, wrapping her hands around her youngest daughter's shoulders, standing behind her like she's a hostage while the little one peeks up, inspecting the family; she's about five years old, Dennis ascertains.

Haleigh only smiles with her lips, as if she's deliberately trying not to reveal teeth; discernible crow's feet faintly appear with each grin, which may be the reason she's trying not to smile too drastically, to avoid emphasizing wrinkles.

"We're so happy you're all here," Haleigh adds, smirking again with her bashful country smile, endearing and homely; she looks old and tired, as if she's just finished making lunch for the kids, folding the laundry, and emptying the dishwasher.

Her weathered brown hair is pinned back, exposing her micro profile, forcing her button nose to be the focal point of her face. She's welcoming yet inexplicably defensive, like a momma bear. And it finally dawns on Dennis why his brother left his wife to be with a woman much older than him, emanating from his lack of tenderness and compassion, unresolved issues with their mom; he needs someone to fill that role.

####

As they gather around the rustic drop-leaf dinner table in the ranch-style house, Tommy remains standing as everyone sits. Clinking his wedding ring against his wine glass, he holds his drink up in the air.

Dennis unfolds the napkin on his lap before pulling himself closer to the table, inching his chair forward. He looks up to watch his brother, perceiving his shining bald head and bushy goatee; he smiles at him, observing his stereotypical stepfather appearance. He remembers how much he used to admire him when they were younger, how he wanted to be just like him some day; he wonders if his brother is truly happy with this life that he created.

"I'd like to make a toast," Tommy announces, engaging eye contact with everyone.

When he stares at Dennis, an uncanny familiarity washes over him, an ominous realization; it's a startling déjà vu that raises the little hairs on the back of his neck. Panic punches his gut, spiking his pulse. A wave of angst engulfs Dennis as an eerie sinking sensation takes over, like something real fucking bad is about to happen. A full-blown anxiety attack ensues with alarming palpitations, causing him to hunch over.

"First, I'd like to thank my beautiful wife, Haleigh, for making this all possible."

Dennis winces and wheezes, squeezing his elbows with his fingertips, trying to tame his senses. It's a verifiable panic attack, he can tell, a crippling assault of uncomfortable nerves, occupying his full attention, like he used to experience years ago; he fears he's finally regressed, closing his eyes slightly, trying to avoid being noticed while Tommy carries on with his speech.

"We're so happy to have everyone here today to show their love for our Faith."

Fidgeting in his chair, anticipating watching eyes, Dennis frantically tries to recall the tips his old therapist shared to prevent the panic from escalating. He remembers to take note of the time, establishing a point of reference, so in fifteen minutes, he'll be able to reassure himself he isn't going to die, since most heart attacks are instant. It's 7:02 P.M when Dennis pulls out his phone to set an alarm for 7:17 with the title, "You're okay I promise."

Unfortunately, his present state is petrifying. He's been sober for over twenty-four hours now, agitated by the rigid confines of an unaltered nervous system and a dreary mind, a hypersensitivity to overhead lights and intrusive thoughts. He doesn't have pills, weed, or some other vice to abate his mind or calm his psychosomatics since he didn't want to risk bringing it on the plane, so he's going to have to really talk himself through this. Beads of sweat roll from his neck, dripping down the crevice of his back, a warm, uncomfortable presence, creating a wet, unsettling irritation, so he rubs it; he's probably going to die, he thinks. Unbuttoning his cuffs, Dennis rolls up his sleeves, wrapping the fabric around his elbows, tucking it taut against his skin; this is what he needs, to feel less constricted and hot, he tells himself. He imagines standing up only slightly before he would collapse on the dinner table, his face landing in the bowl of mash potatoes, splattering cream corn and peas on the guests all around, including Tommy's wife's elderly parents.

"We just want to say we love you all, and may God bless us," Tommy states, holding his glass up and nodding his head.

Dennis needs a distraction or else he's going to crumble, and the gross dark dated wooden paneling in the dining room is only making it worse; he feels like he's in a legion hall or barn, but they are just down south, it's perfectly normal, he reasons. He glances over at his brother John; his two kids hanging around his neck as he tries to pay attention to Tommy's monologue, clutching a kid in each arm. Maybe Dennis needed a child, something to constantly supervise and keep him busy, he thinks; maybe then he'd be too preoccupied to remember he was panicking.

Manic heart flutters harass Dennis, seizing him every time he drifts, and now he's sure he's going to die; he's certain his arm is going numb, his right arm; no, it's his left. Both arms are going numb actually, so he's going to need to excuse himself to amputate them and go die somewhere else because he doesn't want to die in the dining room surrounded by little Christ porcelain figurines. He takes a slow steady breath; his chest feels constricted, he thinks, and he can't remember whether he's supposed to breath in through his nose or his mouth, he remembers the nose is supposed to act like a filter, so maybe that's best to begin a breath. But he's not sure if exhaling out of his mouth or nose feels better, one might actually be worse for him. He thinks maybe he's too compressed, so he hyperextends his torso, pushing his pelvis forward, leaning back in his chair as he attempts to crack his back.

Tommy says something about Jesus, but Dennis has missed it because he's too panicked with himself, debating on whether he's having trouble breathing too or if he should take a sip of water; maybe he's dehydrated, he thinks. He's real aware of his heartbeat, thudding in his chest like the bass at some underground night club, striking with force, reverberating all the way to his stomach. Perhaps his serotonin levels are depleted, and he should gorge on a biscuit; he grabs his water instead, struggling with a doddering hand as he holds the glass to his lips. The cold bite of the flowing water against his toasty, hyperventilating face surprises Dennis as he sips, spilling liquid out the side of his mouth. He tries to focus on setting down the water as steadily as he can, a task that requires attention, the perfect distraction, but it's not working. He's splashing water, and he's pretty sure Grandma Jackie, Beverly, or whatever the fuck the lady's name is with the pixie cut sitting next to him is watching and judging, condemning him to hell, and being criticized by someone's grandmother is not the best feeling. He's really got to stop drawing attention to himself because that'll just ruin him, speculating his heart will explode as soon as anyone notices his distress.

He can't excuse himself during Tommy's virtuous toast or everyone is going to think he's impolite, and he knows Tommy will take it personally, chiding him at some point during the weekend, so Dennis remains seated, rocking and back forth, waiting for his impending doom. He contemplates his possible dehydration and grabs his glass again, taking a frantic sip.

"Water is good for you," he whispers to reaffirm.

Dennis peeks at his watch; the time is 7:06.

"So, cheers to family," Tommy concludes, cheersing before he chugs his wine.

Maybe he should tell someone he's dying; maybe one of Haleigh's relatives is a doctor and that'll make him feel better. They can check his vitals, reassure him that he's all right, but he decides against, excusing himself to the next room, where he has more space to panic.

Lurching into the hallway, Dennis makes for the door; the idea of an exit brings fleeting peace, until he grabs the doorknob, realizing he now has to decide if he's going to open the front door, which is sure to garner attention once he closes it. The clicking of the deadbolt re-engaging with the lock would echo into the dining room, alerting guests to a potential intruder, creating hysteria and a possible dangerous situation. But maybe then Tommy will blow Dennis's brains out with one of his many shotguns, mistaking him as a burglar if he keeps his back turned. That would certainly end his panic attack. But he doesn't really know where he'd go anyway if he left, but he feels trapped, claustrophobic, and running through a wall might be just what he needs. He ponders if maybe he should go for a walk, the silent darkness of the night amplifying the acoustics of his breath might settle him, his lungs filling with fresh air, calming his nerves and slowing his heartbeat.

Dennis strategizes, pressing two fingers to his wrist, feeling for his pulse, a tip from his psychiatrist he rarely follows.

"Focus on your heartbeat. Match your breaths to it," he recites, as though he can summon tranquility through repetition.

But the feeling of his pulse does little to steady him; it's too erratic, too fast. He can't control it, and instead of calming him, the throbbing in his wrist only amplifies the claustrophobia, the sense that he's caged. Every beat seems to press the walls closer, trapping him in a relentless rhythm, unable to escape the prison of his mind.

Scratching his neck and chest, breathing heavy, his heartbeat blistering; he pictures having an aneurysm, hurling over, sprawling out on top of the low pile jute rug to be discovered twenty minutes later, his limbs crossed over his body in a distressed configuration. He needs to leave, he thinks, but he'll need to get a ride. Perhaps a ride back to the hotel, a quest through the capacious lobby and elevator ride up to his floor will demand just enough focus and provide just enough distraction to keep him from expiring. Downloading the Lyft app, Dennis turns and creeps up the stairs, noticing the white tiling of a darkened bathroom at the top with the door opened, the perfect escape, at least for a little while. He realizes he can't leave because someone will notice, eventually, so he's going to have to figure out another solution, perhaps a short respite from human interaction.

Flicking the light on, Dennis closes the door behind him, locking it before he grasps the sink counter, trying to gather himself. He knows being in an unfamiliar environment exacerbates panic attacks from what he remembers, creating a sense of being unsafe, susceptibility. The lurid overhead light rains down on him with a heavy dread, pouring on his shoulders with pressure. Slouching by the faucet, he splashes water on his face and rubs his eyes with his palms, pressing inward on his eyelids, a pressure point he recalls learning from a hot yoga class he took with Christine, the force purported to relieve tension. But his panic is too dense and deep, embedded, he thinks, a worrisome leakage from his subconscious, filling up his body and mind with poison and uncontrollable conspiracies.

Dennis investigates the mirror, discerning dilated pupils, which escalates his frenzied episode more, spiking his heart rate; he knows that an insensitivity to light brings him closer to death, so he clutches his chest, preparing for the final blow, convulsion, explosion, or whatever the fuck he's afraid of happening finally happens.

"You're going to be fine," Dennis recites, holding pronated hands out, opening and squeezing his hands to regain control, taking deep breaths, tensing and releasing.

Counterintuitive, he knows, but he remembers further tensing muscles that are already stressed works like a pendulum swing, swaying back, releasing tightness into a looser state. He's also going to need to reaffirm his well-being and actively divert himself; he needs to stop entertaining the schemes of the mind. He needs to deconstruct his psyche if he wants to mitigate the panic and uncover the root, identify where the recent surge of adrenaline derives from. Chatter and laughs ring out from downstairs, so he knows his absence is not a disturbance; he glances at his watch, noticing that five minutes have passed since the last time he checked; his timer should be going off soon, so he's doing okay.

"Twist the faucet knob, and turn the water up scorching hot, then stick your hand underneath it. Burn yourself, you fucking piece of garbage," a voice commands from the back of his brain, a primitive impulse, but Dennis resists.

He takes out his phone instead because if he's ever in need of a distraction, he can always find one lingering in one of his apps, hiding behind a notification. He's not going to check his email though because the last time he checked it was this morning, opening a message from Monsignor, inquiring about a troublesome lecture from last week along with a text message a mother had received from her coerced son. Maybe that's what the catalyst for his panic attack is, he contemplates, the uncertainty, possible ramifications with his job. "Megan Earhardt," he types into the search field. Megan's profile pops up; it's a private account with a tiny profile pic of her holding a big mug. "Nothing Gold Can Stay" is written in her bio, prompting Dennis to smile, he wonders if that's his influence;

it had to be, what were the chances he just covered that in class and she has it listed in her profile. He exits the app with haste, swiping away and locking his phone, avoiding any compulsion to request her; he already has enough to worry about.

He's thinking maybe he'll text Christine instead, even though it's been a few weeks since they last talked. He would call someone else, but he has no other viable options; everyone else he ever converses with is downstairs around the dining table. His oxytocin levels are non-existent, approaching six weeks since the last time he got laid, which might be another possible impetus for his paroxysm, he poses. The bathroom fan reverberates with a monotonous hum, scratching at his ears, so Dennis decides against the solitude and exits the bathroom, standing up straight, hoping a heightened stature might bring an uplifted mood. A large family portrait hangs just outside, an image he scurried by earlier. He stops to observe the framed picture with double matting: Tommy and his wife sitting on stools, jointly holding the toddler, accompanied by a teenager on each side. Arranged in an arc, they are all posed in coordinating argyle sweaters, their very best smiles on display.

"There you are," Dennis's dad declares from the bottom of the stairs, holding onto the cap of the banister to support himself.

"Aren't the kids just so adorable together," Russ suggests with an adoring lilt, tilting his head and smiling; he's tipsy from the scotch, his favorite cocktail.

"They just love little Faith," he boasts, beaming with excitement, genuine joy; his skin dull, his hair salted, grayer than the last time Dennis noticed his hair.

"Aren't the kids just so great together?" he asks, searching for confirmation before looking down to notice a drink spot on his loose taupe sweater vest, a garment Denis recalls his father wore on special occasions for as long as he can remember.

127

Russ stares at Dennis with a lively, drunken face, happy to be with his whole family. Dennis descends the stairs to meet his father, returning the smile, amused at his dad's adorable saccharine state and his pleated pants pulled up past his waist; he still can't believe how much his dad has aged and shrunk. Gazing at his father's mottled face, noticing more grooves, discolored patches, and a dullness in his eyes, a fleeting vitality, Dennis extends his arms to his father's shoulders.

"They really are, Dad," Dennis confirms, holding back tears as he hugs his father, a comforting embrace that quells his trepidation.

His phone vibrates in his pocket; it's his alarm letting him know he's okay.

6. The Garden of Eden

"Here she comes," Michael whispered, tapping Dennis on the shoulder, grabbing him by the arm; Dennis then nudged Rich with an elbow, alerting him as if a celebrity were about to grace them with her presence.

Giggling, huddled together at the lunch table, they glanced toward the front of the cafeteria, waiting for the arrival of their enchantress. Miss Howard ambled into the cafeteria always toward the end of lunchtime to grab a lettuce wrap, attracting eyes and lewd looks from pubescent students.

And she'd occasionally call out inappropriate stares with a, "Can I help you?" accusatory remark, cautioning kids to stare at their own risk of being publicly humiliated.

The trick was to avoid blatant staring, to already be looking in the vicinity of where she was going. So as soon as the boys detected her entrance, they'd shift their eyes toward her destination, gazing in the direction of the lunch line, already positioning surreptitious eyes toward the queue where she'd be standing, offering an open view on her delicious pear-shaped posterior.

"She's so hot," Rich sighed with a naughty glare, placing his hands on his crotch.

Untoward behavior was always part of Rich's charisma; he once jacked off in a movie theater, a few rows down from a cache of children watching a Disney movie.

Miss Howard was the librarian who also taught English; the quintessential sultry teacher all the boys fancied; she was the protagonist of every teenager's raging hormone-laced wet fantasy. Her perfect C-cup breasts always stood perkily, her curvaceous rump forcing her hips to sway back and forth as she walked down the hallways, magnetizing juvenile eyes as her cheeks snugged against tight-fitting fabrics. She captivated every room she entered with her naturally seductive aura, usually wearing skirts with bright colors as if her exuberance was symbolic of her rousing sex appeal, always speaking with a soft, sensual lilt.

Dennis admired her since she started at the school when he was in sixth grade, adoring her from afar. But he developed a deep fascination with her as an eighth grader on the apex of adolescence since she was developed like a porn star, providing provocative stimulation for all his budding desires. He dedicated countless soiled tissues in her honor, imagining penetrating her in a variety of positions he had seen on the porno tape he stole out of his brother John's VCR.

Ripped off labels replaced with ridiculous stickers rebranded as "Sports Highlights" didn't fool Dennis as he got lost in lustful reveries as a curious kid. Fantasies about entering Miss Howard's orifices occupied him every night, alone in his bedroom, leering at the photo of her he tore out of the teacher's directory.

"Hi, Miss Howard!" Nick shouted, waving his hand frantically like an awkward stalker.

She turned her head to identify who was howling and where the shouting was coming from. Noticing Nick and his enthusiastic greeting, she waved back courteously with a confused expression, shaking her head, wondering why a student she didn't even teach was greeting her.

"She wants it," he chuckled with a grin, a delusional declaration.

"You know she's not married, right?" Nick added, bobbing his eyebrows.

"No shit, her name is Miss, not Mrs.," Rich uttered, licking his lips as he continued his sensuous glance.

"Dude, she looks exactly like Jennifer Anniston but with a thicker ass," Michael drooled, joining in on touching himself, the nascent stages of a circle jerk.

Miss Howard stood in the lunch line, her arms crossed as she looked around, never holding her stare in any direction for more than a few seconds; she pivoted and turned as the line proceeded, switching her bodyweight back and forth on each leg, accentuating her caboose as she tilted. Her full figure and visual assets on display, her breasts nestled in her cotton cable knit sweater, highlighted by her forearms pressing against her chest. Her plaited red tresses complemented her crisp white garment. Like a Greek Goddess, Miss Howard resembled Aphrodite with her divine beauty.

It was a few days away from Valentine's Day, and whether it was his intense hormones or his tenacity to fulfill a deep gnawing need, Dennis was going to make a move past his timorous, "Hi, how are you?" greetings when he checked out library books. Yeah, he was going to push boundaries, get more intimate, more personal and make her a card, something to stand out from the rest of his desperate primal cohorts. He sat at his desk during homeroom on a Wednesday and folded a piece of printer paper in half, cutting off the bottom to create a five-inch by eight-inch card. Opening the cropped sheet, he drew a big heart and carefully colored it in a solid red, making sure not to mark outside the lines, afraid that a slip over the line might make him seem clumsy or incompetent; he pictured Miss Howard being thoroughly impressed with his steady hand and concentration, rejoicing with his gift.

"I hope you have a wonderful Valentine's Day," he inscribed with neat script letters.

Fighting off a hedonistic vision of t-boning her breasts until ejaculation, his flesh pole squeezing between sumptuous fatty tissue, smacking against his lap, Dennis pondered what else to write, contemplating a possible magical phrase or expression that would win her heart. He fabricated another fantasy where she would embrace him with a warm hug at the sight of his card, clutching him close. He would delight in her intoxicating scent, envisioning her reflective blue eyes roaming back and forth on each line as she read, like a typewriter punching words across a page. After a brief brainstorm, Dennis decided the possibility of her extending her gratitude past a simple "thank you" was extremely dismal, so he sighed, settling on the only thing that came to mind:

"Thanks for lighting up any room you walk into with your smile and essence," a natural poet at a young age.

Valentine's Day fell on a Saturday, so when Friday rolled around, Dennis made a concerted plan to sneak out of class and journey to the library to hand deliver the card. He didn't want to do it too early or she might calculate his desperation, so he planned on taking it to her at 1:20 P.M., exactly two hours before the school day concluded. He asked his history teacher if he could use the bathroom, waving a vehement hand as if he were about to muddy his pants, worried she might have slipped out earlier to start the weekend.

With one powerful stride after the next, arms pumping, Dennis scurried down the hallway to the library, furtively landing on top of his footbeds, trying not to garner attention from the other open classroom doors; he kept picturing the special moment, the look on her face when he handed her a thoughtful card. Dennis slid down the last few feet, breaking his quest by skidding on his heels. Arriving outside of the library, he ducked just outside of the doorway, taking a few moments to collect himself and adjust his disheveled attire. Pushing his hair back and practicing the charming smile his mother always said was his most attractive feature, he tried to recapture his breath from the fraught sprint.

Proceeding inside with his chin held high, his shoulders pushed back, he noticed Miss Howard by the printer, donning form-fitting beige pants and a coral-colored cardigan; her iconic crimson hair flowed down her back, an ethereal view of a heavenly goddess gleaming in the sunlight. Standing in the doorway, he struggled to recite any words, continuing his gaze at her from behind, lusting.

"Um, Miss Howard?" he finally whispered, approaching her as if she were a perilous creature that might turn around and attack at any moment.

He continued forward, whispering her name with an outstretched card, his heart pounding, escalating strikes with each step forward.

"Miss Howard?" he stated a little bit louder, gripping the card with angst, nervous fingers.

"Oh," she shrieked, turning swiftly, pressing her hand against her chest.

"You scared me," she remarked before flashing a desultory smile.

"I'm sorry, but I just wanted to give you this."

"Oh?" she said with a raised eyebrow, curiosity bringing her forward.

"Happy Valentine's Day," Dennis said, flashing a zealous, timid smile before turning toward the door, trying his best to walk with a confident swagger, like Stone Cold Steve Austin.

He imagined her smitten and enticed by such a brazen move as he left. Escaping the library unscathed, he had taken his shot, and that entire weekend, oddly enough, he didn't give any more thought to his encounter, almost as if the mission was complete and the only objective was gifting the card. By Sunday night, Dennis surmised she had tossed the card out by the time the school day had ended, laughing at his desperate deed and his inexperienced youth.

That Monday morning, Dennis doodled in his notepad, scripting the "S" that all the kids drew back in the late '90s and early 2000s, the omnipresent graffiti on bathroom stalls and gym locker room walls and benches. It was that discernible sharp, edgy "S" that started out with making two sets of three short perpendicular lines and then connecting them. Dennis was just about to start shading in the symbol when there was a knock on the classroom door.

"Excuse me, is Dennis Clauden here?" Miss Howard asked as she stepped into the classroom, perked up and adorned in a long pastel-colored pencil skirt, a fetching fashionista with straightened hair, resembling a Stepford wife.

"Yes, he's right back there," the homeroom teacher responded, pointing to Dennis parked in the front row.

Shocked at the sound of his voice being spoken by his dream doll, Dennis glanced at Miss Howard, unsure of her presence. He wondered if he might be in trouble for overstepping boundaries or if maybe he was hallucinating; he wasn't sure.

"This is for you," Miss Howard whispered, handing him a card, her two fingers with fiery red acrylic nails pinching the top corner.

Sharing a warm smile with florid cheeks, Dennis was lost in her eye contact; she turned and exited the classroom, and Dennis knew not to visually harass her as she walked out, since it would be too obvious, but his heart fluttered, his cheeks spasming as he couldn't help but smile. He exulted over the thought of telling the boys Miss Howard hand-delivered him a card; he opened the cardboard piece with enthusiasm, diving into the words addressed to him:

Dear Dennis,

Thank you so much for the kind, considerate Valentine's Card. It made my day. Your words were very poetic and thoughtful. I think any girl would be lucky to call you her Valentine. I wish you the best of luck next year in high school. Feel free to keep in touch! Susanna_Howard98@aol.com.

Sincerely,

Ms. Susanna Howard

####

Spacing out in front of the computer screen, Dennis's mind escapes to the past like usual, imagining things he should have said and done. Maybe he could have just given his friend Brian his wallet back instead of stealing the trio of twenty-dollar bills at that party in 2011, discovering his wallet on the floor by the speakers, retrieving it like an angler snatching a fish before he took the money out of the back fold, stuffing it into his front pocket. He remembers bragging about it to Phil who later told Brian, making it the last time Dennis was ever invited to party with him. Shaking his head to clear the unproductive haze and distraction, he clicks on the Word document:

"Flowers for my father," is the name of the first chapter; Dennis relishes the ominous connotation and the slight alliteration of the title. It's understated, dark, and elegant, he marvels.

Scrolling down the pages, he ponders which character he's going to make homosexual since it's now a character requirement for all newly published fiction; he's going to give the politically correct plot line quotas a go, noticing how all literary agents include mentions about inclusivity and sexuality struggles, emphasizing desires to see gay characters, black females, or trans protagonists. Underrepresented voices and diversity for diversity's sake; he knows they're on to something about hating white heterosexual males, because Dennis hates himself.

For creative inspiration, he considers snorting a stockpile of Oxycodone and connecting with someone on Grinder, engaging in a blood-thirsty anal gangbang as research, earning literary credentials. But he's not sure if he can endure penetration, perhaps a finger, or maybe he can numb himself up enough to be a top, if it means he'll be accepted into the secret society of publishing.

Dennis thinks he's going to make the Elliot character suck someone's cock, delineating precise details about the penis entering his mouth; its bloated veins pulsating with rock hard blood flow; the boy's saliva lubricating its exterior, his butthole moistened from a stimulated prostate. Or maybe he'll depict a graphic rough anal sex scene to serve as a metaphor for systemic oppression and racial injustice. He's not entirely sure if it'll make sense or if people will even make the connection, but he's pretty sure if he puts some effort into it and mentions enough trending hashtags like "anti-racist" and "white ally," it may garner some serious attention, meeting all literary agents' manuscript desires.

He probably should be downstairs at the pool with his family, but he told his parents he had to do some schoolwork, so he's going to meet them around 11 A.M. He reaches into his heather gray duffle bag, unbuckling an inconspicuous interior pocket to pull out a bottle of Jameson, grasping it by the neck. He places it on the hotel room desk, letting it drop just enough so it clatters against the protective plexiglass cover, rattling the surface; Dennis contemplates the choice for plexiglass, deducing it's probably easier to clean than traditional hardwood, a non-stick surface, resisting viscous drug residue.

Luckily, Dennis purchased a handle of whiskey after he got off the plane while his parents struggled with the self-checkout at Panera as Russ shouted obscenities at the miniature screen, offering just enough time to slip away to buy an overpriced bottle. His family weekend requires a licit drug, alcohol. After yanking the top off with a pugnacious pull, Dennis fills the two plastic single serve cups the hotel provided, liquid spilling just over the brims; he's now going to indulge in his favorite pastime, the search for literary agents.

Inching the two cups closer to his laptop, providing easier accessibility, Dennis sinks forward in the uncomfortable modern desk chair, slouching over the keyboard with a heavy head, inspecting the keyboard of his dated HP computer. The "A" key is missing its legs, portraying a perfect triangle, and the "S" button is fading, showcasing the appearance of a backward question mark without the period. He glances over to his duet of whiskey downers, calculating that each is filled with just about two shots worth of fluid, just enough to mitigate his antagonizing mind. Retrieving the Manuscript Wish List's website, Dennis clicks on the newly implemented keyword box to search, which makes it much simpler to locate potential agents in particular genres.

"Coming of age" he types into the field and quickly erases it. "Coming-of-age," he reenters for closer accuracy; he ponders the specifics of how adding hyphens designate the phrase as an adjective as opposed to just an expression, giddy with his useless observation. He probably should be writing instead of engaging in fruitless searching, but writing with writer's block is like trying to force a dump; it's cumbersome. Coercing one's brain to create is like straining a colon, an embarrassing and purely bodily function. And a little poop might eventually come out if pushed hard enough, but it's the worst kind of shit, sloppy and unformed, liquid without any real substance.

Two results turn up in the search field: "Jessica Mileo" and "Matt McCoy." Dennis decides he'll click on Jessica first, since a woman accepted his query letter before; he's thinking maybe women are his target audience.

"I am not really into fiction that takes place during the '50s, '60s, '70s unless it's taking place in a country other than the U.S. or the main characters are PoC or LGBTQIA+. I'm not looking for a coming-of-age story from those time periods from a white cis POV," reads the short description of the "What She's Looking For," section.

Dennis decides it's a great opportunity to take his first shot, especially when he reads about acceptable forms of discrimination in society, pondering the consequences if "white" were swapped with any other skin color. Pinching the sides of the first meager cup, he kicks the fluid back, swishing the liquor in his mouth to really soak up the ethanol before swallowing. He cringes and exhales, the alcohol warming his belly with a burning sensation.

He opts to switch platforms, signing into Twitter, refusing to ever call it X, as it's possibly the worst rebranding in modern history. He's going to search the "Coming of Age" hashtag, hoping it connects him to an agent for representation. He shoots his other shot with haste, wincing as he swallows, the malty liquid slipping down his esophagus and burning his chest. He smiles with a masochistic smirk, drawing teeth; he's thinking maybe he'll become an alcoholic like Hemingway since he likes getting drunk and relishes the confidence it imbues, mitigating embedded self-doubt.

Dennis also enjoys a good drinking game; his current favorite involves taking a shot every time a radical political tweet is pinned to the top of a literary agent's Twitter feed or preferred pronouns are featured in the bio, perplexed but amused that an industry enveloped with grammar propriety entertains the dubious concept of accepting single individuals using plural pronouns as identifiers. It enrages him actually, probably because his life would have been much easier in middle school English class, where he lost points on quizzes for using "they" instead of "his or her."

But the game usually gets him shit-faced, so he's only going to stop after four, or he won't make it down to see his family. He'll probably puke in the bathroom instead, alternating between apps like a juggling clown, opening one and exiting before proceeding to the next digital realm, searching for some sort of engagement before passing out, something to fill the void. He's thinking he'll consider using "you," a second-person pronoun, as one of his preferred pronouns if he ever decides to participate, so he can really confuse the fuck out everyone when he tells people he's "you." Maybe he'll identify as an "it" since he's pretty sure he died a long time ago, and now he's just a sentient decaying corpse; he might even use "us," a first-person pronoun, as a preferred pronoun, since he's hearing voices suggesting he hang himself like a jovial Christmas decoration. And if anyone refuses to acknowledge his chosen pronouns, he'll just accuse them of pronoun discrimination, labeling them as bigots.

He really needs to let the manuscript go though and focus on his new short story idea about some depressed asshole drowning in the sea. And if he has to craft another query letter, he's going to ingest all the expired cough medicine his parents still have underneath their bathroom vanity from over the years. The pervasive politics is killing his desire to write, how it's seeping into every facet of life, how clueless people are, thinking that either political party truly cares about anything else except padding their pockets with taxpayer dollars. The tribalism of the literary industry is ruining a timeless outlet he's admired for so long, the last medium of connection people could share, where thoughts, concepts, and dialectics overrode virtuosity and chauvinism. The sanctimonious overtones and nurturing of echo chambers is a pestilence for authentic, unabashed writing, he postulates as he downs two more shots. He grimaces, closing his eyes as the noxious potion dribbles down his esophagus.

"Kill yourself right now," the roommate in his head suggests, whispering into the crevice of his ear canal.

His story sucks. It needs another rewrite. It reads like a clichéd diary entry, a first-person narrative of a heartbroken, chronic weed smoker who can't make it as a writer. Really profound stuff. But the query letter acceptance is what throws him off; there must be something noteworthy if an agent wanted to read the first three chapters of his book, he thinks. He wonders if maybe his writing is so bad that not even a strong query and pitch can redeem it. And maybe he's not a writer at all, just a poser fooling himself, the opposite of imposter syndrome, that social media catchphrase passed around like some profound existential struggle. An hour has slipped by, downing shots alone, dissecting his own words, so he figures it's time to head downstairs, splash in the pool with his nieces and nephew.

The sun is taking command of the sky outside, beating down rays, positioning itself at its highest point of the day, which means he needs to head to the birthday party; he knows his parents are already panicking that he's still in the room. He glances over toward his parents' bed, which is neatly made even though the cleaning service hasn't come around yet. Looking over to his sleep space, bedecked with scattered pillows and bunched sheets, Dennis knows if he plops himself onto the luxurious king size memory foam mattress with the down feather comforter, he's going to be down for a while, sinking into comfort, so he powers off his laptop and springs toward the door, patting his pocket to make sure he has a room key.

They're staying at the Eden, a palatial hotel with castle architecture and a fully modernized interior, beautified with towering turrets and detailed corbels that highlight the exterior. Neutral-colored marble flooring amplifies its capacity while a neon lit bar provides an alluring focal landmark for the lobby. He hopes he'll maybe catch eyes with a lone dame by the bar, enjoying a cocktail or maybe working on her iPad; she'll be there on business, and she won't mind he's sharing a room with his parents. Yeah, he's not just drunk; he's also completely delusional.

Journeying down the woven tufted carpeted hallway, soft, pleasant steps with a hurried stride, Dennis catches his reflection off the golden hardware of each door, oversized entry plates providing stunning décor accents. Polished surfaces capture his blue and black tropical-inspired swim trunks, reproduced in each passing doorway. Approaching the elevator doors, Dennis pushes the call button and steps back to wait. The copper-plated molding entices his eyes, glancing, assessing his appearance briefly; a smooth stately pediment surmounts the gilded double doors, beaming in front of him, spotlighting uncomfortable reflections.

He sways back and forth, fighting a gaseous uproar in his stomach as the whiskey blisters his belly; he turns to notice a stack of apples on a trestle accent table. The column sculpted legs support a thick marbled surface with a display of produce. Accessible fresh fruit definitely exudes luxury, he decides. Associating its brilliance with flavor, he picks the most scarlet one, gripping the apple. He flips the spherical fruit up in the air, tossing with a snap of the wrist; it twirls with a brisk spin before Dennis snatches it, grasping with his palm. He positions his two fingers on the center, imagining textured seams; he thinks back to playing shortstop in high school, grasping a baseball in an identical matter, right before he'd sling it to the first.

He sheds a wistful smile, nostalgic for the simple joy of playing sports and being a teenager, experiencing genuine fun, the comradery of a team and physical competitiveness, an outlet to live in the now. He squeezes the apple, anticipating a firm surface, a dense, solid exterior, conversely, his fingers sink into the skin, breaking off chunks of soggy apple pulp, leaving a spoiled, sticky residue on his hands from a rotting core.

Dennis discards the rancid apple onto the floor, rolling it toward the corner as the tumble spits bruised chunks in different directions. The elevator doors chime open, revealing a vast car with mirrored surfaces. And Dennis can't stand to see another fucking reflection judging him, so he ducks his head away, looking down at the ground after he presses for the lobby. He gazes at the hammered textured floor, the only obscured external that doesn't stare back at him.

Exiting on the bottom floor, he stammers out into the reading area, furnished with ottomans and stacks of beach reads and terrible murder mysteries; he ponders if maybe having his novel offered as a reading choice at a hotel is worse than not getting published at all. He fathoms the destiny of his work becoming recommended literature for happily married couples on an indulgent getaway, nauseous at the thought of some middle-aged female with stretch marks on her stomach from birthing three children turning the pages of his book before falling to sleep on her sleep number mattress. Passing by the blinding bar with striking lights, he slows his pace to search for his fancied female suitor. But all he spots is married couples, affixed as if they were conjoined to form a single entity; they're all reading books, sharing drinks, holding hands, and a combination of all three activities.

Pushing his way through the turnstile gate to the pool, he notices a bachelorette party huddling around pool chaise lounges, a legion of plump pink-shirted women clapping. The presumed bride in a white bathing suit with a body sash emblazoned with a metallic label "Bride" executes an ungainly dance, an awkward twerk and takes a shot. Assessing the commotion, Dennis calculates it's her second marriage based on her gelatinous limbs, her under arms flapping as she moves; her garish makeup overapplied, distracting cheeks with an abundance of blush and no contour, like a washed-up adult actress.

"Uncle Dennis!" Jake hollers as he launches himself into the pool, pulling his knees to his chest as he soars into the water; Dennis being the one who showed him how to perform a cannonball years ago.

Dennis smiles and waves to Tommy in the shallow end; Faith clings to his brother's arm as he gently splashes her, encouraging a playful attitude while showing the innocuity of the water.

"I ordered you a Jameson and ginger," Tommy proclaims with an elevated pitch, trying to catch Dennis's attention; he turns to see his brother waving his hands at the waiter, directing a small server to deliver a garnished drink.

"Oh, thanks, man," Dennis replies, retrieving the rocks glass and holding it up, saluting his gesture before taking a chug.

"Well, damn, bro. Come get in the pool," Tommy rejoices, splashing the water as his miniature meatball-like child roams, elated as she spatters; her amusingly large yellow swimmies transforming her into a bolstered baby raft.

Tommy wears original Oakley sunglasses in bright orange and blue, the kind that were all the rage in the '90s, his skin glowing purple under the blistering sun. Dennis wonders if Tommy is sunburnt or if there's something more concerning behind his strange radiance. The heat presses down on Dennis like a fucking elephant, his tongue hanging out, desperate for water. He knows he needs to hydrate, since he feels his faculties faltering, but he sees the welcoming swimming pool. And he's thinking maybe he can drown himself here, a nice peaceful rest, conducting research for the short story he'll never write. Tommy certainly doesn't know CPR, so maybe this is a great opportunity, a real poetic finish to go out surrounded by his family. A wave of poignancy deluges, tears flood his nasal passage, so Dennis jumps into the pool to rinse the emotion, washing away developing tears, even though the stamped cement clearly reads, "No jumping."

"Uncle Dennis, let's have a jump contest," Jake shouts as he swims toward them, smiling with excitement.

"You really shouldn't jump in the pool unless it's the deep end," Dennis's mother remarks, emerging from the private cabana the family rented.

Dennis ignores the criticism and idles, becoming familiar with the water, urinating as he looks around. He notices John with Reese in the deep end; she's holding onto the stainless-steel pool ladder, her arms clenched around it, like she's hugging a stuffed animal; John's a few feet away, kicking, his arms stroking the water as he instructs, demonstrating how to swim in deeper water.

"Jake, come with Mom-Mom and let's get a sandwich," Mary orders, motioning to the wonderous boy; he's already forgotten about the jump contest he challenged his uncle to and now engages with an underwater toy torpedo, tossing it with joy as he marvels at its journey in the translucent water.

"Where's Dad?" Dennis asks, his head oscillating as he scans the horizon.

"He's getting a drink, you big baby," Tommy jests before he lifts Faith by the hands, tossing her up to his waist side and catching her wrists.

He stands in the shallow water, pivoting his weight back and forth on each leg, tensing his arms as he holds onto his daughter, forcing blood flow to his upper body, creating discernible vascularity.

Tommy entertains his little one, swaying her with his hands, lifting her up and down like a kettlebell, whispering repetition numbers as he presses her over his head. He places her back in the water, holding her up by her arms; he glances down at his newly tattooed pectoral, admiring the inked artwork and his developed striations. His muscle dysmorphia on full display, but it's okay, Dennis espouses, recognizing the fun his daughter is having with her father; he wishes he could get excited about just being in a pool, soaking in the water and splashing in the sunlight.

"Mommy, watch how long how I can swim under water," Reese chirrups, dunking her head to swim a few feet ahead, zealously emerging from the water with a frantic face.

She struggles with the discomfort of water rushing from her nose, but she fights the unpleasantry off with determination, looking over to Natalie, seeking her mother's applause and attention.

"That's great, hon," Natalie replies with an aimless response, absorbed with her device, disheartening her eager child.

Reclined on an off-white chaise lounge, a towel draped over the top, Natalie's holding her outstretched phone above her face, texting relentlessly, too consumed in her own digital space to notice an endearing moment. Dennis watches as Natalie bounces her head from shoulder to shoulder, shielding her eyes from the blazing sun with her iPhone. Positioning a bent leg, she poses as if she's taking a selfie; her vodka and soda water are at an arm's length reach on the small stackable table next to her chair. Low-calorie alcohol is a staple in her diet to maintain her leanness. Flipping to her stomach, pronated, she continues her technology fixation, never breaking her concentration. Dennis recognizes her apathy, detachment; she's gone, he deduces. It's a stark contrast from the impassioned mother she used to be only a few years ago when the kids were babies. Always snapping photos of playdates and family gatherings from her professional Canon camera that adorned her neck; she used to even take her time to adjust the aperture to capture heartwarming moments with the children.

"You're such a great swimmer," John praises with an effusive timbre, holding up his palm for a high five.

"John, where's Jake?" Natalie bawls, inquiring as she switches her smart phone obsession to a concerned, assertive mother, a role she plays only a few hours a day.

"He's with my mom," John snarls, annoyed.

"Maybe take a break from your phone. I hear the blue light might cause brain damage," he quips, smiling at Reese with a playful demeanor.

"Do you want another drink?" Tommy asks, tapping Dennis on the shoulder, already signaling for the waiter before Dennis can respond.

Dennis appreciates Tommy's persistence, providing constant alcohol, even if it's motivated by optics. As long as someone is imbibing with Tommy, he's safe from being lectured about his excessive drinking.

"Dennis, can you take a selfie picture of all of us before we forget?" Mary beseechs, holding up her smartphone device.

A torrential wave of anxiety crashes over Dennis, palpitations prodding his chest as he ponders mortality, blindsided by an intrusive thought, how one of the three brothers will live to see the funerals of both his siblings, one won't see any, and one will have no brothers left to attend his own.

"Uncle Dennis, you promised we would have a jumping contest," Jake whines, holding a cup of water as he frowns.

"The kid has been out in the sun all morning, and they haven't given him anything to drink," Russ scorns as he flops into the pool.

"Well, Natalie's been on her goddamn phone all day like usual. There's no way it's all for work," Mary derides, huddling next to Russ.

"Cheers," Tommy declares, toasting Dennis with another Jameson drink, washing away Dennis's rumination.

"Thanks for being here," Tommy adds in a seemingly sentimental lilt, placing an affectionate hand on Dennis's shoulder, transferring him back to when they were kids.

Dennis flashes an earnest smile, picturing Tommy as the lengthy, long-haired teenager he idolized as a child, recalling how he used to sneak down the stairs to spy on him with his girlfriend, witnessing his first pair of real tits laying on the family's brown faux velvet wrap-around couch as Tommy sucked on her neck. He still remembers retreating up the stairs with an Olympic-paced stride as his girlfriend slipped out of her pleasured trance, making eye contact with him. Her mouth agape with an appalled expression of embarrassment. He still recollects getting drunk for the first time at age fourteen, Tommy handing him a vodka and orange juice as he typed on the computer one Saturday night, communicating with friends on AOL instant messenger, his brother overtly intoxicated with blood shot eyes and a hostile sway. Their parents were out for the night and Tommy had slipped a bottle of vodka from the liquor cabinet and mixed a drink with the only juice they had in the refrigerator. It was either that or milk.

He vividly recalls how close they once were, until adult egos drove them apart, turning life into a competition between siblings. But Dennis wishes Tommy knew he wasn't competing; he doesn't even care. He really just misses having a brother. And Dennis has imagined multiple alternate realities where he and his brother stayed best friends, never growing apart, remaining as close as they were when they were kids. But the universe had other plans for them, and it's becoming more painfully apparent with each passing year. And maybe one day they'll be able to break down the protective walls and be their true selves, without posturing or fear of judgement, but today is not that day, and that's okay. Dennis still loves him anyway; it's what brothers do, even if it's not always obvious.

"You're welcome, bro," Dennis reciprocates before being splashed by Faith, causing him to react in a dramatic fashion, descending slowly into the water.

"Oh no, I'm meltingggggg!" he howls as he slips under the water, waving his hands; Faith laughs and claps before she reaches for Dennis with a lively curiosity.

"Haha, she likes you," Tommy says, still holding Faith by the back of her bathing suit to keep her from falling, bunching her bottom lip, revealing her top teeth, a smile identical to her father's own.

"Ok, guys, let's get a group picture," Mary announces, flapping her arms in the air to command everyone's attention.

"Dennis, please take the photo. I can't freaking figure out this phone," his mother wails, pleading with her phone held out; she's conditioned herself to attest technology and avoid learning how to master it, resenting as if advancement of high-tech is a reminder of her accelerating age.

Dennis trudges through the water to assist his helpless mother, catching sight of the bachelorette party in a rowdy circle. A small Bluetooth speaker sits on the decking next to the pool; the bass from Lil Jon's "Shots, Shots, Shots" faintly reverberating in the background as he watches the bride flapping her arms back and forth in the water as she floats; her face hidden behind oversized aviator sunglasses as she bobs her head. Dennis wonders where Renee had her bachelorette party, probably Nashville, he concludes; she always talked about going there. He debates whether he should try to lure one of the less attractive bridesmaids into a possible rendezvous, seeking a release from the human condition; maybe he'll set one of the dating apps to a one-mile radius to see if any of them are prospects and open to a late-night encounter.

"Ok, guys. Let's go!" Mary yells, holding the back of her palms to her mouth, projecting a vociferous command.

"Natalie, John, come on," she orders as they scurry.

Dennis sets the camera to a ten-second timer, holding it out with one hand to create a wider angle that includes everyone. The family gathers behind him, clutching their kids and pressing close together.

"Ok, everyone, get in close," Dennis instructs, extending the phone out with his left hand, positioning upwards toward the sky, the optimal view for a group photo.

"Please, make sure you take a good one," Mary implores with a frantic pitch, a mother's desperate plea to capture the perfect photo, collecting memories as if a moment doesn't actually occur unless it's captured.

"Relax, Mom," Dennis says before Jake slams into the side of his leg, latching onto him with an impish hug.

"Jake, go with daddy," Mary scolds as she suspires, agitated and flummoxed because she cares too much, assuming the entire trip will be ruined without a family photo; her oversized sunglasses and brimmed fedora mimicking a child wearing her parent's hat.

"Just get in the picture, Mom. Everything is just fine," Dennis assures.

"Ok, everyone I'm starting the timer," he says, still grimacing from the fifty pounds of child impact.

But he's determined to take an ideal picture, one he can already envision being hung on his parents' wall of shadow-boxed family photos, the collage that takes up the entire wall in their foyer.

"Ok, let's count," he directs, inspecting the faces on the screen, ensuring everyone is featured.

His mother's and father's faces are propped in the bottom left corner as they crouch, their gray hair flapping in the wind, their heads turning with every second as if they're unsure where to look. Tommy squeezes in closer to Haleigh with Faith still cradled in her arms; they squish their faces together like fish, smiling playfully. Natalie and John stand on opposite sides, lingering far from each other; each holding a child, a symbol of their relationship, bound together only by their children.

"Ten, nine, eight…" everyone collectively shouts.

As the timer winds down, each second appearing in passing large white letters on the camera screen, Dennis becomes cognizant of the family theme: everyone with their significant others and progeny, an aspect of the family he had no part in creating. A jolt of pain persists at the bottom of his heart, a tight muscle acting up, he supposes, a spasm, but it's tinged with sorrow, and he wonders if Christine should be there, her arms wrapped around him.

"Seven, six, five…" the countdown continues.

Dizzy and drunk, Dennis combats the urge to vomit as he pisses for the sixth time in the camouflaged waters; he's forgotten to put sunscreen on, which is something Christine always did, applying with care. His feels his forehead scorching; his back is already burning as he holds the phone. He should be adoring the moment, Dennis tells himself. His family is all together, which only happens once every year; his parents are pleased, and he's genuinely happy to be with his brothers and their kids.

It's a gathering he's grateful for, but he's too aware, dismayed at the portrait he's about to take, knowing it's going to become a keepsake one day, a relic hanging on his wall when his parents are long gone and he's much older. His smile is forced, barely reaching his eyes, as he recalls the saying about how you never appreciate the value of a moment until it becomes a memory. But he wonders if there's any comforting wisdom for those painfully conscious of a moment that will soon become a core memory, if one can truly appreciate the value of a moment knowing it will one day serve as a bittersweet reminder of life's impermanence?

"Four, three, two, one…"

Sitting in front of the blank computer screen, Dennis is engrossed in his phone, opening and closing apps with no particular order or purpose, just in pursuit of notifications, dopamine boosts. It's a manic cycle he's got himself wrapped up in, clicking, scrolling, swiping. It's an automatic trance that takes a hold of his central nervous system and motor functions, occupying about four hours a day, according to his screen time tracker. He finally exits the ceaseless stimulation, looking up to see if "Gate 28" is boarding; he's got a solid thirty minutes before the plane boards, and he's forcing himself to at least write something. He's gone pretty much the entire trip without writing anything, which is absolutely prodding at his consciousness, like a thousand fucking thorns rubbing over his limbs every time he has a moment of peace because he vowed to at least write a paragraph before the weekend concluded.

"You can't edit a blank page," he had posted to his Instagram last week to remind himself; he checked to see how many likes he got every twelve minutes for the next day.

He's convinced his oxytocin levels are dangerously low because he actually debated fucking his hotel pillow in the middle of the night, slipping into the bathroom while his parents slept, locking the door. He'd dimmer the lights and lay a towel down on the marble floor, placing the bent pillow on top before he kneeled and shoved his derelict dick into the plush creases. So, writing is pretty much impossible right now; he ponders if maybe there's a correlation between creativity and climaxing. Maybe something to do with blood flow, one organ not receiving enough supply, so he's surrendering himself to dating apps instead. His index finger is getting a ton of action, a real overactive limb, swiping across his smartphone screen to express interest or dislike. And he's been satiating his primal needs with explicit incognito searches lately, a habitual indulgent in digital erotica that surely doesn't help, but it's the only thing that mitigates his carnal desires temporarily, now that he's been single for a while. His fingertips quickly dissent from selecting dating suitors to perusing graphic material since it's so easily accessible.

But he's set his dating app settings to search for women ages twenty-one to forty-five within a fifteen-mile radius, convinced a closer range might maintain a wisp of organic dating, a greater chance they could have met without the aid of an app. The dopamine fix is thrilling and spellbinding, driven by the possibility of discovery and the sustained exhilaration of building anticipation, as if something exciting is seconds away and always about to happen. The elevation of his heart rate surging whenever a brunette with mesmerizing sable eyes flashes across his screen, eliciting a pacifying instance of amnesia, a brief reprieve from his regret as if maybe he's a swipe away from meeting someone to numb the pain of existence. Subconsciously, there's a morsel of hope still lingering, like a glitching synapse; maybe Renee will appear across the screen, unhappy with her bland marriage or maybe just out of curiosity, he thinks.

Familiarizing himself with the compendium of dating demographics, Dennis is compiling copious notes on the digital courting realm, noting commonalities and patterns among profiles. The twenty-one to twenty-five-year-old girls all feature brief bios, mostly incorporating five emojis that describe themselves along with their Instagram handles, accompanied by a terse excerpt like, "Not on here often." Its minimalist word content, indicative of the lack of communication skills of Gen Z, the English language becoming too bulky and time-consuming to write out, curating a class of philistines with filters.

"Jennifer, 22, volleyball, sun, doggy face, wine glass, multiple variations of dark-skinned emoji fists, @jensfun95"

Dennis analyzes her tokens before swiping right based on her second photo, which showcases a toned figure and nice teeth, posing against a palm tree on one of Daddy's many paid-for vacations. Jennifer must have played volleyball at some point or was part of some club team. She more than likely loves dogs, probably has one or two, and prefers wine over beer, Dennis surmises. Her simple, flippant Instagram handle reflects her down-to-earth, "chill" personality, and most of her pics portray her drinking at a bar or surrounded by friends, both guys and girls, exemplifying the carefree party phase of an adolescent. Jen likes to have fun, duh.

The multiple black emoji fists symbolize her performance activism. This age group of impressionable saplings also embraces full tribalism, conflating politics with personality traits. Ironically, they declare themselves as "anti-system" yet parrot all the same talking points as major corporations, universities, the media, and Hollywood. Their bios are filled with overt social justice stances or partisan affiliations, with phrases like "Swipe left if you're conservative," "Free Palestine," and rainbow flags. Some even demand proof of vaccination before meeting, acting as unwitting sales reps for Big Pharma. And Dennis is shocked, since he would imagine demanding proof of being STD-free upon meeting would be considered rude. Shockingly, many in this group, particularly Caucasian girls, take it further with radicalized slogans. Acronyms like "ACAB" and bold statements such as "Defund the Police" or "Kill the capitalists" are common, whatever the current boldest hashtags are.

Dennis often smiles at the cognitive dissonance, the hypocrisy of "anti-capitalists" shouting slogans from their smartphones and wonders who they turn to in emergencies or when crimes occur, conferring that a social worker probably won't be able to save them in situations of immediate danger.

The girls a few years older, in the twenty-five to thirty-one age range, contain a little more material in their profiles, exclusively highlighting their projected prestige, their uncompromising pride, and determined desire to find someone respectable along with criticizing stances on one-night stands. This is the most common cadre to find people posing in half-naked photos or in unseemly positions while confusingly mentioning that they're "not looking for sex," like a baffling eBay ad with contradictory selling points:

"Kim, 27, communications manager, Live for the nights I won't remember with the friends I'll never forget. Accomplished, straightforward girl looking for someone who has their shit together and can be my copilot. If you're looking for a hook-up, swipe left."

This second stratosphere of females strategically design their profiles, incorporating a variety of pictures to share interests and hobbies: an outdoor activity photo, usually hiking, holding a yoga pose, most likely a warrior's pose or playing on an intramural coed team to showcase their "active lifestyle," always accompanied with an action shot of running, catching a ball, or volleying. A club photo or a dressed-up pic is also a definite, spotlighting their glamorous beauty and ability to clean up nicely, and always a family picture and or silly photo because everyone loves a "fun family girl."

"Live, laugh, love," Dennis whispers to himself as he swipes right; his motives slowly shifting from possible romance to decent sexual encounter.

The over thirty-three is the last stratification of pursuers; their profiles read like novels, unrelenting monologues, word salads that sometimes morph into biographies and partial resumes, recapping not only their accomplishments but also failures, disclosing job titles, recent relationships statuses, and offspring numbers:

Allyson, 34, HR, recently divorced, mommy first. Hard-worker, active lifestyle, optimist. Concertgoer with a fond appreciation for love, life, and all the unknown. Country music and a little bit of jack makes everything all right. If I'm not in the office or taking care of my Paigey girl <3, you can find me strolling the beach at nighttime, just taking in the waves and cool ocean air. Homeowner and responsible adult that works hard and plays even harder. Not looking for games or bs, if you're real be real with me. #fuckboisnotapply

Dennis sighs. "Really don't need a lecture today," he utters, swiping left with urgency.

The older people get, the more they have to say, apparently; on the contrary, Dennis has nothing to say; he's too busy thinking, really. He espouses that dating app biographies are metaphoric of life's development; the younger are excited, curious, and don't really know what they're looking for, but they're always up for a good time, always interested in experiences and discovery; their bios are short and ambiguous, as if they're still being written. As they age, the descriptions become more precise and direct, transparent, replacing dance festivals for careers and rebuilding from heartbreaks, seeking stability instead of chronic adventure. And the transformation from twenties to thirties is always the most drastic, terse words becoming passionate paragraphs, hoping thoroughness will attract honesty. Because that's what you need when you're a divorced single parent, someone you can trust to sweep you off your fucking feet, telling you everything's going to be okay. A last chance for love, still holding out for the fairytale ending.

The Freudian apps elevate superficiality to incredible heights, reducing each person to mini advertisements, a digital carousel ad with coordinating copy: the main image always the best photo of an individual, presenting a best feature, perhaps a stellar smile with impeccable white teeth, adorable dimples, or captivating blue eyes, perhaps something a bit more hedonistic, objectifying, a delicious derriere or breathtaking breasts.

"What are you looking for?" an incoming message on Bumble reads from Mallory, 30.

"World peace," Dennis responds, accompanied by an earth emoji before he closes his app, realizing he's about to board a plane back home, putting him 500 miles away from Mallory.

Dennis should probably focus on the mirror selfie profiles from now on if he's going to tend to his testicles before they approach hazardous PSI levels. The jaded ones always pose in front of their vertical back-of-the-door mirrors, pushing their hips out and arching their backs to accent their bottoms. Either that, or they're squeezing their chests together to emphasize their ballooned busts as an array of boxes and a mattress without a box spring sit on the floor in the background. This environmental mess typically symbolizes their personal disarray, possibly due to a recent breakup, which required only boxing up household essentials for new living arrangements.

Shaking his head, he glances up to see if any progress has occurred or if people are congregating by the gate. He's still got at least twenty minutes but that's not enough to write anything of substance, he tells himself. Not only has he not retained a single new verb, noun, or adjective over the weekend, but he hasn't written a single fucking word either; he drops his phone on the airport floor and clutches his face in his hands, scratching his fingers at his brows. He's desperate, he knows, and there's nothing floating around in his frontal cortex, no creativity or story concept; the only thing moldering in his mind is where Renee went for her bachelorette, so he's ready to find out. Yep, he's going to rip the band aide off once more, he decides, just peel it right back with a scorching hot iron if it means it'll draw some blood, some genuine pain, authentic inspiration. He remembers his heartbreak being an artistic tonic, spilling words from his hurt, filling pages with minimal effort as he indulged in catharsis.

Before he can be interrupted by posts from a teacher he slept with as an underaged teenager, or updates from middle school acquaintances hawking rejuvenating cream, or anecdotes about their babies' first full defecations, he quickly types Renee's name into the search box, edging his hand closer to the fire.

A picture of a couple outside a massive suburban house with a three-car garage pops up like a brash retargeting ad for a realtor. But there isn't terrible associated copy plastered anywhere on the picture. No, it's not an advertisement at all; it's her and Carl outside of their recently purchased abode, arms intertwined as they both face forward, smiling for the photo. Dennis clicks to uncover, learning about her life, holding the flame, torching his hand in the blaze; they own several homes, he discovers, and her brother Mark had another kid, a boy, only a year and a half ago; her parents got a new dog, and her grandmother aunt Mae passed away in 2020.

"Aww, how sad," he whispers.

Carl's a successful accountant; he's won several business insider awards, posing in multiple pictures with big poster board checks valued at over $20,000. He's short and pudgy, openly flaunting a hairy chest while sporting button down shirts with the top buttons undone.

They've traveled the entire world, riding elephants in Africa and kissing in front of the Eiffel tower, their lives resembling an eHarmony success story; she looks genuinely happy as she holds his hand, kissing him with her eyes closed in almost every other post. Renee has aged and thinned, no longer as sinuous; her face looks smaller, but her smile is the same. He can barely recognize her as he peruses, advancing through her profile pictures, studying a familiar yet foreign face, zooming in on her countenance, trying to identify the woman that haunts and poisons his presence, but she's not even that attractive, Dennis decides.

He's not even sure how he feels or if he still desires her. Maybe her memory is just embedded in his mind, a symbol of his cohesive trauma. Maybe she's just the personification of all his shortcomings, a collection of his failures and disappointments, the voice in his frontal lobe, his harshest critic, relentlessly rehashing what a piece of shit he really is with acrimonious monologues. She's the constant reminder that he hasn't become what he wanted to be, a scar that reminds him he's been burned; she represents it all. And nothing is really motivating him at this point. He's not feeling a creative stirring of any kind as he clicks, nope. Now he's just bleeding out in the middle of the fucking airport, a real crime scene.

"You couldn't afford to rent out their basement," he whispers as he closes his laptop; he holds it closely to his chest, hugging it under his arms with a doleful wince.

He wonders if he could even split half the mortgage to live in one of their homes, like they did before when they lived together. Opening his laptop again, he's going to find out exactly how much they paid for their home; he bets Carl has some rich fucking parents to leech off. His heart is beating heavy, resounding every couple of thumps, a herald of a panic attack looming, but he's distracted by a new notification; Natalie Clauden is selling ten items on Facebook Marketplace. Dennis looks, browsing the eclectic assortment of table placemats, furniture pieces, and more extraneous things she's listed for pick-up only.

"Now boarding flight 382 to Newark," the overhead speaker trumpets.

Standing up to look for John, Natalie, and the kids, the yells of Dennis's niece and nephew draw his attention as they bustle toward him. His brother John follows, helicoptering as Natalie strolls a solid thirty steps behind John, holding an extended phone as she types away, bobbing her head back and forth from her screen to the surrounding areas.

"Slow down, kids," John demands.

"Uncle Den!" the kids shout as they crash into his thighs, relishing the last day of their trip, especially since they love to fly.

"You guys are nuts," Dennis remarks as he laughs, amused with their careening energy.

He sticks his tongue out at Jake, a playful antagonist, and Jake reciprocates the gesture, blowing raspberries back.

"Jake, don't stick your tongue out like that, it's rude," Natalie reprimands, catching only Jake's puckish bearing, an unprovoked act.

"Mom, he started it," Jake groans, pointing at Dennis with a scowl.

"Just cut it out, Jake, or I'll take your Switch away," Natalie threatens with a half-presence, as if she's reciting a statement she's said countless times without real consciousness; her mind, an autonomic soundboard, triggering responses based on individual and subject, Dennis speculates.

"Natalie, I saw that you're like having a garage sale on Facebook?" Dennis probes.

Her eyes widen as her face reddens with a discernible hue, looking up from her phone; she shakes her head.

"Oh, no I'm just selling a few old things," she stammers, crossing her arm against her body; her left hand clutches her right elbow like a fulcrum as she hunches over, holding her device like it's on a platter.

"What things are you getting rid of?" John inquires, tugging Reese with his left arm as she saunters.

"Um, I can't even really remember. Just like old furniture pieces," she spurts with a blushed visage, agitated at the question, seemingly caught off guard.

"Oh, ok," John shrugs, focusing his attention on Reese; he picks her up and positions her on his hip like a holster as she nuzzles into his shoulder.

As they head down the jet bridge toward the plane, Dennis follows behind, smiling at Jake, who glances back over his shoulder every few steps. Dennis taps him on the left shoulder, quickly looking away to avoid Jake's gaze. He nudges Jake's right shoulder next, dodging his glance again. When Dennis taps his left shoulder a third time, Jake immediately leans into him with a playful yelp, like a Kamikaze pilot. They laugh, and Dennis pulls him into a hug.

"Jake, you cut it out right now," Natalie instructs, reacting to the shrills.

She scolds momentarily with a stern arm gesture, swinging her arm like a bicep curl and clenching a cantankerous fist; Dennis hasn't seen her eat anything but crackers and grapes the entire weekend.

"It's not his fault, I was egging him on," Dennis admits with a smile, patting Jake on the back.

"Can you carry me, Uncle Den?" Jake requests with a languorous drawl; the kid needs a nap.

"I got ya, buddy."

"Wait, so we're having a garage sale?" John pries as if he's just been reminded, carrying Reese as they approach the entrance of the plane.

"What, no. I'm just selling some things on Facebook Marketplace, no big deal," Natalie mutters, rolling her eyes, eager to end the discussion; Dennis wonders what she's up to, what she's hiding.

"Welcome aboard," the animated stewardess and pilot greet, synchronizing as they smile at each person that enters the plane.

"Enjoy your flight," they announce after every fifth person appears.

Dennis notices the pattern to their dialogue as they proceed through the plane, how the shortest flight attendant with monolid eyes reaches out for a high-five from any child under eight years old, responding with "All right!" after each engagement. Dennis wishes he could be celebrated with such a salutation; he misses how friendly people were when he was a kid.

"Our seats are over here, Den. What number seat are you?" John asks as he sets the children down and buckles them in; he starts putting the bags in the overhead compartment, activating responsible dad mode.

The economy plane is a smaller aircraft with only three seats per row: a single window seat on one side of the open aisle and two seats on the opposite side. He's probably going to have to get super cozy with a fellow passenger this time, given the limited space.

"I'm 30A. I'll meet you guys at the baggage collection once the plane lands," Dennis replies, passing by to get to his seat; he sticks his tongue out at Jake while doing so, provoking a growl while Jake shakes his head.

"Uncle Den, I want to sit next to you," Jake pleas, reaching his arms out.

"No way, man, I'm going to be bombing the whole plane ride, you don't want to be next to me," Dennis quips, holding his nose while making a silly face, as if he smells something putrid.

The term "bomb" being a euphemism John has been using since the kids were babies to refer to flatulence.

"Nice, Dennis," Natalie remarks with a contemptuous glance, handing Jake his tablet.

Dennis gets to his seat, which is a few rows back from the family and settles by the window; he's still mulling over his Facebook investigation, envious of the luxurious lifestyle his aged ex is living; his heart is fluttering again, that nervous, uncomfortable energy is swarming. He knows his breath is feeling constricted, and he's literally confined on a plane, so there's no escaping. His mind churns with wayward thoughts, imagining he'll have a heart attack mid-flight and die right in his window seat, his last meal being a single serving of peanuts and a mini Coca-Cola.

"Excuse me, is someone sitting here?" a tall woman with cobalt eyes inquires with a courteous demeanor, a soft tone and folded arms, respecting personal space.

She cradles a purse in her arms and smiles, revealing perky cheekbones and a long sinewy neck, placing her in the early forties age range for Dennis's estimation.

"Uh, not that I know of," Dennis breathes, barely articulating; he hopes she's a nurse because he's going to fucking die soon, he just knows it, and maybe she can resuscitate him.

"Oh ok, my seat is 30B, so I guess that's here," she smiles again, pausing as if she's waiting to be granted permission to sit.

"Did you want the window seat?" Dennis asks with a worried cadence, respiring after each word; he's thinking maybe the window seat is making him feel restricted, and maybe the aisle seat might ease his claustrophobia, making him less likely to freak out.

"No, that's ok," she shakes her head, maintaining eye contact with a curious bearing; her body posture attentive, leaning, ostensibly trying to interpret body language.

"I had the window seat earlier this morning, so I don't mind," she follows up with a friendly nature.

She's wearing a business suit, so she's not a nurse; he's definitely going to die now, he's sure of it. Welling with worry, he starts thinking maybe his parents will get into a car accident on their drive home. He told them to fly, but no, they had to go visit Mary's retired friends who moved to North Carolina, the same friends she's had since kindergarten. She's always been good at keeping friends, unlike him. Maybe if he'd learned a thing or two from her, he wouldn't be so alone. His parents are going to need him, he knows it, and he'll be stuck on this fucking plane, convulsing from cardiac arrest.

"Unless, you want to trade?" she asks with an affable disposition, a kind smile, exuding a calming aura.

"Some people get spooked when they sit in the window seat."

Dennis smiles and shakes his head.

"My friend always freaks out," she chuckles, sitting next to Dennis; her leg brushes up against his, the firm warmth of her pressing against his quad rousing his libido.

"I like to look out the window, the view is welcoming. It makes it easier to think about jumping," Dennis replies, cueing his facetious charm.

"Hahaha, yeah. I've been feeling the same way lately," she replies, reaching into her bag to pull out a neck pillow.

"I'm Brittany," she states as she holds her hand out, sustaining eye contact as if she's trying to look deeper into his soul, a character inspection of the pupils.

"Nice to meet you. I'm Dennis," he replies, grasping half of her hand, shaking it lightly with a gentle touch, careful not to overdo it; she might be skittish, he speculates.

"Check out this cool pillow I bought on Amazon for my trip," she announces with a gregarious pitch, handing him a rectangular bolster as she places it in his lap, prolonging physical contact as she grazes his arm.

"It's called the Turtle," she smiles.

Dennis picks it up and gives it a squeeze, watching the memory foam slowly return to its original shape.

"So, check it out," Brittany remarks as she snatches it back and unwraps the shawl.

"You take it and wrap around your neck like so," she flashes a theatrical grin as she demonstrates, overly annunciating words with a playful drawl, smiling, as if she knows her dimples are her most attractive feature.

"And then you close it up, and this little arch lets you position your neck to any side. So, you never have to lean up against something to support your head," she adds, closing her eyes to pretend she's sleeping.

"Why is it called Turtle?" Dennis questions with urgency, sitting up.

She shrugs her shoulders, smiling as she cocks her head to the side; she gazes with fluttering eyes, leaning forward in her seat to address Dennis, transitioning to a more serious compunction.

"So, what do you do for a living, Dennis?" she asks as if she's about to start taking meticulous notes.

Dennis senses her keenness, a tacit indication of intrigue and possible attraction, but he's bemused by the name of the travel pillow, and he's kinda pissed she'd didn't answer his fucking question. It's a terrible brand name, completely unfitting. The pillow is a contouring memory foam fill stitched into a resplendent role of soft fabric with short Sherpa texture.

"Wait, that doesn't make any sense. Out of all the animals in the wilderness, why the hell would they call it the Turtle?" Dennis demands.

"That's a good question," Brittany smirks, chuckling as if Dennis is joking.

"Out of all the creatures found in nature, they chose a fucking reptile that lives inside a slimy coarse shell? Pick something that at least looks or feels comfortable, something fluffy: sheep, kitty, rabbit but not fucking turtle. Even the name sounds dull and heavy, like a ribbed double-sided dildo," Dennis pontificates, articulating with amusing ardor, debating whether to continue his manic outburst.

"Hahaha," Brittany laughs out loud, tapping Dennis's leg as she cackles.

He knows Brittany is flirting. Cognizant of the escalating body contact, her haptic communication of interest; Dennis wonders if maybe he can persuade her into a bathroom break for high altitude intercourse, offering her membership to the Mile-High club, but he's not sure how to broach the subject.

"You're a pretty funny guy, Dennis," Brittany smiles, playfully bumping him on the side of his shoulder with the back of her fist; her face still dimpled with a persistent smile.

"Never would have thought after the shitty morning I had that I would have been lucky enough to sit next to a hot guy on my flight home," she adds as she gazes, forfeiting her remaining mystique.

Dennis knows that she wants him to pose questions, ask her things, listen, really get to know her, but he doesn't want to; he's done this too many times. Realistically, he can play along, act interested and get her number. They'll meet up for a few drinks, dinner, and after one or two dates, he'll use her as a flesh receptacle for his deviant sexual compulsions, probably for a month or two. She'll want a relationship, eventually, she'll want something more than being a moistened womb for his sensual pleasures, a chamber for his bodily fluids, and he'll decline, her self-esteem and worth becoming collateral damage. But Brittany is kind and caring, and even if she's desperate, Dennis recognizes her welcoming outlook and amiable personality has kept him occupied, distracted from panicking; she reminds him of Christine, just not as pretty.

"If you clap when the plane lands, I will punch you in the mouth," Dennis whispers, smiling to emphasize his frivolity.

"Oh, we're getting physical now?" she replies, raising an eyebrow in a frisky manner; her eyes racing as if she's perceiving an obvious flirtation.

Dennis likes Brittany, she's cute, and he's grateful for her geniality, but he knows he needs to quash the conversation before it goes any further. And he doesn't want to hurt anyone else, so he responds to her questions with only one- or two-word answers, cutting off banter and avoiding reciprocal communication for the rest of the flight. Brittany pries, but Dennis evades until she finally gives up.

"Well, I guess, this is it, Dennis," she asks as the plane touches down, breaking the thirty minutes of silence, Dennis relying on his visible headphones as a chatter deterrent.

She's hoping he'll ask for her number, Dennis affirms by the way she leans forward, trying to establish eye contact and any further implicit flirtations.

"What's your Instagram?" he asks for a less direct line of communication; it can't hurt to have one more follower, Dennis decides.

"Add me," Brittany replies, offering an insipid smile, far less enthusiasm than the overzealous beams from earlier in the flight, with dimples not as discernible; she's probably upset, Dennis infers as he opens his Instagram app.

"Brit dot rose six, but the B in Brit is a three," she explains.

"Is that Brit with two tees?"

"One," Brittany clarifies, holding her phone, waiting for Dennis to follow her.

"Got it," she smirks as she looks at her device, noticing his request.

They walk side by side down the gangway, the long drafty corridor with musty carpet, slightly sticking to his shoe after each step, the fall wind sneaking inside the tunnel from the wall crevices. Brittany glimpses at Dennis every few feet, inviting interaction, but Dennis proceeds without heed, noticing the back of John's head up ahead; he's already looking for the baggage claim sign.

"So, I guess this is it," Britany publicizes as they approach the end of the air tube; she stops and faces Dennis, eager for a climactic goodbye.

Dennis extends his hand, grasping Brittany's for an amicable farewell, a gesture to soften a possible blow to her ego.

"Take care, Brittany," Dennis smiles as she turns, flashing a wide grin before walking away.

And Dennis is frozen, stupefied with an epiphany; it's a temporary paralysis elicited by his interaction, a painful revelation that strikes him to his core: losing Christine is far worse than losing Renee.

7. The Catcher in the Rye

Sitting at the classic classroom desk, the traditional steel design with nonadjustable seat and surface space for writing, Dennis held the card in his hands, clutching it as if he were holding a winning lottery ticket. He didn't know who he was going to tell first. If he told Mike, he knew he would lose his shit, harassing him with repulsive questions, like how her pussy tastes. If he told Nick, he would have probably called him a liar and slapped him in the dick with an accusatory manner. And if he told Rich, he probably would have suggested they email her together, destroying any chance of developing any sort of relationship with her. Dennis knew immediately he couldn't show his friends the card or they'd certainly take her email address down and annoy her with salacious soliloquies, sending her inappropriate messages from random emails they created. And she'd know right away who the culprit was, since she only gave her email address to him.

It was going to be hard, a fucking impossible feat, like a teenager going twenty-four hours without masturbating, but he knew if he was going to have any hope of his fantasy coming to fruition, he needed to be completely discreet, shielding his operation from any potential sabotaging spectators. On the bus ride home, Dennis gaped at the dense Hallmark card gifted to him, inspecting with a diligent eye, flipping it over, investigating for a secret message or some sort of clue, an Easter egg that indicated special interest. Maybe a little heart inscribed somewhere secretly, a little surprise for him with his name written inside. He flipped the thick pasteboard card over, admiring its weight as it propelled a slight breeze when waved; it had to be an expensive card, he speculated, wondering if she gave the "Thank You" card a lot of thought before choosing, considering the happy bears that adorned the front. Dennis conjured up a radical connection of her being like Goldilocks and he was the burly bear coming to pillage her honey. Alighting from the school bus, Dennis continued marveling at the card, envisioning her sedentary at a traditional bureau as she crafted her words with grace, equipped with a fountain pen, wantonly wishing his face could be her seat.

Snaking inside, slithering past his mom before she could interrogate him about the particulars of his day at school like she always did, Dennis slid down the stairs to log onto his computer, focused on his mission; the gears in his prefrontal cortex moved with urgency, calculating the next steps.

"It was a good day. I've gotta get started on this paper though," Dennis echoed to his mother upstairs as he set his backpack down, retrieving the card with a dizzy excitement as he turned on his computer.

Opening the note, he reread the words to himself again and again.

"I think any girl would be lucky to call you her Valentine," he mused, closing his eyes, smiling as he enunciated.

Entering his screen name and password into AOL, Dennis gazed at the card with a licentious urge, admiring her handwriting and skillful dexterity, her neat execution with sharp cursive characters; the wrapping of script letters triggering an erotic image of his limbs interlaced with hers. His hard-on raged, and he could barely refrain from touching himself as the raucous ring of dial-up sounded, a harsher white noise associated with connecting to the Internet, an unmistakable clatter from the early 2000s.

"You've got mail!" the spirited male voice announced.

But Dennis wasn't logging on to view his email; nope, he didn't give a shit about that. He had the ultimate plan, a clever machination to connect with Miss Howard, an easier, more effective approach. He typed the first portion of her email address into the AOL search box, double checking the underscore and the ending numbers in her screen name, hitting the enter key: **"Susanna_Howard98"** appeared in green lettering, indicating she was currently online. Goosebumps ran rampant along his forearms, settling into his fingertips as he typed into the chat box. His hands tingling as he imagined conversing with her; this was his chance.

"Hey, I just wanted to…," he typed and deleted before he could finish the entire sentence, deciding he needed something less direct, something to extend the chat past a simple, "You're welcome," response.

"Hi, it's Dennis Clau…." She may not respond if she knew which Dennis was messaging her.

"Hey, it's Denni…." Nope, he needed something more mysterious.

"Hi Miss Howar…." No fucking way, he deleted, second-guessing his tone; he wanted to avoid referring to honorifics, eliminating the association of school or protocol with Dennis.

"Sup," he typed, deleting again before sending, too casual and tacky.

"Hi." Nope, too passive, he decided.

"Hi, Susanna," meh; too bold, he deduced and deleted; he didn't want to sound like a fucking telemarketer.

After deleting his messaging prompt several times, Dennis hung his head, rethinking every possible salutation, unsure of his method; he couldn't think of a clever way to initiate the conversation without finding a flaw in his tactic. She probably wouldn't even respond, he inferred; she did say keep in touch next year, so a premature message would probably come across as desperate and she'd want to rescind the offer.

"Think you, fuck," Dennis whispered.

He needed to think of something casual but intriguing, cool but apathetic, like he wore a black leather jacket and rode a fucking motorcycle. Either that or he needed to come across as Will from *Good Will Hunting*, a smart, sophisticated tough guy, but Dennis fucking sucked at math; he could barely add fractions.

"**Claudjr11:** Hey," he settled on, typing quickly before he could question himself; his heart rate skyrocketing as he pressed the send button.

"**Susanna_Howard98:** Hi. Who's this?" she responded almost immediately, prompting Dennis to hesitate; he wondered if he should wait a while to respond, building suspense and mystique, but he couldn't resist.

"**Claudjr11:** It's Dennis, just wanted to thank you for the benevolent card," he sent as he smiled nervously, placing his face into the palms of his hands as he leaned over the keyboard, staring at the screen, already anticipating a response.

This was the defining moment, he told himself, wondering if she'd respond. He was proud of himself for using such a mature adjective like "benevolent." He envisioned her dirty talk involved captivating vocabulary like copulating with a prostitute from London in the eighteenth century; a torrid fantasy of him shucking her in an alleyway penetrated his mind, envisioning yanking her chimney bustle up and pulling down her bodice, exposing her bundled flesh while ravaging.

The 134 seconds that followed were the longest, as if Dennis were waiting to find out if he had terminal cancer or if the pregnancy test from a one-night stand was positive; barely breathing, his heartbeat reverberated, aligning each strike with every passing second, pure torturous moments.

"**Susanna_Howard98**: Oh, hey! No problem at all."

Dennis rubbed his eyes and tilted forward in his seat, providing limpid vision to confirm she responded. She even included an exclamation point; maybe she was excited, he fantasized. He knew that the next message was crucial to perpetuate the conversation.

"**Claudjr11:** what are you up to this weekend?" he typed, sending without consideration, proceeding with a casual transition.

Extending back in his rolling chair, pressing the lower lumbar support into his shoulder blades, stretching his torso, Dennis placed his arms on his head, opening his airways as he watched the computer screen, expecting her response as he attempted to abate his tensing chest. Ten minutes passed; each minute chipping away at his confidence, transferring his nervous energy into a sorrowful state, thinking he had failed. Curling in his seat, Dennis swayed, rolling his chair back and forward like a comforting rocking chair, trying to calm his racing mind, and just like that, his plan had been foiled, quashed before it could be implemented. And as soon as Dennis was ready to concede to his defeat and exit the chat, a resounding chime broke his catatonic sulking.

"**Susanna_Howard98:** Going to visit my parents. How about you?" she responded after 840 seconds, fourteen maddening minutes, reviving Dennis's ploy.

"**Claudjr11:** Just hanging with some friends, probably get into trouble :)," Dennis sent the message with a smiley face. Not the modern emoji, since those didn't exist yet; it was one of the three classic text expressions, created with a colon and a parenthesis.

"**Susanna_Howard98:** You like to get into trouble, huh?"

Dennis sank into his seat, sliding down like a deflated lawn decoration after Christmas; he had exhausted all his talking points and was running out of cool things to say. He scanned his basement for inspiration, faltering; he contemplated a witty response but had nothing; he slapped his head, like trying to get the flickering picture of an old television to focus. He tried to think of something someone cool would say, like his older brother.

"**Claudjr11:** I like to do a lot of things, actually."

"**Susanna_Howard98:** Interesting."

"**Claudjr11:** What do you like to do?"

"**Susanna_Howard98:** I guess that depends on what kind of mood I'm in."

Dennis's eyes widened with amazement as he engaged; his heart fluttered, racing with exhilaration, epinephrine releasing into his bloodstream as he struck the keys with fervent fingers, creating conversation. And the innocuous chats continued almost every day, mostly surface level exchanges with mutual banter, encouraging Dennis to persist. They'd talk online weekly about trivial matters, but Dennis felt ten feet tall, completely aggrandized; he'd stare at the school clock, counting down the minutes until he could venture home to his computer and slip on his disguise, becoming the cool, confident messenger behind the computer screen, initiating dialogue with a woman almost twenty years older than him.

He'd see her occasionally at school and wave, keeping a distance, terrified of an actual face-to-face encounter where he'd be put on the spot to come up with a droll response, reducing him to his veracious fourteen-year-old self. Dennis was addicted to the AOL chats, which enabled him to become whomever he wanted. Erasing his timid self, he entered a realm where he could take his time talking, crafting perfect sentences, laced with clever undertones, experimenting with tactics to see which elicited the quickest responses and longest discourse. He even had his mom obtain some Men's Health magazines for conversation inspiration at the Drug Fair, sneaking them into her purchase. They were a reliable resource, as he read about the recommended strategies for chatting with the opposite sex; women liked confidence but not cockiness, punctuality but not eagerness, he scribbled in his composition notebook, consulting articles with samples, jotting down salient facts and personal insights Susanna shared.

He knew she loved Dr. Pepper and only liked her pizza with pepperoni; he learned she was married once, divorced five years ago, and that her ex-boyfriend looked like Jason Statham, a celebrity Dennis was told he possessed a striking resemblance to with his short crewcut hair. He bubbled with heart fluctuations every time they chatted, the best kind; his first experience with intoxicating butterflies. And any time he was around his friends, he felt like he could burst from the over-restraint, as if he were desperately holding his breath under water, but he endured, keeping his online endeavors a secret and his eyes on the ultimate prize; he'd rather drown than be pulled up too early.

Their companionship progressed after a month, bolstered by covert confabs, and Dennis became more relaxed, emboldened by their consistent conversations. His hormones urging him to act, his fantasies intensifying as he pleasured himself during almost every other talk; Dennis felt connected with her as he kept the chat box maximized. It was as if she were there while he fondled his phallus.

And then a mild Friday night rolled around in April, almost two months before he was about to graduate from middle school. The spring air acting like a warming aphrodisiac, filling Dennis's head with all sorts of titillating thoughts, hormonal compulsions and possibilities. It was his first night home alone since Tommy and John were both away at college, and his parents had dinner reservations with friends. The perfect opportunity presented itself, an unoccupied home. Before he could even fully strategize and plan out his scheme, he messaged Miss Howard on AOL to prompt dialogue right after school to ensure she was available. She had seen him in school that day, gifting him an authentic smile, a genuine flushed face with full pearly whites on display; it wasn't his imagination anymore.

"**Claudjr11:** What are you doing tonight?" he typed with frantic fingers, his stomach turning with uncertainty.

"**Susanna_Howard98:** Not really sure. Just got home from school! It's still early."

"**Claudjr11:** You should come over and hang tonight," he typed with perfect execution, sending the audacious message.

Pressing his face to the palms of his hands, Dennis closed his eyes, vowing to keep them shut until she answered. He waited until he could hear the chime from her response, a superstitious exercise as if he were trying to summon a divine intervention.

Only the chime wasn't ringing, even three minutes after, so Dennis woke from his meditation, shifting from excitement to fear; his circulation ceasing, creating cold limbs and chattering teeth as he opened his eyes to check the volume on his speakers; maybe she had responded but somehow the sound powered off.

"Fuck, fuck, fuck," he shouted as he vaulted from his computer chair, checking the speakers, realizing they were not the problem

After fifteen minutes, Dennis stood up and began pacing on the clear office chair mat. Fretting with worry, he wondered if he ruined it all; he knew his approach was too daring and pushy. Hyperventilating in front of his computer, Dennis speculated that Susanna was calling the police or his parents, telling them what a sick little prick their son was for trying to lure a woman twenty years his senior over to his home. He was going to be expelled, that was for certain, maybe placed in jail; his naïve mind manufactured all sorts of irrational outcomes. But it wasn't police sirens that caught him off guard; no, it was the discernible sound of an incoming message, two of them, revivifying his temerity.

"**Susanna_Howard98:** What time?"

"**Susanna_Howard98:** What's your address?"

"**Claudjr11:** 7:15; 10 Wooden Pine Road," Dennis typed with a thunderous heartbeat, heavy fingertips and sweaty palms.

"**Susanna_Howard98:** Ok, see ya then ☺ ," she replied right away.

Jumping up from his chair, Dennis raised his arms like a zealous referee declaring a field goal. Bouncing up and down in front of the computer, he celebrated like he just witnessed an incredible Superbowl victory, a tremendous triumphant; his hands quaked with excitement, elated like he'd woken up on Christmas morning.

Processing the boundary he had just pushed, the wall he had just penetrated, the hurdle he had just leaped, like a seventy-two-inch box jump, he stormed upstairs, meeting his mother in the kitchen, realizing he had one last task to ensure the evening would ensue.

"Mom, can my teacher come over tonight? I'm really struggling with English," Dennis queried with a poised presentation, not to reveal any sort of emotion, which might indicate he was up to something he shouldn't be.

Turning through the circular, dabbing her finger on her tongue before flipping a new page, his mother glanced at him only briefly, unsuspectingly. Her short blonde hair framed her ageless face; she sat at the tempered glass kitchen table, surrounded by white wallpaper with green vine imagery, her kitchen style resembling a café in a European village.

"As long as she's okay with us not being home," she replied, resuming her reading.

And Dennis knew right away that his plan was officially in play, a real mastermind. He knew his mother was picturing an old portly woman with gray hair and bifocals attached to a chain necklace, a nice elder volunteering for an hour to help her son improve his grade. She surely had no idea about the youthful full-figured woman, the radiant beauty he chatted with online almost every day, who was about to come over and hang out with her unsupervised son.

Dennis hears his parents yapping overhead, so he tosses and turns a few times, squishing a pillow against his head to drown out the reverberations of Russ's voice; he's gabbing about coffee grounds in the bottom of the Keurig or something. But Dennis can't sleep anymore anyway; his mind keeps him awake, playing his past like some kind of fucking playhouse purgatory, reliving random moments, like the time Renee asked him to steam her work pants the night before she had a very important presentation the next day; she always trusted him with tidying her clothes. He remembers when Christine spilled a splash of red wine on her navy-blue cashmere sweater, imploring Dennis to get the stain out with pouty eyes. He did so, after spraying it with Shout, rubbing the stained part against another portion of the fabric before tossing it in the wash, a technique he developed over time, the pre-scrub helping activate the bleaching properties.

He can't fully decide if he's conscious or still asleep as he rolls onto his side, but an arbitrary memory of a nasty woman with melasma and hyperpigmentation on her face from the parking lot of a ShopRite in 2019 plays in his mind, appearing like a pesky YouTube ad demanding payment for Premium to eliminate further commercials. The bottom-heavy woman with discernible darkened cheeks dinged his car by opening her door in a hurry, a reckless swing as she stepped out of her vehicle, making eye contact with Dennis. He was returning from the Verizon store, and the synchronization of pressing the unlock button on his keyfob with the aggressive civilian flinging her driver's side door into his car immobilized him,

178

rendering him completely perplexed. He thought maybe the cosmos had linked his smart entry system to producing random acts of negligence. And just like everything else in his life, he wondered if it was partly his fault.

"My bad," she shrugged, tossing her hands up with indifference as she passed by Dennis; her disregard vexing him more than the actual damage.

Baffled, Dennis just stood there as she casually walked away, so now he revises the encounter. But this time, instead of remaining quiet, he walks around to the other side of the car and flings his door open as hard as he can into the disingenuous woman's olive-green Volvo sedan, a real whack of the rigid steel door against aluminum, telling her, "Now it's okay."

He sits up on the basement bed finally, acquiescing to never sleeping past 6 A.M. again since his parents talk so loud. And that's a damn shame because he'd rather sleep than be awake. The air is brushing outside, wailing against the windows, and the livid sky is bucketing, dumping torrents of rain, making it much more difficult to get out of bed. It's the second day in a row he's failed to get up in the morning to write; he's been avoiding going into school early, ever since Monsignor paid him a visit on Monday, beseeching him to tone down his lectures and tread lightly with offensive consternations to avoid embarrassing the students.

The elderly honored cleric entered Dennis's classroom at the end of the day, taking a seat in one of the student's desks. Proceeding with a disarming, gentle smile, the bald interlocutor with sagging skin surrounding his neck and face, obscuring a definitive age, spoke to him, addressing his concerns about the recent feedback from parents, donning his clerical collar like a badge of authority. But his criticism wasn't like a typical boss's feedback; no, it felt grave, heavy, and critical as if God himself were admonishing him; he imagined a celestial glow beaming around Monsignor's silhouette as he orated, a reminder of how inferior

Dennis's existence was. So, Dennis just nodded, ensuring he'd take some heat off his disquisitions and channel his passion into a more productive approach, ingratiating himself, making a deal with the divine father, hoping to still be allowed into heaven.

Dennis sinks back into his sheets, drowning himself in the assortment of pillows and a cheap polyester comforter. Mornings are hard for him; waking up with low Serotonin levels and excess cortisol coupled with unaltered neurotransmitters amplify his self-loathing and cogitation. Reality really stings without the influence of narcotics; his critical awareness is too much, reminding him with each passing minute that he's back living at home, unaccomplished, and lonely.

His reluctant eyes open as he swaddles in his sheets, pulling the covers over his head instead of reaching across the bed for a significant other, like he's done for so many years. He snoozes his first alarm, thinking he'll get some solid REM, but all he's done is ruminate and rehash; he hasn't had a solid night's sleep without the aid of his lorazepam, an old prescription he was able to refill without having to revisit a psychiatrist. All he had to do was call it in, knowing his inattentive shrink would just permit whatever request came from the Pharmacy. He's been chewing the little white oval pills like Flintstone vitamins, popping them whenever the noise seems too loud, overwhelming, and the compulsion to let the steering wheel go feels too convincing. The benzodiazepines help muddle the sounds and cynical suggestions, and a hit of THC every hour or so provides temporary relief from a mind assailed by memories and apprehension.

The emotional avalanches are worrisome, but the increasing urges to cry aren't unmanageable; he thinks it's better than feeling nothing. He's not entertaining as many thoughts of Renee, ever since his Facebook reconnaissance; the only time he really thinks of her now is when he sprays his Calvin Klein Reaction cologne or uses his Neutrogena face scrub, which he's been using ever since they were together. He still vividly recalls her proclaiming how wonderful the aromatic nuances were as she caressed his face in the shower, kissing his lips as she pressed her nose close.

And Dennis knows he should have switched his fragrance and skin care products a long time ago, ever since a therapist told him it was a subconscious way of holding onto her, reluctant to let go of her influences. But Dennis doesn't care about what a fucking swindler suggests. He appreciates the light musky undertones of the scent mixed with citrus notes and the effectiveness of the anti-acne wash. He loves how it clears the patches of small pimples that accumulate in common areas on the face from sweating, like the eyebrows and temples, even if the formulas weren't powerful enough to prevent Renee from leaving.

But he's come to accept the inevitable; he thinks he totally gets it now, that everyone carries pieces of those they've met, fragments of each person imprinting themselves, especially those who've touched their hearts. Heartbreak, he thinks, is kinda like cancer, how it never really goes away. Even after the relief of chemo, recovery, and distractions like dating and debauchery, it still lingers in remission. Life moves on, and the hurt slowly learn to love and rebuild. And then one day it returns, but it's not like before; it's metastasized, spreading with ravenous malignancy, relentlessly feeding on insecurities and old wounds. It consumes with a slow, torturous hunger, devouring vitality and leaving nothing untouched. It's an atrophy of the soul, a heartbreak that never truly heals.

####

He's at his desk, and it's the end of the school day. The drafty room with dismal lighting and creaks of old classroom furniture create a Dickensian atmosphere, echoing in between his thoughts, and he can barely remember a single interaction from the day. He knows he should brainstorm on the lesson for tomorrow before he leaves, since he's having a hard time getting work done at home, but he's browsing on Amazon instead, looking for an hourglass. He's thinking an invertible device with two bulbs dispensing sand in sixty minutes is just what he needs to improve his concentration; a timeless tool from the eighth century to help conceptualize transience and concretize time ought to do the trick. He's going to turn it over on his desk before he starts writing, signifying the start of a creative race, triggering ambition and more productivity with his hours, but he still hasn't checked out. It's still in his cart because he can't decide what color to choose for the sand; he can't figure out if time should be white, blue, red, or black, which are the only options.

"Mr. Clauden?"

Dennis blinks, emerging from his thoughts to find Jeffrey Haymaker sitting across from him, rambling about comma usage and its subjectivity.

"Uh, yeah. Sorry, what were you saying again?" Dennis mutters, scrambling to recall exactly what was being discussed.

Jeffrey clears his throat.

"Well, I'm just trying to understand why I keep getting points off for my comma usage. Commas could be used to emphasize pauses, and a lot of what I write, I like to slow the reader down so they really take it in."

Dennis squints, realizing Jeffrey is wearing a bow-tie and not the standard tie; he wonders why exactly he feels compelled to deviate from the uniform, what exactly he is lacking in his life that he needs to dress himself up like a fucking cocktail waiter.

"No, Jeff. The issue isn't your pauses. It's that you're creating comma splices," Dennis states, standing up to assert his point, looming slightly over Jeffrey.

"And commas aren't some gender-fluid punctuation, some social construct that can be redefined at will for inclusivity. Okay?"

Jeffrey stares up at him, wide-eyed.

"There are rules to grammar, just like there are rules for commas. You use them to separate independent clauses when paired with coordinating conjunctions. You use them after introductory clauses. You use them in lists. You use them to set off non-restrictive clauses."

"But Mr. Clauden…"

"No, Jake, that's it," Dennis cuts him off sharply.

"Practice proper punctuation, and you'll get a better grade. Commas aren't decorative accents you sprinkle around for flair. They're functional."

Dennis pauses, feeling his phone vibrate in his pocket.

"Now if you'll excuse me, I have a very important phone call to take," he declares, already pulling the phone out.

"I'm not Jake, I'm Je…"

"Thanks, Jason," Dennis interrupts, staring at his device.

"Close the door on your way out."

A message on Tinder lights up his phone, flashing an eye-catching banner with a red flame that Dennis can't resist.

"2 truths and a lie," Cassie, 28, writes.

"There is no God, there's no better orgasm than autoerotic asphyxiation, and Epstein killed himself," Dennis responds before tossing his phone into his desk to avoid further temptation and distraction.

His mood has improved since the morning; he's a bit manic now, and it's not because he's still high from the controlled substance or the fourth cup of coffee; no, it's because he's spelled "autoerotic asphyxiation" correctly for the first time without having to use the autocorrect feature. He usually puts the "p" before the "s" in "asphyxiation," sounding it out as he types but never fully listening to his enunciation. He also enjoys responding to trite ice breakers, which are shockingly more common than not on dating apps, more corroboration that interpersonal communication is moldering, like a delicious cheese that's been picked on and left out on an exposed counter for way too long.

He knows he's going to have to scale back the mordant jesting if he's ever going to get laid without having to consult a prostitute, but he's not sure if he's ready for intimacy, things always escalate and get complicated. He's pretty sure everyone just gets hurt and that he's developing a drug problem. But really, he's gotta figure out what he's going to do with his lesson for tomorrow. His manufactured scrutiny is weighing on him from his lackluster lectures, which he attributes to his toned-down lessons; he's starting to question his teaching ability since he's been chided by God's messenger. He's never failed at teaching before. He's thinking he should put the students into groups to discuss John Milton since he read on a teacher's blog that designating kids to smaller, more personal groups helps encourage class engagement, a good conversational warm-up.

Dennis pulls up the blog post to study the talking points again and notices the share date: September 9, 2018. He scrolls down the page and tries to look over the paragraphs, but he's thinking about his life back in September 2018; he and Renee were engaged and starting to plan a wedding. And he's been doing this for a while now, where he'll take note of a particular date and try to picture an epoch from around that time as best he can. It's a shitty habit, he understands, but he's thinking it's just residual damage.

Three nights ago, he cleaned out his black messenger bag, tossing an old newspaper article about eCommerce from 2020 that had been crumpled at the bottom. As he crushed the clipping, a memory resurfaced from that same year: taking Christine to her first Broadway play, *Wicked*, just before COVID hit. But it wasn't the entire night he remembered, not a single detail of the play, actually. No, the only thing that lingered was a glimpse of her: the gorgeous girl crossing the street, glancing back at him before scampering down the sidewalk. Her radiant smile, her perky cheeks, and the sharp, eye-lined gaze that cut through him, stirring a warmth that felt like pure, unfiltered love. He gazed back at her and couldn't help but smile, drunk from the drinks but truly intoxicated by her beauty, wondering if someone as stunning as her could ever love him.

The blaring chime from his laptop shakes him from his inertia, rattling his reverie; it's an email alert from school, so Dennis opens it, partially believing it's a notice of his termination.

"St. Vincent's welcomes, Mr. Fairchild," the bold header of the email reads.

Monsignor had mentioned earlier that week they hired a replacement for the other AP English Teacher, the recently retired Mr. Di Fiorre, who had announced an abrupt retirement to take care of his terminally ill wife.

"Mr. Michael Fairchild is a 2014 graduate of UVA with a double major in English literature and creative writing. He has published over five short stories," the first few lines of the introductory email states, and Dennis speculates that the new teacher is self-published because he's a year younger; he's also thinking the school is trying to antagonize him with the new hire, pitting him against some rival intellectual.

"His acclaimed story 'Hangman' was published in the New Yorker," the unctuous email continues, and Dennis feels a fiery rage lighting, a visceral impulse to fucking punch something, so he shuts his laptop with force, using both hands, exhaling as he curbs the building anger.

He's getting really good at repression, burying things in his subconscious like dead pets in the backyard. Yeah, he's just shoving it all into the back of his mind, cramming turmoil into the corners of his heart, an emotional hoarder. Placing his hands on his head, he recalls a breathing exercise he read about on Reddit. Closing his eyes, he stands up and begins counting down from ten, inhaling deeply through his nose. He really thinks he should call Christine, even if they haven't talked in four months; he's dying without her.

"Mr. Clauden?" a voice from the doorway echoes.

Dennis opens his eyes, his elbows angled up and outwards, turning to see Megan Earhardt. She's knocking gently on the side of the door, standing just outside the classroom; fraught with shame, Dennis wipes his eyes, digging the back of his hands into his orbs, clearing the anxious incursion, concealing his current state. It also dawns on him, Jeffrey failed to follow instructions by not shutting the door.

"Yes, please come in," Dennis instructs, clearing his throat and straightening out his tie; sitting in his chair, Dennis pushes his shoulders back, projecting his chest out, placing his hands on the armrests to elongate his posture.

He turns his head swiftly, attempting to crack his neck; he's thinking the release of facet joints will imbue relaxation, assuage tension, and he'll be able to listen. He's been doing this a lot lately, which makes him wonder if it's a subconscious nervous tick he's developed since he rarely achieves relief from the movement but still does it.

"What's up?" Dennis asks casually as Megan nears, promenading as she smiles.

He avoids eye contact as he looks down at his laptop, hoping he didn't break it with his belligerence; the last thing he needs is to have to tell the school he requires a new Surface Pro.

"So, I was umm confused about..." she discloses, talking hastily as if she's maybe rehearsed her introduction and she's nervous.

The gussied girl's long cascading hair converges into curls at her shoulders, a striking style as if she's come from the salon. She speaks to him from off to the side of his desk, standing just about a foot away in the classroom, offering a clear view of her exterior; Dennis notices her amply applied makeup and glossed lips, as if she were about to put on a performance.

She continues explaining her confusion, discussing Poe's hidden subtext, but Dennis isn't retaining much; he's focusing on her appearance and body language, dressed in uniform. She's got her hand placed on her hip, emphasizing a shapely figure; pushing her hip out in a somewhat uncomfortable pose, she combs her hair with her left hand, running fingers through her tresses, preening as if she has ulterior motives. Perhaps she's trying to present herself for viewing, to be admired, Dennis ponders.

"But what's the symbolism of the raven?" she asks; Dennis catches a fragment of her monologue.

Dennis isn't concentrating; no, he's zoning in on her mannerisms, the prurient twisting and turning of her stands of hair, the intertwining of elements coiling like limbs wrapping together during sex, rubbing in concert. Her moistened lips purse and open while she talks; he hates that he's attracted to her; he's disgusted with himself.

"Ok, wait, we're not even covering Edgar Alan Poe right now, nor is 'The Raven' on our curriculum," Dennis states with a puzzled visage, shaking himself from an inappropriate digression.

He floats above the room, like he's watching the interaction from outside of his body; he wonders if it's possible he forgot that he included a portion of Poe's poetry on the syllabus.

"Oh, I know. I'm just so fascinated with Poe, like I've grown to admire Frost, but I find I can't resist his words."

She speaks with ardor, conviction, a gentle voice, soft and soothing, angelic-like as she prattles on. She's retained a lot from her reading, and she's moving often, fidgeting, and soon it becomes apparent she's trying to draw attention to her chest, leaning forward on occasion, keeping her hands on her hips. Her taupe sweater is only buttoned halfway up, jutting her cleavage forward, creating an arresting focal point, commanding attention. Flipping her hair quite often as she speaks, a nervous flick, Dennis can't decide. Her skin is soft and clear, glowing like a freshly painted canvas, new and untainted.

"Mr. Clauden?" she asks with a devilish smile, a precocious expression as if she's partially aware of her tantalizing effect.

"What about Poe?" Dennis asks, fluttering his widened eyes, reaching for poise; he's not paying attention, which is something he remembers Renee saying he needed to work on.

Closing his eyes and crossing his arms, he drifts back to the night he played Monopoly in the dark with Renee, or maybe it was Christine; fuck, he can't remember, but it doesn't really matter. It was during a blackout from a turbulent storm, leaving them without electricity or hot water for an entire week. Going without simple utilities made him realize how much he took for granted, and while most people would have been absolutely miserable without Wi-Fi, Dennis recalls how happy he was with none of it, living the entire week with literally nothing except the person he loved, an organic high, a natural bliss.

"Mr. Clauden, are you, ok?" Megan whispers, waving her hands in front of his face as she bows, examining his distracted gaze with an inquisitive look.

Dennis finally snaps out of his daydream, wiping pooling eyes before the tears fall.

"Uh yeah, I'm sorry Megan," he mutters, harrumphing as a distraction; he peers at his wrist and notices it's 3:15.

"I have to get going, but if you want to continue the conversation, we can finish discussing tomorrow," Dennis states, standing up from the desk to make a departure.

He's crashing and losing control; he needs to get home before he says or does something stupid.

Walking by her, he makes his way to the door, unfazed by her loitering.

"Wait, so, do you think you can tutor me?" Megan asks with a confused countenance, creased facial features, as if she's pondering a riddle.

Apparently, she had asked for a tutor during her long-winded declamation. Her question catches Dennis off guard, and he pauses, turning to her with a nonplussed expression, eyebrows raised.

"You have an A- in the class right now. I don't think you really need a tutor," Dennis counters, remembering her essay on "The Cask of Amontillado" being the only tolerable paper he read, commending her seamless transitions with supporting examples and her proper formatting of block quotations.

She argued that the strongest trope of the story was the connection to the Golden Rule, treating others the way you wanted to be treated, he recalls; she also proposed that Fortunato's fatal flaw is the sole cause for his downfall, his affinity for wine. Dennis found it a bit straightforward, but he appreciated her effort and the way she'd included so many excerpts, easily surpassing the ten-page length requirement.

"Well, yeah. But I'd like to get an A," she smirks, flashing a tight-lipped smile.

Dennis shakes his head and moves into the hallway, unsure of the encounter as Megan follows.

"Come back tomorrow after school, and we'll go over some study questions," he capitulates, shutting the humming fluorescent lights off.

Grabbing the handle of the classroom door, he swings it shut, shoving it with his shoulder. The old, lopsided wooden door with its faulty hinge requires considerable force to close.

"Oh my God, that would be awesome," Megan applauds, clapping her hands in a cute, feverish manner like she just won an Instagram giveaway by tagging three friends in the comments.

Dennis finishes securing the two heavy locks, putting his keys back into his pocket and turns around to see Megan still standing around. She's twirling her hair, smiling; Dennis forgets if his last statement required a response or further instruction, a reason for her to still be lingering. He looks at her, making direct eye contact, unwavering, she continues her excessive smiling as they stare at each other, sharing an awkward silence and gaze.

"So, are you walking out this way? Are you leaving for the day?" Megan asks with a probing pitch.

Dennis can't figure out if he's high or dreaming or what the fuck is going on, but the girl is now following him as he journeys the hallway with his hands in his pocket, scanning each open door for spying eyes while he passes, keeping his head tucked.

"Uh yeah," he replies reluctantly, avoiding eye contact as he continues his walk, checking his periphery to see her still trailing.

"Ok, cool. I'm parked in the back lot too," Megan responds with eagerness, immediacy, as if she's trying to prevent Dennis from hanging up the phone on her, shadowing him with a keen step.

Trekking through the halls, turning corners, and traversing through double doors and corridors, Dennis can't seem to shake the young admirer as she blabbers, keeping herself entertained. It's starting to become obvious he's not making this up; she's definitely following with intention, her hands pulling on the shoulder straps of her backpack as she moves.

"I love to read at nighttime, what about you?" she asks with a relaxed attitude, conveying comfort and familiarity like they're besties.

Dennis ponders if he possibly looked at her Instagram story the other day when he was high, revealing that he's watching her, but he remembers her profile being private, so there's no way he could have viewed it.

Glancing over toward her periodically as they travel, her eyes always gazing; he recognizes the affectionate look, the attentiveness, like she truly cares and wants his attention.

"Poetry has always been my favorite. There's something cool about finding the exact words to express something clearer than you can," she shares with passion, earnest enunciation, like she speaks from the heart.

"Writing helps you better understand yourself," he replies, admiring her decent observation.

Megan beams, and it's not a tight-lipped smile; no, it's wide, exposing, full and sincere, like she's showing herself, expressing desire.

They walk for another five minutes, silent as they pass through the lower parking lot. Megan holds her backpack in her arms, clutching it like a comfort pillow; she's kicking her short legs to keep up with Dennis's pace. And he's happy she's allowing there to be silence, because he loves to listen to the sound of residual raindrops after a rainstorm, trickling against the leaves as they fall. The pavement is wet, but the rain has stopped, leaving behind just the soothing sounds of sprinkling water and a petrichor that fills the air, grounding him in the peaceful aftermath of the storm. The upper lot is girdled by tall coniferous trees, beautified with the colors of fall as they voyage up the long passageway; the fulgent sun is peering through the thunderheads, providing just enough shimmer to spotlight the vividness of the autumnal trees. And Dennis thinks he should get a Starbucks, a pumpkin spice latte, because a serving of 300 mg of caffeine is just what he needs at 3:35 P.M.

"Here's my car," Megan announces, interrupting Dennis from his wandering mind and daydream of specialty coffee.

His mind is really fucking drifting, like a wayward sailboat bowling through surging tides; Dennis is not exactly sure what has transpired or why Megan has become so interested, but his nose detects a whiff of skunk aroma, possibly a wisp of weed. He stands, rising to his tippy toes, sniffing to see if he can detect where the ambiguous scent is emanating from; he wonders if it's him that smells.

He loses interest in the marijuana odor when he looks at Megan, standing with her adorable smirk and youthful gaze; she's still holding her backpack, squeezing it against her chest; the bottom of the shoulder strap catches a part of her skirt on the side, exposing a portion of her thigh. She's standing in front of her car, leaning against the driver's side door, waiting for instruction. She waits for Dennis to say goodbye; he senses her seeking approval.

He remembers being her age, transparent and pure, untouched by the harsh elements of life. A guileless form, free of pretenses and agendas, brimming with optimism and possibility, intrigue and geniality. He longs for the days of living uncompromised, true to his authentic self, without any traumas to identify with, not jaded by disappointments. It was a time before he was forced to conform to societal pressures, before he was manipulated to fit molds, before the world dictated who he should be and dimmed his light. It was a time before the vibrant colors of life became muted, leaving him to ponder if anything is still worth looking at when it's not as colorful or bright.

The pungent fragrance arrests Dennis once again, pulling him from his philosophical propounding, and he's now 100% sure the smell is weed, spotting a tall, dark silhouette across the way, outside of the gymnasium with a cloud of smoke hovering overhead. The anonymous individual sits on the stairs, reading a book; Dennis debates if he should go and write the kid up, but there's not enough fucking time; all he wants is that fucking latte.

"I guess I'll see you tomorrow," Megan suggests, trying to elicit further conversation and recapture Dennis's attention; she's hanging onto the interchange with a sense of desperation, as if she's obstinate and won't accept anything less than her high expectations.

She doesn't yet understand the psychological warfare of attraction and its power dynamics, the need for strategy, a calculated approach to access the limbic system and spark intrigue. She hasn't grasped the potency of inaccessibility, the most effective method, which exploits self-consciousness, feigns disinterest to intensify desire, and programs the psyche to crave what it can't have. She's unaware of the calculated moves: the delayed responses, the brevity, the aloofness tempered with clever sarcasm and playful banter. Because feeding breadcrumbs ensures insatiability, a habitual need, establishing loyalty by creating dependency. But it isn't Megan's fault she doesn't know; she's still untouched by these games, wholly open in her communication. She hasn't been broken yet, and Dennis admires that; he appreciates her unspoiled beauty.

"Ok, Megan. Get home safe, I'll see you tomorrow," Dennis voices, captivated with her charm; he reciprocates a genuine smile.

She waves as she pulls out of her spot, driving a blue Volkswagen Jetta; it looks rather new, except for the missing rear hubcap. Dennis watches as she drives away; a discernible "Hang Loose" sign decal pasted on her left side bumper, depicting the front of a three-fingered fist with an extended pinky and thumb. She must surf, Dennis theorizes, as he continues his hike to the far end of the parking lot. Yeah, he parks as far away as he can to avoid any dings or dents in his car by inconsiderate fucks.

Approaching his deserted luxury vehicle in the last row, covered in tree debris, Dennis notices the kid is still smoking weed on the stairs outside of the gym, now reading a book. He stops and squints, trying to get a better look at the figure, focusing. He realizes it's not a student, it's actually the school's electrician or janitor; he's not sure what his official role is. Dennis can't recall his name either, but he's seen him a few times in passing. Jay or James, a younger black guy who's always changing light bulbs and smoke detectors, forever in the hallway standing on a ladder, his head up in the ceiling. Dennis wonders if maybe he might be a good connection, since he's not sure how much longer Christine's friend is going to keep selling to him, especially since the last ounce was rife with stems and seeds.

Dennis ambles his way toward the gymnasium, accepting that a latte is now not going to happen since it's almost a quarter to four, and if he has caffeine too late, he'll never be able to go to sleep. Taking furtive steps, a steady stroll, Dennis doesn't want to startle him, so he tries to walk naturally, letting authentic footsteps occur as he proceeds.

"Krishnamurti" is inscribed with striking red letters on the back of the book, which he's holding with his right hand, placing it against his knee; his other hand clutches a cellphone as he sits in a surprising lotus pose.

Before Dennis makes his presence known, a strange command sounds, an abrupt voice:

"Kill yourself," a speaker tone announces.

"Kill yourself," the tone continues until the swarthy fellow picks up the phone; the startling, irreverent expression is his ringtone.

"Hello?" he answers with an irritated voice, a bark at the speakerphone.

"I said I hate fucking rye bread," he shouts, yanking the gym door open.

He charges inside, grasping his book under his arm with his phone pressed between his ear and shoulder.

Dennis stands there for a little while, feeling the remnants of squishy grass under his feet, damp and lush. The cushioning is disappearing, and the ground is becoming solid, cold as winter looms. Perplexed and amused, Dennis springs on the wet grass before he turns to leave, concluding that anyone with a ringtone and disdain for processed grains like that must be an awesome individual, someone he would enjoy being friends with.

8. Paradise Lost

The compact box he called an apartment smelled like wet cardboard, stale and stuffy, the leaky pipes emitting a musty aroma. The sporadic dripping of the kitchen sink nettled him during quiet hours, keeping him up at night; his crooked mattress, a block of cement, cold and unforgiving, creating stiff, groggy mornings. But Dennis knew it was only temporary and that it would be worth it, eventually; besides, it wasn't like he had moved back home with his parents.

He retrieved his phone from his unstable nightstand, one of the only pieces of furniture he actually owned; it was a wooden miniature accent table with a single drawer that he bought from Goodwill his senior year in college. The thing wobbled since the day he bought it, but he developed a connection with the piece, an affinity for its charm; it was pretty much the only thing from college that still remained in his life. He needed something for his bedside anyway, something with accessible surface space; he was getting tired of hanging off the edge of his mattress to grab his phone from the charger, since he'd rather not leave his bed.

"Oh stoppppp," the last message from Renee read, received at 11:30 P.M.

Dennis couldn't remember what they were talking about or what she was referring to, but he knew it was part of some passive aggressive banter, which was all they exchanged since he had moved out. The one-bedroom, one-bathroom apartment Dennis had been occupying was like a coffin, cramped and constricting. He felt himself becoming lifeless, feeling even more dead inside as the days passed, waiting for Renee to text him or knock on his door to tell him to come home, finally resuscitating, bringing him back to life. He decayed in the bleak suite; it was all he could afford with the money she'd given him as reimbursement for the down payment of the house they had split. She made it seem like she took it from her savings, but Dennis knew it was her father's money, too prideful to admit her dependency. But he didn't really care about how decrepit his dwelling was; he hardly paid attention to the setting, ignoring the derelict details, never fully perceiving its appearance. It wasn't his, and he'd be leaving any day, as soon as Renee realized how much he meant to her.

Scrolling through his messages, he cringed at the ratio of sent to received texts, noting the long melodramatic blocks filled cliché romantic quotes and jealous ramblings, asking who she was with or what she was doing. He remembered the whiskey talking, his overly active sympathoadrenal system antagonized by loneliness coalescing with alcohol, a potent stimulant for repressed emotion.

"A person that loves you will truly never let you go, no matter how hard the situation gets," one of the images read, displayed in bold black letters against a white background, emphasizing its significance with a contrast of colors; Dennis had sent it to her last night amidst some histrionic monologue.

He felt nauseous, and it wasn't because he drank a bottle of Jack; no, it was from reading his desperate pleas and embarrassing texts. Dennis had been forcing himself to sleep every night to avoid the obsessing, the uncontrollable texting; he was an addict, helpless with his words, shooting messages like desperate arrows from cupid's bow, trying to connect and rekindle their romance. He knew there had to be something he could say, some eloquent paragraph he could construct, some resonating, inspirational quote or some evocative image he could send her that would make her come to her senses, bringing clarity about how they should be together. He'd type out memories in detail, recalling moments they shared together, ones he knew she would remember fondly, times they laughed, like when he literally screamed out loud after being spooked by a zombie at Six Flags Fright Fest.

But nothing seemed to elicit any substance; he just couldn't figure it out, like a Rubik's cube, every combination seemed to get him nowhere; no anecdote worked as an antidote for her indifference. Manic with insubordinate fingers, he'd text throughout the day, unable to deal with the distance, the disconnect; he needed to know where and what she was doing at all times, fearing that if the conversation ended, they'd eventually cease all communication. But that particular night was a disaster; he suffered a moment of weakness, a caprice, as he fired off aggressive messages like a psychopath. From spiteful anger to pitiful bargaining, Dennis laced his tangents with uncontrolled emotion, humiliating himself in the digital space. And even if he deleted the evidence, the damage had already been done, his ego battered and bruised, his insecurity and self-consciousness revealed, the power dynamic completely lost.

Grabbing his phone from the nearby unsteady table, the legs juddering as he retrieved the device with force, he dialed Renee, the phone ringing twice before going to voicemail. Calling her number again with an irascible vigor, the dial tone sounding two times before her greeting picked up.

"Hey it's Renee, you know what to do," her nasally voice spoke.

And Dennis wanted to tell her how much she hurt him and how much of a fucking cunt bag she was for doing what she did, separating them, ruining their future as she explored relations with some fucking dweeb that slid into her DMs. He wanted to scorch her and tell her what a simpleton she was for being wooed by a digital stranger, but Dennis couldn't garner the patience to wait for the beep, so he hung up, and dialed her again, hanging up each time he got her voicemail. He repeated calling, always clicking off as soon as her voicemail started, placing about forty straight phone calls, his anger escalating.

"Jesus. Why are you calling me so many times?" Renee's voice finally whimpered over the phone.

"Where the fuck have you been?" Dennis shouted, wondering if she even glimpsed at the photo of the stuffed lion toy he'd Snapchatted her.

It was the first prize he won for her at the Jersey shore; it was supposed to be the lion from *The Wizard of Oz*, since she always teased Dennis about needing more courage, a baseless claim, but condescending repartee was part of her charm that he adored.

It cost him sixty bucks trying to win the carnival bean bag throwing game, since he told her he had played baseball in college. Dennis hadn't played baseball past eleventh grade, but he had bragged to Renee when they first met that he had been recruited by a Major League Baseball team his senior year and even made it past two tryouts before being cut. Maybe he wanted to impress her or maybe he was insecure, possibly both, but he blurted it out during their second conversation at the gym like uncontrollable vomit, half embarrassed after he spewed the lie while they were stretching. And he could barely hit anything, landing only one can in three throws, costing him five dollars each time he tried. Each toss whizzed low and off to the right, prompting cackles from Renee as she teased him

"Come on all-star," she quipped like a smug cheerleader, feverishly clapping, playful provocation.

He kept coughing up the cash because he needed to win, his lie was part of his identity, an almost-professional athlete. And after handing over his third twenty-dollar bill, Dennis finally zoned in on the target while the excitable drumbeats and notable guitar riffs of "Semi-Charmed Life" by Third Eye Blind boomed overhead. It was serendipitous, and it unlocked his athleticism somehow; the tiny pellet-filled pouch shifted in shape, no longer unfamiliar and awkward as he gripped the bag, manipulating it in his hand. It brought him back to an unforgettable freshman night in college, when he and his buddy Brandon dominated in beer pong and snorted the freshest powdery lines of cocaine he had ever sampled, the same catchy chorus bellowed in the background.

The floor's RA had returned home to attend a funeral, so they had the 3rd floor of Potomac all to themselves one Thursday night, a small gathering in the dorm room. He remembered taking the closet door down to use as the board and playing against Heather, the blonde from room 219, the one with the lustrous green eyes and a puka shell necklace. She bet him a blowjob he couldn't beat her, so Dennis had to sink the last shot with an ostentatious showing, setting the celluloid orb on fire with Brandon's Bic lighter before tossing it. The room erupting in pandemonium as the fireball dropped into the final cup, extinguishing in the beer bubbles. And Dennis couldn't even recall the blowjob from later that night, but he vividly remembered feeling alive, free, and fearless as he won the game, his voice rattling in his ears as he cheered with friends.

"I want something else, to get me through this," the catchy chorus echoed as Dennis wound up, whispering the words.

Channeling the warm memory into physicality, motivated movement, the redolence of kerosene mixed with ammonia notes rushed into his nasal cavity as if he were back in the dorm room, snorting a fat wintry line of stimulant residue. Exhilaration pumping, stimulating an energizing poise, his first throw emulated a magic bullet trajectory, crashing into the middle tier of cans with a downward force, causing a bottom tin to ricochet and knock off the remaining bunch. Ecstatic, he waved his fist in the air, gazing at Renee as she smiled in disbelief, shocked but impressed. He was the star that day, a brilliant constellation in her sky before he faded out, losing his luster.

"Why are you calling me like a mad man?" Renee whispered over the phone, wincing with pain or groggy from just waking up; Dennis couldn't decide.

"Why are you ignoring me?" he growled, unchained.

"I'm not ignoring you. I've been trying to sleep. I didn't go into work today. I've been experiencing unbelievably painful stomach cramps."

"Do you think it's your period?" Dennis foamed, mimicking her sarcastic monologues; his words slipped out before processing, like Tourette's, partially satisfied with the clever rebuttal.

Snorting over her whimpers, Renee chortled, a perceived expression of amusement.

"I think I know what having my period is like and it's not this," she uttered, still entertained.

"Well, are you going to tell me what the psychic said to you last night?" Dennis pried, like a desperate car thief with a crowbar.

He needed to know what the psychic said; he tossed and turned the entire night, contemplating the scoundrel's supposition. Renee had acquired tickets to a private reading with the TV personality and clairvoyant Veronica Visionary, the celebrated psychic with over one million followers that all the celebrities raved about. Her job always offered Renee special perks and discounts to top attractions and events, which is how they got to see the Michael Jackson's cirque du Soleil rendition; this private meeting was an opportunity Dennis knew she wouldn't turn down, since he knew how superstitious Renee was, highly analytic but inanely spiritual. He knew whatever the charlatan claimed was going to greatly affect her and Dennis chances at a reconciliation.

"Ugh, is that why you have been calling me?" Renee moaned, losing her tickled spirit.

"No, I just haven't heard from you all day. Am I still allowed to be concerned?"

"Ugh, I really feel like I'm going to throw up. Can I call you back?" Renee deflected.

"What's going on? Talk to me," Dennis implored, switching from a hostile disposition to more concerning.

"I seriously feel like there's something wrong with my stomach. I'm in so much pain," she muffled, as if she were holding her breath.

Dennis pictured her curled up in her black and white zebra printed sheets; she had Snapped him a picture of her new linens a month before during a heated exchange, captioning with a cutting remark, something along the line of "new linens, new me." But Dennis interpreted it further, the symbolism, the subliminal messaging, as if she were sharing sheets with someone new, no longer her fiancée.

"Let me take you to the doctor," Dennis beseeched, since he knew Renee wasn't the type to exaggerate; maybe she really needed him, Dennis thought.

"I'll be right over," he asserted, waiting only a few seconds before hanging up, just in case Renee objected.

The car ride to the doctor was filled with the silence of strangers, as if they hadn't been in love once, engaged, or even lived together, an awkward drive in close quarters, like public transportation. Slouched over in the passenger seat, Renee stared out the window, antipathic to Dennis's presence, immediate proximity yet separated by figurative distance. Flipping through radio stations with desperation, searching for the House song "Clarity," a tune that was gaining popularity and caught Dennis's attention because of the lines being applicable to their tumultuous relationship. He imagined she'd hear the powerful lyrics paired with melodic beats, and it would bring her back to the wild nights they shared when they first started dating, rendering her defenseless and her walls would crumble, resulting in her finally opening up. So, he turned the radio dial in pursuit for the techno piano chords in an A major key and apropos lyrics: "Cause you are the piece of me I wish I didn't need."

He wanted to hear it play, hoping it would provide some perspective, but Dennis couldn't find the song, and he couldn't find his ex-fiancée, even though she sat right there beside him in the car. She was too busy, occupied with her phone in between the casual glances at the scenery outside, her head resting against the window with her hood pulled taut. They had exchanged only a few words when Dennis showed up, shattering his vision of the heartfelt reception he'd anticipated as he rang the doorbell. But Dennis knew about unconditional love and its complexities; he just wanted her to know he was there for her.

As they checked in, apparently fifteen minutes late, the contentious receptionist instructed them to take a seat in the waiting area after demanding proof of insurance and payment for parking. The anteroom was a stuffy container with murky waffle textured carpet, furnished with uncomfortable plastic chairs, and surrounded by random modern art, a real sterile chamber. A large canvas print with splashes of red paint was set as the focal point of the front wall, an equivocal display of creativity or perhaps just the glorified scribbles of a toddler.

"Jesus, my stomach is seriously killing me," Renee groaned as she sat down, clutching her abdominal.

Reaching for her hand, Dennis attempted to grasp her clammy paw, which she withdrew upon the warmth of his hand, but only a partial retreat, as if she were too weak to refute his affection.

"Excuse me. Ya'll need to fill out this paperwork," the pleasant administrator instructed, standing up from behind her desk, holding a clipboard.

Dennis fetched the papers like an obedient dog, returning with a pen for Renee to fill out the forms.

"You're going to be okay, I promise," Dennis whispered to her, offering support despite her animosity.

"Are you guys married?" an older lady with curly gray hair sitting across inquired with a genial tenor and a warm smile

She reminded Dennis of his grandmother and how comforting her smile was, how gentle and inviting her demeanor was, assuaging all of his worries.

"No," Renee snorted if she were repulsed, taking a break from filling out forms to correct her, not making eye-contact with the curious civilian.

And Dennis felt a sudden urge to scream at her, rebuke her inconsideration and shitty fucking attitude, and possibly leave, abandoning her there. But Denis knew it wasn't actually his grandmother because he watched her die in the Hospice, withering away like a diseased flower; a sharp wave of heat tinged in his diaphragm, a fire igniting, compelling him to clench his fists, closing his eyes to invoke tranquility, a non-reaction, like a stoic. He convinced himself it was Renee's sickness speaking and not her heart and he still needed to find out what the psychic said.

So instead, Dennis snatched the pen from Renee's hand, standing up and tossing it across the room with a devious grin. He looked back at her, studying her reaction.

"What the fuck?" Renee snapped, rising from her chair; her brows furrowed, her face pale.

The elderly pedestrian withdrew, turning her head down and away, avoiding further conversation.

"Renee Podava?" a tall white guy in a white coat asked, emerging from the hallway with a rising pitch, signifying a question and not an announcement

Holding a tablet and equipped with a stethoscope around his neck, he scanned the waiting area.

"Yes," Dennis replied, turning to address the doctor, pulling Renee by the hand.

"You must be her husband?" the doctor inquired, smirking, offering his open palm as a greeting.

"No, just a concerned ex-boyfriend," Dennis uttered before Renee could add a backhanded comment, like how he liked girls' posts on Instagram when they were together and that was the reason he wasn't her spouse.

The doctor retrieved his hand, avoiding further awkwardness.

"Well, maybe things will change," he rebutted before bringing them to the exam room.

Streptococcal pharyngitis, better known as Strep throat, was the reason for Renee's severe abdominal pain, which required five days of antibiotics. Dennis stopped at the pharmacy while she waited in the car before he drove her home, ensuring he provided complete care, so she could never accuse him of being calloused or negligent; he kept waiting for her to express some extension of gratitude, some indication of appreciation, but it just never happened. The ride back home was filled with deafening silence as Dennis gave up trying to find any inspirational songs, make small talk, or do fucking anything to keep her present with him. The tepid air of March was palpable with the windows down, mild gusts suffusing the cabin as the vestigial snowbanks on the corners of streets melted. The burgeoning spring was on the horizon, and Dennis wondered if there would be any renewal of their relationship by the time summer came around.

"I think I'm just going to go to bed," Renee drawled with a lethargic blink as they stood outside of the house they'd bought together; she had slipped out of the car as soon as he parked, a desperate getaway, which was thwarted by Dennis following her to the porch.

Holding both of her hands at her sides on the front porch, Dennis gazed at Renee swaying in his grasp, like a reluctant child wanting to go play with friends instead of spending time with a parent. He hoped she'd invite him to watch a TV show while she fell asleep or at least let him use the bathroom, even though he was ambivalent about being back inside the home they used to call theirs.

"I need to get some rest," she grumbled, turning toward the front door.

And Dennis couldn't help but feel defeated with her resistance, her hesitation to even look him in the eye or thank him. He kept hoping there would be a moment of recognition, a remnant of affection still lingering somewhere inside her, but she was a ghost. Dennis surveyed the portico, architected with Roman Tuscan columns and crowned with a Greek-styled pediment, the exterior highlights of a place he used to call home. He gazed at the floor, expecting the first purchase he made for the home to be still there, a coir doormat that read "Welcome," in Times New Roman font, but he noticed it had been replaced with a florally feminine door mat with blush colors, slapping him in the face with disillusionment.

The faint rumbling of her smartphone sounded, and Renee extracted the device from her pocket with haste, attempting to shield the caller ID from Dennis, but he already saw the name and accompanied picture: Carl was calling.

"Are you fucking serious right now?!" Dennis growled as he threw his hands up, turning to leave, scurrying down a few steps before stopping.

"Oh stop. I'm not answering it," Renee tried to placate, shedding a critical smile and shaking her head.

"So, you're clearly seeing him," Dennis accused, shouting from the steps, his body lateral with his head turned to Renee.

Renee pivoted and headed toward the door, ignoring Dennis's fit.

"I fucking come and take care of you and for what. You're fucking some clown," Dennis spewed, spitting as he spoke; his heart striking with manic flutters and provoked anger, his teeth chattering with overstimulated nerves, becoming unhinged.

"I never told you to come take care of me. You just showed up," Renee chided, pulling out her prescription from her front sweatshirt pouch to retrieve her keys.

His heart sinking, mired in the mud of his illusion, his expectation of a rekindling completely destroyed; Dennis felt himself convulse, quaking with repressed irritation, a boiling teapot left unattended on a stove, steaming; he couldn't get that little fuck Carl's face out of his mind.

"At least tell me what the psychic said?" Dennis quavered.

"This was a mistake," Renee replied, frowning as she glanced back at him, her typical disappointed expression.

She finally put her key in the top lock, her back turned to Dennis, uninterested in his question, the last impudent demonstration Dennis could withstand. He could feel a fleeting energy, a dissipating force escape his core. And he couldn't tell if it was the realization that she was gone, truly no longer his or if it was heart breaking even further, a shifting of the already severed halves, putrefying as he watched her purposely disregard his existence. Opening the door, Renee removed the key from the latch without turning to him, her contouring yoga pants highlighting her nourished backside, teasing his suppressed lust.

"You know what, fuck you!" Dennis squawked, hurling the heavy disparagement from deep within, a visceral release of frustration, like a damaging drug with the quickest high and lowest low.

And just like that, all the good Dennis had done the entire day was tarnished, all the work wasted. Renee froze as if she were paralyzed, still holding the door open, her back turned. She then swung herself 180 degrees around with a threatening dynamism, displaying a sinister grin as she proceeded down the steps. Flashing a menacing smile, she cackled with a nervous, excitable vigor.

"You wanna know what the psychic said about you, huh?" she taunted, face-to-face with Dennis, the closest they had come to intimacy since they broke up.

"Do you wanna know?" she asked again, antagonizing, her face florid, her hair disheveled from being tucked into her hood.

Dennis nodded, acquiescing to the punishment, defeated.

"Oh, it has nothing to do with you being ruined because you were raped by your middle school teacher," Renee smirked, her eyes lit, malignant, brilliant, and terrifying.

"Oh, no. It's deeper than that."

Dennis's stomach plunged, a quicksand of sadness swallowing him whole as he braced for the final blow, like a condemned man awaiting the firing squad. His vision blurred, pixelating under the mist of forming tears; the first time suicide ever slipped into his mind.

"She said you're a fucking serpent," she rebuked, heaving with fury, making an S-like sign with her three fingers and holding it against her forehead.

"You have the devil inside of you, Dennis," she delivered before turning back and entering inside, leaving Dennis decimated in front of the house he once thought was home.

####

Grating the spoon around the ceramic bowl's rim, he scoops his Frosted Flakes and turns it over, dumping the milky cereal back into the miniature basin. He likes the difficulty of retrieving the miniature sugared chips from the filmy liquid and the sound of the milk trickling as he pours it. It reminds him of being five or six years old again, sitting at the kitchen table in little footy pajamas at his parents' house, the place they occupied before the condo, when he used to be excited to start his day and head to school to see his friends. So he slides the spoon around, operating a time lapse, repeating the cycle, collecting cereal remnants and tossing it over as he's always done, invoking familiarity, a feeling of being young.

It keeps him occupied while he scrolls through listings on his smartphone with his left hand, but he's really not paying attention to the two-bed, one-bath townhomes Pete has sent him. No, he's focusing more on the leftover milk and cereal bits for some reason. He's been eating with the same silverware since he was a kid, gripping the white angled plastic handle and stainless-steel body tool from Mary's classic tableware, the spoon he's been using to consume countless meals from the past twenty-five plus years. But that's not entirely why he's relishing the repetition; he's thinking there's more to it than just a habit hemmed in nostalgia; maybe it's the symbolism, and he's just a sentient spoon; yeah, sliding around in circles looking for cereal bits, maybe he's just a fucking utensil;

he's been gliding, gathering things for what seems like forever, picking up stuff and just trashing it, discarding it over and over again without a clear purpose or objective. And perhaps it's time to just finish up breakfast and put the cereal bowl in the fucking sink. Shoveling the last remnants of high fructose corn syrup, one last go around, he studies the spoon; it's loaded with scraps, carrying multiple alphabet letters, spelling out a shocking suggestion:

"Kill yourself," the soggy flakes of cereal display, the space included between the two words for intelligibility, a direct recommendation.

Dennis shakes his head, realizing it's not Alphabet cereal, so he shouldn't be receiving any messages from his breakfast. His phone chimes, which prompts Dennis to drop his spoon back into the bowl, abandoning any further interpretations.

"This 165 unit has a garage, and the neighborhood is FLOCKING WITH MILFS," the Facebook messenger banner reads, an incoming communication from Pete.

And a garage is important because he didn't have one in the apartment he lived in for a while after Renee, so he's not about to take a step backwards; he's also going to purchase a two bedroom instead of a one bedroom; he's hoping that'll make him feel validated.

"Thanks, Pete," Dennis responds.

Pete is his realtor, Dennis thinks, he's not entirely sure if it's official or if he's just advising. They actually went to high school together and were friends on Facebook. Dennis messaged him after watching one of his live streams, which had nine views. He was doing a walkthrough of a condo, using superlatives to describe the place, shouting adjectives like "magnificent" and "extraordinary," as he smiled with emphasis, showing his bottom teeth. His hairline had receded significantly since Dennis had last seen him, flapping in the wind like diminishing feathers on an aged bird as he walked through the front door of the "perfect starter home." Pete had also grown a beard, perhaps to conceal his clefted lip, Dennis concludes.

Clicking through a couple of evocative photos of satisfied clients, posing in front of their homes, holding pairs of keys with beaming grins, he stopped to study one photo, a still image of a couple jumping in the air, legs flailing and arms pumped in a fit of excitement. And he's ready to jump for joy; he's ready to be excited about something. This is just what he needs, something to own, a reward, a hefty dose of dopamine from an accomplishment, tickling neurotransmitters into content, so he's ready to buy a home, anything, really. It doesn't even need to be completely modernized; he'll even settle for popcorn ceilings or Formica countertops.

Dennis is convinced he's saved up enough money to move out, even if he could save more if he stayed home for at least a year more. But he'll never make it; he decides. He's been picking up too many bad habits that he's not happy about, like watching Youtube videos he doesn't even enjoy, clicking recommendations in a vortex of visual stimulation. He's also been frequenting Facebook for an extra two hours of social media, looking at people's lives, comparing, scrolling past uploads of babies, colonial homes, and #much-needed vacation photos. Searching through archives of individuals from his life, he's been reexamining people from the past for any clues, looking for missed signs, further directions on an old road map, any connection to making things make sense.

Maybe it's closure he's looking for, but he discovered in his quest that Chelsea Ewing, the girl he dated from college for a year, is now obese and shares encouraging quotes about moving on along with unflattering selfies, ironically starving for attention. He feels terrible because he cared for her a long time ago, and it wasn't just because she used to swallow his load without stopping while she sucked, providing tremendous release as she devoured his seed; no, he actually loved her, for a little while, he thinks.

He fucked her up permanently by cheating on her his senior year, he just knows it; he still recalls the stifled chords of her Jason Mraz ringtone echoing outside his locked bedroom door as he plowed a drunk sophomore from his applied ethics class on his futon; his pecker pulsating as he anticipated the door flinging open at any minute; the smacking of cheeks, pounding flesh filled the room as the thrill of being on the edge, almost being caught, heightened his climax. But the door never opened, and he never saw the sophomore or Chelsea ever again. They're not friends on Facebook either; no, she blocked him a long time ago, cutting off communication, but he saw her blackened name tagged in a recent photo, uploaded by a friend of a friend at someone's wedding she attended without a date. Switching to his mother's Facebook account, the one he made for Mary two months ago, he accessed Chelsea's profile, wasting days puzzle piecing her life together.

But his Facebook activity isn't all entirely bad, actually; Dennis shared a black rainbow fist post to combat climate justice or global warming, he can't remember. It might have been to save the ozone layer; he's not sure if that's still a thing or if global warming and climate change are the same. But he knows he's helping out either way, and that's what matters most. He's also helped his parents sell a few things on the Marketplace, like vintage picture frames and decorative curios, crafting compelling copy to entice people within a twenty-five-mile radius.

He's saved a text message draft he's been working on in his notepad, crafting a heartfelt letter he'd like to send to Christine, adding to it whenever poignancy prods or her delicate face surfaces in his memory, like a distant echo. But he's vacillating, second-guessing himself, and he's also run out of refills for his medication, having been dropping the tiny tabs like breath mints. Now, he's drinking cough syrup before bed every night, consuming five tablespoons of dextromethorphan. This equates to approximately 4000 mg of an active dissociative anesthetic, inducing a sensational warmth in his entrails, a magnificent complacency, as if he's being massaged with 1000 sumptuously soft cotton balls and nothing really matters. It's not good, he knows, since he can only go to sleep by taking downers and only stay awake by taking uppers, so he's dependent, addicted to it all, apps, validation, dopamine, serotonin, endorphins, whatever trips the cognitive wires.

He is worried about the emerging nihilism, which is creeping into most of his optimistic thoughts like a terrible aftertaste. He's troubled by how hard it is to see the point in doing anything, the undertones of insignificance, how simple and inconsequential everything seems. But he's not worried about dying or substance abuse because he's done the math and calculated the components and quantities, ensuring he knows exactly how much to take, avoiding a possible overdose by using handy yellow measuring spoons for accurate gauging. He walks a confident tightrope, happy there's no safety net to catch him.

"You look so handsome," his mother praises in his periphery

Glancing up from his haze, Dennis espies his father donning a new sport coat in the kitchen, turning, modeling off a snazzy fit in front of the vertical hanging wall mirror, and it's moments like these that capture him, bringing him back to reality, a grounding, a realization of what he's missing out on.

"Fits like a glove," Russ raves, adjusting his cuff, visibly impressed with his new look.

"You look like a real stud, ya know that?" Dennis remarks with reverence and smiles, standing from the table and carrying his cereal bowl to the sink.

Russ's two briefcases are set in the foyer, indicating he's traveling up to Hartford for his monthly meeting. Dennis packs him a lunch each time, reversing roles by filling a brown paper bag with an apple, tuna sandwich, and water bottle to keep him energized and hydrated for the long drive.

Despite being in his eighties, his father is still working. He has to; an ex-business partner sued him almost twenty years ago, winning a default judgment because his incompetent lawyer never answered the summons. His wages were garnished for years, crippling his retirement funds and any chance to save, especially since he committed to sending his three sons to private high school and college. Dennis often thinks about how the best years of his life may have been some of the worst for his father as he struggled. He contemplates how many fake smiles his father had to feign when he wanted to just break down, how many fake laughs he had to force when he just wanted to cry, and how many times he felt truly alone in a crowded home but had to keep it together when he was really falling apart. Yet his father never revealed the dire predicament to his family nor let it negatively affect them, an admirable strength Dennis wishes he possessed. Holding back a surge of emotion, Dennis reflects on how courageous his father truly is, the quiet heroism of a man who bore his burdens alone to shield his loved ones from pain.

"Just call when you get there, hon," Mary says as she kisses him on the cheek, pulling at his lapels to tidy his look; she hugs him briefly and tightly before she heads downstairs to take a bath.

"Den, you said pleats were out, right? That's why I got these new pants," Russ smirks, pulling at his pockets to emphasize the straight leg design.

Dennis runs the faucet; the water rushes into the bowl, rinsing out the vestigial cereal flakes, emptying the milk into the sink. And he watches the stream of filmy liquid run, leaking into the drain, transporting sugary scraps into the abyss as he fights the urge to cry. He turns to his father, still admiring himself in the mirror; his coat is little, tailored to fit his miniature frame, shrunken in age, a carcass compared to the built formidable man he used to be. Dennis approaches, watching his father; his reflection morphing in the mirror, replaying a slideshow of him from over the years, an exhibition of age. And Dennis watches as his father transforms from solid dark hair to salty gray, from slender to thick and scrawny, a virile man in his forties to a weathered elder into his eighties, maturing in seconds. So Dennis reaches out and hugs him because he doesn't want him to disappear; he can't bear to lose him.

His father chuckles with laughter, smiling, he embraces him back, grasping Dennis's forearm that's wrapped around his collarbone.

"I love you, Willy Loman," Dennis whispers, clutching Russ around the shoulders.

####

He's at his desk again, wondering when lunchtime is, but a glance at his watch tells him it's 3 P.M.; school ended 20 minutes ago. It doesn't really matter that school is over or that he's hungry, eating feels like a chore, a demanding, tedious need. Dennis is more concerned with monotony, wondering how many more times he'll sit in the same clunky chair before he dies.

If he lives to the average life expectancy of eighty, he'll most likely retire around sixty-five. That gives him about thirty more years of teaching or approximately 10,950 days. If he works five days a week for the next 360 months, that's about 7,200 days. Factoring in holidays, two weeks of vacation, and yearly sick time, he estimates he has about 6,900 days left sitting in the same mahogany wooden chair with a spindled back. It's a long time, so he's turned notifications on from his dating apps and all social media platforms, streamlining the connection; now he receives chronic updates throughout his day. Brian Doberman uploads a photo smoking a cigar while fishing, and he's got a new match on Bumble, Arianna, 27, from Staten Island. Dennis hasn't talked to Brian since he was in the middle school and Staten Island is way too fucking far, so he clicks his phone off, disheartened by the lack of appeal.

Dennis is really craving a chemical reaction, something that can settle his brain, since he's got no one to talk to, not a single fucking friend; only his algorithms truly know him. They know what makes him laugh, slapstick humor, videos of people slipping or falling. They know what gets him riled up, like videos of coverups, conspiracies that are all too coincidental. And they know what keeps him engaged, the anticipation of not knowing what's coming next, throwing reels at him like a dopamine dealer shuffling cards, each one more random than the last. He's hooked on the unpredictability, the way his feed feeds him in a world that's all too predictable.

He rarely uses his phone as an actual phone anymore, more like an access tool to an alternate world, as if his surroundings are simulated. He opens his Bumble App, his finger swipes, administering like syringes entering his bloodstream, eliciting a sense of bonding, fulfilling his oxytocin deficiency. And it's only about four swipes until Dennis catches a photo of Renee with a friend, like a reminder email about leaving something in the cart. The profile depicts Ashley, 32, a girl he doesn't recognize with her arm around his ex-fiancée. Scrolling through her photos, he notices there's no other photos of his ex and an empty bio, only indicating she's thirteen miles away; Dennis wonders if maybe Renee recruited Ashley to make a profile to connect with him.

The blistering shrills of the fire alarm pierce the silence, wailing overhead, flashing bright LED lights; Dennis drops his phone and covers his ears, scanning his classroom for an impetus only briefly before the alarm seizes. Bewildered, Dennis keeps his hands on the sides of his head despite the reprieve from the jarring sound. A few seconds of silence pass while he keeps his palms pressed against his ears. A loud knocking on the back door captures his attention, a steady, erratic beating. Dennis ambles toward the noise to answer the old courtyard door. Behind his classroom is a private quad, a cloister used by priests in the 1960s. He's only been out there a few times since he started teaching at the school, and from what he remembers, it was overgrown with fescue and brittle cobblestones. Shrouded in weeds, the designated garden features a monolith with an affixed Jesus statue, covered in moss, so Dennis can't imagine who might be out there.

Peeking through the small glass panel on the door, Dennis notices a distraught James without a jacket, the maintenance worker; he wonders if maybe he's out there blazing.

"Hey, what's up?" Dennis asks as James enters the classroom holding the top of his head with both hands.

"Did the fire alarm just go off?" he asks, trying to catch his breath as visible sweat leaks across his brows.

"For like a second."

"Oh fuck. I think I set the fire alarm off," James expresses with concern, pacing, taking four steps to his left and then four steps back, like some sort of manic square dance.

His crooked beanie lay to the side of his head, exposing part of his hair. And before Dennis can even think of a response or fully process the strange encounter, James storms toward the classroom door.

"I gotta go, man. We'll talk soon," he shouts over his shoulder, opening the door and dashing out into the hallway, leaving a perplexed Dennis behind.

"Mr. Clauden," Megan utters, appearing in the door frame, mere moments after James's exit; she's clutching the Norton Anthology of English Literature.

Accoutered in form-fitting clothes, still wearing her uniform skirt and coordinating knee high socks, Megan's loitering and must have been lingering around outside his door; she's slipped on a pull-over sweater since he saw her earlier in class, a verdant color, bringing out the hazel hues of her eyes. Dennis is befuddled, deliberating on the surreal successive interactions; he does recall promising to tutor Megan.

"We're doing tutoring today, right?" she asks with an eager enunciation, drawling her words with an elevated tenor.

Rubbing his eyes to gain focus, he pulls a nearby desk next to his and extends his hand outwards, an inviting gesture, vaguely recalling their agreement for after school sessions on Mondays and Thursdays.

"Yes. Come on in, Megan."

"What can I help you with?" Dennis asks, his reluctant gaze meets her benign eyes, free from the weight of affliction or dismay.

Pain, Dennis postulates, always leaves a mark in the eyes, a glossy film, a shield that guards against seeing the world through a sober lens. He studies her, wondering if she's ever worn that veil.

Dennis has been struggling with Megan, finding her increasingly appealing, especially after getting a blowjob a couple of days ago from a divorced mother of two in the Applebee's parking lot following three dirty martinis. He finished in her mouth, though she pulled away after the first shot, catching the rest with her hand. Now, Dennis feels insatiable, even worse than before, and it's not just because Lea didn't let him finish fully. He's thinking it's more like a new addiction, a drug he can't shake

"Well, I was hoping we could go over *Paradise Lost,*" Megan replies, taking a seat and placing her book on the desk.

"We're not covering Milton until another couple of months though, not until the end of the school year. Is this your new thing? Overachiever?" Dennis jests.

"Oh, I know. I just got a head start on the syllabus. I really love all the titles you selected for us," she adulates.

She smells like scrumptious cotton candy; her sweet, mouth-watering aroma infuses Dennis's nasal cavity like a love potion, compelling him to move closer and pay attention. Her slick lips sparkle in the fading sunlight that glimmers through the spaces of the horizontal window blinds. Her face, dotted with faint, adorable freckles, frames a peerless mouth, a perfect specimen compared to the worn receptacle of Lea.

"I guess, we can do that. It's not like any other students are as ravenous with their reading as you," Dennis rebuts, smiling, aware of his overt compliment.

Megan receives the commendation with vigor, perking herself up like a veritable TikTok, displaying a dynamic smile and radiant energy as she flips the book open, turning the pages with intensity like she's being timed.

"Ok, so I had a few things underlined that I wasn't entirely sure about," Megan states, scrutinizing a selected page in the book, one that's littered with annotations and pink-highlighted sentences.

Dennis peeks over the binder of the book, noting the copious notes inscribed on the first page of George Milton's work.

Moving closer, positioning his head to decipher her script, Dennis accidentally brushes his foot up against hers underneath the desk. He keeps it there, pressing against hers, testing to see if she reacts, but she doesn't even flinch. No, she's emboldened, locked on Dennis as if trying to communicate telepathically, her intermittent blinking and composed comportment exuding confidence. He casually tilts his leg to the left, positioning his shoe away from hers.

"First and foremost, what language is this written in? Archaic English?" Megan speaks with an ambiguous delivery, blending an interrogative sentence with a declarative statement, like some sort of grammatical transformer.

Dennis senses she's comfortable now, as if the inadvertent touching of feet was some sort of tacit consummation.

"Yes, that's common with works from the 1600-1700s. If you go back to Geoffrey Chaucer in the 1400s, that language was even more complex. Go back to like 500 with Old English, and your head will really be spinning," Dennis replies, crossing his arms and leaning toward her, drawn by magnetism, lured by her seductive scent and polished presentation.

Separated by inches, Dennis inspects her flawless face, admiring her budding beauty: her perky cheeks and smooth forehead, the contrast of darkened eyeliner with glowing eyes, and the soft sensuality of her dampened lips.

"How does language change?" Megan asks with assured curiosity, speaking clear and poised, her eyes gleam with intrigue.

"Well, there's a few variables that contribute to how a language changes and evolves," Dennis replies, avoiding eye contact, purposely not providing any further encouragement.

"But like how?" Megan pries as if she's challenging him.

Dennis stiffens in his seat, contemplating his response; he stands from the desk, twisting his torso with swinging arms to generate force, cracking his lower back.

"Over time, phrases and idioms are added and tweaked, and even the interpretation of words becomes altered. Certain slang finds its way into common conversations, morphing our colloquial language, changing how we communicate on a regularly basis," Dennis proclaims as he positions himself on the edge of his desk, sitting with his hands extended outward, balancing as his legs project, assuming an assertive pose.

"You keep this going on for hundreds and hundreds of years, and you'll notice how things start to really transform. But you'll also find that the overall foundation is still there, like a fossil," Dennis concludes.

"Wow, you're just like the smartest guy I think I ever met," Megan blushes, sitting back in her chair, twirling her hair; her cheeks mantling with nervous attraction.

"Thanks," Dennis blurts and withdraws, rising from the desk.

He saunters to the classroom door with his hands held behind his back, turning his head over his shoulder to notice Megan's frown and discernible disappointment. Dennis feels bad, but he can't help toying with her; besides, it's not like she's even cognizant of the manipulation, he decides.

"So what are you confused about with *Paradise Lost*?" he asks, glancing at his watch as if he's pressed for time.

"Oh, um, yeah," Megan flusters, flipping the pages in her book.

"Um, I guess like the main thing I wanted to know was like, is this a prequel to the Bible?"

Dennis steps out into the hall, spinning 180 degrees to get a glimpse down each direction, wondering where James went; he wonders what he was so upset about it. He's losing interest in tutoring; he realizes he probably should have charged her, but he can't remember if that's against school policy. But either way, he's feeling done for today.

"There are two narrative arcs in the epic poem. One of Satan and the events that take place after he is banished to hell by God, which could be considered a prequel if you want to say that. But the other narrative arc follows Adam and Eve, which is a slightly varied version of the one found in the Bible," Dennis decrees with a domineering energy.

He approaches Megan, who's on her phone, texting. Her phone rings, and she answers it instantly.
"I'm busy right now, Jonathan," Dennis thinks he hears her say.

She hangs up, and Dennis stops a few feet from her, wondering if she'd be capable of swallowing a load or if she'd cough it up, spoiling the orgasm, pulling away before taking it all.

"Did you go to catholic school too?" Megan asks, ignoring her illuminated phone, catching Dennis in his lecherous daydream.

"I did actually," he replies, crossing his arms.

"I knew it," Megan grins.

"So, you know a thing or two about forbidden fruit?" she quips with a wry smile.

Dennis cackles, nodding his head with amusement, admiring her creative humor. He's really starting to enjoy being around her, so he's thinking it's time to wrap up the session, even if it's only been fifteen minutes; he ponders of an excuse to cut the meeting short.

Perhaps he can tell her his grandmother died, but she's already been dead for eight years now, and Dennis knows this because his mother still cries every year on her birthday and refuses to sell her car; it's still sitting in the visitor's parking lot. But Dennis doesn't want to think of MiMi because he still feels terrible, remembering how he used to steal twenty dollars from her every time she went to the bank when he was a teenager. He would snatch a loose bill from the white envelope left out on the counter after she returned home. She always had so many bills, and Xbox games were expensive, so Dennis didn't mind taking one whenever he saw an opportunity, even if it made her question her own cognition. It was a terrible payoff for a lifetime of remorse.

"Last question, I promise, and then I'm gone," Megan says, rising from her seat.

"What does the snake represent in the story? I know he's more than just a snake," she adds, closing her book.

"It's a serpent, and he's the devil," Dennis replies flatly, slinging his messenger bag over his shoulder.

He pauses, glancing at Megan's expectant face, but offers nothing further. With a silent nod, he heads out through the back exit into the old courtyard, leaving Megan behind, her curiosity hanging in the air like an unfinished sentence.

9. Inferno

The buzzing of cicadas filled the muggy air as they strolled along the sidewalk. The distinct sound of summer conjured memories of playing manhunt as a preadolescent, darting through the darkness to evade the silhouettes of friends. The musky, earthy notes of a morning rain shower permeated the air, mingling with the smoky ash aroma from a fire the night before. A little old lady named Maryjo had left a fruitcake in the oven and dozed off while watching TV, nearly burning down half her house. The smell of soot suffusing Dennis's nostrils felt fitting; he had been smoldering for a while now, itching and burning with each passing day. Cooper led the way, chest puffed out like a proud pack leader, sniffing, pulling, stopping, and inspecting every sound and scent, happy to be outdoors with the two of them. His anxious excitement always putting smiles on their faces, but Dennis's adoration for the dog was fading, becoming annoyed with how much the dog shed and how often he had to pick off strangling hairs from his shirts, rolling through lint rollers like rolls of toilet paper. Perambulating at least one lap together a day around the development, Christine and Dennis decided on two loops with Cooper, since it was officially the first day of summer.

"Come on, Cooper," Christine remarked with a high-pitched tone, a lovable cadence, directing him away from chasing a squirrel.

Shifting his excitable energy into some other interest, intrigued by any movement, noise, or particular breeze, Cooper followed Christine's guidance with a short attention span. He pivoted from each striking stimulus, sniffing the lush grass with urgency. As they approached the arch bridge overlooking the lake, Cooper pounced his paws onto the cement ledge, fixated on a new provocation.

He stuck his head through the rails to scan the currents below. This spot was usually a place to pause on their walk, stopping to marvel at the breathtaking vista. They'd admire the setting sun behind the trees and the passing wildlife, crisp white swans with their cygnets cruising by, casting an effervescent shine on the rippling water; they always stopped to soak in the moment.

However, Dennis was impatient this time around, anxious with a hole burning through his pocket, a broiling urge to check the dating apps he had downloaded. He'd been surreptitiously swiping while he pooped or went to work, skulking his flirtations and stimulating his insatiability with attractive strangers whenever he was away from Christine.

The novelty of their romance had been rubbing out like a losing scratch-off ticket, revealing undesirable numbers and burdens, like a messy canine to care for and a poor family to inherit, unlike the bourgeois parents of Renee.

"Look at the Swans," Christine gushed, pointing toward the lake, encouraging Cooper.

He pedaled his paws against the pavement, trying to get a closer look as he sensed Christine's elation, his nose pulsating with each sniff.

"Look babe," Christine remarked, turning to Dennis as she bubbled.

But Dennis was uninterested, faltering, detached and occupied in some other existence. He glanced back at Christine, her hair tied in a ponytail, exposing her cartilage piercings. She leaned against the metal posting, her body angled to access both Cooper and Dennis. She stared at Dennis with a searching face, alerted, attempting to recognize her aloof boyfriend with his hands in his pockets.

Scanning Christine with a cynical eye, Dennis focused on the faint grooves of the slight cellulite that ran along the back of her legs. He discerned creases in her forehead as she squinted, holding her right hand along her brow, shielding her eyes from the pouring sunlight; the urge to flee to one of his dating apps intensified.

"What's wrong?" she asked with a concerned lilt as she pulled at the tugging canine.

Barking playfully at the swimming swans, Cooper pattered along the concrete siding, trying to get closer to the bevy. Surveying the last stretch of street ahead, Dennis noticed a female approaching a short distance away, a possible sprouting Jane, ambling with a small dog.

"Dennis?"

"What?" Dennis replied, emerging from his daze momentarily, gazing at Christine.

He usually felt comfort when they locked eyes, a synergy that made him feel they belonged, a settling warmth. But things had changed; it had been different for a while. Now, it was more like a slow burn, and it was already way too hot outside. He couldn't figure out how to keep a flame lit ever since Renee, and he wasn't entirely sure what to do since he discovered she was married now.

Dennis stared vacantly as the techno beats reverberated in his heart, the music still playing in his mind. He recalled kissing Renee passionately inside the club's bathroom, Avicii's thumping beats in the background, the throbbing vibrations resounding in their chests as they embraced with lovers' lust: "All this time I was finding myself. And I didn't know I was lost."

Walking parallel at a decent pace, Dennis looked at Christine, the constructed pillar of hope and optimism for his post-Renee life. But that pillar was cracking, crumbling. Dennis had become too proficient in identifying her flaws, picking out foibles like dead skin cells. Her loquaciousness, once charming, had become a big distraction, killing his creative thought process and interrupting

226

silent contemplations on word choices and possible plot lines. A future with her would require a lot of work, a different lifestyle than what he envisioned for himself.

Even the adorable dog that used to make his heart swell had become a chore, constantly shedding long curly hairs on the hardwood floors, vexing his OCD to unbearable proportions, always idling by and whimpering whenever Dennis was eating, a perpetual pest drooling for a portion. An unsettling feeling had been stirring within Dennis for a while, like a hurricane forming, ready to wreak havoc. He wondered if ending up with anyone other than Renee would be settling; it had to be since she was his first choice. Maybe it was a pathology, an inability to love any longer, but he had grown accustomed to his brokenness. His heart hurt whenever he saw a beautiful sight or experienced a cherished moment, realizing he could never fully appreciate anything with his condition, his perennial ache, like a torn meniscus, still trying to figure out how to walk without applying too much pressure.

It was a defining moment for Dennis as he locked eyes with Christine, sensing her brooding. A hyperconsciousness occurred, a revelation that there was nothing left to save him any longer. All the temporary salvations were just illusions, hallucinations of a rescue plane hovering overhead, circling a survivor on a deserted island or the mirage of a boat floating ahead to save a shipwrecked sailor, clinging to driftwood. There was no saving him; he was a goner.

"Kill yourself," a scoffing whisper echoed, jarring Dennis.

It was a voice he hadn't heard in years, reemerging from the back of his brain, unleashing an avalanche of sadness. Startled, he fought back overwhelming emotion; it had been years since such recommendations floated in his head. His knees buckled as he wondered how long it would be until his meniscus finally gave out and his other knee became disabled, crippling him completely. In that moment, he decided he'd rather end his life instead of living confined to a wheelchair.

Sensing an approaching dog, Cooper jumped back down to the sidewalk, yanking Christine with curiosity, emitting frisky growls.

"Cooper, stayyyyy," Christine cooed, shifting focus, pulling Cooper back with both hands, pacifying the roused pooch.

The lassie lingered, letting her chirping Chihuahua lead; she flashed a neighborly smile and retrieved the rat-like creature, clutching it in her arms. Her long tawny locks flipped with her quick movements; her biceps flexed as she cradled her pet, spotlighting her young, athletic composition. Gawking at her contoured black shorts, snugly accentuating her developed features and strong legs, Dennis imagined her legs wrapped around him as he sucked on her nipples, piercing her fresh flesh, penetrating her deeply as their fluids mingled, unrestricting secretions.

He gazed up at the boiling sun, his soul on fire, the blinding rays forcing him to close his eyes. Dennis stood on the sidewalk, sweat seeping from his lower back into his T-shirt. Tuning out Christine's words from her friendly exchange with the passing girl, he continued glancing up at the sky, his head tilted backward, allowing the light to blister and beat down on his face, toasting his eyeballs. His body felt heavy on the pavement, his limbs baking with discomfort; he envisioned this was what hell felt like upon arrival.

Smiling with an elongated tongue and panting from the heat, Cooper remained collected. With his paws placed in front, he lowered himself to the ground, wheezing with his tongue hanging out, his face emulating a smile. Cooper's attention was locked on Christine, unbothered as another small puppy passed by.

"Good boy," Christine cheered as she knelt beside him, rubbing his back.

"Isn't he such a good boy, babe?" Christine asked, looking up at Dennis, shielding her eyes from the obtrusive sunrays with her hand, hoping to catch her taciturn boyfriend present and available.

Dennis knew Cooper was a good boy, he really was, especially since he would always bark at oncoming dogs, annoying Dennis every fucking time. His manic behavior always causing Dennis to tug and scold the cute Collie in front of strangers, but no amount of decorum could fix Dennis's mental incongruity. Nothing could make it right.

"He is, and he loves his mommy," Dennis uttered, smiling to conceal his turmoil. Returning home, with Christine filling the silence with gab, the sun weighing down as it crested the sky, Dennis remained silent because there weren't any words to be said; his laconic state spoke louder and clearer than he ever could. Escaping to the guest room he had transformed into an office, Dennis closed the door behind him, proceeding to re-download the Tinder and Bumble apps he had deleted earlier, desperately abating his guilty conscience.

Plopping down in the middle of the room with a mischievous grin, sitting cross-legged on the soft shag pile rug, he embarked on the temporary fulfillment of carnal impulses, swiping right on every girl he could imagine satisfying his desires. His eyes expanded with each salacious scene that flashed in his head, pondering whether to masturbate in his aroused reverie.

Dennis contemplated turning his sexual needs toward Christine, but her flesh had been worn, already devoured and scavenged. Her womb, like a sweater washed too many times, no longer fit him. Dennis was desensitized, and he needed something new to ruin.

He swiped right on Sarah, a plump literary agent wearing bifocals. An animated "It's a match" message in tawdry green letters popped up, juxtaposing their profile pictures like two missing puzzle pieces being connected. Dennis quickly sent her a message:

"Hey 😊 "

Pondering which agency she worked for and if he had maybe queried her before, Dennis envisioned her on all fours. He pictured her tonguing at his skin pouch drenched in saliva, glimpsing back and forth between her lower back, watching her haunch and reading his manuscript, reciting the first three chapters aloud as the sound of smacking and sucking spit echoed.

Slipping his pants down, Dennis began handling his phallus, already preparing to load up a "BBW" video on Xvideos.com to play while he pleasured himself, his preference shifting to a heftier size; anything to get his book published, he committed.

A light knock on the door interrupted his titillating trance, imbuing him with embarrassment.

"Babe?" Christine's delicate voice echoed from behind the door.

Jumping up from the ground, amplified with animosity, Dennis quickly put his phone into his pocket before answering the door.

"What?" he demanded, holding it open, taking in the vision of a wary Christine with her arms crossed, the adorable beauty that had saved him from the throes of heartbreak years ago.

Dennis felt a sting in his chest from the sight of his distraught girlfriend, but it was quickly displaced by a floating thought, a speculation on whether Carl had written his own vows for Renee or if he had just Googled trite sentimental words.

His anger was rising, the repression of aggression no longer a sufficient solution, and he could feel a malicious Molotov cocktail of rage lighting, his restraint to throw it diminishing.

"What's going on? Why are you being so distant?" she inquired with a slight tremble and troubled eyes, her lips quivering as she waited for a comforting response.

Dennis stared back at her with a wry face. Her selfless nature, a perceivable weakness, and her consistency a bore, a stark contrast to the tumult with Renee. Christine had become the scapegoat for his failure to become a writer; her naïve amiability numbing his clever, witty words, he believed, and her passiveness in the bedroom, a direct catalyst for his inferior climaxes. He was playing the same movie over and over, and as much as he appreciated the footage, it wasn't something he wanted to watch forever. Standing in front of Christine in an opaque pose, his arms dangling at his sides with his fists clenched, he was positioned for any external or internal battle.

"Please talk to me," she beseeched, looking up at him with concerned eyes and a quaking expression.

He wanted to tell her how much he cared for her and how none of this was her fault; he was just too damaged, incapable of being healed. No matter how many stitches were sutured or medicine applied, his injuries were permanent, terminable. Scanning her face, shooting his eyes back and forth, he wondered when he had changed and become so impatient, wicked, and cold; she had been a light in his bleak world. He skimmed the back of his hand against her somber cheek, wondering how much of her deterioration he was going to cause, how much life he was going to extinguish inside of her. She didn't deserve it, and he didn't deserve her, he knew that. She was the angel he had been sent, and he was the devil, the darkness she never should have known.

Sensing her qualm and confusion, Dennis reached out and pulled her close, clenching her tightly, clutching her; his hands dug into her shoulder blades as she shook like an injured animal.

"I'm sorry. I just don't know who I am anymore."

####

"This is going to be quite the bachelor pad for you, bro," Pete chortles, turning the key into the lock and flashing a goofy smile at Dennis, perhaps trying to distract him from how difficult the distressed door was to open.

The condo was originally built in 1984, the only real detail Dennis retained from the email. Entering, Pete flips the light switch on the side wall, triggering a dismal overhead jaundice glow. Marching to the uninhabited kitchen with parquet floors, Pete pulls the pull-chain of the lamp in the corner of the counter to produce a brighter ambiance. Turning to Dennis, he holds his arms out in dramatic fashion as if revealing a beautiful tenement. His sarcoline sport jacket buttoned in front, spotlighting his paunchy belly, and the light above, raining directly on Pete's head, severely highlighting the bald patches in his hair that he had failed to conceal.

"Newer appliances, bro," he smiles with an exaggerated smile, his mouth expanded, as if he's preparing for someone to take his picture.

Dennis wonders if maybe there's a social media consultant filming the encounter, hiding in one of the nearby closets, capturing all his good angles; maybe he's live streaming.

Dennis ate a hash oil brownie for lunch after fasting for the entire morning, so he's starting to feel edgy with paranoia, like he's gazing down a precipice and flints of vertigo are swarming. He needs to focus and convince himself there's nobody else in the condo except the two of them, but he's feeling self-conscious and a bit loopy, like anything can happen. He's thrilled though because he's acquired new narcotics, a vial of cocaine he discovered underneath Jonathan's seat along with two plastic wrapped pot brownies tucked in a brown paper bag. Dennis spotted it as soon as class ended, scooping it up like a loose fumble before anyone could come retrieve it. And he probably should have known the brownies weren't dessert, given their earthy floral fragrance, and that the white residue wasn't some sort of tablet cleaner or enigmatic Juul powder. But as soon as he dabbed his fingertip in the chalky dust and rubbed it around his gum, the familiar, succoring numbness and neuropathy tingled like an endearing memory, a hug from halcyon days, enticing him to indulge in plump lines of paradise, even though he swore he'd never do blow again.

"Direct access to all major highways, bro, and the bustling town is within walking distance, in case you woo a cutie from the bar back home," Pete cackles, walking around the empty premises, flipping light switches on and opening doors for display.

He's been calling Dennis "bro" a lot since they first reconnected, which makes Dennis wonder if they're on a path to friendship; maybe they'd grab beers after the showing, Dennis speculates. They did hang out a few times in high school, frequenting the same parties, and they even egged a kid's house together when they were sophomores after binge drinking at a party, so the possibility of a companionship might come easy, since they share some memories, Dennis hopes.

"Both bathrooms have been updated recently, so don't let the kitchen deter you, bro."

The zesty fragrance of citrus makes Dennis crave orange juice, and he thinks that's a good sign because it means the place is clean and good for him. Dennis can't remember what he's supposed to be looking for in a home, since the last time he shopped for a place, Christine did her due diligence, researching neighborhoods and school systems, as well as preparing questions for the realtor. But Dennis can't remember if a septic tank is good or bad and if eight grand a year in taxes is acceptable. He does remember that Pete went to some local college to get his business degree, worked in the city for a few years before becoming a real estate agent, returned to the area he grew up in, and married some average chick named Lisa.

It was about an hour and a half that Dennis spent studying Pete's Facebook, learning about his two kids, Jillian and Ryan. His wife often tagged him in photos of their baby boy, posting a picture of the mushy figure on his back as he glanced up at the camera; the coordinating caption detailed some personal birthing experience and mentioned how many months old he was. But Pete was pretty active on Facebook as well; besides featuring real estate content, he often shared slapstick humor videos of people slipping off ladders or tripping in public, commenting with laughing face emojis. He also posted memes with puns, like a big bear sitting at a picnic table with a speech bubble saying, "I built this with my bear hands." Or a standing sink outside of someone's open front door with the caption in block letters, "Let that sink in."

Dennis could compose a complete character profile on Pete with the amount of material he shared on social media. Technology makes it possible to meet people before actually meeting them, while also enabling individuals to portray themselves as the people they want to be or wish to be perceived as. They upload materialistic posts, spotlighting new purchases to depict success and affluence; share scenic views from different countries visited, projecting an image of a world traveler, an artistic wanderlust. It's all to paint a picture, to play a role for their audience, creating personas by what they choose to share.

Dennis never wants to be one of these people. He doesn't want to be generalized; he likes to think he's special and beautiful, like a fucking exotic bird with exquisite feathers. But he's got nothing to share. His life has passed him by, he's pretty sure of it.

"Central air and dual vanities in the upstairs bathroom, just in case down the road you want to move a lady friend in," Pete lauds as he peeks into each room, flickering his rehearsed realtor smile.

And it's the third refence Pete has recited about Dennis being single, so now Dennis is feeling a bit embarrassed, like he's inferior because he's not committed, as if matrimony was a caste for the elites. But the dwelling isn't far from St. Vincent's, so his commute is going to be shorter, Dennis thinks, selling himself on the place. He hates the phallic chandelier hanging in the designated dining room space; it's an elongated glass cylinder protruding from a spherical base, like a bulging ball sack, and he's wondering how much it's going to cost to swap with something more modern. And now he's fixated on the hanging penis and the dust accumulated on its transparent shaft.

"Cozy place with killer potential, right bro?" Pete boasts, signaling to Dennis, turning his body toward the laminated stairs, a tacit positioning, implying the upstairs is next to tour.

Dennis just nods because he's not really paying attention; he's trying to picture himself living in the place. He imagines watching TV, perusing Netflix on the couch in the cramped living area, cooking breakfast on the kitchen stove, burning his omelets like he always does, vacuuming the beige carpet, and checking his smartphone every six minutes with a crackhead-like tenacity. All he wants is hardwood floors, but he's thinking laminate will do. Maybe he'll put down engineered wood one day, after he's figured out a way to cook meth and sell it to his students, paving the way for a lucrative future, getting children addicted early to create a habit.

"I like it a lot," Dennis proclaims with a perfunctory interest, following Pete up the stairs.

"Technically it's not a three bedroom, but that's only because the one room doesn't have a closet," Pete speaks with a didactic mannerism, using a softer tone and pointing his finger.

Dennis still recalls how he and Pete printed out and plastered naked photos of Anne Hathaway from the movie *Havoc* on her brother's locker, guffawing together at the end of the hallway as they watched her brother frantically rip the pictures down while shouting obscenities. He's thinking they'll probably reminisce and laugh about it at some point in the day, but he's not really sure how to bring up the memory.

"Nice natural lighting up here," Pete continues his parade.

"This development is flocking with fine ladies too," he adds, cupping his hands and placing them in front of his mouth, as if he were talking into a megaphone.

"That's always good news. Although I'm not quite sure If I'm up for ruining anyone else's life," Dennis deadpans, feeling scintillas of antagonism, sensing Pete's patronization.

Pete flashes an awkward smile, not expecting the dark humor.

"Oh nonsense, it's always a good time to meet someone new," he espouses with a condescending tone, cocking his head to the side like he's a parent trying to offer sound advice.

And for some reason, Dennis really wants Pete to like him, even though he looks like a five-pound shit in a ten-pound bag. Yeah, Pete resembles the archetypal catfish, not a complete deception, but the type of person who shares a photo from ten years ago and then shows up thirty pounds overweight with a receding hairline that's passed the halfway point of his dome. Pete looks like a caricature of his high school self, just bloated with a flushed face, his belly jutting, which Dennis ascribes to his habitual drinking. He's wearing pastel colors too, like an '80s car salesman, and his blazer features shoulder pads, offering a semblance of a built upper body. He's got a skinny fat build, and every time he raises his arms, his feeble hairy forearms slip out from underneath his sleeves.

"You're probably right," Dennis smiles, self-abased.

"How long have you been married for?" Dennis asks, as if he didn't already know Pete and Bridget met in 2014 and got engaged in 2017, holding their "Dream wedding" at an old winery in Rhode Island on a beautiful pastoral land.

Raising his eyebrows, touching his wedding ring with his right hand, Pete pauses to ponder the question.

"Just about five years," he crows.

"It's a lot of work, bro. I can tell you that," he discloses, puffing his chest out and placing his hands on his hips, glancing up at the ceiling as if he's in deep contemplation, reliving each memorable challenging time of his marriage.

"But it's been the happiest I have ever been. Especially since we just had our second child," Pete effuses, now rubbing his hands together like he's just washed them with Purell.

"Crazy to think we're at the age now when we're having kids. Feels like yesterday we were back at St. Michael's Prep, putting naked photos of Anne Hathaway on her brother's locker," Dennis comments, chuckling with a smile, anticipating Pete bursting out in laughter.

"Your memory is better than mine, bro, but sounds like something I'd do," Pete grins, shaking his head as he crosses his arms.

"Haha or when we egged Anthony Pecora's house on Halloween?" Dennis gasps, nudging with the back of his hand, tapping him on his shoulder.

"High school was definitely fun," Pete appeases, opening the master bedroom's closet.

"Closet is capacious, offering space for a serious wardrobe," he praises.

And Dennis excuses Pete for not remembering egging houses on Halloween, since he used an admirable adjective like 'capacious' and also because they had been drinking stolen liquor from his parents' bar cabinet that night. But he can't believe he doesn't fucking remember harassing Ben Hathaway for two years straight in high school over his famous hot sister because that's something that doesn't just get forgotten. Apparently, Pete's life had been just like a fucking movie, like all the *Hangovers* and *Van Wilder* films rolled into one. And he's done so much cooler, crazier shit that teasing a celebrity's sibling in a variety of pranks wasn't even worth remembering. There wasn't enough room in his entire hippocampus to hold onto any mediocre memories.

Dennis enters the closet, inspecting the cracks and crevices, looking for unsightly discoveries, like dead bugs or droppings. He's disappointed in Pete, but it's his own expectations that crush him; he should have known by now that everyone fucking sucks.

"So how old are your kids?" Dennis asks, attempting to revivify the conversation, as if he didn't already know their ages.

"Hmm, let's see," Pete said looking up from his smartphone, holding his chin with his thumb and pointer finger, slowly scratching his stubble.

"Well, Jillian is four and Ryan is just about a year old, now," Pete reflects, gazing up into the left corner of the room, an implicit sign he's being sincere, accessing images of his children.

He shares an affectionate smile, his lip curling under his teeth like he's imagining his little rugrats crawling over him as they play on the couch, and Dennis admires his sincerity, his obvious adoration for his family.

"That's awesome man. Can't even imagine how fulfilling it is," Dennis remarks, bouncing on the soft low pile carpet, relishing its elasticity and cushiony feel, speculating that the previous owner must have put the new beige carpet down.

It goes nicely with the other neutral colors of the home, and Dennis debates lying on his back to really enjoy the new carpet, making a snow angel, since he's starting to feel dizzy, like a delicate dryer cycle, slow and escalating.

"Must be amazing to create another living being that is half of you and half of another person that you love," Dennis emotes, feeling an emotional onslaught as he dawdles to the bedroom window.

"It's probably just cool enough to be in love with someone so much that you would want to procreate with her," Dennis elucidates as he glances out the window; he's struggling to get the theme song from the cartoon series *Rugrats* out of his head, the acoustic sounds and synthesizers synchronizing, a real whimsical melody floating in his ears.

He catches the low winter sun suffusing a pink hue behind the partial clouds, radiating vibrant rays in all different directions, like reflective broken glass across the sky's canvas. The sight captivates Dennis as he reminisces, the thuds of reverberating bass from a passing car playing Wiz Khalifa's "Black and Yellow" elicits vivid memories of nights driving out to Pennsylvania to visit Renee's parents. The song was ubiquitous on every radio station during those trips. An hour in the car together, listening to tunes and talking, they shared childhood memories and embarrassing stories, like how Renee used to steal her neighbors' mail and leave half-eaten pizza crusts in their mailbox, or how Dennis once told his preschool class his grandmother was struck by lightning because he was upset another student was getting too much attention for her grandmother's sickness.

A passing couple walks by with a white boxer, across the street from the condo. The two hold hands as they talk and laugh together, their puppy pushing forward with curiosity. Dennis remembers a fleeting time when he was content with a stunning girl and an unconditionally loving dog; his heart swelled for a period when it was still whole. He feels a sense of regret, a terrible sorrow, like he made a dreadful mistake. He misses his imperfectly perfect family, thinking how he'd probably give anything to take Cooper on a walk and listen to Christine blabber about nonsense. The ache is bittersweet, that hollow realization of a moment's worth only when it's lost to memory.

"So do you still keep in touch with anyone from high school?" Dennis asks, wiping away the tears forming.

Rubbing the corners of his eyes, he turns to look at Pete. Holding a finger up to indicate his current preoccupation, Pete continues texting on his phone, engrossed in his device. And he's not paying attention to a fucking thing Dennis has said; he doesn't want to be friends, he just wants to make a 6% commission fee from selling the home, Dennis concludes; the sudden compulsion to jab Pete in his portly belly entices Dennis, envisioning him gasping for air after the blow, watching his dwindling hair scrunch.

"One sec, bro," Pete stalls as he swipes and clicks on his phone.

Dennis recalls how Pete used to partake in self-denigrating humor back in high school, always dropping his pants in the hallway or tossing himself into a locker as a teacher approached. He loved to make a fool of himself and make a scene, which makes Dennis wonder if his proclivity transferred into sexual humiliation. Maybe his wife Lisa puts on a ribbed dildo and pegs him while their precious children are asleep, inspiring wholesome Facebook posts as she penetrates his loose sphincter, he contemplates.

But it's a deeper cogitation that comes to Dennis, when he ponders over the preponderance of Facebook material Pete shares and the associations he holds dear. He wonders who Pete would be if all his "likes" disappeared, if his shared memes were erased. Without his favorite football team or primary political party, no tribes to pledge allegiance to; without his children's favorite nursery songs or his wife's cherished vacation spots, no immediate family to cling to; without the echoes of his high school sports glory days or the pride of his vocation and big house, how would he truly define himself, if none of it existed. What vestiges of authenticity would really be his, if all the pieces were stripped away.

The sound of a doorbell chimes, sounding from Pete's phone, which he answers, pressing it to his ear,

"Stan, the man! I got a great home for you to look at. Let me call you back in an about an hour. I'm just finishing up with a client," Pete responds, pacing as he glances at the ground, listening to the warbling voice on the other end.

"Ok, sounds good, bro," Pete exclaims, smirking as he hangs up.

"I'll take the place, you motherfucking piece of shit," Dennis says with a wry smile, giving a thumbs up.

####

Immersed in their reading assignments, the students bow their heads in concentration; the classroom is super quiet except for the echoing clicks of Dennis striking his ProBook's keys with an aggressive tenacity. Sitting upright in his chair, his brows furrowed and legs coiled around the base, Dennis leans forward with a focused, hostile expression as he fires off responses.

He's arguing with people in the comment sections again on Instagram from a blank burner account he created, fixating on fallacies and hitting them hard with statistics and diatribes. His anger escalates with each @ or mention, replying with belligerent run-on sentences and big words, constructing sesquipedalian speeches in a rage, a pointless psychosis that elevates his heart rate to manic proportions. The lure of a new notification has him opening his app every thirty seconds despite the presence of his class, checking for a rebuttal, a challenge, a chance to prove his intelligence. He relishes calling people "eunuchs" when they resort to insults and ad hominem attacks, aware of the irony as he calls out their repressed masculinity and insecurities, their need to lash out to compensate for their lack of discourse ability. It makes him feel aggrandized, intellectually superior, when he gets more than ten likes on his comments or when the opposing interlocutor retreats without further provocation, signaling defeat.

He's only seen a few faces peek up from their desks while he's been engaged in his digital discourse, curious countenances afraid of making eye contact, which makes him feel less guilty that the students aren't objecting to the direction. Dennis knows he should probably focus on actually teaching instead of just having them read, since he's had them read for the entire fifty minutes of the past two periods, handing out a printout of Dante Alighieri. He made copies of *Inferno* in the annex after snorting a line off the xerograph surface, trying to capture the sequence by taking a few images to create a flip book, but it didn't quite come out as anticipated; instead, it just produced a bunch of awkward shots, his face crumpled and his eye squinting, the scanner failing to even pick up the lines of blow.

He's finished his short story though, so he figured it was the perfect time to celebrate with an illicit substance, especially one that he remembered so fondly before he gave it up after college. He once felt like life might be worth living sober enough to feel it all, to experience its full scope without the need for escape, but that was a very long time ago. The transition from downers to uppers has been quite productive for him the past couple of days, now that he's only getting five hours of sleep and arriving at school at 5 A.M. to write. "Swimming" is the name of the short story he's completed, which he's feeling good about; he's feeling pretty good about anything, now that he's taking bumps of coke whenever he feels discouraged. Yeah, he's been feeling good, but he knows life is just like taking drugs, and no matter how high he gets, there's always a chance of a freak-out lurking, festering under the surface, ready to wreak havoc and turn his fucking world upside down.

He should probably tell John that his wife has been uploading additional items for sale on Facebook Marketplace, like his favorite Yankee recliner upholstered in blue and white leather, or how a man named Luke with gray hair has been sharing office memes on her Facebook page and posting heart-eye emojis on her pictures. But Dennis is too occupied with his ego. It's becoming more apparent, too, he's even uploading pictures of himself after his daily ritual of fifty perfect pushups, flexing his bicep with his sleeve rolled up. He props the phone against a water bottle, sets the camera on a timer to capture his image, staunchly insisting he never technically takes a selfie. He incorporates a coordinating hashtag like #fitgoals or #fitlife and uploads a picture of his breakfast avocado toast, checking every two and a half minutes to see who has viewed his story.

And it's maddening because he knows he's engaging in a mindless obsession, needing validation for some reason or another, but he can't resist. It's like a parasite has attached itself to his cerebellum, controlling all his motives and actions. The narcissism is blighting, accelerating his disassociation.

The first part of *The Divine Comedy* is *Inferno*, which is 150 pages; more than enough reading content for a few days. He should probably assign it as homework and dedicate the class period to actual instruction or discussion, but he doesn't give a shit. He's sick of his job consuming his creative hours. Besides, he's going to give them a quiz on Thursday: ten open-ended questions on plot summary and the specific circles of hell, especially about the middle ring of the seventh circle, having them elaborate on the significance of suicide souls turning into trees. The final question will ask them to explicate the symbolism of colors in the lines, "No green leaves but black in color." And he'll be able to tell who hasn't read after the first couple of questions, but he's willing to give extra points for effort in the interpretative analyses.

Megan's been out for two days now, and Dennis has checked her social media for some indication of the reason, but he's had no such luck; her Instagram is still private, and her Facebook is pretty limited too, except for a recent profile picture update of her with an older woman, possibly her grandmother. Dennis speculates that grandma might have died and she's mourning with her family, but there aren't any heartfelt comments on the photo, and people in the digital realm never miss a chance to emote and express their condolences, so maybe she's just under the weather.

Sifting through his work emails, Dennis scrolls to locate the sample quiz he sent himself last week, but he's engrossed with a floating quandary: the unanswered text he sent Christine a day ago: "Hi Christine," he texted in a semi-conscious state, abandoning any further communication after several hours passed with no reply.

He probably should have gone with a softer approach, more sincere, maybe an apology, not a cover letter opener like he's applying for a fucking job, but he floundered, too disconnected from reality. So instead of sulking, he opens a recent email from Mallory's mom to project his disquietude. The pestering parent routinely floods his inbox about her precious daughter's academic performance; Mallory is a dull crayon with purple hair and an inability to follow directions on assignments. Her mother's persistence is intrusive, hounding Dennis about extra credit opportunities since she's barely passing. Her incoherent emails are even more troublesome, which makes Dennis realize her mother is just as incompetent as her daughter. He often struggles to decipher the illegible fragments in her bickering emails, similar to how he tries to piece together the non sequitur sentences that plague Mallory's essays.

Reading on, Dennis rubs his temples in a desperate attempt to alleviate his frustration. The concluding paragraph of the email mentions how "Mallory needs a C" to get into such and such college and how she isn't going to be studying English anyway.

Shaking his head, Dennis expounds internally on the concept of education, how people tend to take school and its influence on life too literally: forcing students to absorb lessons, learn times tables, pivotal points of historic battles, and proper punctuation, which some will argue lack any real intellectual depth. But school is just a microcosm for life, really, teaching that there are things people have to do, even if they don't want to. Whether it's working a monotonous nine to five just to pay your bills, burying a loved one, or living the rest of your life with a broken heart, you have to do things you don't want to do if you want to survive.

Dennis takes a quick glimpse at the class to ensure everyone is consumed with their reading before bending down and opening his bottom desk drawer to retrieve a lightly foil-wrapped brownie, even though it's twenty minutes until lunchtime. The tangy reek saturates his nose as he devours the baked pot treat, shoveling collected crumbs from his hands into his mouth, chewing with a rapid jaw. He closes the bottom drawer and returns to a sitting position, taking a swig of his cold coffee to wash down the chalky substance.

Dennis sits, constructing a compelling response to Mallory's illiterate mom in which he delineates that a lack of interest in a particular subject isn't justification for not participating or completing any of the work correctly. Pondering his approach, Dennis scans the room once more, his head wavering as he peers at the field of adolescent faces, capturing a leering mug from the back of the classroom. Jonathan's face returns an ambiguous look, resulting in a steady stare; his coiffed hair slicked back, and it's not a pensive glimpse as if he's deliberating on the reading. No, it's hemmed in aversion with a snarled lip, like he's picturing punching Dennis in the balls. He wonders if Jonathan knows he stole his stuff.

The bell rings, rattling Dennis's concentration and signaling the end of the class. Dennis continues his stare-down with Jonathan, his adrenaline spiking with each passing second, tensing as if bracing for battle. The tapping of his right foot produces muffled squeaks, fretting with a springy bounce; the rubber sole of his cognac shoes pecking against the vinyl floor like some backwards-ass woodpecker.

A large potato stands up, blocking their line of sight, causing a surge of epinephrine in Dennis's bloodstream because he certainly shouldn't be seeing any personified potatoes. This vegetable is not cartoonish, like Mr. Potato Head. Nope, it's a round, meaty potato, starchy, brown, and bruised, wearing the blazer and tie combo school uniform. The second brownie is probably kicking in, so Dennis clenches his eyes closed for a few seconds. When he opens them, he sees a hefty student instead, not a potato. It's an honest mistake since it's almost lunchtime, and he's probably just hungry.

Jonathan is no longer staring at Dennis; his arms are retracted, holding the straps of his bookbag with a staid expression, not the previous antagonized state Dennis observed. He looks uninterested as he moseys down the row.

"Watch your butts," Dennis comments as Jonathan rounds the class aisle row to exit, locking in on the unaware student.

"What?" Jonathan utters, halting, turning to look at Dennis with a puzzled face.

"What?" Dennis replies, his eyes expanding.

"Did you just say watch your butts?"

And Dennis can't figure out if he really just said what he thinks he said. His short-term memory is fried, and sometimes he's not sure if he's speaking out loud or just thinking his thoughts. But it's now obvious he vocalized, as the room is empty, all the other students dispersed, leaving only a confused Jonathan in limbo.

"Excuse me, Jonathan?" Dennis exclaims, crossing his arms as he leans back in his desk chair, homing in on the perplexed pupil.

"I thought you just said…"

"You thought wrong, Jonathan. Now go, mom's spaghetti," Dennis instructs, pointing toward the door as he pivots his attention to his laptop, no longer looking at Jonathan.

"What the hell man?" a visibly frustrated Jonathan whispers, shrugging as he leaves, tossing his hands up.

And it's a foreign feeling that besets Dennis after the interaction, a surge of blood rushing to his head, a burning paranoia coupled with tension in the lungs, squeezing every time he breathes. He's way too fucking high, and he's been reading about aneurysms and how they instantly kill people of all ages. Now he thinks he's wheezing, and that's really never happened before, so he starts bargaining, like he's communicating telepathically with a higher power or some cosmic deity, attempting to abate the uncomfortable waves of panic. He tells himself he'll stop indulging in daily narcotics and possibly go to church, even donating to a children's fund. Thinking back on how many times he's made similar deals and always failed to fulfill his promises, he debates whether this instance, this particular type of discomfort, is the one that kills him, like a sniper picking him off. He's been thinking he would probably die on a Friday, since he despises the weekends, often feeling obligated to venture to a bar or somewhere social with real human interaction to show he's not alone.

"Dennis Clauden?" a voice travels from the classroom door.

Looking up from his desk, clenching his chest in worry, he notices a slender man with glasses, ducking under the door frame as he proceeds.

"Yes?" Dennis remarks with a tenuous cadence, standing from his chair with uncertainty.

He contemplates whether the stranger might be a plainclothes detective here to arrest him for the drugs he has in his possession or maybe for the few seconds of foot rubbing he engaged in with Megan. Maybe that could be confounded as some sort of foot molestation.

"Nice to meet you," the tall individual smirks, branching down an open palm.

"I'm Michael Fairchild, the new AP English teacher," the individual announces, flashing shards of teeth.

Michael has the quintessential balding man's haircut, a fuzzy asymmetrical landscape with hair missing on the top but thick and dark around the sides. His bulging bald forehead resembles a roasted peanut, and his ostentatious blue bowtie is vivid, coordinating with his eccentric argyle sweater. The grooves on his wrinkly white T-shirt underneath distract Dennis because they're fucking untidy and unbecoming.

"Welcome to the team," Dennis recites with a desultory demeanor, switching on his autonomic interpersonal communication, using cliché phrases.

They shake hands for a brief greeting. Michael's weighty, clammy hand engulfs Dennis's, swallowing his entire row of fingers like Godzilla snatching a village. Dennis becomes uncomfortably cognizant of his small stature, a further indication of Michael's greatness.

"So the other staff were telling me you're also a writer?" Michael asks with a full smile, revealing more splinters of faded enamel, peeking out like shark teeth.

He places his hands on his hips as if he's positioning himself to really pay attention. He reminds Dennis of a Picasso painting, haunting scenery put together in appealing colors.

"I'm in the review process with a few literary agents for my first fiction novel," Dennis lies, a self-defense mechanism to mask his insecurities and shortcomings.

He knows he's not really a writer unless he's published, but pending a review sounds much more promising than disclosing his manuscript was rejected about one hundred times. He can't even remember.

"That's inspiring," Michael remarks with a crooked smile, an affectation of admiration, Dennis assumes, since he always expects the worst of people.

"Who is your favorite author?" he follows up, crossing his arms and placing his weight on his left leg.

Dennis is all too familiar with this kind of inquisition, the question that feels less about genuine curiosity and more about writers trying to pin other writers down, attributing their styles or themes to whoever they choose to name. It reeks of pretension, as if acknowledging a favorite author somehow reveals whether you're a true creative or just a mimic. Dennis doesn't have a go-to answer, but the absurdity of it makes him want to reply with something provocative, like "Adolf Hitler" for *Mein Kampf,* just to see if Michael's face would drop or if he'd try to mask his shock with polite indifference. Or maybe he could name "Moses," the author of the first five books of the Bible, where a harsh, almost tyrannical God hands down Draconian laws, punishing disobedience with brutal consequences.

He can't say "Hemingway" because that's way too predictable and blasé.

"Palahniuk is one of my favorites," Dennis declares, recalling *Fight Club* and *Survivor.*

"Ah yes, I was really into him about five years ago. And as a queer writer myself, I felt compelled to study his work," Michael pontificates.

Dennis knows Palahniuk is gay, but he's not sure sexual orientation should factor into assessing whether the writing is quality or not; he wonders if straight and gay authors write differently.

Dennis doesn't know how to respond to Michael's declaration, and he debates whether he should mention that he's heterosexual, thinking that reciprocation is the key to any successful friendship. But Dennis isn't entirely sure he wants to be friends, and it's not because Michael is gay, not at all. To Dennis, a mouth is a mouth, really. What perturbs him more is Michael's comment about being into Palahniuk five years ago, as if he's now moved on to more intellectually stimulating authors, undergoing a marvelous transformation into ultimate omniscience. Dennis imagines this sort of conversion is required to be published, but he doesn't see why one should no longer enjoy an author's work. Part of him wishes he had mentioned Moses now, specifically his work in Leviticus 18:22, the verse that bluntly condemns homosexuality as an abomination, just to see how Michael would have reacted, if the irony would strike him, teaching at a Catholic school.

"Much of Palahniuk's sinister take on life inspired me to write my story, 'Hangman,'" Michael adds, whipping out his accolade like a big throbbing cock, ready to rub it all over Dennis's tiny face.

Flashing an awkward smile, Dennis knew it was inevitable that Michael would mention he was a published author, but he didn't expect it to be within the first five minutes of their interaction. The pretension oozes from Michael's eyes, glinting as he anticipates Dennis asking him about his short story that was published in the New Yorker. But Dennis doesn't care; he's disgruntled, thinking the only reason Michael was accepted is because he fits the desired intersectionality.

"I saw that. I would love to read it," Dennis replies politely, diplomatically, swallowing his caustic thoughts like poison.

Maybe he'd learn something from reading Michael's story, he ponders. Their dialogue concludes as Dennis forces a tight-lipped grin, leaving the classroom to access the back corridor, a new emergency exit he can escape through whenever he wants to get the fuck out of a situation. He doesn't care that he's left Michael in his classroom. No, he's more concerned about getting to the secluded roof space above; it's a small terrace with a view of the entire town, a panorama of bushy greenery and scattered buildings poking through the horizon. He wants to catch the brilliance of the skyline as the sun sets earlier now, to watch the incandescent diamonds scattered overhead, sprinkled across the velvet night, reminding him of the vastness of the universe, like maybe there's a place he can go to get away, as if somewhere, maybe, he belongs.

A ping from Dennis's phone sounds, interrupting his attempt to take a photo of the sky; he's thinking he's going to share it to his story and maybe incorporate an obscure caption like "Starry Night." The banner on his phone flashes, revealing a new email from Michael with a paperclip icon affixed to a document titled "Hangman." Dennis wonders how Michael managed to send him an email since he never gave him his address, until he remembers that all the teachers' school emails follow the same format: first name, period, last name, followed by @St.VincentKnights.com. He finds this rather eager of Michael, picturing him sprinting back to his classroom after Dennis departed, impatiently punching in his first and last name and attaching his celebrated story.

Clenching the phone with angst, Dennis wraps his palm around the screen, clutching the sides with his fingers. He debates launching his phone but settles on grinding his teeth instead, realizing the phone is his whole fucking life, and it's going to cost $500 to replace since he never got insurance for it. Maybe he'll send Michael his story "Swimming" to read, he considers, a test to see how pompous he really is, whether he'll even bother to reciprocate.

The purple falling sun emits mild rays, tickling his skin with fading warmth, deploying to the back of his neck and traveling down his forearms, eliciting goosebumps, a feeling submerged in nostalgia. He approaches the edge of the roof, gazing down at the pavement below, which is the student parking lot. The blacktop looks like a dark, daunting sea in the fading sunlight, a twenty-five-foot drop into the unknown. His legs quake as he imagines his body smacking the current, creating an indelible splash; sinking momentarily until his survival instincts take control, his arms shoveling water. He wonders how long he can resist the urge to survive, how long before he truly panics as his lungs fill. But

Dennis knows none of that matters because his body isn't going to end up drowning. No, it's going to end up contorted, splattered against the pavement, blood splashed around like a glorious Mortal Kombat 2 fatality.

"Jump," a whispering wind says, sailing through his ear, and it's a suggestion that's not as crazy as it sounds; his heart rate slows with the thought.

Raising his arms out in a crucifix pose, Dennis closes his eyes, wondering if the blackness just stays black when it's over.

"You won't die from this height," a voice sounds from behind him, breaking his concentration.

Opening his eyes, Dennis turns to see James sitting in a beach chair with a bag of Cheetos, munching with a crisp chew as he dumps orange chunks into his mouth. He licks his discernible orange fingertips after each handful, vibrant crumbs dusting his zipped-up bomber jacket.

"I tried it once a couple years ago. I broke my arm and a few ribs," James remarks, crunching away, standing from his chair, crumbling up his empty bag with the Krishnamurti book in his right hand.

"Hurt like a bitch too," James adds.

"Haha, well I was just taking in the scenery. It's super nice up here," Dennis attempts to deflect, hiding his embarrassment like he just got caught masturbating by his parents.

"Sure," James rebuts.

"You ain't serious about doing something like that unless you close your eyes."

"That's the first step," James comments with an amused smirk.

"You really jumped off this roof before?"

"Oh yeah. Fucking cannon ball," James laughs briefly, an equivocal cackle, and Dennis can't entirely tell if he's being facetious or not.

"You need to go to a higher height if you wanna die," James says.

"But before you find a higher spot to jump off of, start distancing yourself from your thoughts, and maybe read this book," he states, pushing the book into Dennis's chest before walking off.

10. The Picture of Dorian Gray

Shaking his Cool Water cologne bottle to ensure it was fresh, Dennis glanced at himself in the mirror, beaming at his reflection, soaking in the surrealism. He wasn't sure how much to spray, but he remembered reading that the wrists and neck were optimal spots for misting, something about the pulse points being the warmest parts of the body and heat helping release the scent, like a wax warmer. But he didn't want to overdo it. He didn't want to repulse her, fearing too much pungency might deter her from getting close, so he pushed only slightly on the cap, emitting a half spritz on his neck and wrist, like a scientist applying a precise formula.

Buttoning up his nicest blue Calvin Klein shirt, Dennis smiled, thinking he looked handsome, admiring his choice of coordinating polo jeans. His blue eyes popped from the deep hue of the shirt; the rhythmic chords of the acoustic guitar from Foo Fighters' "Furling" sounded from his stereo. The third CD in his three-disc changer was a mix of only acoustic versions of songs. He figured it was the perfect soundtrack to listen to while getting ready for the evening. It still didn't feel right; it still felt like it wasn't going to happen, like she wasn't going to show; maybe her car would break down or her mother would require immediate medical attention, something arbitrary to prevent the night from occurring. Dennis floated with excitement though, imagining being alone with his crush, his first real flutter from anticipatory intimacy, a possible romance. And he knew he needed to control himself and that even the thought of intercourse might ruin his chance.

By the time 7:15 P.M. came around, Dennis had changed his shirt several times, only to revert to his original choice of attire. Reapplying cologne, frantically scrubbing away aromatic overtones to reset his fragrance, Dennis paced the small foyer of his parents' home, bouncing in and out of the dining and delicate china room, a special room full of exquisite figurines and expensive keepsakes that he and his brothers were forbidden from playing in as children. Peeking out the window of the designated decorative room, Dennis spied a silver Saturn sedan turn down the street of the cul-de-sac, slowing to the front of the house, pulling alongside the curb.

The off-white headlights flipped down as the car shut off; a bright interior light turned on inside the cabin revealing Miss Howard checking her face in the visor mirror. Dennis backed away from the window in a nervous manner, almost tripping over the lavish linen upholstered ottoman, closing the curtain panels before heading for the door. Peeking through the peephole of the door, Dennis watched Miss Howard as she walked up the driveway; her purse with short handles hung on her shoulder as she flipped her hair out with the ends of her hands, gussying herself. Approaching the porch, she proceeded with a sway, adjusting her shirt and waist, her physical attributes constricted by tight fabric, accentuating her physicality, a voluptuous vixen. The outdoor light illuminated more details of Miss Howard as she drew close, her puckered chest and shapely figure, a glowing sex angel in the night.

She stopped to adjust her cleavage before ringing the doorbell. Dennis remained, still peering through the aperture, deciding he would count to ten before answering, so he could soak in the anonymous sight of his eighth-grade English teacher at his front door. Miss Howard continued her preening, combing her hands swiftly through her hair until Dennis opened the door.

"Hi," she smiled a dimpled grin, appearing shorter than her usual stature since she wasn't wearing heels.

"Hey, come on in," Dennis greeted, stepping back to wave her in, not sure if he should offer to take her purse or something.

"How's it going?" she replied, stepping inside.

Maintaining a steady smile, she stood in the vestibule; her aroma of ripened fruit wafting Dennis as he closed the door. And it wasn't the typical saccharine scent he was acquainted with from the girls his age, nor was it the abrasive fumes of an elderly lady, like his grandma or aunt's perfume at Thanksgiving. No, it was a subtle yet potent fragrance that crept in, enticing with light floral notes followed by a cinnamon finish. Like an invigorating clove, it cast an intoxicating spell that instantly stimulated his libido.

"My parents aren't home, they're away for the weekend," Dennis blurted out like premature ejaculation, taking in the vision of the woman he dreamt about.

"Oh, well I hope they know I'm here, right?" she asked, looking around as if she were trying to figure out if he was really home alone, inspecting the peripherals for any parental occupants.

"Of course," Dennis muttered, nodding his head, confused about her concern, pondering the possibility that she might just be there platonically, making all his fantasies fruitless.

He felt defeated and stupid, embarrassed about how long he took to pick out his outfit and how high his expectations had been for the night; he was a fool, he thought, for thinking she'd ever do anything with him.

"Yeah, I was just about to start a movie. Do you want to come watch?" Dennis asked, attempting to recover, returning to his plan, invoking a cooler demeanor; he knew he had to be resilient.

"What movie?" she inquired, puckering her blushed lips.

"Office Space," he smiled, trying not to convey too much intrigue.

He had discovered the Blockbuster DVD in Tommy's room after school that day; leaving earlier that week, Tommy had forgotten to return it before he went back to college.

"Oh, that's such a good movie," she flashed a disarming smile, a tight-lipped smirk with a tentative vigor, like maybe she was nervous but really wanted to watch the movie with him.

"Cool," Dennis smiled, hoping to prompt her to proceed further into the house so he could see behind her, get a full view, but she remained standing, as if she were waiting for instruction.

"Let's do it, follow me," Dennis encouraged, ambling to the cellar door as he gazed back at Miss Howard.

Venturing into the basement, Dennis felt like he was luring prey into his lair, watching as she followed him, sustaining an inviting smile, like Montresor coaxing Fortunato, except Dennis wasn't interested in deception or walling her in. No, he was driven by pure sexual impulse, the possibility of attaining the impossible, every teenager's ultimate fantasy fulfilled. Strolling through the finished basement, Dennis noticed she had taken her shoes off, unveiling baby blue socks as her feet pressed into the fawn carpeted floor, and Dennis debated whether there was a subconscious meaning behind her action, like maybe her willingness to remove her footwear would escalate into further disrobing, if all went well.

Reaching for the remote, Dennis turned on the TV and started the DVD. Periodically, he glanced back at Miss Howard, who had taken a seat on the oyster-colored sectional couch, her hands folded in her lap, as he adjusted the input and volume.

The catchy rattling of maracas matched with the upward melody of trumpets blasted from the speakers as the opening scene of the movie played, creating a lighthearted atmosphere. Dennis had already turned off the invasive overhead lights, switching on the standing lamp and the two small desktop ones an hour before she had arrived, setting the mood, a strategic move to avoid the possible awkwardness of having to turn down the lights for the movie.

After setting the volume to an even number for good luck, a desperate superstition, Dennis took a seat close to Miss Howard, but not too obtrusive, about a foot away, testing to see if she'd move, which she didn't. The movie rolled, portraying a nerdy white guy rapping along to Scarface's "No Tears," cocking his hand up and to the side, exclaiming with urban dialect and a deep voice. The pasty actor with glasses then locked his doors, ironically, turning his music down as he saw an approaching homeless black man begging for change. And it's a scene that caused them to giggle nervously, looking at each other.

Dennis felt pretty anxious, sitting without talking, watching a movie with the fragrant smoke show breathing next to him, and he couldn't fathom just staying there for an hour and half more, so he stands up.

"Want me to get you something to drink?" Dennis offered, looking down at her, his body already facing the other direction.

"Oh, um, a water would be nice," she replied with a cheeky smile, a febrile, friendly gaze.

"I'll be right back," Dennis whispered, beaming the best flirtatious smile he could deliver, a curled upper lip, revealing the top corner of his teeth.

And Dennis ventured upstairs, rummaging through kitchen cabinets to find a suitable drinking glass for his queen, a deserving vessel fitted for her lush lips, still fighting off licentious reveries from entering his cerebral cortex. He pinched his skin, wondering if maybe he'd wake up from the circumstances and find himself in his bed, engulfed in his sheets with a raging hard-on, compelling an extemporaneous pillow humping session.

Yeah, he wasn't into traditional masturbation; he preferred fucking inanimate objects, preferably plush soft items with give, mimicking the rhythm of real intimacy rather than the routine pull and tug most teenagers settled for. The motion felt closer to actual fornication, far more satisfying than the usual, tiresome yanking with a weary hand. He even slipped a condom on a few days ago after stealing it from the local grocery store to simulate a realistic encounter of having sex with a contraception on. Although he wasn't entirely satisfied with the numbness of latex smothering his sensitivity, he did enjoy ejaculating into the bubbled tip instead of emptying into a wad of tissues.

The butterflies swarmed his chest, flying him back downstairs as he clutched the medium-sized mason jar of water.

"Here you go," Dennis announced, making his presence known; Miss Howard hadn't moved, her arms still positioned shoulder width apart with her hands folded in front.

"Oh, thanks," she purred, leaning forward to put her purse on the hexagonal coffee table before accepting the glass.

The returning amorous aroma consumed Dennis once again, so he sat down much closer to her, brushing his leg up against her yieldingly soft jeaned thigh, sending an electricity to his genitals; the thought of her weightiness, her flesh pressed against his arrested his imagination.

"Would you like some gum?" Miss Howard asked, unzipping the top of her purse.

"Yes, please," Dennis responded immediately.

Reaching into her purse, she scooched over, creating more space between the two. Holding his hand out, Dennis smiled as she placed the unwrapped piece of gum in his hand.

"Thanks, Miss Howard," he recited, putting the dextrose stick into his mouth.

"Oh, fuck," he uttered, realizing he referred to her with a title.

"Haha, what's wrong?" she grinned, chewing her gum with a sexual munch, snapping her tongue into the sugary substance, although everything Dennis perceived was sexual with his hormones raging.

"Nothing," Dennis breathed.

Miss Howard sighed an amused gasp, leaning her head back as she smiled.

"Do you want to call me Susanna?" she asked, tilting her head with a smirk; her porcelain skin reflecting in the dimmed ambiance; her oceanic eyes engulfing him as he sat.

"Can I?"

"Go for it," she replied, turning her focus back to the movie.

And Dennis tried to think of something really cool to say, some witty one liner, but he was exposed in person, unable to hide behind a screen name and take his time with a response; he could feel himself imploding under the pressure as the silence persisted and the movie progressed to the iconic therapy session:

"So, every single day that you see me, that's on the worst day of my life," Pete uttered with a blithe disposition, compelling Susanna to giggle.

Dennis reciprocated a giggle, resisting the urge to look at her; she was as hot as the sun, blinding with her beauty, and every time he looked at her, he experienced an intense heat emanating, so much so where he needed to look away. Susanna lifted her glass with grace, wrapping her lithe fingers around the clear vessel, bringing the rim to her pressed lips as she drank; her back slightly arched, her busty chest and ballooning backside protruding in opposite directions; Dennis could feel himself growing, blood flowing to his regions.

Placing the cup back onto the coffee table, Susanna glanced at Dennis with a friendly smile, as if fully aware of his observation. Retrieving her purse, she extracted a hair tie. Leaning forward, her hair flowed and followed, revealing her back and the top strand of her white underwear. With a swift movement, she launched her tresses backward and tied her locks up.

"You look so pretty," Dennis murmured, eliciting instant embarrassment as he blushed.

"Aw, thank you," she replied, rubbing his chest quickly with her flattened hand, her sensuous fingers scrubbing his shirt, a gesture of appreciation.

"Oh, I probably shouldn't be touching you," she uttered, withdrawing her hand.

"Oh, stop. You know it's just us," Dennis remarked, shoving her with a playful touch, relishing the euphoria of physical contact.

And Susanna remained quiet, confusing Dennis because he wasn't sure if he should continue the conversation or let it go since the movie was still playing; it wasn't his fault he was clueless; he was just inexperienced with transitions, unaware of how to proceed; he imagined this was his opportunity to advance, but he couldn't figure out the appropriate move. He felt like a failure. As the movie began winding down, Dennis grew agitated, frustrated with the lack of development; the night was shaping up to be a big nothing. As Milton unwound on the beach chair in the Bahamas, Dennis brainstormed on how to extend the night, fearful that she may leave at the conclusion of the movie. He spotted his old stereo propped on top of the bookshelf, a bookcase that was utilized as a console, housing all their entertainment devices.

Once the screen faded to black with credits rolling, Dennis reached for the stereo remote, distracting her from looking at the Mickey Mouse belt clock on the wall; it was one of those collectible items his mother had to have when she saw it, purchasing it when they were in Disney world. It was a silly mechanical clock, mimicking an oversized wristwatch with Mickey in the center of the dial, his arms as the minute and hour hands. And Dennis knew the radio antenna had broken years ago, so the only other option was playing whatever burned CD he had left in the player. Still chewing the flavorless gum, his jaw became tense from the fatuous champing of the rubbery substance, the taste fading faster than his patience.

"Want to listen to some music?" Dennis suggested, clicking on the stereo while simultaneously shutting off the TV, a seamless transition.

"What kind of music do you like?" he followed up with persistency.

"Oh wow, it's almost 10 P.M.," Susanna noted, yawning with a breathy exhalation, the wind from her vocal cords resounding in her throat.

"Wow, someone can't even hang," Dennis quipped with a defensive tone, shaking his head as he turned up the stereo, hoping whatever songs he had downloaded from Kazaa were decent.

The echoing guitar riffs followed by the marching drums of "Kryptonite" rang from the speaker followed by the opening verse, "Well, I took a walk around the world to ease my troubled mind."

Cocking her head to the side and whipping her ponytail, Susanna looked at Dennis.

"Well, aren't you just a wise guy," she sneered, nudging his shoulder as she leaned into him.

"Why did I see you in detention this past week?" she inquired, squinting her eyes at him with an admonishing look, possibly out of concern.

Dennis had only gotten detention because he was late for class, but he saw an opportunity to evoke sympathy, a purported aphrodisiac he had read about.

"Yeah, but it's no big deal," Dennis replied with feigned reluctance, hoping to provoke her to inquire further.

"What happened?"

"Let's just say, I had to fuck these kids up," Dennis boasted with a cocky grin.

And he'd never been in a fight his entire life; the whole story was a complete fabrication, a lie meant to make him seem bold, masculine, with a hint of grit. He was aiming for that elusive blend of sensitivity and toughness.

"Oh my god, what happened?" Miss Howard gasped, pressing her gentle hand against her chest, revealing her slender digits; the same hand Dennis often fantasized about clenching his shaft, jerking him off with an aggressive vigor, the same technique that started off every porno scene he watched on the videotape inside John's VCR.

"These two kids were picking on this girl at school, so I had to teach them some manners," he huffed, holding his hands in front and rubbing his knuckles as if recalling the fight.

The smacking of fists pummeling flesh, like a real-life Fight Club, but Dennis wasn't a Tyler Durden; he was a compulsive liar desperate to lose his virginity.

"Are you serious? Who were the kids? Do I know them? Who was the girl?" Susanna rattled off questions, perking up in shock.

And Dennis hadn't given the story much thought or consideration, especially since had there been a significant fight at school, teachers would have obviously been informed; he couldn't think of two kids he would have fought either, so he really needed to abandon his embellishment before he revealed himself.

"It's just, I guess I have these demons," Dennis uttered, hanging his head in a coy manner, committing to his role of playing possum.

"Demons, you say?" she whispered, leaning forward with a comforting cadence, an approachable position with her shoulders open.

"I don't know. Sometimes I feel like I'm lost," he emoted, rubbing his eyes as if tears were forming.

"Oh sweetheart, it's okay," she consoled, embracing Dennis, pulling him close, hugging him is his arms.

Clenching him close to her body, Dennis wrapped his arms around her, resting his cheek on her breast; the soft tissue welcoming him with warmth, radiating up his entire body with rapturous tingles. Her scent surrounded him, filling his orifices with every inch of her essence. Continuing his fake sob, Susanna rubbed his neck with the back of her thumb while he remained pillowed into her. Her skin was soft and supple, complementing her incredible physical features; the heat from her chest transferring to Dennis's body, completely enthralling him, but he had no idea what to do next; he hadn't ever gotten this far.

Their hug continued for at least a couple of minutes, the pressure consistent, never breaking, and Dennis wondered how long he could pretend cry until she would relinquish the hold, so he knew this was his only chance. This was going to be the closest he'd ever be to her again, and her uninterrupted hug had to be an implicit invitation. Inching his hands down her back as imperceptibly as he could, slowly manipulating fingers against the fabric, Dennis pursued his destination as Susanna held him in her arms.

"It's okay," she comforted, cooing.

His hands approached her behind, spiking his heart rate and producing a frantic thudding in his chest. Dennis acted quickly, placing his hands on her ass. Sliding his hands onto each cheek, Dennis cradled her behind, waiting for a reaction, but the hugging continued and so did his fondling for a few moments as his grip intensified, rubbing methodically, relishing every second of the pleasure. His erection poked the front of his pants, creating friction against the fly; and he could feel the sticky residue building up, the pre-cum in his briefs every time he humped forward while he played with her full, firm yet compressible buttocks. The sybaritic enjoyment consumed him, debating whether he should escalate the scenario, possibly slipping his hands down the back of her jeans, encroaching her desirable crack.

And right before Dennis felt like he could ejaculate from the pure tactile stimulation of massaging fabric-covered flesh, she quickly released her arms, pushing away from the huddle, breaking from his grasp. So Dennis dove in like a kamikaze pilot, kissing her on the lips; Susanna froze, the life escaping her as she stared down at the carpet, her mouth closed and her eyes vacant.

"What's wrong?" Dennis whispered.

"We can't do this here," Susanna trembled, her head hanging and pressed against her sternum, as she crossed her arms.

"Why not?"

"I have to leave, Dennis," Susanna asserted, jolting from the cushion, tossing her purse over her shoulder.

She whisked past his legs to exit before he could react, marching her way up the stairs. The clamor of the front door closing shook the basement ceiling, leaving a stunned Dennis on the couch, surrounded by her lingering scent, trying to figure out what had just happened.

####

Nebulous chatter plays as background noise to the clinking of utensils and bowls being emptied by the trash cans. Metal spoons scrape against ceramic plates, dishing out remnants into the whooshing, plastic-lined bins. Plastic trays slap as people pass by, tossing theirs onto the counter, creating a spastic drumbeat. A jazz instrumental buzzes with a distinctive saxophone sound, rattling the overhead speaker and the mineral fiber ceiling tile above Dennis. He's been fixating on it since he sat down, looking up from his laptop for the tenth time in five minutes to see if his coffee is ready.

"Dorian!" the broad barista shouts, commanding almost everyone's attention.

The meaty employee has been announcing names with a vociferous delivery about every minute, disturbing Dennis's concentration as he corrects papers. But he's been severely vexed for two days now, even though he's bought a condo; Monsignor informed him that another parent complained about his lectures, citing a casual indifference to teaching. And Dennis is a neurotic individual in general, but now his reputation is slowly crumbling, which is going to lead to unannounced observations, like he's a first-year teacher all over again. He should probably just shake it off and turn his act around, but he's faltering, diminishing his appetite, and it's killing his creativity. He hasn't been able to write or even think about creating.

"Thanks," the apparent Dorian patron says, slicking back his dark hair.

He scoops the cup in one hand, raises his phone, and snaps a selfie while taking the first sip, another protagonist; Dennis wonders if the moment will make it to his story or land as a permanent post on Instagram.

The aromatic atmosphere of Arabica coffee notes pervading the air brings a slight solace to Dennis, reminding him of early mornings when he was a kid, when his mother used to prepare a pot of Joe for his father over breakfast. He's hoping a change of scenery like Starbucks will imbue productivity, focus, and distraction from his self-loathing. And it's a shame, because he was making progress, even taking temporary pride in his purchase, the completion of a short story, and his thought-provoking reading.

He's been digesting chapters of Krishnamurti like nourishment, chewing on the concept of the human psyche and how people tend to live either in the past or the future and seldom in the present, losing all control of their thoughts, obsessing over existences that aren't actually realities, never fully aware of the now. He had been thinking how profound that postulation is, how enlightening it is to understand the impact of thoughts. But now he's thinking he'll be unemployed in a matter of time once the school dismisses him, living off credit cards, just like his father did for a few years during the lawsuit, struggling to stay afloat. The water is calling his name, even louder than before, promising eternal peace. And it always takes something bad to happen for Dennis to realize how good things were before.

"Apollo!" the binary marshmallow declares, holding up a small cup.

Launching himself from the booth, Dennis beetles to the counter to collect his latte, enjoying hearing his faux name, since he's been unable to finish a meal, relying heavily on craft coffees as sustenance and consistent pick-me-ups.

"Have a great day," the barista responds, adorned in a pin-covered apron, bedecked with activism buttons like "Free Palestine" and "Gays for Gaza."

Dennis nods in amusement, because he knows wearing these pins will make a real difference, playing a significant role in ending the crisis in the Middle East. The "Gays for Gaza" one strikes Dennis as rather odd though, since he's not sure Gaza is for gays, given the reported criminalization and persecution of homosexuality for decades. But maybe that's just right-wing propaganda, he ponders, recalling a CNN headline he saw on Instagram.

The perceived male's stubbled face, accented with eyeliner and pierced ears, renders his gender ambiguous as he holds the drink out to Dennis. Dennis isn't surprised by the pronouns labeled on the name tag; he understands that's a thing now. However, he's confused as to why someone would need to know a person's third-person pronouns when they're conversing face-to-face in a two-person conversation.

"Thank you," Dennis replies, debating whether to use an honorific like "ma'am" along with his expression of gratitude.

It used to be considered a sign of respect to address individuals with a title, and he thinks it should work since the name tag says, "She/Her," but he's not entirely sure. He doesn't want to be potentially lectured about his inherent misogyny if he does, so Dennis shares a tepid smile instead, appreciative of the coffee.

And it's not a reflection of his feelings toward the server at all. No, he's just struggling to smile in general and that sucks because he usually feels immense joy when the barista doesn't suspect a phony name, which is most of the time. Except for the instances when he used "Zeus" and "Aphrodite" and was served with a cackle and a smirk.

It's a heavy discomfort that's bedeviling him, like he's got an anvil on his chest and there's a timer affixed to the front, counting down to eventual self-destruction, which culminates with being fired. And he can't stop mulling about the fact that if it weren't for Renee, he'd never even have a career; he'd still be working for fifteen dollars an hour as a shitty editor if she hadn't helped him become a teacher, so in a way, he's forever indebted to her. Maybe that's why she's haunting him, he wonders. His phone has been ringing all day; it's his mother calling to vent, and he usually listens, understanding she needs to let off steam about his aunt, her sister's declining mental state, Natalie's callousness toward John, and her frustration with Tommy's wife not calling to thank everyone for coming to visit, but Dennis needs a break before he breaks.

"Don't forget to call your mother. Love Mom," an incoming text reads, accompanied by several heart emojis.

Sinking back into his booth, trying to evade the swarming guilt from ignoring his mom, since she's been so helpful too, helping decorate his new home with little accent pillows and drinkware. He clutches the piping hot coffee in his hand, debating how intense the burning would be if he were to douse himself in the steaming liquid. Experiencing excruciating pain would certainly distract him from his existential angst, even just for a moment. Sipping his tall brew and licking the foam away from his mouth, Dennis opens his laptop. The Starbucks is filling up as the afternoon progresses, and he still needs to find an attorney for his closing, but he's not sure how many more free consultations he can tolerate with pompous pricks posturing, patronizing in their explanations of the process, justifying their $400 an hour fee with legal jargon. Dennis feels nauseous when he contemplates how much money he's going to have to cough out just to get a home that's his own, but he's surrendered to the leaching, the financial draining and enervation, if it means he can finally move on with his life.

The hankering to pick up his phone itches at his fingertips like a burning urge, pulling at his hand with a magnetic force. He's disgusted with his addiction, his increased screen time, and how much of his daily life involves frequenting social media and dating apps. Mindless, wasted hours of stimulation as he swipes, scrolls, and reacts, skipping through stories and recommended videos. So he's forcing himself to resume grading, now accepting email attachments from his students, thinking it would give them more autonomy and freedom to submit their papers with a designated deadline each month; he's speculating this innovation in the grading practice might help redeem himself at school.

Opening his recent Word documents, his last saved response, the one he crafted in a manic fit of rage the night before, spending the evening hours ruminating about his latest infraction before projecting his hostility into hypercritical feedback:

Sorry, Stephanie, but the reality is nothing we do is unique, and no experience is unshared. We are literally recycled stimuli that are subjected to constant stimulation Along the way, we establish patterned behaviors, reactions, and habits that essentially define our personalities and egos. We create relationships with other living organisms, acquiring likes and dislikes. We engage in experiences, reproduce, assign ourselves goals, and develop desires to distract ourselves, filling our time while we exist. And we repeat this ever-varying ritual and routine until we cease to be, repeating the cycle with our offspring. And while we tuck away memories and loved ones as we progress, none of it is actually significant. There was and there will always be someone who goes through the same things and shares a similar story. No life is truly your own. There's a reason there's a fucking rush hour; we're all just doing the same goddamn things.

Grade=C+

Sighing, doubling over, Dennis cradles his forehead into his hands.

"What the fuck is wrong with you?" he whispers, holding down his backspace button with his index finger, deleting his absurdist tangent about the human experience.

Clutching his brow and shaking his head, Dennis settles on a "B" along with an encouraging note, "Wow, this was compelling," even though he found her paper on a "life-changing cruise" the most vacuous bullshit he had ever read. He assigned a five-page paper on a seminal event, a formative occurrence, inspired by Frost's "Stopping by Woods on a Snowy Evening," which she then turned into a vapid anecdote of a five-day cruise she went on last summer with her cousins, drinking and smoking pot with a cute boy she met from Australia. And he knows his melodramatic digression about existence, simplifying it to a pattern of tendencies and behaviors isn't going to achieve anything except get him in more trouble, implicating himself with something tangible, incriminating writing, something he's been doing since he was a kid.

Exiting the grading portal, Dennis hovers to his desktop, selecting the Word document in the bottom right corner of his screen titled "Catharsis." It's the name of the new manuscript he's been working on, the title derived from the fact that it's the only thing bringing him relief or at least the only thing he was working on before he was reprimanded, another blemish to his tainted ego. So now he just stares at the display for a while, watching the white screen like freshly fallen snow since he can't bring himself to write a word, second-guessing his syntax structure and hating his limited adjective variety.

Closing his laptop and pushing it away, since he's tired of looking at fucking screens, he glances to his left, peeking at the vast windowed walls, a more appealing screen offering a view outside. The sun setting behind the building casts shadows on everything; creeping silhouettes configure against the pavement, colored with fading amber daylight. Dennis watches without turning his body so it doesn't look like he's staring at the older man at the bar top by the window.

Several napkins are haphazardly tucked into the man's collar as he scoops his soup, blowing on each spoonful before sticking it into his mouth. After every other mouthful, the man scans his vicinity, looking for a face to connect with and smile at. His slicked-back hair stays perfectly in place, even when he hangs over his soup bowl. Dennis has already smiled at him once, so he's not doing it again.

A middle-aged man passes by outside, along the sidewalk next to the window, pulled by the leash of his feisty pooch, a French bulldog tugging its way with energy similar to Cooper. Dennis watches wistfully, subconsciously frown smiling with pursed lips.

"Leave it," he hears the man bellow to the spastic dog, echoing through the prodigious glass window.

Dennis knows the dog is just excited to greet every person that it encounters, and the guy should probably think about shortening the leash to have better control. But Dennis knows he shouldn't be giving advice to anyone, since he can barely keep it together; he often thinks about his father and how he kept it together for years, never letting his retirement fund draining and financial bleeding from litigation affect his composure or destructively impact the family; the weight of the burden his father carried would have crushed Dennis instantly, and he knows it. The thought alone of losing his teaching job is crippling him; hypotheticals are just enough to ruin his present moments.

Wearing the blue Express sweatshirt he purchased seven years ago, thinking Renee would love the way it brought out the blue in his eyes whenever she resurfaced, Dennis is quickly running out of distractions, and he's always looking for distractions, distractions from distractions, a modern aesthetic man, anything to avoid boredom. So he turns his body completely, swinging his legs out into corridor from the booth. The hoodie strings are ragged, the tips peeled and fraying, the vibrant blue color, now a muted hue. He latches his eyes on the large canvas print hanging on the side wall, hunching over to peek his head out, sitting in an awkward position as he stares. His legs out in front of him as he imagines dangling them off the edge of an edifice, one with impressive facade windows, towering above a city below; and it's amazing how his heart flutters, feeling an anxious rush as if he's really hanging off the side.

The decorative wall displays contemporary art, lifestyle images with evocative photography. A commanding portrait of an athletic woman, her head tilted back and upward, obscuring her profile, holding her arms out in a celebratory pose as a raining waterfall splashes in the background, gushing waves spraying out, misting the rocks below. Across the scene in bold shadow letters it reads, "Travel." It's supposed to imbue inspiration, Dennis knows, but he's smarter than that, he thinks, to be motivated by oversized cliched photos and trite call-to-actions, because people think traveling is just some big escape, a way to get away and start new. But he knows there's no evading himself, no matter where he goes, no matter how far he ventures; there's no exit, there's no avoiding the mind.

The rectangular digital print adjacent to the waterfall image depicts a juxtaposition of pictures: a youthful pair embracing each other with adoring stares and innocent bliss on the left, and an older couple in the same endearing position, presumed to be the younger couple years later, on the right. Their hair is peppered, and creased skin surrounds their eyes, but there's still a youthfulness in their gaze, portraying a lifetime of infatuation. Dennis muses: no other emotion has been more commercialized than love, and it's a wonderful depiction. The shading is vivid with crisp white outlines, really leaving a lasting impression. But Dennis is getting so fucking tired of being retargeted by advertisements for the timeless concept, supraliminal shaming, making him aware of the consistently empty seat across from him. And it's the guilt that really gets him, knowing these are the days he'll eventually look back on, longing for his youth and his parents still being alive.

He probably should have ordered food, since he's already surveyed the coffeehouse, fixated on the overhead speaker, and listened to the scraping of spoons and forks against bowls and plates by the trash. He's already read his email, graded some papers, and inspected all the wall art, gulping his latte with unwitting haste. Now its discernible emptiness weighs in his hand, reflecting an internal hollowness, like a deep, darkened cavern, coercing him; he really has no choice.

Unlocking his phone with possessed fingers, drumming against the screen, he opens his Instagram, submerging himself in reels, a carousel of stories, eleven second clips of people's lives, characters he has either never met or hasn't seen in years. The stimulation is ceaseless, passing hours and occupying uncomfortable minutes. Dennis fucking hates himself for his dependency, its comfort and diversion from his own essence. He seeks insipid engagement, refreshing feeds to discover that people often marry their high school sweethearts because it's the only relationship they've ever known, afraid of being alone, finding comfort in familiarity and years of experience.

It's all pretty depressing, discovering how self-absorbed the average person is and how often people share countless cluttered story blocks of their daily routines. They record clips from a selfie view, usually hiding behind a filter that makes them more attractive, plumping lips and smoothing out wrinkles as they recap every little fucking thing that occurs, vignettes of vanity from self-proclaimed influencers, as if they're the most important people in the world. It's technological solipsism, something he even reinforces and encourages by watching regularly. And it's real sad to see how easily manipulated people are, sharing articles and news headlines without researching, believing anything that aligns with their confirmation biases and pushes propaganda to promote their associated tribes.

The acoustic chime of his phone sounds, sending Dennis into a frenzy as his dopamine surges, only to cease after he realizes it's a notification of Natalie selling more stuff from their home.

"Dude, what is your wife doing on Facebook?" Dennis texts John because these aren't significant items, they're odd knickknacks, like five-dollar placemats and napkins, children's coloring books and stuffed animals, exuding desperation and possible financial hardship.

And Dennis recognizes the growing tension in his chest, the heaviness and elevated heart rate, so he quickly tries to pull up a meditation video on YouTube, but he's subjected to several five second ads instead because he's not fucking paying for premium, exacerbating his condition as he clicks repeatedly to skip. And he's starting to notice a pattern, too many coincidences and inhibitors, like how he always seems to catch every red light when driving or always chooses the slowest check-out line in the grocery store, despite picking the shortest queue; the passive nihilism is bleeding into his perspective like a pernicious leak, and it's fitting because he's been feeling like the captain of a sinking ship. It's all extremely discouraging to think about, really, especially since he's been trying to quit the narcotics, and the drugs used to soften the blow from his intrusive thoughts, kinda like a chaser for hard liquor, so now he's too painfully cognizant of his own existence, swallowing burning sober realizations that just wreck him, like he's probably going to die poor, alienated, and alone.

A striking glare from the glass door swinging reflects on the floor, shaking him from his pessimistic haze as a trio of girls enter the Starbucks, one of which is Megan. He's surprised he recognizes her, since she's not wearing her school uniform, making it the first time he's seen her in plain clothes, and she looks nothing like a student. Her volumized hair curls against her shoulders, cascading down her back, drawing attention to her thin waist; her red shirt brightens up her brunette locks, and she leads the triad into the line to order like the red Power Ranger. Dennis peers out from his booth, undecided on whether he wants to be seen. She's smiling, laughing as she stands with her two assumed friends, whom Dennis doesn't recognize from school. Megan clasps her hands in front, clapping her palms as she speaks to her peers, reciting some anecdote, an amusing account they all appear to be engaged with. She's chirpy, animated, and undeniably attractive; her eyes gleaming, oozing with life as she advances in the line, and Dennis wonders how come she hasn't been to school the past few days, trying to get a closer look, which captures her attention as they lock eyes.

Megan waves fervently, smiling with excitement as she excuses herself from her friends, her face visibly flushed. She scurries over to him, smirking with radiant cheeks and endearing dimples. Her focus on him elicits a timid disposition in Dennis as he retreats into his booth, defenseless against her beauty and zeal.

"Mr. Claudon! How's it going?" she asks, pushing her hair over her ears, disposing a curious, attentive demeanor.

Standing in front of Dennis, she places her left arm on the table like a kickstand, breaking the proximity boundary with only a few inches of separation. She gazes at him with a warm, affectionate stare, as if genuinely happy to see him. It thaws the coldness of his mind, offering comfort, and he's thankful for her presence yet also shocked and uncomfortable with how pretty she appears.

"Is anyone sitting here?" she inquires, leaning toward the seat across from him.

"No, please sit," Dennis smiles, flourishing his hand as an invite.

277

"How are you, Megan? You haven't been at school the past few days. I was starting to become worried."

Descending into the booth, Megan's feet skim over his legs, grazing his shins as she positions herself on the leather cushioning.

"So, I went on vacation with my family down to Florida to see my cousins, but don't tell school because I called out sick," she rebuts, continuously combing her hair back, exposing anxious energy.

"I don't know. It's going to cost you," Dennis quips, moving his laptop away from obstructing their path across the table.

"Oh my God, I'll do anything," Megan chuckles, blushing with her declaration, pushing back creeping curls behind her ears.

A myriad of responses run through Dennis's head, varying degrees of appropriateness, but he composes himself, deflecting any untoward replies. Dennis discerns her peeking at the wholesome portrayal of a lifetime of love hanging on the wall, her eyes lingering thoughtfully, as if lost in the evocative art.

"Have you ever been in love?" Megan blurts out, her voice carrying a soft, ambiguous lilt, somewhere between a question and a statement.

"I have," Dennis responds without hesitation.

"Have you?" he mirrors the question.

Megan purses her lips before answering, her gaze meeting Dennis's with earnest intensity.

"I think I have," she replies, her eyes tender, as if unveiling a cherished secret.

"I just don't know how to make him love me back," she adds.

Dennis feels a warmth creeping up his cheeks, knowing he must shift the conversation before his emotions become too transparent.

"Men fall in love with what they see, and women fall in love with what they hear," he says abruptly, trying to change the subject.

"That's why women wear makeup and men tell lies."

Megan raises a curious eyebrow, leaning forward.

"Why do you think I'm wearing makeup right now?" she jests with a playful smirk, revealing her bright smile.

Dennis flashes a quick grin before letting his gaze drift toward the line, seeking a gentler transition.

"So, are you here with friends?" he inquires, changing the subject.

"Yeah, just some friends from my old school," she answers, looking at his laptop.

"What are you working on?" she asks, tilting her chin and placing it on her pedestaled palm; her face clear and contoured, polished and smooth, much more appealing than the throwaways he finds on dating apps.

"Trying to finish up my novel," Dennis mutters, uneasy with his confession, knowing his latest work needs serious revisions and colloquial synonym changes for better readability.

"Oh my gosh, are you like a real writer?" she perks up, fawning.

Her face beams, and Dennis nods, relishing his temporary aggrandizement, since the only other instance he refers to himself as a writer is in his Tinder bio.

"Can I read it? Please?" she insists, sitting up tall.

She places her hands on the computer willfully, with an enthralled, enthusiastic nature and a lively energy that reminds him of Christine.

Megan's leather bracelets and gilded bangles press against the back of the computer screen, provoking a fleeting image of her wrists pressed against his chest as he cradles her in front, penetrating her in a passionate pose. Dennis pauses, shaking the evocation from his mind, pondering over the consequences of sharing his manuscript, contemplating the overt cynicism and explicit language laced in the prose. But he really can't make a decision, since he's ogling at Megan's physical features; she looks nothing like a teenager but rather a sweet, sensuous woman with inherent charm; his libido is capricious, his self-restraint tenuous, compelling him to dismiss her. And it's weird for him not being high, feeling natural flutters of joy from an interaction.

"I tell you what, you go back to your friends, and I'll think about sharing some of the chapters with you," Dennis smirks with a reddened visage, avoiding any further engagement.

"Deal," she smiles.

Stepping out into the row in her coordinating red Chuck Taylors, Megan ascends from her seat, as she turns and waves.

"See you at school, Hemingway. Byyyyee," she drawls, looking over her shoulder and revealing her fit composition and jean-tight backside, as if luring him with her looks, leaving a helpless Dennis exposed.

Exhaling with relief, he resists watching her walk away, not wanting to be interpreted as checking her out. Instead, he checks his phone and uncovers a text from John:

"I have no idea," the apathetic message reads.

"Me neither," Dennis mutters, shaking his head as he gathers his belongings.

11. The Stranger

The uncomfortable silence was overbearing that night, keeping Dennis awake as he tossed and turned in bed, trying to shake off his pessimism, flipping back and forth on each side to prevent worrisome thoughts from sinking in. There was a good chance he was going to be arrested the next morning for attempted rape, underage consensual fondling or something, he speculated. He wasn't too familiar with the law, but he was pretty sure he was going to be locked up for years for his bold advances toward Miss Howard. He knew he wasn't going to last more than a month in jail either, since he'd seen snippets of the TV show OZ on HBO, never forgetting the graphic scene of a new male inmate who was in for drunk driving being forced to give a blowjob to his cell mate, sucking for only a few seconds before biting his dick off, spitting a chunk of penile flesh at the camera. And Dennis wasn't too sure if he possessed the poise or gumption to bite someone's cock off, but maybe he could settle on the death penalty and be put out of his misery, he pondered.

Dry eyes and stinging permutations beat him down for hours as he lay in bed until around 8 A.M., sliding down to the basement, which was still filled with the residual scent of sweet, ripened fruit, fragrant lust, evoking a bittersweet memory of molesting Susanna's delectable derriere, a heavenly haunch, the closest thing to complete euphoria he ever experienced. And the brooding weighed on him like a ton of bricks, forcing a slouch as he recalled how she had given him permission to call her by her first name. Logging onto AOL Instant Messenger, he eagerly pulled up his friend list to see if she was online, hoping to rectify the previous evening before the police showed up to haul him away in handcuffs in front of his parents. But she wasn't online; she was probably filing a police report, Dennis conjectured.

Leaden eyes and a heavy conscience weighed as Dennis tried to distract himself with whimsical games on eBaum's World. Impassive and on edge, he switched back and forth to his friends list, toggling between the two, until finally the sound of a creaking door rang from the speaker, prompting him to check immediately, which revealed the screen name "**Susanna_Howard98**" illuminating in green. The descending sensation of his heart plummeting encroached, like he had just been double bounced on a trampoline.

Unsure of his strategy, Dennis debated messaging her first, but he was addled, not sure what to even say, so instead he stared at her name, letting his eyes settle on the green, slipping into a fog as he theorized on the significance of the numbers "98" in her screen name. His concentration quickly wandered, moving to a new focus, the yellow stick-figure running man at the top of his friends list, abreast the big AOL lettering. His eyes transfixed on the big bobblehead, blurring the oval shape and empty yellow space; Dennis wondered what the yellow figure was running from, wishing he could also run away, rehashing in his daze, thinking he should have just let her leave after the movie.

A white box appeared, occupying his whole screen, lagging for a second as it loaded and formulated into a message bubble after a few seconds, accompanied by a chiming tone.

"**Susanna_Howard98:** Hey."

Dennis jolted in his pneumatic computer chair, stiffening in disarray, rubbing his eyes in disbelief.

"**Claudjr11:** Hey," he typed, letting his instincts take over as his abdomen filled with nervous flutters, anticipating her response.

"**Susanna_Howard98:** I'm sorry about last night."

Dennis exhaled, feeling a temporary relief, a mitigation of the anxious tension in his chest.

"**Claudjr11:** It's cool."

"**Susanna_Howard98:** I hope you didn't take it as rejection."

Typing out only a few letters, the beginnings of possible responses, Dennis erased his chat box, unable to conjure up a witty rebuttal. Reclining in his seat, Dennis placed his arms up, interlacing his fingers behind his head as he brainstormed. After ten uninterrupted minutes of unsuccessful meditation, another chime rang.

"**Susanna_Howard98:** We just couldn't do it there."

"**Claudjr11:** Couldn't do what?"

Dennis responded with fervent haste, hitting all the correct keys without needing to fix a typo.

"**Susanna_Howard98:** ;) oh well. What are you up to today? I have nothing planned..."

The abrupt transition perplexed Dennis, prompting him to throw his hands up and spring from his seat, trying to figure out what he missed, which implicit part of the dialogue he failed to decipher. He felt like a dehydrated nomad on a quest to quench his thirst in a barren desert, approaching a fresh brook only for the water to vanish just as he was about to drink. Scrolling back through the short conversation, Dennis tried to identify any area of communication he might have overlooked, but there was no oversight, she had completely changed the topic.

A perturbed disposition took hold of him, assailing Dennis with heated anguish, an angry internal hotness. He wondered how he could pivot back to his question, but after taking a few breaths and invoking a poised demeanor, he realized she had dealt him an ambiguous proposition, something he needed to capitalize on.

A few fraught minutes passed as Dennis deliberated on a plan; he knew he needed to allocate four to five hours, so he would have to get dropped off somewhere by his parents. He couldn't have her pick him up at his house because his mother always watched him leave, verifying he got into any car that picked him up, glimpsing through the dining room window. He couldn't go to a friend's house because his mom always made sure he entered the front door after dropping him off, always double-checking he got inside before driving away. Dennis knew he would have to be driven somewhere public but not too populated.

And just like an artist receiving precise inspiration and creative direction when needed, the perfect machination emerged from his mind.

"**Claudjr11:** I'm going to the library at 1 P.M. Maybe I'll see you there ☺ "

He typed before purposely signing off, cutting off the conversation.

####

The car ride over to the library was filled with anticipatory excitement and nervousness, hoping his plot would come to fruition and his mother would let him out without any further inquisition into his schedule.

"What time am I picking you up?" Mary asked, pulling alongside the curb and stopping in the yellow-lined designated fire zone space.

"Can you come get me at five? I'm going to have to do a lot of research, and I'll probably just write the report up in the annex afterwards."

"Ok," she smiled back with a proud countenance, protruding her chin forward in a nod, as if she was impressed with Dennis's ambition.

"I'm very proud of you for getting your work done on a Saturday. You're definitely preparing yourself for high school, aren't you?"

Dennis grinned, consciously fighting back a giggle, realizing his plot might provide several rewards, ranging from parental hubris to premarital intercourse. He told himself he was a genius as he closed the car door, lugging his backpack for dramatic effect into the library.

Pushing the doors open to the building with force, Dennis glanced over his shoulder, catching the fleeting bumper of his mother's car exiting the parking lot; the coast was officially clear. For some reason, Dennis imagined being greeted by a crowd of admirers ready to snap his photo as he entered the library, commending him on his ingenuous strategy, but he knew there was still much work to be done and the possibility that she wouldn't show up lingered in the back of his mind.

Peering through the glass windows of the library double doors, Dennis's heart yo-yoed as he scanned every car that passed in the parking lot; the silver Saturn sedan was embedded in his brain as he desperately searched for its presence. It wasn't much longer until the compact car idled by, revealing Miss Howard in the driver's seat, wearing large black sunglasses as if she were trying to thwart the paparazzi. Stepping out from behind the concealing doors, Dennis dawdled over to the passenger side door of her car, parked in the back of the lot, bending down to investigate the window.

"Need a ride?" she commented with a flirtatious, mischievous voice.

Pulling the door open, Dennis hopped into the passenger seat; Miss Howard immediately pushed his head down with a forceful shove from the back of his neck.

"Do you mind just hanging down low until we get out of town?"

"Sure," Dennis replied with a zealous smile, coiling down like a Jack-in-the-Box as they pulled out of the library parking lot.

He glanced up at Miss Howard on her veritable pedestal, taking in the exotic essence of the goddess that occupied his wildest dreams. After a ten-minute drive, she reached over, grabbing him by the arm with surprising strength. Dennis thought she clearly wasn't timid with touching him anymore.

"Ok, you're safe to sit up now."

Miss Howard's bulky sunglasses and voluminous, flowy hair obstructed her profile, scarlet coils escaping in all directions, creating a celebrity-like disguise.

"You can put on whatever station you want," she beamed, pointing to the radio dial.

Reaching into his pocket, pulling out a CD he had burned a few nights ago, Miss Howard being the muse for his song selections.

"I made you this CD," he replied with a tentative tone, his voice cracking, seeking her approval as he slid the CD into the slot.

And Dennis had completed almost one hundred dumbbell curls before he left for the library, so he tensed his arms, trying to emphasize their vascularity and definition; his short sleeve shirt slightly rolled at the edges, hoping to highlight his biceps as he flicked through the tracks, putting on "Wonderwall."

"Oh my God, I love this song," she declared, placing her warm, soft hand on top of his, turning the volume up to amplify the acoustic guitar; the electricity from her touch radiated to every corner of his body, tingling his insides like a feather, an organic intoxication.

"That was so sweet of you," she remarked, smirking; her glossy lipstick accentuating the plumpness of her lips.

And for a split second, Dennis envisioned her mouth around his penis, his untouched phallus finally submerged into a sensational niche.

The crisp, refreshing wind filled the car as they sped along the highway with the windows down, freezing time, creating a vacuum in existence, and Dennis delighted in the aura of being in the presence of a pretty woman, savoring her touch, a rainfall of affection. He felt like a man, unchained and limitless, a moment of liberation he decided was the feeling of complete happiness.

Sinking into the passenger seat, Dennis basked in the flutter of butterflies as he fixated on the New Jersey Devils bobblehead swaying from the rearview mirror. The goofy character sported a silly smile that seemed to grow wider with each bump the car hit, spinning aimlessly.

"Are you a hockey fan?" Dennis asked, pointing to the bouncing figure.

"What? Oh, no," Susanna chuckled, shaking her head.

"I just think he's cute. I kinda like him."

"You like the devil?" Dennis smirked, his grin sly.

"Maybe," Susanna quipped, teasing.

"Maybe you like the devil?"

"Yeah, what's there not to like?"

"Please, enlighten me," Dennis replied, leaning into the playful banter.

"Well, you know the devil was a fallen angel, right?"

"Huh?"

"Oh yeah," she continued.

"His name was originally Lucifer, and he was the most beautiful and powerful angel. God's perfect creation, until he got kicked out of heaven," she posited.

"And what's not to like about an underdog who rises above rejection, carving out his own kingdom?" she proclaimed, flashing a devilish grin.

"Interesting," Dennis muttered, contemplating her words and surprising answer.

Whipping gusts filled the cabin as she accelerated down the freeway, their hair blowing in all directions. Dennis alternated between watching his reflection in the side mirror and glimpsing Miss. Howard as she sang to the lyrics, pondering where they were off to, but it didn't matter. He was completely content with simply sitting next to her in the car and hoped the ride would never end.

"So, how long do you have today?" she asked, turning down the volume as they pulled off the freeway.

"I told my parents around 5 P.M. but I'd call them. Honestly, they were just thrilled I was going to library," he cackled.

"Ok, good," Miss. Howard smiled a devious grin, removing her sunglasses, revealing vivid blue eyes as bright as the ocean; she gazed at herself in the visor mirror, biting the bottom of her lip.

"Are you nervous?" Dennis bantered, turning toward her to show his best smile, a perfect opportunity to poke fun, his arms still flexed, exhausted with lactic acid building up.

Her eyes widened as she gasped, pushing the visor mirror up and away; she stared straight ahead, as if she were pondering the consequences of being discovered or caught by the police.

"We haven't technically done anything wrong yet," she resumed, turning toward Dennis, her eyebrows dancing as she spoke, exuding an excitable, manic energy, a stark contrast to the reserved demeanor she usually displayed.

As they pulled down a residential block of older colonial homes pushed closely together on opposing sides, Dennis questioned the proximity of each house, wondering why they were so close, since his home was much bigger and featured sufficient surrounding space.

"We're here," Susanna stated, turning into a long, extended driveway with several other cars parked haphazardly.

He wondered if they were all her vehicles, unsure if teaching was a lucrative career or not. And Dennis started feeling an uneasiness impinging his stomach as they parked, a nervousness, still trying to deconstruct her expression of "not doing anything wrong yet." The "yet" portion had a lugubrious effect, an ominous feel to it, like maybe they were going to do something completely irrevocable, something permanent with lasting impressions and ramifications.

Removing her seat belt and opening the car door, Susanna peered back at Dennis.

"Are you coming, nervous nelly?" she pried, smiling with a taunting mien.

His heart fluttered with insecurity and hesitancy, realizing his tentativeness was apparent. Exiting the car, Dennis followed Susanna, debating whether they were truly going to have sex. Something just wasn't quite right; in his dream, he was the assertive one, dominating her during intercourse, barking out orders and penetrating with confidence. But now, Dennis felt helpless, like a child who wandered off in a grocery store, away from his parents, panicking around strangers.

Advancing to the back of the home, Dennis tailed reluctantly, fighting off anxiety as he lusted over her voluptuous form. Her form-fitting jeans emphasized her full figure, hugging her hips to accentuate a slender waist and juicy rump. His hormones raged, eliciting a slight drool as he fixated on her features; his temporary meekness mitigated by his escalating libido. Forcing the back door open, shoving it with her shoulder, they proceeded inside.

"So, this is your house?" Dennis asked.

"No, it's a split family home, and I live downstairs," Susanna remarked as they stepped inside to a dated kitchen

Dennis didn't quite understand what that meant, wondering what splitting families entailed. But his focus shifted, quickly becoming concerned by the derelict conditions of her appliances, discernible dark blemishes in the corners of the white utilities, screaming for a clean wipe down. The vinyl flooring, detailed in a paisley print and dainty scrolls with muddled grout.

"Let me give you a tour," she smiled, pulling him by the hand.

Entering the adjacent room, suffused with the familiar fragrance of her perfume, they passed by a cramped bed pushed up against the wall and stepped onto a red, weathered carpet. It reminded Dennis of his great-grandmother's home, eliciting a forgotten fret as he remembered how she used to scare the shit out of him by telling him he'd develop worms in his stomach if he ate too many snacks before dinner. The wooden paneled walls exuded a claustrophobic '70s feel, emphasizing the compact proportions of the 700 sq. ft. room, which felt like it was closing in on Dennis. Ornamented with an array of old furniture pieces, the walls were styled with striking red, orange, and antique-colored hues, overwhelming stimulation with garish tones from all directions.

"Here, let's sit on the couch," she said, yanking him like an incessant current and positioning him down, relinquishing any control.

The antique sofa was detailed with soft felt upholstery, which was surprisingly comfortable. Small nailhead accents ran along the edges, and across from the couch was a miniature-sized TV. The whole room felt cramped, with her bed only a couple of feet away, creating a compressed atmosphere, disappointingly different from the spacious settings he fantasized about fornicating with her in.

"Do you want a beer?" she inquired, standing in front of Dennis as she glanced down at him, towering above as he lay scattered on the decorative settee.

Her robust bosoms hung over him, dangling like forbidden fruit; a pink bra strap slipped from underneath her top, commanding Dennis's attention.

"Do you have Corona?" he asked, recalling the only beer he could think of, even though he really didn't care for a drink.

He had tried beer before, sneaking sips of half-drunk bottles at holiday gatherings, always wincing after each gulp.

"I don't, but I'll definitely have that for you next time you come over," she replied, frowning slightly but then perking her puckered lips at the corner of her mouth.

She leaned forward toward Dennis, creeping in closer, exuding an exuberant energy, as if she were a wild lioness about to pounce on her prey. Her eyes widened, vast, and while she had been discouragingly restrained the night before, her playful, touchy demeanor was now completely transparent. She pulled Dennis by the collar, meeting his lips and kissing him with fierce execution, slipping her tongue into his mouth, sloshing it around from cheek to cheek. He felt confident with his reciprocating kiss and was reassured that she had already determined there would be a next time.

Her jasmine scent swallowed him once again, devouring him in her aroma as he sank into the soft fabric. He focused on her hips as she departed for the kitchen, coveting her sinuous cheeks, better than the porn star bodies he had seen in the few videos he'd watched.

Strolling back into the room from the kitchen, she placed an open Bud Light down on the coffee table with gilded banding.

"So, what do you want to watch?" she asked, squeezing next to him, her hands falling carelessly across him, eliciting a full erection as her sensuous smell lingered.

"Ohhh," she gasped, sitting up straight.

Dennis boiled with embarrassment as he covered his crotch with his hands.

"Wait," she declared, pulling his hands apart.

"What are we going to do about that?" she suggested facetiously, scooting closer as her hands ventured to his waist, prompting Dennis to spring up and pull his pants completely off before returning to the couch.

"I want you to just sit back," she smiled at his eagerness, whispering as she slithered down, keeping eye contact as she descended.

Her hair had been tied up in a ponytail since she left for the kitchen, perhaps in anticipation of the encounter, Dennis thought. Her hands progressed slowly, triggering heated tickles in his limbs and torso that amplified the closer she got to his pulsating pillar. She wrapped her right hand around his shaft like a zealous anaconda, caressing with a gentle yet firm undulation, twisting and turning with softness as she stroked. Dennis reveled in the heavenly pleasure, a foreign hand, not his own, grasped around his member, a transcendent sensation of a building climax.

She pulled his stimulated phallus deep into her mouth; her lips drawing tightly around his shaft as she bobbed, saliva soaking his foreskin. Dennis exhaled intensely, overwhelmed with unprecedented intense enjoyment. The heated suction and her humid orifice caused Dennis to quiver in euphoria, sending scintillas of delight up and down his legs. He released bated breath as he burst in her mouth after only a few divine moments, sending a hefty load down her throat. Moaning as she swallowed, she continued sucking with a devilish grin, relishing her control over him, his body convulsing from the sensitivity.

"You came fast," she whispered with a slight chuckle after releasing him, slithering up from the ground, gliding onto his chest.

Dennis breathed like a newborn, emerging into a novel realm, exposed to an existence enhanced by hedonistic indulgence; his lungs chugged from quick respirations; he felt light and dreamy, completely changed.

"I only came fast because you were really good, but I'm only getting started," he declared, reaching his hand down and around her back, sliding his fingers between her legs.

He clenched her crotch, a technique he witnessed male actors performing on their partners before intercourse in the pornographies.

"Oh wow," she responded, jolting up; his penis still throbbing, discharging residual semen.

Susanna retreated, pulling Dennis by each arm until they stood, embracing each other tightly. They kissed aggressively, their tongues slippery with spit, engaging in belligerent intimacy and fierce groping. Dennis grabbed at her goods, her sweet sultry scent dancing around him, enticing him further with every kiss and touch. Her felt-like milky skin pressed against his body as Dennis tore at her clothes, grabbing at her flank and digging to get to her distended backside, struggling to strip her from her bottoms.

They pulled and rubbed their faces together, kissing crazily. Susanna assisted Dennis in removing her pants, bending at the knee and parting for a few seconds to wrench them off before returning to their romantic rage. Breaking from his grasp once again, she gazed at him with a licentious look as she backpedaled, her lips pursed and her eyes fluttering, standing in her underwear. She moseyed over to the archaic stereo player stuffed in the corner on her nightstand, sustaining eye contact.

"This is my favorite song," she stated, turning to press the play button on the bulky box, hunching over to read the dimmed lights on the screen.

Dennis immediately disrobed his shirt and socks, rendering himself completely nude before the song even started.

With her eyes closed, Susanna turned back toward Dennis, holding her hands against her chest as the slow dramatic tones of a violin sounded from the speaker. She twisted and turned in a hypnotic state, synchronizing with each sound of the strings, rubbing her covered nipples. Staring lustfully, moving her eyes back and forth as she undressed, releasing her locks by pulling her hair tie with one hand, flipping her tresses around as they cascaded down. She then proceeded to pull off her panties, twirling the lacy bottoms before tossing them aside.

Swaying from side to side, she stared at Dennis, massaging her bosoms to the dramatic melody, until she finally freed her perky pink breasts. The realism of her naked body shocked him, as he usually had to hide or keep quiet whenever he viewed graphic imagery. But there it was, right in front of him, raw and explicit, bestial.

"At lastttttt…my love has come along," the speaker reverberated as a big grin emerged on Susanna's face.

The old cheesy romance song scratched, creating an awkwardness, causing Dennis to grow uncomfortable as he listened to the saccharine lyrics.

"My lonely days…are over," the song belted, temporarily tossing water on the blistering fire of his hormones; Dennis tried to ignore the kitschy tune and its overbearing sound, focusing on the naked Susanna bent over on the edge of the bed, crawling onto the mattress.

"So, how do you want to do this?" she asked submissively, turning her head back with her area exposed.

"I want you from behind," Dennis chirped without hesitation, imagining the countless videos he masturbated to.

"Come get me, tiger," she roared, squatting her bottom back, revealing her anatomy, an open womb, a punchy patch of multi-tonal skin.

Dennis wondered how his penis would be able to fit into the multitude of flesh folds, since he never really studied the insertion process in pornos.

"Just scoot on up, and I'll guide you in," Susanna whispered, luring Dennis in with a wink and flipping her hair back.

An uneasiness gripped Dennis, a fear of the unknown magnified by the haunting lyrics and tacky instrumental. The reddened vagina stared back at him, a daunting image, like a convoluted lotus head with harsh details amplified by the daylight, spotlighting its ornate intricacies and gradations. He had never seen a vagina before, and it was striking, more intense than its simplified presentation on the television screen. It scared him, reminding him of his inexperience and immaturity. Maybe he really shouldn't be there; maybe this wasn't right, he pondered.

"Should we…use a condom?" Dennis whimpered, pulling at his penis, still aroused despite his hesitation.

"Only if you want to," Susanna replied with a confused cadence, as if his question was foolish.

"We probably should," she added, sitting back on her hind legs.

"See the side table next to the bed," she instructed, pointing her index finger, possibly annoyed.

Dennis reached over, opening the drawer and pulling out an unopened box of Trojan ultra-skin condoms. He wondered why she had readily accessible condoms.

"Do you want me to put it on for you?" she offered.

Dennis shook his head staunchly, angered, perceiving condescension. He knew how to put a condom on; he had practiced. Dennis slipped his hard-on into the silicone wrapper with precise application, as if he were being graded.

"Now come here, let me guide you."

Moving onto the bed, creeping closer to her blushing gash, she reached between her legs and grasped his shielded hard-on. The cackling of rubber sounded as she wrenched his penis, maneuvering it inside her.

"I found a dream that I could speak to, one that I can call my own," the dramatic words of the singer echoed, pouring from the speakers, filling the room with a tawdry lover's ambiance.

Dennis closed his eyes as he entered her, gliding into her succulence, sliding inside. It was his first dip in the forbidden water, the onslaught of warm moisture and tightness enveloping him. Jarring his mouth open in a state of euphoria, he glanced down at the back of a glistening Miss Howard, absorbing the vision of his first sexual encounter, the loss of his virginity as he thrust.

Pounding his pelvis into her cheeks, slapping against her bare behind, his hands holding her hips, Dennis fixated on the fantasy transforming into fruition. The owning of another body, the exchange of fluids accumulating, noticing the creamy viscosity building up on his shaft every time he retrieved his sword from her sheath, increasing with each stab as Miss Howard erupted:

"Oh baby, fuck me, fuck me. I've been dreaming about you inside of me."

Shocked at her revelation of also dreaming about him, Dennis tried to think of something super depressing to delay his ejaculation, like the image of his rotting grandmother's corpse being consumed by maggots. But the rapture was too powerful. The ecstasy of his penis inside a warm, suctioning orifice captivated him in a cosmic state of pleasure and sexual stupor.

"And here we are in heaven, for you are mine at last," the creepy retro song continued sounding as Susanna huffed and hummed.

"Oh baby, it's just me and you," she muttered, reaching underneath to cradle his rising scrotum, approaching culmination.

The ancillary sensation of his testicles being cuddled stimulated his prostate tenfold, releasing immense built-up pressure. Right before he came, Dennis shook his head at the absolute absurdity of it all. The visceral, primitive nature of pounding flesh, fusing private parts to create friction as he penetrated the mature woman he dreamt about on her full-sized bed in her cramped apartment. His climax approached with incredible, mind-blowing elation, tinged with festering embarrassment, realizing his first sexual exploration was anomalous and how this occurrence would never be believed for the rest of his life, even if he tried to share the story. He was using her for pure sybaritic urges while she was living out some romantic fairytale, a quixotic consummation, something much deeper than sensual pleasure, something much more consequential, something that would change him forever.

####

The scariest thing about life is that there is no finish line, so you never really know where or how far you have left to go. Living out each day, assessing the past and present while eyeing the future, we choose directions based on impulse and prudence, decisions that guide the run. And it starts out like a sprint with fast-twitch ambition and energized strides, until the eventual fatigue sets in, a realization that it's actually a marathon, requiring both stamina and endurance, a steadier pace. And subconsciously, we're convinced tomorrow is expected, assuming there's always another day, more time to catch up. But you never really know if there's a lifetime ahead, another mile to go, or if you're experiencing your last conscious breaths, and maybe that's the beauty of it all.

Dennis sits back in his faux leather office chair, which took him two hours to assemble from Ikea. He considered purchasing from Wayfair but refused to pay for shipping and support a business he believed, based on his social media algorithm, was involved in sex trafficking. So, he settled for the difficult assembly, which included a one-year manufacturer's warranty. He stares at his computer screen, his coffee mug beneath his chin, the aromatic java notes wafting up. He's disgruntled with how his manuscript has devolved into a collection of short paragraphs, terse word vomit like some assortment of haiku poems. This most recent piece, he calls "Run." He thinks he has the right idea about running, even if he has bad knees, but he's not sure what he's running from or where he should run to, maybe into oncoming traffic.

Dennis deliberates on whether to add to his drabble or delete the micro-narration, envisioning it pinned to some motivational Pinterest board curated by a "conscious" influencer on a letterboard. But at least he's writing again, he concedes, and maybe he'll receive some feedback sooner or later, some direction on his short story from his sexually fluid superior, his adroit colleague Michael Fairchild.

He's thinking maybe he'll write another short story, but he has no interest anymore. He knows depersonalization is the first sign of a pathology, especially since every time he sits down to commence, he feels this urge to venture into his new one-car garage and not to program the LiftMaster so he doesn't have to keep manually opening and closing it. No, he feels a compulsion to start his vehicle up and sit in the passenger seat with the windows rolled down instead, inhaling exhaust with the garage door closed. He's read that it's quite peaceful to go out under the influence of carbon monoxide, drifting off to an eternal dreamland, and that the fear associated with approaching death just dissipates as the abundance of toxic fumes perfuse the lungs, creating a serene, undisturbed sleep as the breath slows, and it all ends, just like you're taking a nap.

He's hoping his Facebook will feature one of those memoriam mentions at the top, an in remembrance, like he's seen on the profiles of deceased people he knows. He wonders how that notification gets triggered or added to someone's page; he thinks someone in the family has to reach out to Mark Zuckerberg directly to make that change. So he's envisioning his will go years without any sort of notice on his passing since he'll never be able to explain to his parents how to log onto Facebook, let alone contact anyone.

The bags of groceries still sit by the door, two large mesh carry bags piled with items from Costco. He should probably put the eggs and yogurt away before they spoil, he thinks, knowing he'll have to go back to the store this week. He never seems to get everything on his list, always missing one or two items he discards in the check-out line, stressing about spending too much, trying to save money at the last minute. He usually chucks the string cheese or the avocados, leaving them by the register, a tragedy because he really enjoys guacamole and finger food.

Dennis perks up from the desk he bought on Amazon to finally address the warming groceries. The desk, a functional design made with laminate wood, dual side storage shelves, and an aged gray finish with a dark metallic frame, was put on a credit card he just opened with 0% APR. Along with a bunch of other furniture pieces and home décor items, he's starting his own life, and everything has to be new, he decided. He doesn't care if he's up to five grand in debt because he'll just open another credit card with 0% APR and start charging things to that card while paying off the other. Then, he'll open another card in a few months, so every time an annual percentage rate is expiring, he'll have another card to put expenses on to avoid interest, jumping from one credit card to another like some financial ninja warrior.

His phone is in his hand, retrieved from his pocket with eagerness before he can tend to the mesh taupe bags packed with produce and household essentials, like Spring-inspired plugin scents to infuse his home with the floral essence of the blossoming season. He thinks a refreshing fragrance emblematic of renewal will channel into his life, and if his place doesn't smell magnificent at all times, he's just going to lose it. He still can't endure more than three minutes alone without his phone, fixating on dopamine feeds and updates to keep him occupied.

He's staying off Facebook for a couple of reasons, and no, it's not because he cringes every time Tommy shares some rambling post. Nope, he's creeped out every time he sees Susanna's eight-year-old kid, uploads of her and her geeky husband wearing a fanny pack and New Balance sneakers gathered around the center island in their kitchen, conducting a science experiment for Harrison's school. Despite his old man name, Harrison looks like a cherub in glasses with pebbled teeth and a goofy smile, just like his father. And Dennis wonders if the child will fornicate with his English teacher in six years to complete the cycle of life, or maybe he's supposed to seek him out and molest him, return the favor. He's not sure how it should go for it all to make sense.

It's been a rough couple of nights for Dennis, barely getting any solid REM sleep, as he's been anguished by a new recurring dream. No, it's not the one where he's back in college, forgetting something dire like a final exam or a class he's neglected to attend, eventually causing him to fail out. This one is more vivid and debilitating: he meets up with Renee and Carl for some strange reason, and they're having cordial dialogue, catching up like long-lost friends. Secretly, Dennis tries to gauge whether there's still chemistry between him and Renee when Carl's not paying attention. This sends a rancorous pain into his stomach's pit, waking him up instantly and ruining his morning with a nauseous dream hangover.

It feels like an augury, he thinks, a push to check Carl's Facebook since Renee's information is private. But he knows if he continues the investigation, it'll only be a matter of time before he uncovers that she's pregnant. And that's a serious ramification, something permanent that can't be annulled, unlike a marriage.

Kicking the loaded soft-sided carriers across the floor to the kitchen, inching along as he scrolls, Dennis smiles at a new "like" notification that pops up in the top right-hand corner: a miniature banner with a white number one next to a heart, a prompt elicited by "MegsGotit," which he quickly recognizes as his student

Megan. She's found his Instagram, finally, even though she hasn't requested to follow him. He suspects she accidentally liked his post while browsing his profile, since the image she liked was a month old: a picture of the anthology of Edgar Allan Poe lying on his nightstand. He wonders if she's aware she liked his photo, whether she'll request to follow him, or maybe he should request to follow her, since her account is private. He'd love to stalk her photos. Dennis knows there's a high probability she liked his post knowingly, attempting to provoke him into following her, the quintessential cat and mouse game.

The bags finally reach the refrigerator, sliding across the floor as he thwacks the side of his foot against the paper towel pack stuffed into the side of the carrier, providing a soft impact for his forceful punts. Reaching down into the oversized sack, shoving the crowded contents apart, he pulls out an overturned pallet of steaks and a package of blueberries that was concealed under the white liner at the bottom of his bag. Chuckling mischievously as he retrieves his loot, admiring his guile and audacity, Dennis puts the steaks in the freezer and tosses the berries into the back of the fridge. He doesn't care if he's considered a petty thief; technically, he's just proficient in finding loopholes and exploiting them, like recognizing how inattentive the attendants are in the self-checkout lines and how easy it is to bring an outside nontransparent grocery bag and tuck away goods before approaching the checkout. All he has to do is scan three or four items and bring the bag to the end of the conveyor belt, tossing the purchased items on top of the hidden commodities. He doesn't feel bad about it, nope; he spends at least $150 every time he shops there, so he's developed his own rewards program. It's called external shrinkage in corporate terms, and he feels good about it, just like he does about not recycling. It's his way of getting back at the world, he believes.

It's almost 4 P.M. by the time he organizes his merchandise, tossing the eclectic assortment of items he purchased into random kitchen cabinets and drawers, unconcerned with their placement. The only real area he takes pride in is his linen closet, which he's stocked with an abundance of cleaning supplies and home essentials like WoodWick candles for a soothing ambiance, paper towels, toilet paper, tissues, Shout, Febreze, toothpaste, and more.

He'd love to vacuum and Swiffer his floors for the fourth time this week despite there being little to no visible dust or debris present, but he's pressed for time, since he's supposed to go over to his parents' place for dinner. He's been blocked from using Bumble, apparently reported for a cavalier remark. He asked a girl who claimed to not have any social media if she was an overweight black non-binary individual named Destiny with a septum piercing attempting to catfish him, a pretty innocuous comment, he thinks, but it's clearly too incendiary for an application that elevates superficiality to massive proportions, basing attraction solely on physical features.

It's probably for the best though, having one less app to frequent, and he's still got Tinder to engage in caustic dialogue and cynical conversations. These either end in a heated debate about some arbitrary infraction, like incorrectly using "your" or "you're," or asking banal questions, like "What do you do for fun?" and "What are your favorite movies?" because he's answered them all with a variety of responses. Diversity is a good thing from what he's been seeing on social media. From knitting wool cardigans while sitting cross-legged, listening to Sisqo's *Enter the Dragon* album to naked underwater basket weaving, playing tetherball with blind autistic children, and reading daily obituaries to guess the causes of death, Dennis has shared an assortment of creative hobbies and fabled movie titles like "Good Will Gathering" and "Armadillos on a Plane." His irreverent replies have either yielded awkward fellatio or being blocked/unmatched, always cutting off communication before emotions materialized but still gaining a follower on Instagram before moving on to the next classified, collecting profiles like trophies.

Venturing into his master bathroom with old bulb vanity lights, which he fucking hates but has promised himself he'll update as soon as he finds a contractor he can verify with at least ten five-star reviews on Google, he twists the faucet to warm the water up to shave. The whooshing waterfall sprays like a spastic sprinkler, gushing into the basin; the steam of scorching water rises, settling on the mirror, creating an opaque dew on the glass surface. He runs the badger barber brush under the faucet, blasting the dried, crusted soap suds off. Swishing it into the small wooden oval dish, mixing and swirling the soap to create a lather, Dennis glances into the foggy mirror as he applies the shaving cream. His face becomes muddled, but his bright eyes remain apparent; the water runs, boils, and steams as it pours into the sink.

He remembers his freshman year in college, how he and his floormates would huddle in the bathroom under a similar faucet of hot flowing water, taking hits from a colored ceramic bowl. They'd run all the faucets as high as they could to mask the marijuana smell with steaming condensation, always alternating a lookout amongst each other every ten minutes for lurking RAs. Blowing clouds of weed smoke into the running water, the smog turned into fleeting vapor as the cackles of friends sounded in the echoing chambers of the capacious bathroom. They'd float above in their elevated states, getting higher and higher with each toke, laughing at the odd pronunciation of simple words like "faucet" and "water," articulating with flippant drawls: "FAW-SET," "WAH-TERR" they'd repeat, chuckling uncontrollably as they passed the bowl. Eventually, their frivolity would shift to more profound dialogue, discussing their ridiculous interpretations of life's meaning, their futures, aspirations, and how they couldn't wait to be on their own, having the freedom to do whatever the fuck they wanted, completely unaware that those casual nights would become their best memories.

Dennis is lost in his distorted reflection, dripping with shaving soap from his face. He runs the stainless-steel blade under the water, slipping into a vivid state of contemplation, realizing all of the people he experienced his most cherished memories with are no longer in his life. His grip tenses around the razor, and a compelling suggestion creeps into his mind, reminding him he's fucked up everything that was ever good. It persuades him to remove the metallic blade from his handheld razor and press it against his wrist. The sharp burning sensation of scorching steel against his skin stings, a brash reminder of mortality. He presses the blade harder into his pulse, not sure exactly how to execute exsanguination. The mist grows, surrounding Dennis as he sweats, and he can no longer see any semblance of his reflection, losing himself in the brume.

"Push harder, do it already. You'll never be okay," an antagonizing voice whispers, sending goosebumps down his neck.

It's a terrible vision that overcomes Dennis, a prescience: splatters of blood sprayed all over the bathroom, indicative of panic and pain as his body lays on the floor, bleeding out on linoleum tile with his eyes open. But he knows he's not going to die from a self-inflicted wound. And no, it's not because he doesn't possess the temerity to sever both his wrists. It's because he knows it's going to be an overdose in a few years, after his parents have passed, on the sedatives he's been prescribed or the magic mud he's been sipping on, ample servings of Kratom tea, which he discovered on Reddit as a recommendation to emulate opioid effects. He can purchase this new vice at the local smoke shop for only sixty dollars since it's not FDA-regulated, enough to last him a few weeks at ten grams a day, lifting the heaviness on his heart and the tension in his shoulders while muting the critic in his mind, like he's floating on a cloud of content.

It's really the only other option at this point, since he doesn't know any drug dealers and he'd rather not rob his notorious students, raiding lockers while they're in gym class. He's been a bit loopy with his new dosages, unsure of the consequences of ingesting multiple controlled substances, combining an herbal stimulant with a depressant. He thinks he's either approaching psychosis or enlightenment; he's not quite sure. The hedonic wheel is his major problem, he believes, and he needs to become more cognitive of his tendencies to revert to disappointment if he wants to improve his intrusive thoughts or at least that's what he's been reading. It's pretty much science, you know: everyone's happiness is adaptive, a survival technique. That's why on average, a lottery winner and an amputee will experience the same level of happiness years after the drawing or the tragedy, because psychologically, everyone eventually adjusts their happiness stability to suit their situations. So he's thinking maybe he'd be the same way, even if he wound up with Renee. It's pretty troublesome, he thinks, how checking off milestones seems fruitless, unable to alleviate the throes of meaninglessness.

He's also thinking about the latest chapter he read in the Krishnamurti book earlier, but he can't really recall the entire analysis on fear. Something about fear being the root of the most harmful thoughts, despite being another psychological survival tactic, ingrained in the past, based on experience or at least preconceived notions. Fear can cripple the present with anxiety because we're all just afraid of the future, afraid of uncertainty, fraught with worry about the imminent and possible. He knows all of this, really, he completely grasps the antagonism of the mind, and how he needs to free himself from himself, being too reactionary to his thoughts, but he just can't execute. He can't implement the insight and make an update to his software.

He's floating in the fumes in the bathroom until the glow of his phone rattling on the vanity catches his attention. It's a text notification and a missed call, a text he sent to himself about an hour or two ago, some arbitrary soliloquy on wanting to buy a goldfish. But the missed call is shocking; it's from Christine. He grabs his phone, not to launch himself into a fidget spinner of social media cycling, opening Instagram and exiting to open Facebook, then exiting to open Gmail, restarting the pattern by opening Instagram. And no, it's not to upload a story to see who's still watching him, because it's truly a tragedy if no one is paying attention. No, he stares at his phone to make sure he's not hallucinating, that Christine legitimately called, and she did; her name appears just as every number stored in his phonebook does, first and complete last name. Wiping away the fog on the mirror, smiling, he decides he'll call her later after he's shaved, visited his parents, and not killed himself.

Arriving at his parents' home for the first time since he moved out, even though he's been out for a month now and swore he'd come over for dinner at least once a week, he greets his mom at the door, holding out a bottle of White Zinfandel with a guilty smile, cheesing teeth.

"What's this, honey?"

"It's a bottle of wine."

"Are you going to drink it?" his mother asks, kissing him on the cheek and holding the door open as he enters.

"Maybe. I brought it for us," Dennis says as he hugs his mom.

"You didn't need to bring wine," she replies, pushing the front door closed but struggling to get the deadbolt to catch as she attempts to shove the door with inadequate force.

"I'd never come empty-handed. I'm not like John," Dennis jokes, jostling the door closed with a shoulder and taking control of the handle to get it to shut.

"Who is it?" his father cries from the kitchen.

"It's Den," she turns, shouting with her arms flayed.

"Who?"

"Your father is in the kitchen, and he's having a hard time hearing," she remarks with a frustrated tone, smirking, shaking her head.

Following his mother, Dennis stops to glance at the accent wall filled with digital prints just outside the kitchen, recalling how Christine gifted his parents most of the pictures hanging, the sleek shadow box ones. She knew how much his mother adored photos. The ones with Christine in them are still on display, three pictures of her with the family from the last three years they were together. Christine is not a topic that's really been talked about since they broke up, which has made it a bit easier for him, even though he knows his mother is disappointed. He smiles at the images; he wouldn't want it any other way. She looks happy in every pic on the wall, and he's glad she's still there every time he comes home because there's a vivid memory of Christine that's burned into Dennis's brain, one he knows will haunt him for the rest of his life: her melting in front of his eyes, her hair ruffled from hyperventilation, her mascara a mess from crying, standing with her arms crossed in a defensive pose, reflecting her hurt as she quivered, a crushing visual of a broken angel, a beautiful soul crumbling.

"We're not all perfect, Dennis, and I'm not sure if you'll ever be okay with that," her voice still trembles, echoing in his ears sometimes, when it's quiet.

And he's really hoping her phone call wasn't a butt dial from earlier and maybe she'll speak to him; maybe there's still time to make it right or make right by her. It's really exciting too, the new development of Christine reaching out and how a simple missed call can create hope, brightening things for a bit, like a tighter turn on a flickering light bulb. He hopes to hold onto the feeling for as long as possible because the bliss of optimism is far more intoxicating than any narcotic and more potent than any stimulant he's ever tried.

The sizzling of breaded chicken being cooked resounds, and Dennis views his mother sitting at the kitchen aisle, his father slogging away at the stove with an apron on.

"You know, your brother John is out with Natalie today looking at new houses," Mary announces, flipping pages in a magazine.

"Hey, Dad," Dennis says, wrapping his arms around his father's shoulders, pulling him into this chest; his upper body feels slim and angular, like he's lost weight since the last time they hugged.

He's indirectly to blame, he knows because he always made his father a sandwich for lunch, so he's pretty much a fucking piece of garbage for neglecting his nutrition; his nose starts itching, his sinus stimulated as the tears begin to formulate.

"Oh, I didn't even hear you come in," Russ replies, jumping backwards into Dennis's arms, chuckling.

"He's really having a hard time hearing," Mary repeats, this time with a deliberate tone, pausing from her page turning.

"I heard you, Mom," Dennis responds, sneering at his mother as he pushes back on his escalating emotion; her gray, moody eyes gaze back at him; a dark blemish about the size of a quarter pinned on her right cheekbone is highlighted by the overhead recessed lighting.

"What's that spot on your face?"

"Oh, it's just something I had removed," she waves her hand at him, returning to her magazine.

"What is it?" Dennis asks, shifting to a concerned manner, moving closer to inspect his mom.

The splotch saturated in cover-up makeup, beige powder tamped into the creases on her face, his mother's attempt at concealing the mark.

"It's just a little melanoma, nothing really," she says, patting the area with her index finger, deflecting attention.

Dennis holds his mother's hands, moving them away from shielding her face, and she turns her head, avoiding eye contact as if she's ashamed. His mother's arms feel light, brittle in his hands, like she's been shrinking, and he sees the area that's been scraped, her cheek has a small crater from where the cancer cells were dug out.

"How come you didn't mention this? We talked a few times this week," Dennis pries, letting his mother's arms go.

His face scrunches, he's bothered; his parents are withering away, he concedes, and he's been too busy manufacturing hypothetical problems to realize he's not paying attention to the important things.

Mary looks away, like a timid child, and it's a feeling that never feels right, since he still always feels like a kid, the reality that the caretaker roles reverse, and he needs to be the one to take care of his parents.

"John and Natalie are looking to move," Russ announces, turning to place a plate of cutlets on the counter.

"Apparently, Natalie was out looking today."

"I thought you said the two of them were out looking at houses today?" Dennis asks, confused.

"Oh, yeah, well just Natalie," Mary mutters, taking the plate of breaded chicken, holding the sides of the plate in a certain way, her elbows angled out to ensure the greasy paper towel flaps don't touch her hands or sleeves.

"She was out looking by herself?"

His mother gives a perfunctory nod, placing the stacked plates in the center of the table.

"And where is John today?"

"He's home, watching the kids," Mary replies, holding out an outstretched smartphone.

"I'm having trouble with my Starbucks app," she sighs, positioning herself alongside Dennis so they can look at her phone together.

"Your brother is home today," Russ interrupts, stirring the sauce.

"They are looking to move," he adds, bouncing skittishly from saucepan to the last simmering cutlets.

"He knows, hon," she remarks, rolling her eyes.

"This is what I mean with your father," Mary whispers, speaking out of the corner of her mouth as if Russ has even a remote chance of hearing what she says.

"I couldn't use my Starbucks app the last time I went in. It says I need a password," she pivots back to technological frustrations.

"Natalie went out by herself to look at houses," Russ discloses with his back turned, still stirring the pot.

"Russ, he knows," Mary says as she taps him on the back.

"What?" Russ says, bouncing up from patting the last of the cutlets.

"Hon, he's trying to help me with my app," she whimpers, flipping her hand out in annoyance, a back swipe at the air.

"Well, what's your Starbucks password?" Dennis asks, attempting to log in with her email address and the only password she's ever used for any technology: tiffany10, inspired by the name of the beagle his parents had when he was a toddler, the only dog they ever owned.

But Dennis can't remember if it's a capital "T" or if there's a special character after the zero, like an asterisk or an exclamation point, maybe an additional two numbers to expand it past ten characters. He told her to write it down the last time he had to reset her password, and he usually has to do this every two months, so you'd think he'd write one of her passwords down by now. But he's too distracted with tumultuous thoughts, possibilities, like maybe he's going to die completely alone.

"I don't know. I thought you knew it?" his mother sighs, throwing her hands up in protest.

"What?" Russ exclaims, turning away from the stove.

The swoosh of the front door opening sounds, accompanied by a double beep, the installed alert for any door or window being opened in all the units of the fifty-five and older community. John barges in, stumbling into the kitchen, opening the refrigerator door to retrieve a Coke Zero, which he chugs.

"How did it go? Did you guys see anything good?" Russ asks, smiling as he holds a plate of freshly cooked cutlets, his apron riddled with grease splatter spots, his oval bifocals slipping down the bridge of his nose.

"Where is Natalie and the kids?" Mary asks.

Standing in front of the center island, his soda on the marble slab, John bites his nails, gnawing with a spastic vigor, an anxious mannerism Dennis recognizes.

"What's going on, John?" Dennis asks, stepping toward him, attempting to make eye contact.

Hunching over the center island, pivoting from biting his nails to drinking his soda as if he's relying on carbonation as sustenance and comfort, swimming in his oversized clothes, his Sherpa sweatshirt draped over him like a cloth. John continues his anxious chew, spitting his fingernails like sunflower seeds.

"John?" Dennis demands.

"Natalie and I are getting a divorce."

"What?"

The shrills of Mary's scream resound, a visceral screech, a similar shriek to the indelible shout she emitted when a sheriff knocked on their door years ago, serving them a summons for Russ's lawsuit and taking inventory of their possessions. Only this time, the yelp is met with the commotion of a plate of cutlets slipping out of Russ's hand, crashing onto the floor, sending shards of ceramic and thin, crispy chicken breasts in every direction.

12. Brave New World

The days passed, and the rendezvous continued. Every weekend, Dennis invented new projects that required research at the library: a book report on Thomas Jefferson, a paper on World War II, a presentation on Christopher Columbus, even at the end of April, long after the holiday. He conjured up assignments that demanded several unaccompanied hours each Saturday so he could escape to his sybaritic world. Occasionally, they'd meet during the week, especially after he downloaded a new pornographic video on Kazaa, enduring a grueling nineteen-hour wait, eager to try something new.

As the school year drew to a close, Dennis knew his report card would soon be finalized. If he didn't earn straight As, his parents would start questioning his routine library visits. To avoid suspicion, he read and studied with determination, ensuring his grades were good. He immersed himself in the American Revolution, the Battle of Bunker Hill in 1775, and how it confirmed that any reconciliation between England and the American colonies was no longer possible. He also dedicated focused hours to studying FDR's New Deal when necessary. He'd memorize all of the series of programs, public work projects, financial reforms, and regulations it enacted if it meant he could continue to shove his erect penis all the way into the mouth of the English teacher at Williamson Middle School, pushing it as far back as it could go, tickling his bulging mushroom head against her uvula until he discharged a body-warming soupy load into her throat. He was willing to put in the extra hours, solving practice problems for algebra, finding the value of both X and Y if it meant he could continue exploring and sinking his throbbing rod inside her anus, sucking it in like a vacuum because the rectum isn't like a vagina, he learned; the sphincter doesn't self-lubricate, so applying ample lubrication is a necessity for a seamless insertion. And it was a different sensation, he perceived, a tighter suction with more friction, causing euphoric tension in his scrotum when he ejaculated.

Two months of continuous sexual trysts taught Dennis the meaning of life, instilling a purpose, he thought; seeking hedonistic impulses, indulgent pleasures, disconnecting the body from the mind, so it could experience pure undisturbed gratification and bodily release. It influenced all aspects of his life too, no longer invested in video games or hanging out with friends, like a typical teenager. No, he even opted out of PAL baseball because he didn't want to devote his weekends to anything less than pornographic debauchery.

Yep, he was way more interested in fulfilling every single sexual fantasy he could imagine, losing himself in the ecstasy of carnal delights, focusing on transcending previous climaxes, surpassing each orgasm with something more perverse, more degrading. Relishing his burgeoning sexuality, the newest discovery of human engagement, purely adulterous copulation, using someone else's body for pure pleasure, disconnecting a person from servicing orifices. Dennis embraced his id, giving this psychic apparatus full control, an early programming to seek urges, sexual satisfaction at all costs, like most adolescent boys. But there was nothing typical about his circumstance. His feat of breaking the barriers of teacher and student appropriateness was unfathomable and unrealistic, accomplishing the impossible, attaining the unattainable, unaware of the psychological ramifications of realizing an anomalous fantasy at a budding age, instilling distorted, quixotic expectations of the world.

A girl was all he needed to feel good, he established at a young age, continuous sexual satisfaction. He wondered how long this would go on for, how long the encounters would occur; he hoped he'd always have a girlfriend, a sex doll for his needs, his inflated ego suggested. Their online conversations continued, but nothing ever happened at school; Susanna was adamant about keeping their activities strictly extracurricular.

They'd pass each other in the hallways without a glance, except for when she had ventured further down the corridor. He'd always turn to watch her walk, savoring the sight of her conquered territories, igniting his fancies, evoking the sounds of her sensual moans, images of her cardinal curls whipping against his face as she bounced up and down on his lap. Evocations of her marshy yoni soaking his concrete tool consumed him during the day, her juices trickling down his legs, pooling in his taint. He pined for the panting, heated breath, and sweat meshing together as he counted down the minutes until their dalliance could resume on the weekends. He acted on impulses during intercourse, like spitting on her anus as he penetrated her from behind, massaging saliva into the starfish with his thumb, or how she synchronized intense moans with each of his ejaculates, swallowing his seed while maintaining eye contact.

His parents didn't suspect a thing, but he always prepared himself for an interrogation when they picked him up, entering the car with papers tucked under his arm, as if he had just completed an extensive project. He had several facts readily accessible to recite, just in case he was asked about his topic. Like clockwork, he'd get dropped off around 11:30 A.M. on Saturdays, and Susanna would pull in around 11:40, returning him to the library around 5:30 P.M., leaving just enough time for his mom to swing by fifteen minutes later to scoop him up. By the tenth weekend, Dennis had started to care less about being prepared, ditching the bogus research papers and sometimes not even bringing a bookbag. He'd become too confident, brazen, like a seasoned criminal becoming comfortable with his craft, associating normalcy with their relationship as his fanciful existence persisted.

The brisk summer breeze of the morning tickled his skin, sending shivers along the back of his elbows and trickling down his forearms as he sauntered to the murky glass doors of the library. The redolence of sunscreen permeated the air, leaving a salty scent in his nose, reminding him of the shore. His mother waved to him as she pulled out of the parking lot. The buzzing of cicadas thrummed, warming up their vocal cords for the day, a soft humming practice.

Dennis figured he'd take a leak before Susanna picked him up, so he ventured inside the cooled library, entering the dampened atmosphere. The air's moisture brushed against his face as he passed by the open-concept library space, a rough-piled carpet ornamented with aged wooden desks and chairs. The discernible scent of wet paper infiltrated his nose, wiping away the nostalgic fragrance of summer, like there was a stack of molding paperbacks stashed in the room somewhere. Dennis stopped by the same open space before leaving, after his tinkle, noticing an elder librarian organizing books with her glasses attached to her chain necklace. Oversized bifocals sat on her nose, causing her to tip her head backward to get a clearer glance at the titles. Her purple cashmere sweater, besides being decorated with two antique silver brooches, was half-buttoned, like she had given up during the process. Dennis thought she was adorable, smiling at her momentarily, long enough to draw eye contact. She kind of reminded him of his grandmother, although any cute old lady seemed to remind him of Mi-Ma.

"Can I help you, sir?" she announced with an aggressive tone, scrunching her face as she addressed him.

Attempting to diffuse the unwarranted hostility, Dennis flashed another warm smile, revealing his straight, appealing teeth, his most alluring feature, besides his eyes, as his grandmother always told him.

He surveyed the open room and saw there was only one other person in the library, a kid he recognized from school. This outsider always wore Slipknot T-shirts and spikey bracelets from Hot Topic. He didn't talk much, and Dennis couldn't remember his name since they seldom interacted. It used to be something unusual, like Helberth, and the kid was always self-conscious about answering to it during teacher attendance, which may have been the catalyst for his introversion. He eventually changed his name to something like Richie or Mickey, some other Little Rascal-like name, but it didn't change much. He still sat by himself at the lunch table, voluntarily sequestering in the corner as he drank his miniature milk carton. The damage was already done; he was still always Helberth, unable to escape his moniker. Two classmates living antithetical lives, Dennis decided, standing and staring at the loner.

"Sir, can I help you?" the crumpled-faced curmudgeon invaded again, unaffected by his infectious smile, immediately spoiling his affinity for her.

A ferocious desire to tell her to "fucking eat shit" slipped into his cerebral cortex, almost sneaking out of his mouth.

"No, you really can't," Dennis rebutted before turning and leaving the library.

He was a beer drinker, he thought to himself, always having at least two or three on the weekends. Even though he wasn't entirely fond of the taste, he craved it every time he went to her place. He felt like a real man whenever she came back from the kitchen with a cold one for him, setting it down on the haggard coffee table, the blue Bud Light can moist with condensation, just like in the commercials.

He always swished some mouthwash before he returned home, but not because he was afraid of being caught drinking. His mother's dad had died from alcoholism, and he didn't want to elicit any emotional triggers. He never really felt the urge to drink, except when he was around Susanna, but his thirst could never be quenched.

Kissing and fondling, slapping tongues, they ran rampant hands all over each other's bodies, like ardent searchers, exploring each nook and crevice with curious fingers, nascent foreplay. Tugging at her waist, attempting to unbutton her pants, Dennis could never execute a seamless removal, always requiring assistance, but it wasn't his fault. It was her hourglass shape and voluptuous rear that demanded extra effort to navigate. And he'd feel an intense burst of fluttering in his chest as she pulled off her pants, a nervous excitement, the denim peeling off from her smooth skin, like the skinning of a succulent fruit. Her shins still shining from freshly applied lotion as she untangled her legs, revealing her open womb, a jarring visual for an inexperienced adolescent.

He'd proceed with caution, smiling nervously as she beckoned with her index finger, extending and retracting, signaling the only unenjoyable moment of his encounters. Exchanging sexual acts in a promiscuous barter, all he had to do was lick the conical flaps of flesh until she signaled him to stop. This was usually preceded by a quick convulsion and an increase of perspiration on her inner thighs. She would then pull him up from below, offering anything he wanted in return, teaching him the art of reciprocation, acts of service. Perturbed by the piscatorial pungency, Dennis tongued the lotus folds of flesh, dabbing only the outside layers, avoiding the acrid, moist center, evading its sour stickiness. He'd lick until his tongue felt like sandpaper, burnt and sore, and it wasn't all bad, really. He learned delayed gratification, the genesis of industrious behavior, instilling a work ethic to achieve greater rewards in the long term, like attaining the divine sensation of emptying inside Susanna's warm mouth. Her lips sealed around his shaft, sucking while she moaned, his legs quaking on the couch, his body quivering with choppy breath, her crystalline eyes always fluttering at his reaction.

"I have a surprise for you," she whispered, rising from the ground, wiping the corners of her mouth; her lips flushed and her eyeliner running.

Dennis lay on the cramped cushion of the armless couch, the grooved filigree patchwork scratching at the back of his neck. His penis still pulsated from the immense release, blood slowly decreasing from his nether regions; he let himself wiggle and breathe, disconnecting his mind completely as he idled, emptied. He drifted to a serene state, supine on the awkward settee, his right foot flat on the ground, his left leg bent, pressed against the lumbar support as his deflating phallus leaked residual ejaculate, but he didn't bother to move. He was enjoying the inertia, forgetting he was even alive, a taste of ataraxia.

And he couldn't even imagine what kind of more wild sex awaited for him when he got to high school and college; he'd already pictured all the orgies and how he'd probably be able to pick a new girl to have sex with every night of the week, sniffing lines of cocaine off some inexperienced freshman; he'd certainly show her the way.

"What do you think?" Susanna's voice echoed.

Dennis could only see her in the corner of his peripheral, out of focus as he drooled on himself.

A white silhouette and the light swishing of satin compelled Dennis to awaken. He finally glanced at Susanna, adorned in a white wedding dress, inching forward as the long skirt scudded behind her.

"What is that?" Dennis asked with a concerned inflection, springing up from his reclined reverie, his prick shriveling into an acorn.

"Well, I went shopping the other day and picked out this wedding dress," Susanna smiled, holding the sides of her gown before twirling, revealing a laced-up back as she flashed an infatuated smile.

"I don't get it," Dennis whispered, sitting up with his arms crossed and legs turned, obscuring a view of his shrunken self, becoming ashamed of his naked body.

"Well, you're going to be eighteen in four years. That's not a long time," Susanna articulated with an affectionate tone, soft and seductive.

"And what does that mean?" Dennis inquired, his heart sputtering, sensing something serious, his hands covering his chest, bewildered.

Smiling, Susanna crept toward Dennis, placing one foot in front of the other, tangoing over to him. Pushing him back against the backrest, she pulled up her gown, positioning each leg on either side of him, tossing her ruffles onto Dennis. She lowered herself, wrapping her arms around his neck as he acquiesced to her dominating pose. Tilting her head from side to side as she straddled him, her hair cascaded like scarlet waterfalls, engulfing Dennis as he stared impassively, awaiting an explanation.

"Well," she said with a dramatic facial expression, opening her mouth wide and enunciating the second syllable, inflecting an ambiguous mood.

Dennis couldn't tell if she was being serious, playful, or sarcastic.

"Do you want to marry me?" she whispered before coiling herself against his body, sucking on his earlobe.

He wasn't exactly sure what sort of obligations he had to fulfill, since he made a deal with the devil, but the sound of the word "marry" shocked him, like he was about to get into a stranger's car or sign a long contract filled with esoteric language and serious stipulations. It sounded permanent, like maybe he should consult with his parents before he committed to anything. Placing her hands on his face, palms on each cheek, Susanna glanced at him with a solemn stare; her eyes darting back and forth, a psychotic gaze, deliberating, as if she was trying to read his mind. Her legs tightened around his sides, trapping him as she anticipated his response.

"What do you say?" she asked, lingering her lips closer to kiss him, holding back as she awaited his words.

A nervousness manifested, like little fires catching in his collar and sleeves, as he looked over the edge of a veritable precipice, staring into nothingness, a long leap down. Stressing over an answer, Dennis thought he didn't really have an option but to jump as Susanna nudged him. Staring into her forceful cerulean orbs, reflecting an unrecognizable coldness, a vivid contrast from her usual warmth, Dennis felt a leak in his lap, an alarming wetness emanating from Susanna's privates, pooling on his flaccid genitals.

Dennis's anxiety quickly transformed into fear, a vulnerability, realizing there were consequences for every action. Maybe exchanging "I love you" every time they parted meant something deeper than just reciprocal affection; maybe sex wasn't as objectifying for her as it was for him. Perhaps intimacy was more complex, that porn wasn't accurate, and that every vice came with a price, he concluded.

"Of course, I do," he whispered, petrified, feigning an amorous smile before kissing her.

####

Dennis is supposed to meet James at 1:25 outside of the library, so he's idling, slouching as he stares down at his phone. He scrolls Instagram as he waits, cringing at validation-seeking posts saturated in narcissism, like Marena's recent one, where she's taken a selfie of herself writing down her "2025 goals" in script letters with accompanying hashtags like #goals #bossbabe and #moveinsilence. She was the first girl he tried dating after breaking up with Renee. But he couldn't keep a hard-on when he slipped inside the condom, his erection deflating like a decorative lawn inflatable after the holidays by the numbing agents. She was a good sport about it, minimizing his erectile dysfunction with laughter, blaming it on the whiskey, but Dennis knew returning his member inside of a silicone casing after years of unprotected sex was a plight for any hyperactive libido.

And he was willing to relegate his release to strictly oral copulation, but she required reciprocation, which Dennis avoided since he read on WebMD that HPV could be transmitted through cunnilingus and is linked to Oropharyngeal cancer. Her last text about joining her on a hike went unanswered, since Dennis would rather play Monopoly with a group of blind children than leisurely traverse up a mountain without a destination. "Unfollow," Dennis clicks.

He's groggy, swaying on his feet, fighting the urge to close his eyes and attempt a standing nap. And it's not that he's now hooked on reels of civilian confrontations ending in fistfights, finding release in watching others act on impulses he keeps buried. No, it was last night's discovery that sent him spiraling, keeping him up all night as he fell down a black-hole algorithm about the FDA and overly processed foods. At first, he was fine, scrolling with mild skepticism. But when he saw a side-by-side comparison of food ingredients from ten years ago versus today, now packed with over forty additional chemicals, including food dyes linked to cancer, he just fucking lost it.

He tore through his pantry and bathroom, tossing out anything containing Red 40, Blue 1, and Yellow 5, which is literally fucking everything, filling garbage bags with snacks and toxic household items. Now, he's itching, convinced he's somehow poisoned himself, harboring some form of cancer. Part of him tries to resist the conspiracy, rationalizing, like how could the FDA intentionally make people sick just to fuel Big Pharma's profits through palliative treatments. It's absurd to think the world could be one massive business venture.

Still, he feels slightly better knowing there were fact-check labels from Politico marking the claims as false, determining these facts were taken out of context. And that should be enough for him to look the other way, especially since he knows people like Bill Gates only act with integrity.

Scratching at imaginary irritations, Dennis occasionally looks up to scan the perimeter, returning to his phone with a sour face, pretending to have received an urgent email, just in case anyone is watching. Pacing back and forth in front of the library's double doors, he evades the librarian's attention by never staying in one place for too long. The librarian glances over periodically but not long enough to question his presence. The library doors are propped open, offering a panoramic view of the hallway. Inside, Dennis spots Megan at an oval table by several rolling carts in front of the book stacks, returned titles waiting to be shelved. A book lies open in front of her, pages fluttering like a pinwheel as she stares upwards, distracted, possibly annoyed, while Jonathan leans over the desk, smiling and nodding in apparent dialogue.

Ducking off to the side of the doorway, Dennis cowers, trying to decipher the context without getting too close. He squints, attempting to perceive the interaction, positioning himself against the door, sleuthing. Megan occasionally looks up to address Jonathan, who looms over her, blocking any easy exit. Oscillating between her book and the obstinate boy, it's clear Megan isn't interested in discourse. She offers no eye contact, letting her hair conceal her face. Jonathan leans forward, pointing his finger at Megan as if the conversation has turned personal, possibly confrontational. Dennis starts creeping forward.

Megan closes her book and pushes her seat back, grabbing her backpack off the floor. A familiar chime sounds, annoying Dennis, as he always keeps his phone silent. Frantically retrieving it, like feeling a cockroach crawling in his pocket, Dennis turns away from the interaction, looking at the recent banner notification.

"Sorry, I missed your call, call me sometime this week when you get the chance," reads the message from Christine, sending swarming butterflies through Dennis's insides, a nervous joy.

And even though he doesn't know her disposition, he's relieved either way. He mustered up enough temerity to call Christine the other night, conceding to the perceived time limit for returning someone's call before it was no longer anticipated. He didn't leave a message though; he didn't know what to say. Her voicemail picked up, and Dennis thought about possibly making a joke, perhaps saying something about butt dialing, but he ditched the idea, since he wasn't sure if jesting was the best approach. He hung up right before the beep sounded, second-guessing himself minutes after, ruminating about not leaving a clear message, since he knows he has to work on being a better communicator.

Christine's text is a spark of needed optimism, enough to replenish his emptiness, at least for another day. He's starting to think Christine is what he needs now. It's her memories he finds himself revisiting when he's at his lowest. Maybe he can take her out, tell her how he really feels, and rekindle their brilliant flame through a night of revelry and conversation. Maybe they'll reconcile with fireworks bursting and the stars finally aligning, clearing cloudy skies. He's convinced it's just what he needs, envisioning a heartfelt reconciliation as soon as he spills his guts, apologizing for his mercurial mind state. He is confident that Christine is the only girl who truly loves him unconditionally. He's hoping, and that's great, he thinks, because hope is something he hasn't had in a long time.

But he's got to learn to see the glass as more "half full," he's been thinking, invoking more Krishnamurti sentiments and taking an active approach to his perspective. He's starting to fathom that happiness is a state and not a destination.

His optimism has been glitching, like a shorting in the wireframe of his mind, a misfiring of neurotransmitters. No matter how many times he practices distancing himself from his thoughts and the past, he finds it easy to revert, sinking into pessimism; there's a cruel sense of comfort in the melancholy. It's depressing how a little misfortune sends him into a spiral. It probably has to do with the vivid dreams he's been experiencing, incorporating characters from his past, like splinters in his fingers, reminding him he'll never escape certain memories, no matter how much time elapses.

He's back in his junior year, feeling betrayed and hurt again as Ralphie stands in the kitchen of their college condo, telling him that the guys are moving out because of his impetuous behavior and temper while drunk. They're all renting a shore house together, and he's not invited, but they're still friends. Dennis is going to be one of his groomsmen one day, a nervous Ralphie insists, flashing cursory smiles and toothy smirks with his arms crossed as he speaks. The memory crumbles, and Dennis wakes up in bed, but not his; it's Diedre's twin bed at her parents' home in Delaware, since her parents wouldn't let them sleep in the same room when he visited. Her teeth are chattering as she clenches her hands underneath her arms, cradled on the bed, and Dennis pulls the blanket up, wrapping it around her again, kissing her on the forehead. It's one of their last weekends together before she discovered him soliciting sex from Craigslist ads. But her face is warped when he kisses her this time, and she's no longer freezing; she's frozen and completely faceless with her glasses still on.

The dreams are warped, inconsistent in details, skewed with spurious additions, like how the condo's kitchen has a desk instead of a sink and Diedre's bedroom doesn't have walls, just encased with dark space, like an abyss. But none of these fragmented dream memories come close to the outlandish portrayal he experienced last night, possibly the biggest catalyst for his erratic behavior. He's at a baptism party for Renee and Carl's baby girl, honored as the godfather, dressed in all white and taking photos with the infant in his arms as he smiles. He's pretty much ditching the thought exercises in a manic pursuit of serious narcotics to cope with his rogue mind.

It's 1:35 P.M., and Dennis is wondering if James bailed and how much longer he should wait. Opening his text message app, Dennis scoots down the hall as he sends James his third consecutive text without getting a response; the texts appear with green background fills, indicating James doesn't have an iPhone.

A toxic thought floats from the back of his mind, like a fucking mosquito, sinking its stinger into his forehead, reminding him that he's been exfoliating with rich cancer-causing shower gel and mouthwash infused with Red 40 for years. Yeah, he's been lathering and rinsing with poison, which might explain the dreams about his teeth falling out. But he's not entirely sure why it's bothering him to such a magnitude, since he's abusing substances like candy lately, but it's the principle, he thinks. How he's been manipulated, lied to by the FDA, misled by the very sources he's supposed to trust.

So he buries his head, returning to his feed. Dennis scrolls aimlessly, noticing an influx of dating app acquaintances getting married and having babies, girls he's only added in the past year. He's amazed at how quickly people seem to settle, how eager everyone is to choose a permanent partner by a certain age, as if the ark is leaving soon and only couples are permitted for salvation.

He debates sending John another text message, inquiring about his current emotional state, but he's been disappointed with his brother's lack of reciprocation. Dennis had imagined they would have connected, becoming closer by now, and his brother would confide in him, knowing he understands what it feels like to be completely destroyed by a female. He even took time to craft a sentimental text to his brother, empathizing with his situation, letting him know he's there for him if he ever wants to talk. But his brother's response was terse, apathetic, as if he was annoyed: "Thanks, just concerned about the kids." A sharp sadness fills him, thinking the ordeal would have brought them closer, but maybe he's destined to always be the little brother, no matter how old they get.

"You order this cheeseburger?" James shouts, jumping out from behind the row of lockers with a goofy smile on his face, his hands up like a mime.

"Goddamn, you're late," Dennis huffs, shaking off the surprise, his eyes widened as he holds his phone by his side.

"You got the list?" James asks, crouching with an army green duffle bag with metallic grommets tucked under his arm.

His eyes are bloodshot, barely open, like he just woke up from a nap or is already high as balls.

"Each student with their prescribed medication," Dennis announces, flashing a post-it note with five names, a compendium he compiled after sneaking into the nurse's office early in the morning since she never locks the door.

The list stars the most desirable prescriptions like Adderall and Benzodiazepine, with big scribbled inscriptions.

"Good look, my dude," James mumbles, elated, chewing with a snappy munch.

"I saw your texts, but I couldn't read them. My phone doesn't encrypt punctuation."

James pulls out a silver flip phone, one Dennis remembers his freshman roommate having, the memorable model with the two-in-one texting option, equipped with a full keyboard that ejects and can be easily accessed by sliding a thumb across the device.

"Holy shit, that thing is a relic," Dennis quips, recalling a girl from his freshman psychology class he dated briefly, who used the same phone before their relationship ended when she asked if he'd be open to water sports.

"Hell yeah, it's great for texting, but I had to buy the last fifty batteries available on Amazon since it dies every other month."

"Why not just upgrade your phone?" Dennis asks, flummoxed yet fascinated.

"No fucking way. You think I wanna become glued to my phone like all these parochial creatures walking around?"

"I don't need that shit in my life," James shakes his head, sliding his phone back into his pant pocket.

"These fucking lemmings and their technology," James exclaims.

"All right dude, chill," Dennis laughs, putting his arm around James's shoulder, pushing him forward as they walk down the hall to shield him from any curious onlookers.

Dennis peeks over his shoulder, consumed with paranoia.

"All right, let's do this," James declares, stopping in place.

He stands up straight, taking a deep breath, a semi-meditative practice to cleanse himself from aggravation, Dennis supposes. His dark complexion contrasts sharply against the white undershirt that pops out from his open collar, and Dennis partially wonders about James's political beliefs and if he's a dedicated tribalist like the media suggests people with certain complexions should be.

"Here's the list," Dennis whispers, handing it to James with a closed fist.

James crumbles it up in his hand and reaches into the front pocket of his janitor ensemble. His haphazard facial hair is oddly well-groomed, like he's purposely manicured his look with patches in his beard and a trim that doesn't connect.

"You want some jellybeans?" James asks, shoveling a handful of colored candies into his mouth.

"What's that? Is that molly?" Dennis asks, intrigued.

"Nah, they just straight jellybeans. But none of that wholesale shit. This that gourmet Jelly Belly goodness. You know, with those precise flavor names."

"Uhh, no, I'm good," Dennis replies politely, his eyebrows raised, anticipating a punchline or some further explanation.

"What, you don't fuck with no Chili Mango?" James demands, shifting from a frivolous demeanor to a more serious mien, pushing his shoulders back.

"You too good for Toasted Marshmallow?" James's face scrunches in distaste, like Dennis just stomped on a nest full of baby bird eggs right in front of him.

"You too bourgeois for some Sunkist Lemon and Cream Soda confectionaries?"

"What? No, I just don't want them right now," Dennis responds, puzzled, not sure if James is goading him.

"Well, shit, open your hand up and store these for later," James persists, reaching into his pocket.

"All right, fine, fine," Dennis acquiesces, holding his hand out as James dispenses jellybeans with a shaky hand, dropping several as they clack against the floor.

"Just hurry, the class ends in twenty minutes," Dennis says, sticking the handful of sweets into his pocket.

"Shit, I'll be in and out just like a robbery," James comments.

Yukking as he scurries away, his keys jangling from a blue carabiner clipped to his rear belt loop, he frolics down the hall. Pulling up his pants as he hops to the gym locker room, the canvas bag wrapped around his shoulder, James holds his hand against the white tiled wall, grazing the grout with childish wonder. Dennis watches in amazement at the eccentricity of this character, an individual connected to the present, reveling in the simple joys of his surroundings.

"Fucking A, man," Dennis remarks, admiring, wondering if James is on some sort of substance.

Glancing at his watch, Dennis estimates he has about nineteen minutes to kill, which he decides to use productively by using the restroom before class. He has to urinate almost every twenty-five minutes ever since he started drinking a combination of Kratom and coffee, a potent diuretic, the only elixir that keeps his mind somewhat tamed. He contemplates whether he should wait for James, but he can't risk being caught in the hallway when the bell rings.

Lurching down the vacant passage, Dennis tries to recall a more intellectual synonym for the word "hallway."

"Corridor," Dennis announces, smiling, admiring his memory and quick thinking.

And it's a great feeling, a transient moment of joy, since Dennis has been working hard to improve his lexicon, hoping it will enhance his writing. He's even stocked up on a selection of academic reads in his Amazon cart like a fucking summer reading list, imagining if he devours enough literature from renowned authors as sustenance, he'll be able to cultivate his malnourished mind. He's almost done with the Krishnamurti read, so he must be prepared. Perhaps he'll even discover some groundbreaking concept or a timeless notion, a perfectly formulated sentence that resonates in his soul, transcends his perspective, and makes him feel connected, like he isn't the only one that feels the way he does.

He enjoys the tumult of his temperaments, from inert depression to manic bursts of bliss. Take, for instance, his delight upon discovering the iOS update that allows users to type a phrase or word and receive a recommended autofill with an applicable emoji, simplifying communication with entertaining convenience. He relishes typing out "curious" to elicit the monocle emoji, which reminds him of Uncle Pennybags from Monopoly. It's enough ephemeral delight to distract him from his mother's relentless laments about John and Natalie's divorce during their phone calls. He could ignore a call or two to avoid feeling like a stress ball being squeezed, but he knows one day he won't have that option, and he'll regret ever missing a call from her.

The narrow, neutral-colored halls of St. Vincent's create a timeless setting even as the years go by; stiff corners and waxed tile floors have seen generations of kids in the same space. Dennis ponders what could differentiate classes from different decades since their uniforms have always been blazers, and hairstyles and facial hair have always been regulated. It's like a time capsule with no definitive date.

As he saunters closer to his classroom, just a little way from the bathroom, Dennis feels a calmness settling inside, no longer anxious about the pending heist. He's distracted by the ornamented walls, filled with flyers about upcoming pep rallies, fundraisers for the forest fires in Australia, and combating climate change. He notices the dates: March 10th, May 8th, May 24th. May 8th was his and Renee's anniversary date, but Dennis doesn't dwell on it. He's still intoxicated by Christine's text and transfixed on the array of senior headshots that adorn the walls. The expiring quietness of the hallway suggests the impending stampede of students, moments away from bursting out of classroom doors like wild animals flocking to a trough. Dennis stands, staring at the tacky bulletin board, made of construction paper and bedecked in the blue and white colors of the school.

"Meet our 2025 Seniors," reads the headline atop a row of glamour shots.

Savoring the last minutes before the storm of trampling students, Dennis stares at the photos; all young faces filled with hope, aspirations, goals, and delusions of grandeur. Each photo is paired with a cliché bio, outlining trivial accomplishments and inside jokes with friends. Dennis starts to feel nauseous, like he could just puke all over the display, unleashing a hot mess of chunky food debris and bile, coating the walls with his stomach contents.

Gravitating toward Megan's feature, Dennis examines her photo and blurb: her permed locks flowing around her shoulders, enclosing her face perfectly. Her fizzy eyes exude life and optimism; her bio reads like an Instagram caption, mentioning her passion for reading and "nights she won't ever forget with friends."

His phone buzzes in his pocket, signaling several notifications, which he retrieves with haste, since he rarely receives anything significant. He's got three new messages on Tinder and an email.

"What are you looking for?" reads a message from Lori, 26, on Tinder.

Dennis accesses her bio, which leads with the quintessential header for most women in their late twenties, "not looking for a hookup."

Perusing her pics, Dennis cringes at her four zoomed-in selfies from the neck up, the typical hefty girl mirage; makeup caked on like a carnival clown and the classic kissy face as if a ridiculous animated expression is going to detract from the possibility that she may or may not just be a floating head without a body.

"I'm actually looking for the opposite of a one-night stand, one that's rooted in crippling dependency where we fuse our identities together to become one single entity for eternity. We'll get married in eleven days and possibly attach ourselves together via a conjoining operation, which probably won't be covered by our healthcare."

"If you had to take a road trip today, where would you go?" the next message reads from Kimberly, 29.

Swiping through her pictures, Dennis has a difficult time identifying who Kimberly is since every photo depicts a group of different girls, a common tactic used by unattractive individuals for deception, camouflaging themselves amongst a group of appealing people, psychologically implementing a greater chance of a viewer finding at least one of the girls in the group attractive, compelling them to swipe.

"I would take a trip to the George Washington Bridge, Kimberly, and I would invite all of your friends in your photos to tag along. We can make it an elaborate venture; we'll pack sandwiches and soft drinks, and once we get there, I'll take a swan dive right off the bridge to my demise."

"Are you down for going to Taco Bell at 2 in the morning?" asks Lindsey, 23.

"Nope, but I'm down with the sickness. OHH WAT AT AT AT," Dennis types, contemplating if the embryonic being will even understand his Disturbed reference.

After sending his satirical comments, Dennis opens an email from Cheryl Earhardt, which he determines is Megan's mother, causing his heart to sink like he's about to open test results for a terminal illness. Sweat suffuses his palms, and an uneasiness seethes in his stomach as he reads the opening line with palpitations:

Dear Mr. Clauden,

I'm Megan's mother, and I'm emailing you in regard to possibly tutoring my daughter outside of school. Her interest in English studies has really taken off this past year and I haven't seen her this passionate about anything in a long time or at least since we moved. Please feel free to give me a call at your earliest convenience to discuss. 908-555-2150.

Dennis closes the email before he can fully process what appears to be materializing, breathing a sigh of relief as he apparently hasn't done anything wrong, yet.

"Dennis," a deep voice resounds in the hollow hallway.

A lofty bald head glistens under the fluorescent lights, flashing a jagged smile enmeshed in a spotty beard. Michael Fairchild stands there, his pink ostentatious bow tie tucked underneath his protruding chin; wrinkles run up and down his slacks, implying either he's been wearing the same pants for a few weeks without washing them or he isn't skilled with an iron. A small rainbow pin with debossed lettering is affixed to his collar, reading "Pride," and Dennis wonders if it violates the school's non-political accessory policy; theoretically, a sexual orientation isn't a political affiliation, he deduces.

"Hey Michael," Dennis returns a perfunctory greeting as he turns to head to the bathroom, hoping to discourage any further talk.

"Oh, good idea. I could use the potty myself. I'll walk with you," Michael remarks with a joking demeanor.

Dennis would prefer to use the bathroom alone, really, and it has nothing to do with Fairchild being gay. No, he's just not prepared for dialogue, especially with the accomplished author. His brain is foggy, capricious; he can't even think of one or two impressive vocab words to incorporate into a discussion. He hasn't been sleeping well either, with the haunting dreams, and the fact that his parents are withering away while his brother decomposes is spoiling any waking moments of peace. He can't pinpoint how, but he's definitely to blame for all of it, he thinks.

"Are you working on anything right now?" Michael asks as they both approach the urinals, like synchronized pissers, maintaining an acceptable distance.

Dennis feels a wave of dread crash on his consciousness, provoking him to reply with several inappropriate comments.

He wants to tell him he's working on developing a hot conspiracy theory in which JonBenet Ramsey faked her death to start a sex trafficking ring of pageant girls, but he's thinking he probably doesn't share his affinity for dark, wry humor. Dennis wonders if maybe he should just pull his cock out all the way and they could get the dick-measuring contest over with, because he knows that's what's at the root of their encounters: who is the more intellectual, who is the alpha English teacher, and the ping pong posturing is exhausting.

"Trying to polish up my story," Dennis responds with reluctance, unsatisfied with his verb choice; he wishes he used something more compelling like "refine," as if he's a writing connoisseur.

The discernible splatter of urine splashing against the porcelain walls captures Dennis's attention while Michael stares at him with an odd peculiarity as they both evacuate their toxins. Fairchild is a towering individual, so his height against the urinals is even more conspicuous as he looks down.

"Swimming. Yes, I started reading it, it's quite sharp."

Dennis scrunches his face, turning away to watch his liquids drain, and he finds it rather apropos since his aspirations for becoming a legit writer are on the same path as his piss. He doesn't know what "sharp" writing means, but he's thinking it's a euphemism for shitty and certainly laced with condescending undertones; sharp like a prison shank, and every word read elicits pain like being stabbed in the fucking abdomen. Debating whether to opine about Fairchild's "Hangman" read, Dennis decides he doesn't have the energy for a discussion, nor does he want to decipher any literary jargon.

"Thanks. I'm actually halfway through with your story. Let's talk sometime next week," Dennis rebuts, zipping up his fly, booking it to the sink to wash his hands before Fairchild finishes, noticing one of his blazer flaps is folded back.

"That sounds great," Michael announces, flashing a snaggle-toothed grin as he continues his drainage, turning his head to maintain eye contact.

"I'll swing by your classroom," Michael adds, leaning backward as he continues whizzing, attempting to look at Dennis.

Dennis shares a quick smile, feeling a strong impulse to headbutt the hand dryer on the wall, hoping it will clear his head of insidious thoughts. Dashing from the bathroom before he encounters any more people, Dennis debates going home early, using a half personal day, but he doesn't think "misanthropy" will be an acceptable reason for his dismissal. Instead, he pulls out his phone and notices a recent text message from James:

"I just found some mushrooms," the message reads.

"On my way to your classroom," a second message appears from James.

Shoving the key into the lock with an aggressive demeanor, Dennis struggles to pry the door open, twisting the rusted steel implement into the deadbolt.

"Fucking cock-sucking piece of shit," Dennis blurts as he kicks the door, stressing over time management, realizing class starts in six minutes.

Finally, flinging the door open, letting it slam against the hallway wall, Dennis quickly flips the light on as he approaches his desk.

"Is that you fighting a door?" a cackling voice comments from the doorway.

"Fuck man, you scared me, again," Dennis shrieks as he takes a seat, rubbing his forehead.

"Goddamn, man, you gotta relax," James smiles, tossing the duffel bag onto Dennis's desk, sending office supplies awry.

Dennis watches as term papers and recent printouts of Kurt Vonnegut's *Slaughterhouse-Five* scatter, floating to the ground like falling leaves. It's a trying moment as Dennis endures excessive anger, debating whether to lash out at James, but he resists. Instead, he smiles, letting what's out of his control happen as he reclines in his chair.

"Now you're non-reactionary?" James quips, pulling the duffel bag open.

"What's the point of anything?" Dennis remarks, stretching his arms behind his head.

"Now you're getting it," James states, retrieving a hefty sandwich bag of dried spore-bearing remnants from the duffel and tossing it to Dennis, who catches it in his lap.

"How do you want to split the pills?" James asks, pulling out several orange containers.

"Class starts in three minutes, so how about you just keep the pills, and I'll hold onto the shrooms?"

"You sure? I found some coke too. Do you want that?"

"These fucking suburban white kids have a better supply than the niggas on my block," James shakes his head, laughing.

"Give me the coke and the shrooms and you take the rest. Sound good?" Dennis asks, trying not to overtly stare at the clock.

"Damn, you got it, homie," James says, placing a snowy baggie of residue on his desk.

He tosses the loot back into the bag and makes his way to the door.

"Are you ready for the big surprise?" James announces, standing up straight and closing his eyes, putting on a performance.

"Say hello to my little friend," he impersonates, pulling out a long tubular device.

"Holy shit, is that an EpiPen?" Dennis chuckles.

"You're goddamn right it is. Are you ready to come back to life?" James deadpans, holding the pen upwards in a Michael Myers pose.

"That's all you, buddy. I heard if you stick it up your butt, it works faster," Dennis remarks.

"You're absolutely right. I already have two up there right now." James grins.

"Wait..." Dennis commands, hesitating.

He wants to tell James that he thinks he's his best friend, but he's too insecure to make such a suggestion.

"You don't think anyone will figure us out? You're not worried about being caught?"

James turns his head over his shoulder, looking back with a smirk.

"I ain't worried bout shit," James laughs.

"Any of these pasty motherfuckers accuse me of anything, I'll go full Jussie Smollett and report to the board, the news, social media, the nearest overweight white woman with a BLM hashtag in her Instagram bio, letting them know they fired me because of my skin color while they wore MAGA hats," James chortles, turning to face Dennis, the shoulder straps of the canvas bag crossed in front of his chest.

"Now, I'll be back tomorrow to fix your door. Try not to take yourself too seriously until then," James declares, hugging his torso and flashing a peace sign as he departs.

"Try not to get your ass kicked," James hollers from the hallway as the students start spilling into the classroom.

It's a quiet ride over to six Longacre Drive, just the purring of the engine as Dennis accelerates, hugging turns, admiring the German engineering of his high-performance vehicle. The soft, pleasant brogue of his Waze app recites the directions, guiding Dennis and making it easier to navigate as he multi-tasks. His phone is plugged into Apple Play, allowing him to drive, refresh his Instagram, Facebook, and Snapchat for updates, and swipe for women in different locations. He's never been able to do this before, since he's sworn to never pay for Tinder

Plus; he's drawn a figurative line he refuses to cross, telling himself he'll never become that desperate.

"Weep for yourself, my man, you'll never be what is in your heart," the low chorus lilts from the radio as Dennis shifts lanes, holding the blinker lever up with his finger instead of fully shifting it.

He's defenseless against his craving to check his Instagram, giving peripheral glances at the right lane for oncoming cars as he drives, peeking back at his feed. He can't look away from the mess that's social media: a profusion of people thinking they're main characters, self-conscious influencers revivified by deceiving appearances with filters, uploading "good deed" posts, portraying themselves as virtuous as if they're genuinely altruistic and not just attention-seekers looking for validation.

Like Jaimie; she's not accepting gifts this year for her birthday; instead, she's made a post about only accepting donations to black-owned businesses, posing with a BLM wristband and a thumbs up. And then there's David; he's helping save the planet by only using paper straws and discarding any products made of plastic, standing by a recycling bin outside his house, snapping a selfie while sipping a smoothie. Dennis debates commenting on David's post about forests and if sacrificing trees to make paper is also good for the environment, but he can't type and drive. Dennis is even tempted to make a similar post after donating to the fight for women's rights, but he can't remember if it was to help them get abortions or to keep biological males from competing in their sports, so he resists.

A red dot appears under his photo in the corner of his screen; he's got a new follow request from his niece, Reese. She has social media now, and it's starting to dawn on Dennis that time is passing, life is progressing, regardless of whether he's participating. He's back on Facebook, even though he hurled imprecations at his screen the last time he logged in at the sight of Susanna's offspring losing more of his baby teeth. He really wishes he hadn't, because he's noticing a pattern of people in their late thirties and early forties becoming so bored with their lives that they dedicate themselves to their profiles, uploading constant status updates and sharing posts on their pages. They check in to every location they visit, take pictures of their food, create cartoon characters of themselves, and share quiz results on which Disney character their personality aligns with. It's all ridiculous, mind-numbing, but Dennis is pretty much engaging in any app that occupies time away from being alone with his thoughts.

"In 300 feet, turn left," the eloquent voice instructs.

Turning onto Longacre Drive, Dennis's stomach twists and turns, as if his conscience is emanating physical symptoms, alerting him of an impending bad decision. But Dennis has justified his newest part-time job after speaking with Megan's mother over the phone, especially since it's a paying gig. He's a capitalist, and he'll do anything for money, he thinks, so if Megan's mother believes her daughter needs a tutor when she's getting an A- in the class, then so be it.

The cul-de-sac is comprised of contemporary homes with thick driveways, and even in early April, the lawns are full of lush, muted grass. Patches of perennials decorate the landscapes, burgeoning for the season, waking from their slumber. Dennis wonders if the residents all use the same horticulturist and if maybe he offers a neighborhood discount. A weathered basketball hoop is erected in the space between two houses at the back of the turnaround; the square of the backboard completely faded, the rim level but the net missing. It's odd, Dennis deduces, as the structure looks to be older than the surrounding homes.

"You've arrived at your destination," the Waze app announces.

Megan's house is the second one in, with a big barren tree in the foreground, occupying much of the yard; crooked branches point in different directions.

Creeping closer, Dennis focuses on his side mirror, obsessing over the proximity to the curb as he pulls in front of the house, deciding against parking in the driveway despite there being sufficient space to accommodate his car. Pulling his visor down to check for any residue in his teeth, Dennis notices the dark circles under his eyes, the sunken, aged face of a high-strung man, wondering if this will be the last time he'll be able to tolerate his own reflection.

Traversing the lawn, despite his instinct to travel up the driveway, Dennis isn't going to travel the same path as Susanna. No, he's going to do things differently, despite the frightening notion that maybe he's destined to repeat the cycle. Gazing at the gigantic tree towering overhead, its dark brooding base commanding attention, Dennis wonders if there used to be a tire swing hanging on the longest, thickest branch when Megan was a kid. He imagines her parents pushing her on sunny days, a jubilant child shrieking as she clenched the taut ropes. But there's no indication anything has ever been hanging there, just dying limbs.

Dennis rings the doorbell, envisioning Megan on the other side, peeping through the look-hole. Adjusting his lapel and making sure his Persian knotted scarf is tied securely, Dennis puffs his chest out and rolls his neck as he positions his carry briefcase on his shoulder, posing, trying to invoke a cool calmness, like he's being watched. The porch light pops on and the door opens seconds later.

"You must be the esteemed Mr. Clauden? Come on in," an older lady with ruby hair inquires with an obeisant smile, holding the door open as she steps backwards.

Creases splinter from the sides of her eyes like a jigsaw puzzle; her golden necklaces layered in a fashionable configuration.

"I wouldn't say esteemed," Dennis smirks, nodding his head, noticing the "Home is Where the Heart is" doormat; a navy-blue coir design inscribed with white lettering, the word "heart" transposed with the anatomically inaccurate heart symbol in fire engine red.

Dennis feels immense joy as he stomps his feet on it before entering. He feels relieved that at least one of her parents is home; just in case temptation teases him. He'll be more influenced by his scruples than if they were alone.

"Well, you're pretty much a celebrity according to Megan," the convivial woman adds, which Dennis guesses is Megan's mother.

"A D-list one," Dennis banters, flashing a cordial grin.

The foyer of the two-story home is floored with white ceramic tiles, exuding a late '90s look, but it contrasts nicely with the Oxford blue walls. It's decorated with a mix of themes, an assortment of home décor that suggests they haven't settled on a cohesive aesthetic, giving the impression they haven't lived there for very long. A giant oval mirror with beveled edges hangs at the top of the exposed wooden staircase, and Dennis can see Megan's reflection as she stands at the top behind the banister, attempting to listen.

"So you must be Megan's sister?" Dennis quips, stuffing his hands into his coat pockets.

"Oh, you're funny! I'm Cheryl, Megan's mom. I'll take your coat," she replies, holding out her hands, showing her slight muffin-top midsection and skinny awkward legs.

Obliging, Dennis removes his messenger bag, placing it on the floor to undo his scarf. Taking off his peacoat, her mother holds the shoulders of his jacket, assisting with the removal. Retrieving a hanger from the small closet by the front door, Cheryl wraps his scarf around the hook and drapes his coat before tucking it into the closet.

"Megan didn't mention how handsome you were. Love the sweater," she adds.

And Dennis glows because he picked out the navy-blue merino turtleneck purposely as it accentuates his build and stature while enhancing the vividness of his blue eyes.

"Mom, stop," Megan commands, lingering down the stairs with a contemptuous mug.

She emerges like an Instagram model in form-fitting, ripped jeans and a tapered T-shirt; her make-up applied with bold contrast and darkened eyelids, amplifying the hues of her eyes. Her hair is straightened, enhancing her angular facial features; she looks absolutely stunning.

"What? Can't a mom still flirt?" Cheryl chuckles, flipping her hand in a playful flourish.

"Ew, no," Megan shakes her head, scrunching her face with scorn; her face mantling with embarrassment as she stands with her arms crossed.

"Well, it's nice to meet you, Cheryl," Dennis says, smiling, partly embarrassed by how gussied up Megan appears.

Megan's mother looks like she used to be attractive years ago when she was younger; despite her diminishing physicality, her nose is narrow, her teeth are white and immaculate, and she still possesses the confidence of a good-looking woman, remarking with playful comments. Her pixie-like hairstyle is indicative of the archetypal suburban mom, and Dennis imagines she chopped off her locks in a symbolic ritual, trading long tresses for motherhood and years of attending PTA school meetings.

"So, listen I've got to head out to do some errands, but you are more than welcome to stay for dinner later," Cheryl announces as she retrieves a black shortened trench coat, slipping her arms inside and tying the belt buckle across her body.

And an apprehension catches Dennis by the throat, and he can't conjure up a response or any words for that matter as Cheryl tosses her purse over her shoulder and opens the front door.

"See you guys later," she smiles, waving as she departs, closing the door behind her.

And just like that, her mother facilitates a completely unsupervised, secluded house for her daughter to be alone with a thirty-four-year-old man, and Dennis starts feeling uncomfortable, like maybe he should fake a sickness, perhaps a stomachache, since it's applicable. Turning back to Megan, who's standing with a servile aura, beaming with a semi-flirtatious glance; her eyes vivid with an eager edge; her brows raised in anticipation.

"So, shall we get started?" Dennis poses, shifting the power dynamic to ensure he's in charge.

"Let's do it," she remarks with an animated demeanor, reaching out, pulling Dennis by the hand toward the stairs; the lacy top of her underwear jutting out with the contortion of her body.

"Wait, are we going upstairs?"

"Duh, that's where my room is," Megan sighs, still gripping Dennis's hand, tugging with a zealous force.

Breaking from her grasp, Dennis halts, evading Megan's direction, thinking about how he needs to take control of the situation, something Susanna didn't do.

"How about we do the tutoring in the kitchen?" Dennis asks with a delicate tone, as to not antagonize her.

"We're home alone. Why does it matter?"

"Because, Megan, it would be highly inappropriate for me to tutor you in your bedroom."

And Dennis can see Megan's facial expression escalating into aggravation as she squints, a petulant mien; her eyes expanding as if she's stirred.

"Ugh, you're so lame," Megan asserts, turning her back with a querulous vigor, as if she had just been told she could only get one toy at Toys' R' Us and not three.

"If I'm going to be your at-home tutor for the long run, I have to show respect to your parents," Dennis replies with a placatory response, flashing a soft smile.

"So you want to come see me more often?" Megan smiles, her cheeks blushing as she spins back around to face Dennis; her teeth slipping out between her taut lips, flashing a beguiled grin as she contorts his words into some perceived cunning plan for the future.

"Sure," Dennis retorts, deflecting from her misinterpretation.

"Good, the kitchen is this way," Megan states, brushing past Dennis, almost knocking off his leather messenger bag from his shoulder, eliciting a warm tingling in his chest from the brief contact.

Megan proceeds to the kitchen, emphasizing her curvaceous frame with an exaggerated stroll, swaying her hips from side to side, and Dennis is cognizant of the demonstration, avoiding his focus on her features. The Earhardts' kitchen is a modern masterpiece, the highlight of their home. Engineered with wooden planks and contemporary fixtures, the center island is topped with a granite slab, which is bigger than Dennis's entire kitchen. The sleek stainless-steel appliances look pristine, and Dennis can't stop staring at the magnificent industrial hood that hangs over the impressive stove, wondering how much a renovation like this costs. Megan pulls out a rustic barstool from under the kitchen island and gazes at Dennis.

"We can sit here," Megan says, flipping her hair back as she positions herself on the stool.

Dennis stands, immobilized, transfixed on the glorious space; shrouded with envy, gnawing on the realization that he more than likely will never own a marvelous kitchen like the one he stands in. His thoughts consume him, as he pictures Renee and her pustule, left-brained husband eating their breakfast in a similar structured setting, living the life that was meant for him. Glancing at Megan with snake eyes, Dennis enviously wonders if Megan has any idea of how fortunate she really is. His mood diminished, he feels hopeless, disgusted with his predicament, how everything always seems to come back to Renee and how he's whoring himself out for one hundred dollars an hour to tutor an underage girl he finds extremely sexually attractive. Dennis takes a seat, reticent, wallowing in his rancor as Megan stares at him.

As Dennis gazes at the pendant light swinging overhead with each of Megan's movements, an unsolicited image comes to mind: Michael Fairchild's uncle swaying from his belt like a pendulum, the climax of his short story "Hangman." A creak sounds every time the asphyxiated body changes direction, a bald chunky loner swaying from side to side, and for some reason he pictures him as hairy, a beefcake bear. The autobiographical read details the last few days of his uncle, a guilt-ridden closeted homosexual committing suicide by hanging, unable to endure life as a gay man any longer. And Dennis read the story several times, searching for paramount insight or a clear formula for great writing, a possible equation he could apply to his own stories, and maybe it's his pernicious cynicism, but he's shocked about how insufficient the ending is, how little the prose evokes any emotion, especially with such a haunting finish and heavy subject matter.

"Dennis?" Megan asks, her mouth agape with confusion.

She's been waiting for his response as Dennis indulges in a wayward daydream.

"Don't call me Dennis, I'm still your teacher," he rebukes, shaking his head as he reaches into his bag to retrieve the novel.

"Okay, teacher," Megan retorts with a sarcastic lilt, avoiding further eye contact like a child denied ice cream for dinner.

"It's okay to have boundaries," Dennis coos, placing his hand on top of hers, which is resting on the granite countertop, attempting to calm her combativeness.

"Now, are we covering *Slaughterhouse-Five,* or are you going to wait until next week when we start going over it in class?"

"I'd like to get an early start since I've read a good amount of it already," Megan smirks, as if she's attempting to impress.

Opening her paperback, Dennis notices different highlighted passages in vibrant purple, pink, and orange. Megan's candy-like fragrance of flowers fused with frosted sugar penetrates his nostrils, enticing his senses with zest.

"All of this happened, more or less," Megan recites from the first page of her book, which is highlighted and circled several times for emphasis.

"I feel like this line has major significance with the narrator, but I'm not entirely sure," Megan inquires, like maybe she's looked up sample quizzes or already engaged with ChatGPT about it, tilting her head, turning on her charm with an exaggerated smile.

She gazes at Dennis with a discernible motive on her mind, something beyond classic literature; her cheek resting against her closed fist in contemplation, slowly blinking, as if she's really not concerned about the importance of the opening line. Perhaps her interest is in something more intimate than dialogue.

"It blurs the line between fiction and reality, establishing an unreliable narrator," Dennis explicates, looking away instead of positively reinforcing her approach.

"Oh, that makes sense," Megan smiles, continuing her gaze, twirling a strand of her hair.

"How about the recurring birds that say that stupid phrase. I forget exactly what they say," she asks, bursting out of her stare, turning the pages in her book to locate a specific reference.

"Poo-tee-weet," she shouts excitedly, lighting up with energy as if she's just buzzed into *Jeopardy!* with the winning answer.

"What do you think it means?" Dennis challenges, as he starts succumbing to her animation and enticing, mature look.

He feels uncomfortable sitting on the compact stool; his legs angled to rest his feet on the bottom rung, his body jutting forward, slouching from the unsupported seat, imbuing a timidness, like he's an awkward kindergartener. He adjusts his seat, pushing his shoulders back, trying to maintain a powerful pose.

"I don't know, it's pretty silly."

"Exactly, it's nonsensical. The bird says it after a massacre, meaning there is nothing intelligible to say about war. There are no enlightening words; it's a stand-in for critical commentary," Dennis explains, making eye contact with Megan, who he can tell isn't really paying attention to his delineation.

She's staring at his eyes instead of his mouth, a psychological tell she isn't really grasping what he's saying; she's fantasizing. Dennis stares back, relishing her admiration and adoring her youthful beauty, the smooth, seamless contours of her face and captivating eyes.

"Wow, you're seriously just so smart. I feel so dumb when I talk to you," Megan fawns, gradually inching her seat closer to Dennis.

"Thanks, cutie," Dennis blurts out, allowing a few seconds to pass before he processes the untoward remark that escaped from his lips.

Megan perks up and shares an enticing smile, lingering forward as if she's about to kiss him. Dennis stands up, diffusing the momentum, seeking a reprieve from the escalation.

"Where's your bathroom?"

"Oh, it's just down the hall to the left," Megan instructs, biting her bottom lip as she leans back on her stool, pointing at the small corridor that runs along the living room.

"I'll be right back."

"You better be," Megan replies, flipping her hair back from her face, watching Dennis as he walks away.

Entering the powder room, Dennis closes the bathroom door and locks it, pressing his body against the door as it closes, still clenching the brass handle. Turning to face his reflection, he's engulfed by the familiar fragrance of the Bath and Body works Eucalyptus plug-in; it's the same scent that filled the bathroom of the home he shared with Renee, immediately eliciting an emotional breakdown. Dennis plops himself on the toilet seat, fighting against stirring tears; his cogitation deepens, so he reaches up to run the faucet of the sink, shielding his somber cries. The rapids rush, crashing into the basin as he lets his repressed feelings flood, falling from his face.

Reflecting on causality, he wonders how he got to where he is right now, wondering which series of decisions destined him to the first-floor bathroom of the Earhardts' home, pondering how his life is and how it may have been had he made different choices. He postulates on whether he's been fated to end up in this compact bathroom on 6 Longacre Drive ever since he lost his virginity to the middle school librarian. He ponders what Christine would think of him right now, flirting with a teenager, alone in her home, soaking in the excessive validation. She would tell him he's better than this, he knows it and that just fucking kills him.

Reaching into his pocket, Dennis pulls out the baggie of cocaine James had given him, seeking a remedy for his rumination, placing it on the edge of the sink. Standing up to access the powder-filled pouch, Dennis glances at his glum reflection; his reddened eyes and moistened cheeks glaring back, a depiction he's seen too many times before. Retrieving his wallet, Dennis takes out a dollar bill, rolling it tight but with enough space to ensure an interior passage and access on each end.

Trickling out a small pile of white residue, Dennis holds the straw to his left nostril and snorts a miniature mound of powder, jolting up as soon as he finishes. The vitality shoots through his body as he kicks his head back, gazing at his reflection again in the tempered glass mirror. And it's amazing, really, the feeling of his blood pumping through his veins and how crystallized leaves soaked in gasoline can shift the perspective of the mind, a Shakespearean narcotic, turning a tragedy into a comedy. And it's not like a panic attack; no, it's an excited nervousness, like being in a constant state of anticipation, like something is always just about to happen. It's a defibrillator for the soul, reminding him how great it feels just to be alive. Dennis scours the corner of the sink with the furled dollar bill in his right nostril, sniffing, attempting to snort any remaining grains on the counter. He wipes up the excess with his hand, rubbing his fingertips against his gums for the tactile numbness, ensuring there isn't any trace of coke left on the porcelain.

He pulls out his phone, emboldened by the nasal drip of invincibility, an imperviousness to disappointment.

Dennis finally texts Christine.

"I've typed out so many different messages to send to you, deleting them all before sending. Will you have dinner with me this weekend?" he presses send before questioning his text or proofreading.

After washing his hands and wiping the sink ledge with the washcloth, Dennis emerges from the bathroom with an invigorated disposition, clapping his hands as he returns to the kitchen, tucking his phone away, ensuring it's on silent.

"Ok, so let's deconstruct. Are there any other quotes or theories you want to analyze?"

Megan is texting but clicks her phone off as Dennis approaches.

"We can go chapter by chapter, or we can start with the characters. Protagonist. Billy Pilgrim," Dennis jabbers, as he yanks the barstool out, straddling it as he sits down.

"Who are you texting? Your boyfriend?" Dennis teases, reveling in his boost of dopamine, the mesolimbic stimulation tethered with adrenaline, like he's always post-celebration from just draining the game-winning shot.

"Pshh, I don't have a boyfriend," she announces with an ambiguous tone, rolling her eyes in a theatrical manner.

"Oh yeah, what about Jonathan?" Dennis comments as he rises from his stool, peering down on Megan.

"Oh my God. Ew. Jonathan is a druggie, and I don't date druggies," Megan remarks, covering her mouth and nose with her hand as if she's just smelled something putrid.

Clicking her phone off, she turns her attention to Dennis.

"I mean, it's not like he doesn't want to fuck me, I'm just not interested," Megan comments with confidence, fluttering her eyes with her jarring statement.

"He'd be sooooooo pissed if he knew you were over at my house," Megan adds, breathing in amusement as she smirks.

"Yeah, I saw you two in the library this week," Dennis fires off, his pulse pummeling, speaking with an aggravated pitch.

"Ohhh, is someone jealous?" Megan cackles, her head cocked with a curious look.

Dennis knows he's about to lose his composure with his amplified emotions and escalating tone; he feels his heart beating in his neck, thumping with each heavy breath like he's about to explode.

It's not going to be a good look when he destructs, he tells himself, and it's pretty obvious Megan's landed a punch to his ego; she's relishing her impact on his mood.

"Let's just get back to the lesson," Dennis sighs, counting to three with each new breath, exhaling lightly as he tries to conjure up compunction, a calming technique he learned from his free trial on the Headspace app.

"So you were like spying on me the other day?" Megan laughs, picking up her book as she rolls her eyes.

"So it goes," Dennis states, ignoring her question, crossing his arms and turning his head to read from his book on the island; his body still facing Megan.

"They say that in the book after someone dies. What's that about?" Megan forfeits her inquisition, participating in the conversation; she swings her legs around, grazing Dennis's feet, melting his hostility.

Dennis pivots back; his manic euphoria peaking, the cocaine effects starting to wear as he leers at Megan. Contemplating, he pines for her and not so much as an object, but rather for her inexperience, her current stage in life, excitement for the unknown. The first quarter of existence, where anything is possible and there's always more time; every year that passes is momentous for physical growth and mental maturity, not knowing any other lives except for the first epoch, the one lived less than two decades with no reference to a previous life to miss; the purest time, not guided or influenced by the past.

"I mean, I could tell you my interpretation, but you're too busy gawking at me," Megan utters in a brash display of confidence; she's glowing, animated, and fully invested in his presence as if she knows Dennis is interested.

Dennis realizes his leg is pressed up against Megan's calf, but he doesn't care. He's feeling great, and he senses a connection, even if it's the drugs. Their legs touching feels like no big deal. His attention shifts to the mini figurine hanging from her necklace, a gilded serpent in a coiled pose.

"Is that a snake on your necklace?" he asks.

"Oh, this thing?" Megan chortles, retracting her head to give herself a double chin as she glances down, holding the charm.

"I picked this out randomly at a thrift shop. Think it was a dollar," she says, flaunting her infectious smile.

"Well, it's fitting. You are the forbidden fruit," Dennis laughs, becoming more relaxed with their banter.

"Oh yeah? Does that mean you want a taste?" Megan asks in a monotone, her eyes focusing on Dennis, mimicking his head movement to sustain eye contact, like she's trying to cast a spell with her pupils.

"So it goes," Dennis replies, turning his head to avoid subjecting his lips to accessibility.

"Tell me," Megan pries, her face still lingering forward toward Dennis.

"It's a flippant phrase, satirical. It's like saying 'oh well,' because life is meaningless; we're all just going to die, and there's nothing we can do," Dennis expresses, pushing his shoulders back to position himself further away from Megan's potential encroachment.

"That makes me feel afraid to die," Megan comments, partly frowning as she cradles her arms.

"Are you afraid to die?" she asks, maintaining a drooping bottom lip.

"I think I'm more afraid of dying while I'm still alive," he admits, adopting a softer tone and looking away.

"Are you afraid to die?" Dennis asks, returning his eye contact, feeling the top of Megan's foot rubbing against his shin.

"I was for a little bit after my brother died," Megan confesses, breaking eye contact for the first time; her face freezing from the bitter words.

Dennis can't believe what he's heard; his mouth drops open as he hunches forward with intrigue.

"Your brother died? I am so sorry to hear that," he consoles with a concerned pitch, furrowing his brows; he feels like he could cry, and he's not sure if it's genuine sorrow or the cocaine effects.

"It's okay," Megan whispers, placing her hands on her thighs.

"Yeah, that's kinda why I'm going to school at St. Vincent's. Well, not entirely."

"Wait, what? Tell me what happened," Dennis investigates, fully focused as he inches closer.

"Well, three years ago my older brother died. He was twenty-seven. We tried to live in the same town for as long as we could, but it was just too difficult. Everything reminded us of him: eating at his favorite pizza place, walking past his bedroom, seeing his friends in public. So we packed up and moved here, and my mom thought a private school was best."

"Is your dad still in the picture?"

"Oh yeah, that's another thing. My parents got divorced shortly after. They wouldn't stop blaming one another and all they did was fight. So, my Dad bought my mom this house for us," Megan explains, still looking down at the ground.

"Is your dad in the mafia?" Dennis deadpans, hoping to trigger a smile.

Megan laughs, tossing her head back as she holds her hand over her mouth, engaging eye contact. Her hands return to her knees, much more forward on her legs; her knuckles grazing Dennis's legs.

"No, I wish. Pretty sure I'm paying for college myself," Megan whimpers, sharing a pouty frown, like she's possibly flirting or being cutesy.

"How did he die?"

"He overdosed on heroin."

Dennis sighs in disbelief, deflating into a defeated pose; his shoulders falling forward.

"I am so fucking sorry," he expresses, pronouncing his apology with a slight tremble as his eyes well, imagining how distraught her parents had to be.

Speculating on his death, Dennis pictures Megan's mother discovering him in his bed, attempting to wake up the lifeless corpse she used to change when he was just a baby. Shaking the expired body of the toddler she made peanut butter and jelly sandwiches for, always cutting the crusts off, pleading for him to wake up, shoving him harder as reality set in. For some reason, he envisions her brother still living at home in the house he had grown up in.

"It's okay," Megan replies stoically, as if she's spent the last few years being counseled with the loss.

"What was his name?"

Megan stares for a few seconds before replying, as if she's maybe picturing his face. "Walter," she smiles, smothering her lips together, like she's struggling to not cry.

And it's a distinct poignancy Dennis recognizes in Megan; her face reddens, flushing with suppressed emotion. He can't fathom losing a sibling, especially at her age, and all of his preconceived ideas of who she is are clearly inaccurate; she may even be more damaged than him, he ponders. His heart hurts for her as he leans forward, contemplating some profound words he could possibly say, but he knows there's little solace in speaking, so he wraps his arms around her in a compassionate hug. Megan burrows into his chest, returning her arms around his torso, and Dennis can feel her quaking, emitting a high-pitched weep as he pulls her close.

"Life really sucks sometimes," he offers, his best platitudinal effort.

Megan tilts her head back to look at Dennis, her eyes heavy with desire; she swoops in, initiating a passionate kiss. Instinctively, Dennis reciprocates, caught up in the fervor, thinking she might need this, she's suffered too much loss. But after a few lustful seconds, Dennis pulls away, stopping her from mounting him on the stool, refusing to become an indelible character in her story.

And it's not like he wouldn't love to capitalize on her vulnerability, grief being a powerful aphrodisiac. Turning, bending her over the center island and yanking her bottoms down, penetrating her on the marble countertop with varying gray and white gradations, guiding his inches in and out of her fresh orifice, mere inches away from where she ate breakfast with her family; he could even watch himself in the act, catching their reflection in the polished chrome pendant lights overhead. He'd probably get away with it too, unless there's a small chance they have a hidden nanny camera. But it would certainly be a quickie, not enough footage to implicate him, he presumes. It wouldn't be his fault either. Nope, he could justify it, attribute the encounter to her enchanting flirtations, or he could just blame it on Renee, like everything else, blame it on being abandoned, heartbroken, forcing him to fornicate with a teenager. But he's better than this, or at least he knows Christine would think so. And he's not going to be the fucking creep Megan looks back on in twenty years with disgust.

"Time's up," he declares, standing up from the stool and packing his messenger bag, trying his best to diffuse the situation.

He notices she's no longer fraught; she's smiling.

"Wait."

"You don't want to stay for dinner?"

"No, it's been an hour," Dennis replies curtly, floating in place as he gauges the appropriateness of his actions, wondering about the severity of his offense.

He did decline her, he assures himself.

"Ok, maybe next time."

"Don't forget to take the check my mom left," Megan adds, hurrying over to Dennis as he dresses in the foyer, fumbling with his scarf and adjusting his jacket by the front door.

The setting sun casts a deep orange spotlight through the cathedral ceiling windows, the last shimmer before darkness, and Dennis knows he's racing the sunlight home.

"Thanks," he snatches the check from her outstretched hand, assessing her face for any indication of her demeanor.

He feels like a harlot, just being compensated for a kiss, still trying to get the taste of her tongue out of his mouth.

But Megan's still glowing, beaming with a smile, radiating happiness. She flips her hair back, exposing adorable dimples. And maybe a five-second kiss isn't the worst thing, since her brother died, Dennis rationalizes as he opens the door and leaves.

13. The Road Not Taken

A colossal American flag waved in the spring wind, hanging over the entryway of the venue. The sun, sinking into the estuary of the sky, dispersing light into the flapping reinforced folds; its shine shedding lucid blue and red rays on the double glass doors, casting a patriotic glow on the attendees entering the event. An assemblage of Crown Vics and other first responder vehicles with flashing lights was already in the parking lot by the time they arrived. It didn't daunt Christine; no, she was poised for the fifteenth anniversary commemoration of her father's passing on 9/11.

She had prepared a speech about her dad, consulting Dennis on adjective choices like "heroic," "courageous," and "daring," along with accompanying humorous anecdotes, such as the time her father broke his ankle sliding down the fireman's pole in the station after challenging his unit to see who could slide from the third floor to the bottom the fastest. He was always a competitor, instilling a passion in her for achieving and pushing oneself, she included. She practiced a few times, delivering her address to Dennis, usually breaking down during the solemn peroration, detailing how her father was the first to charge up the stairs of the fiery tower to rescue civilians and how she often contemplated what he was thinking during his final moments, realizing the building was collapsing. Hugging her every time after she finished practicing, Dennis made sure to express how proud he was of her and how her father was looking down on her with a smile.

Christine had everything set up for the evening a few days before, obsessing over every detail, from coordinating cocktail napkins with the firehouse's logo to printing black-and-white photos from her father's old albums, allowing an eager

Dennis to help. Although her father's department contributed generously to finance the event, Christine was determined to take care of the rest, citing her father's tenacity to do everything with a full heart as well as her sister's and mother's lack of expendable funds. Stocking the fridges with beverages and finger foods, Dennis and Christine smiled adoringly at each other, exchanging impromptu kisses every time they came close during the organizing, grabbing waists and arms. The event coincided with the beginning of their relationship, almost five months of dating.

Assembling place settings, playfully whipping each other with the napkins before folding them, they flirted and giggled like school children. Dennis found himself in awe of her natural beauty, an organic vivacity and silliness. Her hair was tied up in a bun as she positioned guest chairs and tidied the dedication table with framed pictures and her father's FDNY gear, still gorgeous with no makeup on. Her infectious smile always commanded Dennis's attention. Her cute mannerisms and constant optimism were always on display, as she was always humming a song or practicing an impromptu dance move as she decorated, like an arm wave, rolling her shoulder, transitioning her movement to the opposing side. An intrinsic liveliness, a fun contagious spirit that Dennis adored.

The event was a significant milestone for their relationship, not just because Dennis was meeting almost all of Christine's family, but because it was the first time in a year that he didn't feel the malignant impressions of Renee lingering on his consciousness. Not even a fragment of their last dialogue festered in his mind. He was falling in love with Christine, finally enjoying his life.

Dennis couldn't remember which were her relatives and which were her father's co-workers, even though Christine introduced everyone he met. The place was packed, filled with people of all different ages, from babies to elders, decorated individuals in uniform to arguably underdressed strays, a testament to her father's popularity and gregarious nature, attracting diverse individuals from all walks of life. Dennis must have shaken a thousand hands, but it didn't matter because all he was focused on was Christine, the absolutely stunning girl draped in a dark navy-blue v-cut dress. Her naturally tanned skin gleamed against the rich hue of her frock; her brilliant white teeth brightened up every conversation she participated in, her smile was radiant.

It felt both surreal and amazing for Dennis because he was involved with a captivating woman, and it had been roughly ten months since his last communication with Renee, a blistering exchange that left him despondent for the longest time. Echoing callous words were always amplified during times of serenity, but that night, he was finally feeling genuine peace, like maybe Christine was the biggest blessing he'd ever received.

The resounding chatter and flashes of photography flickered among the crowd, like little bursts of fireworks as retirees and peers reunited, exchanging signs of affection, handshakes, and hugs. The expansive room with minimalist décor and tall overhead lights exuded a professional aura, an impressionable veneration, a presidential vibe, reducing even the most egotistical to simple anthropoids. Laughter could be heard as work buddies recalled fond memories and encounters while on the job. The prestigious gathering oozed respect with each speech about Roger Ramirez, highlighting his accomplishments and major character strengths, his work ethic, honesty, and dedication to people, a selflessness that Dennis could easily identify in Christine.

Sitting next to her at the table in the back-left corner, closest to the kitchen in case she was needed by the staff, Dennis held Christine's hand under the draped linen cloth. Nothing overly affectionate, just a sign of support, letting her know he was there as the time for her speech approached. He could sense her nervousness, perspiration on her palm.

Flanked by the nasal breathing of Christine's alcoholic mother and overweight sister, Dennis missed a few punch lines and word choices from the esteemed orators. A collection of breadcrumbs and empty champagne flutes accumulated on her sister Jasmine's place setting as she sat, stuffing her face with complimentary bread and imbibing free alcohol. The stout single mother of two took full advantage of a night out. Had it been any other night, Dennis would have been antagonized to explosive proportions by Jasmine's open-mouth chewing and her under-the-breath commentary as she chugged pricey libations meant for toasting. But he was empathetic to their situation; fate had dealt the family a shitty hand with the early demise of their father, and both her mother and sister made poor life choices after his death, spending all the victim settlements they received from 9/11. Her sister dropped out of college and had children out of wedlock, and her mother turned to booze for solace, requiring a handle of liquor a day to keep the pain at bay.

Grief rendered people irrational and impulsive, Dennis knew, and it was another reason why Christine stood out like sea glass polished smooth among a family of rough driftwood, shaped by disaster. Even in the face of adversity, the calamity of her father perishing in such a tragedy when she was young, Christine used the event to motivate her, not deter. Instead she made responsible decisions and good choices, refusing a victimhood mentality and venturing on the right path for a brighter future, the veritable rose that grew from concrete. And Dennis knew had he lost his father when he was young, he'd have gone the other way, off the deep end into despair. He certainly wouldn't have lasted long enough to organize a fifteenth-year anniversary commemoration.

"Our next speaker is a person I remember quite fondly, always hanging on the arm of her father as a little girl. Although she's not as little anymore, I'll always remember the stories her dad shared with us at work about his rambunctious, sporty Christine. Please welcome our final speaker for the night, the daughter of

Roger, Christine Ramirez," her father's close friend announced, holding out a supinated hand toward her seat, triggering a spotlight overhead.

The applause erupted immediately as Christine rose, flashing a recognizable anxious smile as she adjusted to the pouring light overhead. A figurative aureole for the angel, she made her way to the podium; her shoulders pushed back, her posture upright, gathering confidence as she shuffled her cue cards in hand.

"That's my baby," her mother slurred, barely mustering up enough strength to clap as she pressed her elbows down on the edge of the table, anchoring herself to stay upright.

Collecting herself in front of the crowd, Christine flipped her hair and took several deep breaths. A staunch proponent of mindfulness, she smiled at Dennis before she began.

"It seems like it's been forever that my life has been separated into two sections: the time before Tuesday, September 2001, and the time after," she opened, evoking a solemn mood.

She spoke with purpose, an impressive elocution, clear and loud, making solid eye contact as she proceeded, scanning the room with a crisp pitch. She delivered a cathartic, heartfelt speech about her father, resisting tears in some parts as her voice trembled, touching on all emotions with evocative accounts. She spoke of how he was always the first one into a fire, never resigning until everyone was evacuated and how she used to dress up as a fireman for every Halloween as a kid to be just like her dad, even as a teenager. Surveying the audience, Dennis noticed people laughing, people crying, people completely moved by her words.

"Let this be a reminder that you can never tell someone you love them enough, so hug your loved ones as tightly as you can, because one day, you won't get the chance," she concluded, dabbing at her saturated eyelashes.

A thunderous ovation erupted as the crowd stood, clapping for the stirring, resonating speech. Cheers and whistles rang out as Christine paused, soaking in the moment. She smiled, wiping tears from her eyes, and waved to the crowd. A row of firefighters in uniform marched to the front, synchronizing their movements, and saluted as she departed from the lectern. A stern man with gray hair approached, offering her a folded American flag in a glass case. Pausing for pictures, Dennis stood, applauding, welling with emotion. The patriotism emanated in the atmosphere, commanding a sense of connectivity and pride for the country, a reverence for being American. An inexplicable feeling captured Dennis, like he was part of something bigger, something historic and significant, and everyone there was family.

It was a transcendent occasion for Dennis, standing with admiration as he gazed at an ethereal Christine, the spotlight still overhead. She glowed with exuberance and pride for her accomplishment. The electricity radiated as the ovation continued, and Dennis was elated, experiencing a vicarious happiness and fulfillment from the present as Christine promenaded, making her way back to the table. Still clapping and relishing the moment for Christine, Dennis glanced down at the table, noticing his phone lighting up with multiple text messages flashing across the screen, all from the same unstored number. Lifting his phone to check the communication, Dennis was baffled at first by the anonymous number but recognized the "215" area code:

"Hi"

"........."

"Hi Punk lol," the texts read, each sent approximately fifteen minutes after the other.

He must not have felt the vibrations from the incoming messages before, he told himself; he hadn't been paying attention to his phone all day. Musing and staring blankly at his screen, Dennis finally realized who the mysterious messenger was; it was Renee. The realization hit him hard, causing a moment of paralysis, his breath escaping as he struggled to comprehend her motive. It had been almost a year since they interacted, they were moving on, he thought, his conscience was clear.

Like his foot stuck in quicksand, he could feel himself sinking from within. Anxiety swarmed, eliciting the sullen, draining sensation that consumed his insides for months as he thought of all the sleepless nights, the toxicity, the maddening obsession of wondering what she was doing and being glued to his phone. Like a wrecking tidal wave, Dennis was engulfed with evocative flashes of memories, vignettes, fragments of recollections, crawling back into his mind, how she always kissed him behind the ear, or how they used animal emojis to refer to each other; her as his cub, him as her pup.

Dennis typed into the chat box, "Hi," but erased it before sending, shoving his phone into his pocket; he wasn't going to let his ex-fiancée ruin the night.

Christine lingered, beautiful and buoyant, as Dennis quaked from ambivalence, recalling how miserable he was for the few months after he and Renee stopped talking. He remembered how desperate he felt for her attention, checking his phone constantly for some sort of communication from her, and how he felt for the longest time like a part of him had died when she left, how incomplete he felt, like he had a limb amputated; a feeling he never wanted to experience again.

Sighing as she returned to the table, Christine glanced at Dennis, awaiting his response, like an eager child hoping to hear positive affirmation for a job well done, but Dennis was frozen in thought, lost in deep cogitation.

"How did I do?" she asked, her face stuck in a smile.

The question floated through his ears without resonance. The audacity of Renee to steal this moment from him, he thought. He couldn't believe she'd text him after all this time, even referring to him as "punk," like they were buddies who went to kindergarten together. It wasn't fair, he thought. He had deleted her number from his phone; that was the closure. How could she just barge back into his life like nothing had happened? Who was she to think he would just come running back, and how could he be such a sucker to let her, he deliberated.

"Babe?"

A contemplative Dennis spaced out, a kinetic stillness, pondering on a cutting response he could send to Renee. Something about her being poison and how gross she was for settling for someone as physically unattractive as Carl, something real cutting. The hurt was flooding back, but then he felt Christine's hand grab his, resuscitating him from pernicious rumination.

"Are you okay?"

"I'm sorry. You did absolutely amazing. I cannot even tell you how proud I am of you," Dennis replied, pulling her close and kissing her on the forehead.

The heat from the kiss touched his soul, her intrinsic warmth capable of thawing even the coldest of hearts. Dennis soon recognized the most disturbing part of receiving the texts: he was partly relieved Renee reached out to him, he was delighted. He had wanted her to.

"Christine, can we borrow you for a few quick photos?" a woman in a pant suit inquired, escorting her over to a small crowd of people waiting for her.

"I'll be right back," Christine announced to Dennis, sharing a concerned smile as if she knew something was vexing him.

His phone vibrated again, and Dennis retrieved it with annoyance, yanking it from his pocket.

"Helllllo?" Renee texted.

She had to be drunk, he told himself, quickly recalling how she would occasionally text him when they were taking a break and how the next day, she would always refute anything affectionate she had said, reducing it to merely being intoxicated.

A familiar heaviness sank into his stomach, a dreadful weight on his soul that he knew all too well from the months spent desperately trying to win her back. He hated the possibility that this would be his life again; he had come so far, he convinced himself. Fraught with emotion, fighting the currents of nostalgia, Dennis turned and scanned the room to find Christine among the masses, like a drowning voyager looking for a life raft.

"Hello," he typed back into the chat box, pausing before sending.

He mulled over the possibility that she would diminish his text the next day on account of her being under the influence, another condescension, and he wasn't going to grant her that power over him again; she had humiliated him enough. Clenching his phone with angst and turmoil, Dennis deliberated on whether she was really trying to come back into his life and if this was his last chance to venture back on the path to a life with her. Her text messages echoed in his head, the sound of her voice returning to his mind, poking at his newfound poise. Like a recovering addict, Dennis's sobriety was tested with the drug that had derailed him.

Oscillating between his phone and the distant profile of Christine amidst a group of people commending her delivery, the joyous positivity that filled Dennis's insides was extinguishing, a gradual evacuation of contentment every time he looked back at his phone. He could feel Renee's hold attaching to his mindset once again, manipulating its way back into his psyche like a clamp, an industrial vise on his heart, gradually applying pressure, reminding him of how damaged he still was, how unworthy he was of happiness.

Suddenly, meeting someone on a dating app seemed pathetic, even if it had connected him with someone as virtuous and unique as Christine. It felt like a contrived love story that lacked merit compared to how he had met Renee serendipitously at the gym. It had taken him months of hard work to woo her, precisely exchanging small talk, inquiring about her life, and dropping subtle insights about himself while maintaining a cool, confident mystique, a game of strategy. He had won her over like a sought-after prize, he remembered; he didn't need a digital matchmaker.

The new, beautiful life materializing with Christine was becoming contaminated by Renee's pollutive texts, causing Dennis to second-guess himself. He grasped his smartphone in a subconscious attempt to break it, thwarting further communication, but the fortified plastic remained uncompressed, and the unwelcome texts continued to pour in:

"..."

"Hello????"

Tears surged in his ducts as he wondered how he could resist a possible reconciliation when it was all he had wanted for as long as he could remember. But Dennis knew the risk versus reward wasn't worth it. The possibility that her desire might be purely motivated by intoxication, that she might not really want him back, would be the final devastating blow to his fragile ego, a treacherous trail that could kill him. So he reacted to escalating emotion and temptation with tenacity and resistance for once, invoking inspiration from Christine's speech as he faced the figurative crossroad.

Deleting his response from the chat box to Renee as well as all of her text messages, Dennis decided he wasn't going to give in. He wasn't going to choose the perilous road, one he was too conversant with. No, because the view was too damn peaceful and gorgeous on the path he was on, the one less traveled, even if there were obstacles and hazards ahead. He chose the road not taken with brazen optimism at the time, but it would ultimately be a decision he'd come back to contemplate often, a choice he'd always reflect upon, wondering how different his life could have been.

####

The exposed bay window creates a focal point for the front of the house; the convex glass is a lens into their home. It was never covered during the ten years they lived there. No, they didn't even have blinds, just beige gauze curtains that they rarely kept closed. This produced a constant open view into their home, specifically of the empty extended living room surrounded by a perimeter of children's toys. Dennis recalls numerous times pulling up to see his baby niece and nephew with the two dogs sitting in the windowsill, looking out, rubbing their hands all over the glass, producing smudges and making silly faces as they waved to him. But today, he's not greeted by overbearing cuteness. No, instead it's just an empty single-hung window and a bleak front yard, vacant of life. The "under contract" sign from Weichert is stuck in the ground by the mailbox, like a friendly headstone for the marriage that perished.

Dennis is sure "Cindy Collins" is a great realtor; she's probably a doll. But her large headshot with its asymmetrical smile perturbs him. It feels like she's not just happy about her 6% commission on the sale but also about the dissolution of the family.

The burnt grass of an overly cut lawn distinguishes John and Natalie's home from the rest of the houses in the development. The crusty, dried dirt of the plant beds surrounding their nest hasn't been cultivated in at least a year, requiring work they haven't put in. Dennis deduces this as he pictures a disgruntled, anxious John cutting the lawn almost every day, even after work on weekdays. Pushing the lawnmower around for an hour to give himself a reprieve from his racing thoughts and building resentment; John unwittingly killing the grass.

Parking on the street, Dennis isn't sure whether to go through the open garage or try the front door, which is usually unlocked. They often forget about their surroundings, neglecting common-sense security and other standards, instead fixating on iPads, smartphones, or television, anything to avoid each other during their marriage. Perhaps they don't need to be concerned in their affluent neighborhood, but allowing easy access to their home subconsciously signifies they don't care, Dennis concludes.

Standing at the halfway point of the driveway, a hanging gutter end draws his attention, jutting out from the side of the roof. Dennis recalls the summer after he graduated college when he came over to help clean the drains and move their new furniture in. He remembers being envious, hoping he could own a house as large one day. He aspired to have a family when he was his brother's age, thinking twenty-nine was the perfect time to start. Natalie and John had invested a lot of money in the home, renovating the kitchen and replacing carpets with hardwood floors before they moved in, swapping dated designs for dark mahogany cabinetry and cherry oak floorboards. The place appeared majestic to Dennis as a teenager, possessing multiple bathrooms and expansive rooms, luxuries that seemed indicators of a successful, promising life.

He had no concept of money at the time but assumed it wasn't cheap, recalling how they said multiple times it was their most important asset. An investment, Dennis ponders, standing, staring at the broken PVC and desolate landscape, deliberating on the concept of "investment." Reflecting on whether it's an applicable metaphor for their marriage, he considers how they didn't put any effort into their nuptials after the day they moved in, letting their relationship expire, like forgotten lettuce in the bottom drawer of the fridge. Dennis knows a passive strategy is no way to handle an investment; no, it's better to be aggressive with investments while still young to ensure a better return, according to Business Insider. Yeah, he's been reading more, consuming intellectual articles about saving for the future and steps to experiencing a fulfilling life.

He's been trying to better himself, even attempting meditation; sitting on his faux suede couch, paying closer attention to his breath and stream of thought, riding along like a current. But he can't bear the stillness, the company of himself, deviating from the exercise with antagonizing contemplations, like the current location of his birth certificate or when he last checked his 403B and whether he's losing money as he sits there. He's even tried making a bucket list, a plan for the future, something to attain, but he can't think of anything else he wants to do besides meeting an armadillo and catching the moment right before he falls asleep, that fleeting second between cognition and unconsciousness when it's easier to let go.

But it all comes back to trying to be in the present: experiencing every moment, a consciousness of each thought, each breath, each observation. Yeah, he's finished the Krishnamurti book, and he should be feeling super enlightened, making a more concerted effort to take a mindful approach to living in the now. But he's not succumbing to leaps of faith or dogmas, especially theories with significant flaws, no matter how uplifting they seem. He just can't, because unplanned pregnancies and hand tattoos happen when people only live in the moment and so do drug overdoses and drunk driving accidents. Maybe he should read the book again; he's not quite sure. Or maybe he's just too conditioned to see imperfections in everything, identifying with negativity. James probably won't want to be his friend, he thinks, since he can't derive a true epiphany from the suggested reading material.

The sun sets behind the house, the brilliant sphere bursting the horizon with prismatic streaks. The depleting daylight creates cold pockets of air that brush against Dennis's exposed arms, and he can feel a change in the atmosphere, a tension looming. He leaves his phone in his car, locking the door as he walks away, purposely. He swears today is when he reduces the compulsions, breaking digital engagement, stopping the persistent stimulation, the updates and connections, craving dopamine and seeking notifications for five to six hours a day of screen time. Yeah, he knows he's been integrated into a multifarious algorithm, incorporating his searches, views, and online behaviors, but he's going to give it his best shot at disconnecting, especially after his explosive Tinder exchange yesterday afternoon with Kaitlyn, 26, an MBA graduate from Yale, about the Oxford comma. It wasn't his fault, really; he just asked what her position was, whether she thought it was necessary. Her response was light-hearted but trivialized its usage, carelessly relegating its incorporation to formality, like writing a term paper, so he presented a cogent example on its significance, posing a hypothetical question.

"George has 100 pounds of steel, 50 pounds of iron and coal. How much iron does George have?"

Kaitlyn responded with indifference, possibly to change the subject yet still diminishing the example with a terse response, "I'm not solving a math problem lol."

This prompted Dennis to rebut with an aggressive soliloquy: "It's not a mathematical question; it concerns reading comprehension. The omission of the last comma obfuscates the meaning, as it insinuates a special connection between the last two items in the list. This failure to distinguish specific quantities makes it unclear how much iron George actually possesses."

His ardency came across as acerbic, apparently, as she took his discourse as a personal attack, responding with a diatribe about having two masters degrees from an Ivy league school and how she never flaunts her intelligence and he "ought to" figuratively "eat five humble pies because he'll never attract a mate with such pretentiousness." And Dennis was about to apologize for the misunderstanding and clarify he's just a grammar extremist, he really was, but she blocked him before he could fully type his response. She's right about never finding a partner though, he knows, because an existence in the specious realm of perfectly presented selfies is a prescription for disappointment, impossible standards, but that's not why he's attempting to disconnect.

He's embarrassed, really, by how much he seeks out social media. Like passing a trainwreck and rubbernecking, Dennis spends the last two hours before falling asleep swimming in the void of others, watching as individuals project their personas and personalities. He sees how Kelsey, the girl he fingered in tenth grade, is now a purported triathlete. Swiping through her stories, he sees her flaunting her latest gear, posing in her helmet and super official outfit, always giving a thumbs up during her bike rides and swim sessions, her entire identity on display. He remembers her being a bit of a druggie back in the day, so it makes sense she traded one addiction for another, one that's more socially acceptable.

Then there's Brian, the kid who was riddled with acne in middle school like a pepperoni pizza and creeped out all the girls with his stalkerish vibe; he's mastered auto-tune and is now touring locally as the lead singer of a band, portraying himself as some sort of heartthrob. He proudly shares photos of concerts with twenty-five people in attendance, announcing "Cool Brawn Summer," their "debut album" on Spotify, the modern-day equivalent of self-publishing.

Dennis can't help but watch and wonder what happens to Kelsey after she completes "X" number of triathlons or Brian when he releases "X" more albums and they still don't feel fulfilled. What becomes of their constructed identities then? What will they resort to next to seek validation, to fill the endless void?

Dennis feels the same way lately, recognizing the impact social media has on his mood. He's been feeling pretty self-conscious too, so he's been posting more often, relishing the rush of neurotransmitters as he checks for likes every two and a half minutes, rewarded by little hearts that pop up on a miniature screen. It's pretty crazy, he knows, to put such weight on the acceptance of others, but the feeds on Instagram are engulfing, numbing, and he's finding it harder and harder to detach from the scrolling, searching, and seeking the end of ceaseless reels. The waters are deep, vast, and comforting. Ironically, the deterioration of his sociability is setting in; he feels a resistance to interacting with others, a reluctance to engage with anyone. He barely has enough social stamina to small talk with his affable neighbor Carson and his wife Cathy when he encounters one of them as he retrieves his mail from the cluster mailboxes. The alienation is worsening but only because he's starting to actually enjoy it.

He's been thinking, contemplating how crazy it is that people spend the first half of their life learning and implementing behaviors and the second half carrying them out, living with predictable routines and habits. And it's all about behavior, really, and that's what's really agitating him, a nucleus of insanity. He can identify a flaw in his own actions, yet he can't change or execute, just like how he routinely experiences gum bleeding from brushing his teeth too hard. He knows he needs to ease up, but he can't scale it back, no matter how soft a brush he chooses. It's as if his hand takes over when he puts the toothbrush into his mouth, maneuvering the bristles with immense force, his gums receding, his mind stupefied until he rinses out swirls of blood into the sink. He's incapable of relinquishing self-applied pressure, a recurring temperament driven by neuroticism.

It's the same concept of irrevocable behavior when he explores new profiles and personalities in a semi-conscious state, checking follower-to-following ratios as status metrics, looking at likes, accumulations of individual votes for validation, and checking tagged photos for traces of authenticity, connections to others, links to unfiltered, unedited photos shared by others. And it's having a major influence on his outlook, whether he's fully aware of it or not: normalizing instant judgment and criticism of others, formulating opinions on people by their content and appearance, a meretricious existence.

He's done it a few times with his student Megan. Yeah, he's pretty much studied all her vanity indicators, noting only 106 posts since the beginning of her account in 2020, a profile with 300 followers despite following 800. She's matured from bathroom mirror selfies with backward ball caps to suggested candid filtered photos of her looking off into the distance or facing a friend while they laugh and smile ridiculously. And he's been doing a good job avoiding her engagements as she habitually likes an old photo of his; he still views her stories, though, defenseless against the urge to look, a modern voyeur. Things were going well for a few days since the kiss; there wasn't a next day, nope, they didn't even speak. He foiled her attempts to talk, leaving her DMs on read. And they haven't spoken further, as he even minimized interactions during class and thwarted her mother's efforts to schedule subsequent tutoring sessions. So it's almost like it never happened.

And then around 11:30 P.M. last night, as Dennis took a break from scrubbing the corners of his shower to reduce potential mildew buildup, right after he vacuumed his rug and had a revelation about society and its metaphorical connection to cleaning a carpet, positing that each person is a veritable rug: constantly influenced by external forces, embedded with dirt and imprints, inflicted and influenced by others, individual piles manipulated by societal trends, daily occurrences, and years of use, yet everyone tries their best to clean their surfaces, tidy their presentations for appeal, mitigate the impressions and grime that accumulate, neaten their fabricated faces to conceal the effects of an unrelenting world, he opened an unsolicited DM from Megan: a photo.

He was startled as he viewed a nude image, a disappearing selfie of her lying on a bed, her arm extended upward to snap the photo, revealing an exposed breast as her hand covered the other. The lower portion of the picture showcased defined, turned legs, a mantis pose with a diaphanous covering, revealing a minor glance of her shaved canvas. And he spiraled for a moment, grasping the severity of the situation, receiving a naked photo from a female student. But it wasn't the unprovoked message that's been bothering him; no, it's its lasting impression, the vision that still lingers, the flashes of flesh on his mind, and he's ashamed of how often he thinks of it.

He's thinking he'll just never go back on Instagram now; maybe this is the only way to wean himself off the social wasteland. But it's a bit too sobering, and he can't tell if the pervasive negativity is emanating from his steady submergence in social media or if it's the lack of substances in his system to soften the ridges of reality since he's also kicked back on the narcotics, finishing the miniature baggie of cocaine approximately five days ago. He's even avoided ingesting the sporous mushroom twigs he obtained from James, determined to facilitate clearer cognition, especially since he's finally going to be having dinner with Christine tomorrow night. His best foot is going forward, he's reassured himself several times, even talking to himself in aphorisms and Bob Marley choruses, "Every little thing is gonna be all right," he recites, eschewing the precognitive thoughts that something bad is on the verge of happening, hoping Megan just leaves him alone.

"Hello," Dennis announces as he opens the front door.

"Dennis? Is that you?" a quaking question echoes from the hallway, unmistakably his mother's worried voice.

Looking over to the cluttered room, a cramped space packed with memories, Dennis discerns a trophy poking out from the top of an opened cardboard box, stacked onto two larger bottom boxes. The dancer's head prods upward, the ballerina in an arabesque pose, leg and arms level. It was an award that used to be displayed on Reese's dresser in her pink room. He wondered if Reese would still participate in dance once the divorce finalized, since it was her favorite thing to do. She possessed a natural rhythm since she was a baby, swaying back and forth to Mickey Mouse Playhouse in front of the TV.

"We are cleaning out John's house period. It's a mess period. Will call you later exclamation point," his mother's loud, monotone voice booms from the kitchen.

Dennis doesn't even need to see her to confirm. He can envision her speaking aloud as she talks to text, holding the phone close to her face with both hands, like an oversized walkie-talkie, a message relayed to her sister, her best friend, Dennis speculates.

The familiar wall art display that had been divided into three sections is nested in a shoebox beside the ballerina trophy. The butterfly's wings, detailed in curlicues, now separated. Dennis wonders why it's packed this way; maybe they ran out of boxes.

The bickering of his parents sounds from the kitchen, and Dennis hears the agitated remarks from an exasperated Russ as he slams cabinets, rattling their contents.

"She's a piece of shit, she really is," the barbed words escape from Russ, which would have probably been uttered under his breath if he wasn't so upset, sparking with agitation.

"What's going on, guys?" Dennis intervenes, stepping into the kitchen and observing his parents fussing over an oversized box on the island counter.

"See, I told you I heard Dennis come in," Mary announces with a snarky smile, turning toward him and launching her hands up in the air with dramatic execution.

It was as if Russ and she had argued earlier about whether someone opened and closed the front door, and she had been right the whole time.

"Thank you for coming, Den," Mary says softly.

"Of course, Mom," Dennis smiles.

"You know, it's important for you boys to stick together," Mary sighs.

Sensing an oncoming lecture or some kind of platitude, Dennis crosses his arms.

"What do you mean?" he asks, exhaling.

"Things are going to change when we're gone," she says quietly.

Dennis looks at her, confused.

"What are you saying?"

With a small, sad smile, Mary nods.

"You and your brothers... you're the only ones who share your childhood."

Dennis frowns, not sure where she's going with this, but clearly the emotional scene has tapped into deeper feelings, triggering embedded thoughts, a purge from the subconscious.

"After we're gone and you have your own kids, your childhood is over. The only ones who'll keep it alive are you and your brothers, with your stories, your memories," she pauses, her gaze drifting toward the breakfront in the dining room, her next assignment.

"You'll see."

Dennis stands there, speechless, as his mother walks away. He's not sure what to say, but maybe there's really nothing to rebut, just another somber concept to mull over later. Scanning the perimeter, noticing more boxes are scattered around; cartons of various sizes line the edges of the kitchen, overstuffed with household items and random keepsakes that had been shoved into the back of cabinets and drawers for years, forgotten about or deemed lost. Objects without designated places were retrieved during the final clean-out.

The rectangular wooden kitchen table is clear, indicating his parents had been filling the boxes on the floor, rummaging through cupboards and sorting items with non-sensical purpose. The warped center of the table still holds a gray blemish, a stain they could never repair from that one Christmas dinner when they served steaming hot mashed potatoes from the stove to the table, unaware the finish wasn't heat-resistant; Natalie's mother placed the casserole dish on top of a single sheet of paper towel. They used to have Christmas dinners at their house for a few years, Dennis remembers, until they decided to break tradition by going on vacation for the holiday. After that, things were always just too busy, they claimed, so it stopped, concluding family gatherings and special times together, a herald for the beginning of the end.

"What do you guys need me to do?" Dennis asks.

Rubbing his fingers across the grain of the table, Dennis wonders what the last dinner was like. If they ordered in or if Natalie even made dinner; if the sauce was cold from an easy microwave quick cook, if the noodles were tough from being overboiled on an unattended stovetop. All they ever ate was mac and cheese since it was quick and convenient. He wonders if they even knew it was their last meal together as a complete family, if they knew how different life was going to be.

The clash of stainless-steel pots smacking the floor yanks Dennis by the ears, as Russ scrambles to collect the scattered cookware and coordinating lids dispersed around the porcelain tile floor.

"Dad, let me move that stuff," Dennis insists, scurrying to gather the rolling tops.

"Jesus, Russell, you're going to break the only stuff John owns!" Mary exclaims, fretting with a shaky voice, rushing over with her arms folded, escalating the scenario.

"I got it, for Christ's sake," a riled Russ roars, his fogged glasses falling off the brim of his nose as he crouches to clean up, a garnish to his exacerbating anger.

"Well, you clearly don't. You just dropped them all. I really hope you didn't break anything," Mary unintentionally provokes, huffing and puffing.

"Would you just stop!" Russ hollers, clutching several miniature pots against his chest in a flustered exhibition of rage.

"It's his stuff. If she can't, he can get... fucking shit," Russ stammers incoherently, boiling as he staggers around.

"Guys, would you just both stop," Dennis demands, stepping between the two like two quarreling kids.

"I'll pick up the pots and pans. Do you have a box for them?"

"We need to get these out before Natalie and her family come and take them!" Russ hyperventilates, continuing to cradle as many skillet pans as he can.

His face is rouge, pumping with blood; his gray hair appearing lighter than usual, emphasized by the ultra-red hue of his churned visage.

"Dad, Dad, relax. I promise, I'll take care of it," Dennis grabs the items from his father's arms, pulling them away from his feeble grip, flickers of anxiety creeping from the corners of his chest.

"I just thought I'd be able to carry them all," Russ confesses, conceding.

"It's okay, Dad. Here, just go get a box for these."

His father obliges, scampering to the garage, avoiding eye contact with Mary.

"He's been like this all week, Dennis," his mother comments, whispering with an annoyed cadence.

Dennis can't ever tell what her purpose is for informing him about his father's degeneration; he wonders if she's indirectly implying he needs to do something, maybe reprogram him, perform a fucking lobotomy or brain surgery.

"Well, you certainly don't help," Dennis remarks.

"What did I do?" Mary gasps as if she's been accused of treason.

"You don't do anything to deescalate the situation. It's not helping. You can learn to appease the man."

"So it's my fault," she shrieks, victimized, shrugging with her hands held up, her quintessential reaction pose.

Russ returns with a large box, double his width, which he has to carry sideways to see where he's walking.

"Just put it down on the floor," Dennis instructs, the assortment of pots and pans already stacked, ready to be loaded.

"What is going on with the house? Where is John going to live?" Dennis asks, confused but calm, trying to invoke a more relaxed atmosphere.

The kitchen walls, once decorated with numerous drawings made by the kids, are now empty with marks of peeling paint where the pictures used to be. Dusty outlines of furniture that used to be there adorn the floor of the adjacent dining room.

"Natalie and her family are going to clean this whole place out when they get here, so we need to grab all of this stuff before they take it, just like they did in the upstairs bedrooms," Russ ululates, rummaging through the drawer next to the Viking stove, collecting loose gadgets and utensils in his hands, as if time is running out.

"Dad, Dad, just calm down," Dennis attempts to pacify, alarmed at his father's paroxysm and wondering if it's associated with his aging; he's never really seen him panic before.

"We'll get it all figured out," Dennis reassures, using a quieter voice.

Oozing anxiety with evasive eye contact and jolting movements, Russ paces from box to box without any plan. Dennis wants him to know it's really going to be okay, but he knows his father is incapable of truly understanding; the worry is too overwhelming, all-consuming.

"Is John going to still live here?" Dennis asks, rubbing his dad's back.

"He's going to come live with us until the divorce is finalized," Russ responds, a little more subdued.

"How would he still live here? Did you not see the sign outside?" Mary interrupts with a condescending tone, her questions sharp and pointed.

"Well, where is John? Is he sleeping upstairs?" Dennis retorts, turning toward his mother.

"He's taken the kids to Chuck-E-Cheese's."

"You don't think he should be here?"

"He already cleaned out his bedroom this morning. He needs to be there for the kids. He needs to keep them happy," his mom rationalizes, reciting it louder, seemingly reassuring herself.

Dennis knows his mother handles her irritation differently than Russ. It's how she usually deals with grief. Her intentions are well-meaning, but her approach is often destructive; she projects onto others instead of internalizing, creating a cantankerous mood that breeds further antagonism, even when she doesn't mean it entirely.

"And just look at this damn espresso maker, it's practically brand new," Russ declares, slapping the smooth side of the large steel appliance, intensifying his fit.

"Do you remember, we bought that for Natalie because she complained she never had enough time to grab a coffee at Starbucks in the morning?"

"Yes, Russ. I know," Mary yields, responding with a softer tone.

She joins Russ by the bar area countertop, shaking her head as she looks at Dennis. Attempting to wrap the power cord around its base, Mary struggles to manipulate the wire; her infirmed arms barely contain enough strength to open the capsule shoot for inspection. The slate gray Alabama sweatshirt hangs from her neck, revealing her dwindling frame; her lithe forearms spotlighted against the baggy rolled-up sleeves. The pullover of John's alma mater, her designated cleaning attire for yard work or dusting, has been her go-to for as long as Dennis can remember. He teeters to his mother, assisting her with packing the appliance.

"Well, that's his as far as I'm concerned. I don't give a shit, we bought it," Russ hollers, his face still red as he watches.

"Okay, okay, but I'll put it in the box. The two of you are going to get hurt trying to move this stuff."

Dennis can feel his pulse racing, his chest warming, the detectable conception of a panic attack, but he knows he has to keep it together. Someone has to take control.

"Where do you want me to put these?" he asks, hoping to transition them away from further antipathy.

"You know, I don't give a shit, that espresso maker is John's," Russ comments.

"We know, you already said that," Mary replies.

Tuning out the chirping of his squabbling parents, Dennis proceeds to organize the boxes, stretching packing tape across the face of each carton, ensuring a tight seal on the ones that can be closed and tucking the top portions down as far as he can on the ones that contain heftier items. His parents continue their quibbling, expressing contemptuous remarks aloud as Dennis focuses on the task of packing, arranging the interiors of boxes with strategic order, tidying items together, a modern Tetris. It's the best approach to being productive, Dennis decides, as the critical commentary on Natalie continues, their failed marriage, ceaseless word vomit spewing everywhere.

And it's a jarring realization that grips Dennis as he carries the tenth box to the car: how incredibly powerful regret is, toxic, consuming, and everlasting. It's an emotion that has no antidote; it's not like sadness that can be overcome with laughter or coddled with love. It's not like anger; it doesn't ease with time and is never truly forgotten. It's not like fear; it can't be comforted with reassurance. Regret is a peculiar sentiment, ubiquitous around deathbeds, lingering for years in the subconscious, haunting with words never said and actions never taken. It burrows inside your heart, creating a melancholic echo that's always heard, resonating at your lowest times for the rest of your life.

Dennis sets the box inside the open liftgate of his parents' truck, placing it on top of the last piled column, completing the row to create a leveled wall of cardboard, a monolith of memories. And maybe that's all memories are: stacks of boxes filled with moments, things that used to be important to us and things we wish we could forget, stored away in the back of our brains, time capsules of traumas and treasures, laying around to be unpacked one day, for better or for worse.

As he aligns the boxes, ensuring no tip-overs during the drive and imagining the chaos that would ensue among his parents, he notices random objects his mother must have taken from the home before, scattered around the back seat. Peeking between the crevices of the worn divider, he recognizes a few items, like the cartoonish cow cookie jar Jake used to "moo" at as a baby in his highchair, as well as the silver-plated picture frame she gifted them with their wedding photo, a family heirloom she received from her great-grandmother, who gave the same gift to her when she was married.

He reaches for his phone in his pocket, his go-to distraction from the present, but his hand sinks into an empty pouch. No accessible escapism at his fingertips, triggering a feeling of emptiness, as a percolation of thought occurs, dripping with elucidations. He's forced to face reality.

His heart feels heavy as he steps back inside, watching his parents, now reduced to fussy toddlers. But instead of sadness, a strange clarity settles over him, a realization about loss and the futility of chasing validation. And it's not just that his brother now has a place to live, luckily, since he moved out two months ago. No, it's deeper than that. It's about the absurdity of it all, really, life, social media, and how in the end, none of it matters. The likes, the followers, how placing ultimate value on the perception of others is guaranteed disappointment. No, the only real inoculation for the slow erosion of self is learning to accept the apology never received, embrace the applause that's never given, and find peace in the goodbye never spoken, just to survive. Because to hold on to those things is to harbor the past, a plague on the present moment, the surest way of killing yourself.

14. A Modest Proposal

The instant messages became instant, popping up as soon as he logged on; no longer a nervous waiting game of cat and mouse but rather an eager yet vulnerable animal darting into plain sight, desperate to be noticed. No more anxious periods of anticipating messages or quiet uncertainties of not knowing what to respond; no; his speakers chimed and clinked with rapid texts from Susanna continuously, firing away as soon as he became active on AOL. Overzealous communications riddled with exclamation points and love nicknames, the blue letters of her newly created screen name vibrant on the glowing boxy screen: each new prompt resounding with line breaks of additional text, like a musical typewriter.

And it wasn't "**Susanna_Howard98**" anymore, no, she had a different moniker, something more personal that she created, more sentimental, mawkish, something to express her affection every time they chatted.

"**DCCandyBunny2005:** Working on any projects soon?"

Her subtle messages inquired, referring to their covert weekend gatherings, which had been dwindling since the wedding dress ordeal. The strange screen name radiated on the dull Dell monitor; an amalgamation of Dennis's initials and pet names, since Dennis once referred to her as a "sweet bunny" during a coital stupor, both soft and sensual, and the year 2005 to commemorate their consummation.

"**DCCandyBunny2005:** You there???"

She'd pry if he didn't respond after a few minutes, spoiling any potential fascination, reducing herself to a nuisance that required constant attention; an instant surrender in the power dynamic. Pestering instead of seducing, the conversations became one-sided, surface-level, as Dennis felt himself losing interest in Susanna, turned off by her neediness and easy accessibility, which seemed to only provoke further aggressive pursuit by her. He'd avoid conversation, swatting her away like a fly. The messages rang, consistent clamoring as the computer speakers rattled, even more annoying than the siren static that sounded seconds before an incoming phone call. And her strange screen name wasn't even the most awkward aspect of the relationship. No, it was the escalation of oversharing, the confessions, like how she thought she maybe destroyed her first marriage when she was twenty-five because she wasn't as sexually open as she'd become, despite her ex-husband also being an alcoholic.

It was all a big treasure chest of repressed memories and thoughts, baggage dumped on Dennis as the days passed, quashing her sex appeal and quelling his libido. The burden became too heavy to carry, adding more emotional weight with each fornication, each encounter feeling more serious, like maybe it wasn't fun anymore. Besides, he was going off to high school soon, graduating to the next level in his flourishing sex life, the next conquest of sultry flesh and adolescent debauchery, like he'd seen in the movies; she was just the first of many more, he told himself, as he exited out of her intrusive instant messages. His desire for her diminished; her allure no longer captivating, the closer he got. Like a Monet painting, the brilliant vivid brushstrokes admired from afar were just a colorful mess up close; after a while, the glowing sex idol fizzled, becoming a dull flame, and even a folded pillow became more appealing, less complicated to deal with. But she'd go away, eventually, she had to, he convinced himself; just like a hovering bee flying close to his face, all he needed to do was ignore her, pretend she didn't exist, and she'd fly off.

####

It was a successful night of headshots in Halo. Yeah, Dennis racked up at least a dozen kills in each gaming session, spending the night at Nick's house with Michael and Rich, playing Xbox for hours. Belly laughing with friends, shit talking strangers on the internet, and sniping Spartans online occupied the second Saturday night in a row. Boasting about killing sprees and teabagging dead players before they respawned filled the boys with gaiety and careless moments, making nearly everything they said or encountered feel humorous. It wasn't really teabagging; no, the soldiers weren't actually dipping their testicles in the deceased fighters' mouths. It just looked like it: pressing the joystick down to crouch the player near the head of the recently killed, emulating the bobbing motion of teabagging an individual.

And it was real fun, oddly, plasma punching strangers in the face while telling them to "suck my dick" was more enjoyable than having a voluptuous red head actual suck his dick. He'd catch images of Susanna's exposed nates flashing through his mind during gaming; visions of her pasty, shapely pear glowing in the dark, round mounds of tender flesh packed and tied together in a lacy thong. An overhead view down her back highlighted her most appetizing asset, heightening his pleasure as it bobbed with each pull of her mouth in the rhythmic motion of fellatio.

Ephemeral delights were what they were, and he had experienced enough of them the past couple of months to realize he had a whole life of promiscuous encounters ahead with women his own age, younger, and maybe even older. There were sinuous blondes with short hair and tall brunettes with pierced nipples in his future, he was sure of it; and they weren't going to be saddled with drama and dependency, no, just drunk guilt-free college copulations. He had seduced the librarian from school at the age of fourteen, it was all normal to expect nothing less than an Epicurus destiny of venereal ventures. Besides, he had Susanna wrapped around his finger, he believed; she was obsessed, so any time he wanted to take a dip in her warm waters, he knew he could with such omnipotence. But these weekends with friends were different, healthier, better for his adolescent development; camaraderie left a lasting impression, more fulfilling than draining seminal fluids, he discovered. The emptiness he used to feel at the end of the weekend wasn't there anymore; no, he felt full of companionship, more connected, a solidarity with buddies, kids his own age, like maybe he wasn't alone in the world.

Still recalling the last multiplayer round of the evening when he compiled fifteen headshots and Rich kept getting killed by some eight-year-old kid with an energy sword, giggling every time he swiped him, Dennis barged inside the house from the garage door after being dropped off by Nick's mom. Unlike his surreptitious returns from trysts with Susanna, where paranoia gripped him as soon as he touched the doorknob, envisioning his parents and police waiting inside, aware of his illicit encounters, he felt calm entering his home, like he was living the life he was supposed to. With their hands folded at the dinner table, Dennis's parents sat, the white cordless house phone propped in the center of the rectangular tempered glass top.

"Sit down," his father instructed, arms folded against his chest, showcasing bulging forearms, a virile man with zero tolerance for untruthfulness.

"Okay," Dennis yielded, recognizing an apparent severity as he sank into the polyester chair cushion of the rattan wicker set Mary used inside to coordinate with her vinyl kitchen motif.

Positioning his feet forward, he utilized the table's crossbar as a footrest, the tops of his shoes pressed against the ornate plant holder, which housed several faux fern plants. An overhang of leaves bordered the entire base, with the center abundant in greenery, creating a lush vision of vegetation underneath the glass.

"You received a very odd message tonight on the answering machine," his mother said, leaning forward, grabbing the phone, and dialing a number.

Dennis folded into a defensive pose, slouching, placing his elbows on the table, mulling over the impending communication; he wondered if maybe someone had seen him and Susanna together and had finally decided to call to inform his parents, since he imagined the message had to involve her.

Mary placed the receiver back in the center of the table upright as the phone beeped:

"Dennis... Dennis... are you there?" her stricken voice whimpered, sniffling after every other word.

"I'm just having a really bad night, my car got a flat tire, and I'm just stressed," Susanna's trembling voice continued.

His heart welled with apprehension; a deafening pulse beating him down as he listened closely, hoping the message didn't reveal the caller's name.

"I really wish I could talk to you right about now, but I guess I'll just see you at school," she uttered, ending the message abruptly, as if she realized at that point that calling his home phone number wasn't the best idea and she should hang up.

"Want to tell us who that was?" Mary interrogated with an accusatory tone, folding her arms, leaning back in the kitchen chair as if she had just declared checkmate.

"You better think long and hard about your answer if you ever want to leave this house again, especially for your next four years of high school," his father added before he could craft a response.

Dennis could feel slight perspiration forming on the back of his neck, the severity of his father's words beginning to penetrate his façade. But Dennis was always scheming, thinking two steps ahead, sometimes involuntarily, so he was prepared, looking for loopholes and opportunities. He knew Susanna never mentioned her name on the message, since he focused on listening for an indication during the playback. He knew his parents had nothing unless they knew to press "star sixty-nine" to return the call, which he highly doubted. He was playing a flush poker hand that just needed a bit of confidence.

"Oh, stop. That was my friend Ben from class. He always does that womanly voice, it's a joke," Dennis said, forging a laugh and smile, shaking his head.

"Who is Ben? And why would he pretend to have a flat tire and call you like that?" Russ inquired, pushing his seat back and rising with assertive vigor, as if he were the bad cop, turning on the aggression.

"Dad, he's just this jokester from class. I've even pranked him a few times," Dennis deflected.

"That sounded like a grown woman, Dennis," Mary interjected, leaning forward with her arms still crossed, her mouth ajar in disbelief.

Her eyes locked on his countenance, studying his facial expressions to see if he accidentally revealed a non-verbal tell.

The slim cordless receiver was still out of reach, further away since it slid on the table when his father stood up, so Dennis knew he had to be convincing, exact, and steadfast in his delivery to alleviate any further investigation, like his parents checking the phone for additional clues.

"I know, right? The kid seriously is going to be an impressionist when he's older," he announced with eyebrows raised, a convincing charade.

"He even does a great one of Mike Tyson at lunch. Cracks even the lunch ladies up," Dennis embellished further, nodding, as if he truly believed it; his narration manufactured effortlessly, an inherent skillful liar.

Glimpsing at each other with befuddled expressions, eyes squinted and arms crossed, gauging each other's level of persuasion with body language, his parents deliberated briefly without talking, before standing up from the table. Dennis knew he had pulled it off, even if he couldn't hear what his mom and dad whispered to each other. He should have felt relieved, but his anger was building, pulse spiking as he thought of how pathetic Susanna was, how desperate and careless she really had to be to not only call his house phone but to also leave a fucking message. Seething as his parents spoke, partially listening to their warning about cutting out shady behavior if he wanted to be able to go to a single party next year, Dennis conjured up a plan, a malicious device to get back at Susanna. Boiling with rage as he sat at the kitchen table, he fumed, thinking about how much he detested her; the audacity of her to try and tether him at such a young age, like an animal, cornering him so he couldn't escape her clutches.

After passing his parents' interrogation, Dennis stormed to the basement with heavy, hostile footsteps, each stride thudding down the stairs. Logging onto AOL, he sat at his computer chair, tapping his foot in an agitated rhythm, a soothing tic to abate his escalating anger. The screeching of dial-up connecting scratched against his ears as he swayed, deep in thought, wondering what his next move would be. Pulling up his friend list, he noticed

"**DCCandyBunny2005**" was online, as expected.

"**Claudjr11:** So my parents listened to your message on the answering machine, and I'm not sure, but they're probably going to contact the school. Not sure if they're going to go to the authorities. It's over for us."

Slamming each key with furious fingertips, Dennis fired away hyperbolic revelations, but effective ones. He finally realized Susanna was more like a zit, and she wouldn't just go away, no matter how much he tried to ignore her. So he did what he had to do: applying pressure to the infected area. He attacked with an abject narration, suggesting severe consequences, career suicide, jail time, and registering as a sex offender, smothering even the most stubborn, fervent of flames. Pulling the emergency brake on the speeding, careening vessel, he knew it would halt the relationship entirely and possibly destroy the transmission. But he didn't care if the car wouldn't run anymore; he had already reached his destination and was ready to get out, his needs fully satiated, no longer requiring servicing.

"DCCandyBunny2005: I'm so sorry."

She responded immediately before signing off for the last time. It was the final occasion Dennis saw that ridiculous screen name appear online, their parting dialogue. He would only see her once or twice more at school before the year ended, Susanna keeping her distance as much as possible.

It was the first breakup, technically, that Dennis experienced, but it wasn't the archetypal culmination of a middle school romance. No, there wasn't some note-passing to friends of friends to deliver the bad news. It was more like pulling the plug from a video game that wasn't enjoyable anymore, establishing a pattern of behavior that would persist, a propensity for discarding others when they were no longer useful, to be severed the moment novelty ended. Dennis learned early that attachment was a temporary condition, and by the time summer rolled around, he had already erased Susanna from his thoughts, her presence a morsel in his memory. The tendency for detachment became his armor, a quiet ritual of avoidance that would shape his future relationships. Intimacy becoming less about connection and more about control, a game to be managed, and when necessary, abandoned without looking back.

####

Peeking out from the teacher's lounge, Dennis surveys the area, oscillating his gaze, scanning for any possible ambushes in the remaining twenty-five minutes of free time before the next period starts. He's been hiding in the faculty room for most of his days, abandoning his classroom, dodging possible interactions and unwanted attention, managing to avoid Megan.

Vibrating in his pocket, Dennis retrieves his iPhone as he hurries back to his classroom, hoping it's a message from Christine confirming their dinner tonight. He doesn't want to surrender the power dynamic just yet; he's thinking he needs to revert to tactical dating mode, invoke the same strategies that worked with Renee: exhibit slight indifference, poise, and wait until noon before responding.

It's a new follow notification from a JPuleo2 that rattles his device, a foreign alias but a familiar name he can't recall off the top of his head. Opening his Instagram app with curiosity, Dennis clicks on the public profile, noticing a sundry of selfies. It's Jonathan from class; his peculiar aquiline aesthetic: a draped, hooked nose, beaked jaw, and angular neck; his lanky frame resembling an egret. Dennis wonders why the botched abortion is attempting to follow him, grateful that he made his account private recently. Posing in a variety of purported candid photos, positioned in select scenery, like he's the main character in everyone's life, Jonathan's profile features influencer poses, pressed against a brick wall with his arms crossed, wearing a coordinating red sweatshirt to match the background, a cesspit of narcissism. Perhaps he attempted to follow him by mistake, Dennis decides, declining his request.

A new text message comes in from his mother almost immediately after denying Jonathan; it's a picture of the home screen of her Starbucks app, it appears. The top portion of the photo features the date and time; she's sent him a screenshot of a screenshot. There's no other communication, no context, and Dennis isn't sure how to interpret it, so he calls his mother.

"Mom, what the hell did you just send me?"

"I can't see how much money is on my Starbucks account, Dennis. I'm having a hard time with this thing," she carps, exhaling in frustration.

She sounds like she's in the car, an airy feedback echoing when she speaks.

"You just need to hit the tab in the bottom right corner," Dennis responds, hoping his instruction suffices.

"What tab?"

"The little image that looks like a credit card. You see it?"

"Just press it?"

"Yes, tap it with your finger."

"Okay, tap it?"

"Yes, just tap it."

"Okay, I'm pressing it, but it's not working."

"Just tap it, don't hold it down," he adds, picturing his mother holding down the bottom of her screen, perhaps pressing multiple buttons simultaneously, canceling out any prompt.

"Okay, I tapped it," she announces, her cadence tailing off as if she's in deep thought, inspecting her phone.

"Well, did it work?" Dennis inquires, noticing Michael Fairchild emerging from the restroom, still rubbing his hands with a paper towel; the dark four-panel bathroom door swings back and forth through the frame before closing.

"I think so. I gotta go, your father is driving." Mary sighs, muttering additional words that become muffled.

Dennis envisions her pressing the phone against her cheek, moving her face away to look over at his father driving, scolding his performance.

"Russ, did you even see that car?!" she huffs.

"What, of course I did, would you stop," Russ rebuts in the background, annoyed by her accusation.

"Ugh, I gotta go, your father can-not see, love you," Mary states, aspirating, hanging up before Dennis can reply.

Dennis isn't sure if he should continue holding his phone up to his ear to deter Michael from engaging, but he's already waving at Dennis, indicating he's probably going to wait until he's free to talk.

"Okay, I'll call you later," Dennis recites, his device still in his hand, close to his ear.

"Michael, how's it going?" he greets the tall, bespectacled teacher with feigned enthusiasm.

"Doing well, doing well. Was just going to stop by to see if you wanted to talk about our short stories?" he suggests, a stack of stapled printer papers tucked underneath his left arm; he's made a hard copy of Dennis's story to review, something Dennis hasn't reciprocated.

Michael's ruffled collar is folded over on one side, caught behind his ochre cardigan's neckline, an asymmetrical distraction; his ultra-hairy arms exposed in a buttoned-down short sleeve shirt.

"Yes, I'd like that," Dennis smiles, extending his hand and turning his palm upward to direct toward his classroom.

He continues focusing on the ruffled collar of Michael's button-down, wondering if it's going to be too big of a distraction.

It's not a contemptuous indifference Dennis feels, no, he just hasn't been exactly present the past few days. He was doing pretty well too, sticking to his routine, his habits and rituals, vacuuming his area rugs and dusting his shelves, obsessing over cleanliness and order. Then he came home Friday after school, encountering a heavy police presence and caution tape around the deck of his neighbor's unit; garrulous Carson from next door had shot himself while his wife was out grocery shopping, calling in a suicide tip before pulling the trigger. It's jarring, really, and not just that the affable husband took his own life, no, it's the proximity of suicide and how close it is that's alarming, how it's always nearby, perceptible beneath the surface. If the man who always greeted him with a smile and meaningful small talk whenever they met getting their mail couldn't tolerate the voices, the hazardous suggestions, Dennis knows he stands no chance at mitigating the suicidal ideation, that there's no escaping it, no matter how hard he tries to hide.

"So, how's it going?" Michael asks, taking a seat at the closest desk.

Dennis's social intelligence is lacking, and he's not sure if he should sit at his teacher's desk or pull up a seat. He feels awkward, displaced.

He's thinking Carson should have tried getting a semicolon wrist tattoo before giving up; they're pretty ubiquitous on Instagram. Influencers have them, and they're supposed to symbolize hope, a continuation, since the punctuation is used when a writer chooses to continue a sentence instead of ending it. Maybe then he'd have been able to tolerate the dreadful days if he could have that shit easily readable on his wrist. He could have tried sharing motivational quote graphics on his Facebook, preferably ones from David Goggins or Gary Vaynerchuk, real powerful words about "enduring" and "not making excuses" anymore to spark inspiration. Maybe that could have kept Carson alive, Dennis ponders.

"It's going," Dennis jests, smirking as he opens his laptop.

He's decided on sitting in his chair but rolls it out from behind the desk, pulling it by its worn leather backing, a decision he regrets, realizing he doesn't have an elevated surface to place his laptop on, exposed with his Surface Pro folded into a tablet set on his lap.

"It's going?" Michael chuckles with an ambiguous intonation, like he could be agreeing or posing a question, a deviation from his usual agreeable discourse.

"Yeah," Dennis smiles awkwardly as he squints at his screen, searching his recent downloads for "Hangman."

"This is life. It's gotta be going now or it isn't happening," Michael adds equivocally, grinning with amusement, either kidding or trying to be deep, philosophical, like he's just full of profound wisdom.

The overhead fluorescent lights reflect in his Windsor glasses, obscuring his eyes with white orbs; prominent patches of dark hair spotlighted on the top of his bald head, due for another close shave.

He doesn't mean any maleficence either way with his comment, Dennis concludes, so he's not going to follow up with a mordant response, asking if he should consume copious drugs and alcohol, exchange bodily fluids with an assortment of sordid prostitutes, or maybe murder every individual who cuts him off in traffic or anyone that antagonizes him, to make sure his life "is happening," and he's living every moment. Or perhaps he should gamble his entire 403B, putting his entire portfolio on a black even number in roulette, if it will help make sure life is really going.

"I'm glad we're finally sitting down to discuss our stories," Dennis states, placating with perfunctory courtesy, opening a Word document, invoking a cordial disposition.

He wonders if James will burst into the classroom at any moment, possibly high on substances, even though he hasn't seen him in a while.

Michael's cover paper is riddled with red circles, discernible copyediting marks, notes, and comments. Set on the desk surface, the document's blemishes antagonize Dennis's crumbling composure, provoking insecurity, a surge of anxiety paired with perceivable heart palpitations, causing Dennis to hunch in his chair; his right arm crosses against his body, creating a barrier to keep himself from being exposed, vulnerable.

He knows the notes have to be about the poor quality of his work, it's got to be terrible, probably just the worst thing he's ever read. And Michael is about to shred his story with verbose speech, speaking with literary jargon, delineating the "showing and not telling" writing technique and how Dennis needs to adapt this approach, characters connected by sensory details and actions rather than exposition. Oh yeah, it's going to be a clusterfuck of scathing, regurgitated creative writing class bullshit that's going to ignite his emotions, triggering an avalanche of pessimism and dejection, and the stress of having to go back and edit for the seventh time, to pretty much rewrite the whole manuscript he poured hours into and continue to obsess over details will make Dennis never want to write another fucking word again.

"I'll start!" Michael announces, cracking his knuckles as he gazes up at the ceiling and takes a deep breath, like he's constructing a precise monologue, similar to a soliloquy delivered at the weekend writing seminars he attends.

Dennis envisions Michael performing this same quirk before analyzing every story he reads, popping tense knuckles for temporary relief, a release from weighted hands.

"I like to commence workshops by highlighting things that stood out in the story," he begins, folding his hands in his lap as he looks down at the first page, reading his feedback.

"I enjoyed the character arc of 'Swimming.' I was drawn in right away with your descriptions. I must say, you certainly have a strength for capturing scenes with specific details," Michael continues, reciting with a slow, steady tenor, extending his torso upright in a position of power, the pose of a published literary authority, a savant scribe.

"'Shoveling swells of ocean water' was one description that I thought was rather brilliant," Michael comments, lifting the stapled papers with his left fingers to consult his notes.

The lines of text are mirrored in his bifocals, his lips moving with splinters of teeth poking through, like a shark mouth, possibly about to attack with harmful criticism.

"You also have a knack for evoking emotion, especially toward the end, when the protagonist is fighting against the waves," Michael continues, encouraging with head nods and awkward grins, offering positive reinforcement.

"I definitely see a lot of potential in this story," he concludes, rolling his head from shoulder to shoulder in pursuit of bursting additional synovial fluid bubbles, a possible nervous mannerism, meant to deflect the uneasiness of his impending critique.

"Potential" signifies the story isn't anywhere close to being sufficient, merely a rough draft, a rudimentary attempt.

"But I feel like you sold yourself short in some areas. I would have liked to read more about his wife; she seems like a secondary character. The beginning prose mentions a quarrel between the two. What was the argument about?" he poses, cocking his head and scratching his scruffy chin.

Dandruff flakes dance in the air, illuminated by streaks of afternoon sunlight peering through the classroom windows.

Dennis isn't sure if he should respond to each talking point Michael suggests or if he should just wait until he's done commenting on the story altogether, so he just nods, waiting for the uncomfortable silence. Maybe he should be typing notes in a Word document for consideration, to make revisions later, or maybe he should be reviewing his feedback about Michael's story in preparation.

"More importantly, I think the ending was extremely touching, especially the closing lines. But if the protagonist drowns, the narrator of the story, how is he telling us this story as it occurred in past tense? You'd have to change the story to present tense to be clear."

And Michael is right, Dennis realizes, shaking his head in disbelief, shocked by his negligence in missing such an elementary grammatical aspect.

"You brilliant motherfucker," Dennis cheers, shaking his head with a manic motion as he smiles.

Michael grows quiet, folding his hands in front, the quintessential teacher's pose. He's got a peculiar countenance, like he's sucking on a Warhead, a tart face with pursed lips, his eyebrows raised as he glimpses over at the door, his widening eyes struck with wonder.

"Dennis," a soft female voice sounds from Dennis's periphery, commanding his focus.

A disheveled Megan emerges, hanging on the door handle, her chin poking forward with her body retracted, like she's waiting to be acknowledged, granted permission to come in. Standing in a blank tank top, her herringbone sweater draped around her waist, not the school's uniform, Megan raises her voice before Dennis can respond to the first query.

"Dennis?"

"Yes, Megan. We're in the middle of something. Can we chat later?" Dennis snaps, hot internal surges seething, waves of anxiety crashing through his central nervous system, his worlds on the verge of colliding.

"But I need to talk to you," she whimpers, crossing her arms in a petulant manner, her face soured with pouting lips as she stomps her pink canvas shoe, a similar sullenness she demonstrated at her home when he came to tutor, equally as repulsive.

"Not right now, I'll speak to you after sixth period class," he rebuts more assertively, gesticulating with an open hand from his chair, hoping to mitigate any further escalation in Michael's presence.

"It can't wait, I need to talk to you. Why have you been avoiding me?" she implores, proceeding into the classroom with her same defensive pose, dark discernible eyeliner running, sad raccoon eyes.

"Megan, you need to go," Dennis demands with less emotion, scaling back his tone to avoid alarming Michael and perturbing her any further.

Rising from his seat in a desperate last-ditch effort, he approaches Megan with a disgruntled look, eyes enlarged, moments away from humiliation.

"What are you doing?" Dennis whispers, keeping his back to Michael, trying to conceal the interaction as much as possible.

Megan reaches out, attempting to wrap her arms around Dennis, initiating a desperate hug.

"Cut it out," Dennis snarls, swatting her hands away.

"Oh my God, you're so mean to me!" Megan yelps, writhing her arms in a tantrum, emotional turmoil.

"Hey Dennis, I'm going to head out. We can pick this up at another time," Michael interrupts with an uneasy smile, sliding swiftly past the duo, avoiding the imbroglio as he averts eye contact.

Dennis's eyes follow Michael's departure, watching as he slips out into the hallway in a hurry, unable to decipher his reaction to the unraveling situation. Megan stands with her arms crossed, demanding Dennis's attention with her childish mannerisms, attention-seeking limb jerks; her body limp, her head hanging, sulking, the dangling serpent pendant glimmering in the overhead light.

"What the hell are you doing, Megan?"

Scouring her appearance, Dennis analyzes her chaotic presentation, a stark contrast to the mature, budding beauty he saw before. Her juvenile demeanor on full display, a flushed face and bitter profile pairing with her pantomime; her arms crossed, hugging her body tightly, like she's been abandoned at a bus stop, staggering back and forth; the strap of her tank top sliding off her left shoulder, a herald of her sanity slipping; her feet overlapped, emphasizing her blooming V-shape, a dichotomy of emotional immaturity and physical ripeness.

Enmity rises, an internal boiling of rage overcomes his nerves. Dennis tries to collect himself, closing his eyes for a moment to brainstorm a practical solution, taking a deep breath. Before he can conjure up an idea, warm, moisturized lips infused with lingering notes of alcohol meet Dennis's mouth, galvanizing his hostility.

"Jesus Christ, Megan, have you lost your fucking mind?!" Dennis shouts, grabbing her by the arm to bring her out into the hallway.

Swaying back and forth with a gleeful, cunning smile and heavy eyelids, looking down at the ground, her hair partially haggard, like she's been doing somersaults, she flashes an amused grin.

"Are you drunk?" Dennis asks dumfounded, detecting fruity undertones of some vodka-infused alcohol stained on her breath.

"I want to fucking make out with you," she squalls, sadness intensified to anger, sailing into Dennis's chest with her shoulder, an unexpected forward trust fall.

"Stop it right now, or I'm going to call you parents," Dennis threatens, regretting his decision to bring her out into the hallway, still with a hand on her shoulder to keep her balanced.

"Well, I'll just tell them I sucked your cock," Megan murmurs, smiling manically, fluttering her eyes, a wolf in sheep's clothing; specks of glitter on her face twinkling as she ogles Dennis.

The heaves of anxiety quickly transmute into a panicking uneasiness, like a premonition, he's been too reckless, he can see himself falling off the cliff, the same precipice he's been playing along, walking way too close to the edge.

"Please, stop it," he pleads, a tremble in his conclusion, revealing a perceived weakness.

"What, you don't think I could suck your cock good enough?" Megan coils as she slithers her tongue around before plumping her lips, standing tall in front of Dennis, only a few inches shorter than him.

A provoked image of her mouth pulling on his tumescent tool seeps into his cerebral cortex, a vision of her gagging on his privates, eyeliner streaking down the sides of her cheeks, heightening his hormones, sending blood flow to his member with each of her unwanted advances. Locking eyes with her devilish stare, an intoxicated nymphet, he can see her for what she really is now. Behind the facade, an unhinged, pliable teenager, always seeking, her visage still containing remnants of her babyface. And there's no reasoning with her, a precarious personality, he understands now; he's left a mark on her mold for the worst.

"I promise we will talk later, but you need to leave now, Megan," Dennis beseeches, placing his arm around her shoulder in a concession of affection, hoping to persuade her to listen and calm down.

"Why haven't you been talking to me?" Megan whimpers, averting eye contact, her arms still crossed, wrists clenched under her armpits.

"I've just been so busy with everything."

"You haven't responded to anything I've sent you," she continues, drawling with a whiny inflection, straying from her combative nature.

"Where did you get the alcohol?"

"I'm not telling."

"Why are you drinking in school? You know you're going to get caught," Dennis asks, treading lightly, carefully, like she's a dangerous animal that could be riled with sudden movements.

The woozy girl wobbles, her view oscillating between the floor and Dennis's face, leering each time she makes eye contact, the look of both predator and prey.

"Why not? I'm just a dumb teenager, right? Isn't that what all young, naive kids do?" She snipes with a devious grin, a gothic gaze, curling brows and misty eyes, responding with developed sarcasm, his influence on her dialogue.

The bell clamors throughout the hall, adjacent classroom doors fly open; crowds of backpack-strapped kids pour into the corridor, stampeding on the lacquered floor, swimming around the two of them. Megan notices an opportunity as Dennis surveys the sea of teenagers to see if anyone is paying attention to their interaction. She lunges forward in desperation, another attempt at landing a kiss, an effort thwarted by Dennis turning away at the last minute, sensing her energy as he shoves her off.

"You need to go, now!" Dennis demands.

"Fuck you, you're such an asshole," Megan utters vehemently before taking off, removing her sweater from her midsection and pulling it against her back in a scornful snub.

Scurrying off after her failed try, Megan staggers down the hall, veering from side to side, brushing against the lockers until she disappears into the horde. Scanning the masses for a disorderly brunette, Dennis loses sight of her in the crowd and instead catches the eyes of a rancorous glare, a biting lip, and a rumpled brow, the face of an irritated Jonathan. His arms are crossed, fuming with perceived aggression, like he's been watching the encounter the whole time. Maybe this is the reason he requested to follow Dennis on Instagram; maybe he knows something, Dennis debates, maintaining eye contact as an acrimonious Jonathan turns, slinging his backpack over his shoulder, and departs down the other hall.

####

He's been checking his Instagram frequently, glued to his phone, actually, ever since he posted a selfie to his story earlier. It's a real good photo too; he took it with the tripod he ordered from Amazon, which allowed him to prop up the camera on his bar counter in the kitchen to capture the perfect picture of himself. He probably should have made it his official profile pic instead of just sharing it to his story. The vivid cognac color of his skinny tie complements his navy-blue suit perfectly; a chiseled jaw line can be seen through his beard, real masculine and rugged, superhero like. He'd probably receive an abundance of likes, enough to abate his insecurity that's emerging as the minutes count down to his date, but he wants to see who is checking out his story; he needs to know who is watching.

He should probably be more concerned with Megan's tenuous state, the possible ramifications of a distraught female student attempting multiple times to kiss him in public or the several attempts Jonathan has made to follow him on Instagram since their momentary stare down at school. But Dennis is still focused on his short story, recalling the edits he made with frantic joy right before leaving for dinner, like he just figured out the code to a safe of literary insight. Refining like a mad scientist, changing verb tenses, and elaborating further on plot details, he even sent the story to a few publications, hoping for the best.

"You miss 100% of the shots you don't take," one of the motivational quotes reads from his Instagram archive, he remembers, wise words from Michael

412

Jordan, most likely the basketball player and not the actor, but Dennis isn't entirely sure.

He's pretty sure he'll bring Michael Fairchild Dunkin' Donuts in the morning to show his appreciation for his feedback. He can even picture the two of them exchanging book suggestions and sipping coffee together. Maybe they'll become best literary pals; he'll not only have an actual friend, but a gay friend too, and he might even add a rainbow emoji to his IG bio to show his support for the LGBTQ+ community. He'll explain that the whole situation with Megan is just a misunderstanding, since he didn't handle the ordeal in the best way.

Christine's response to Dennis's text wasn't as enthusiastic as he hoped for, so that's a bummer. It was terse and direct, just confirming the time and place, a new restaurant they'd never been to; she always commented on her displeasure with patronizing the same places when they were together, so he's going to do things right this time, he's decided. North Evergreen's grass-fed entrees and chic atmosphere with rustic oak tables and fresh marble floors seem like just the place for Dennis to make the best impression, to introduce the new him, the level-headed homeowner with writer potential who no longer engages with adolescent drama. He might still be an asshole, but he's come a long way, he thinks.

It's unnerving, really, sitting at the table, waiting for Christine to arrive; she's not late, he's just early. Dennis is thinking he's overdressed with his on-trend tie, but he'd rather overdo it than underwhelm. He's turned his phone off because he's done with distractions, and he's going to be present, soaking in every moment of the night. Subconsciously, he's thinking she might stand him up, fitting payback for what a piece of shit he was. So he's fidgeting with the gunmetal silverware laying on the burlap napkins, rubbing his fingers along the prongs of the fork to soothe the latent anxiety, wondering if he'll still wind up ordering food for himself when it's apparent she's not coming. He curls a fork into his hand, the embossed handle sinking into the crevice of his palm, gripping the utensil like a gun, imagining a barrel affixed to the metal implement; what a pretty setting to pull the trigger, he thinks to himself, visualizing blood splatter speckled around the clean contemporary table like crimson glitter; his hallowed head presented on his dinner plate, like unique delicacy meat.

Relinquishing the implement back to its proper place, he runs his hand along the grooves of the wooden planks, the texturized surface of the bucolic table provides sufficient stimulation, soothing grazes against his open palm, a ticklish distraction; he's not even thinking about the onslaught of direct messages that are probably piling up from Megan, since he chose not to block her, thinking that would exacerbate her obsession.

A raconteur catches Dennis's attention a few tables down, an older gentleman in a corduroy blazer, swinging a glass of wine; his dynamic voice commanding attention as the gathering laughs at his story.

"Rachel comes in and she's staring at me, real anger in her eyes too, and she looks at me and says, 'who started the fireplace?'" the orator exclaims, articulating with dramatic gestures, rolling his free hand to emphasize, communicative calisthenics.

The ostensible family cracks up, shaking in their chairs from the entertainment, an assortment of different ages surrounds the table, perceived parents and their kids, enjoying the speaker. Watching as the gray-haired performer continues his comical story, clearly adored by his relatives, Dennis slips into a ruminative state as an arbitrary thought consumes him, whether "debauchery" is pronounced with a "ch" or a "k" sound in the second syllable.

And it's really starting to stress him out, so he pulls out his phone to hear the proper enunciation, holding his device to his ear, which he's happy to learn the word is pronounced with a "ch," sound, his original guess. And maybe it's not entirely random, the confusion on the vocabulary word. No, it's a deflection on his realization, that he used to be just like the gregarious man, a natural storyteller, the center of attention before he was broken, becoming reticent, a skeptic of organic happiness and oversharing. And maybe it's better to be a little more naïve about the world than overly cynical. Because only with openness can innate hope truly exist; to access natural joy requires a willingness to believe in the goodness that still lies beneath life's rough edges, a faith that shields from the slow, corrosive pull of pessimism.

Dennis can't shake the thoughts of his worried mother, her precarious state, and how she had nurtured his vivid imagination as a child. She had always been a guide, providing markers, poster boards, and books to fuel his creativity. Each day, she orchestrated artistic endeavors, channeling his boundless mind with engaging stories, facilitating the future of a writer; he truly loved her for making his childhood so full of inspiration and wonder. He wishes he could say something to ease her distress, do something to calm her unease, but he's beginning to realize that a mother's worry never truly fades, even as she grows older, no matter how old her child gets.

Her solemn words echoing like a haunting refrain when talking about John:

"I just don't want him to be alone."

To which Dennis replied, "Sometimes it's better to be alone than with someone who makes you feel alone."

The table continues to cackle, encouraging the man to persist with his storytelling, recalling additional plot details and related tales.

"You think she's crazy? Well, that's nothing compared to the time Martin forgot he put his goldfish on top of his car."

"Oh yeah, picture him just cruising down the highway as Finny flops about in his bowl, splashing and rolling around on the roof," he recounts, puffing his lips to emulate a goldfish's face, his cleft chin emphasized by the gesture.

The exposition is met with praise, even the kids start clapping with amusement. Dennis can tell the genial man is the glue of the family, the one who engages with all its members, suggests dinners and gatherings, and takes action to get everyone together. The family relies on him, whether they know it or not, the patriarch. Dennis wonders if someone else will step up to become the family comic once he passes, or if there's anyone who could possibly unite the group like the adored entertainer does so well.

His thoughts snowball into deeper despair, thinking about how different his family will be, not just with John's pending divorce, but when his parents pass away and the glue holding them together scales off. He worries that any remnant of the family he cherishes will disappear when they go, the most significant connection to the happiest times of his life. An evocation of the yearly Christmas parties his mother used to hold plays in his mind, a hired Santa would give out gag gifts, featuring inside jokes that garnered cherished laughs, bringing a closeness to the family that can't be replicated, a connection that's been lost since. Those were the only occasions he would ever see family outside of his immediate relatives.

The acoustic friction of a sliding knife spreading butter on a baked roll from the table next to him draws his attention, evoking the memory of his grandmother, a bagel connoisseur who always buttered her toast from across the table while he ate cereal before school. It feels like forever and not that long ago at the same time since she passed away, a distortion of time and memory.

He's pretty sure he read on Reddit that life's all about finding clues and connections. So he's thinking the Shutterfly-style art piece hanging on the wall depicting a chef's table of diced ingredients seems to signal he should start dosing psilocybin, since the imagery showcases an abundance of vivid mushrooms. He thinks maybe he needs to rewire his brain to palliate his pathologies.

Dennis's focus shifts, like an Instagram reel, and he follows the greenery accenting the restaurant to divert away from a potential emotional breakdown. Long, leafy botanicals occupy the cornices of the walls, cascading and creating a fresh, trendy environment. Decorative foliage hangs over the front entrance, forming a natural arbor that frames Christine as she enters, brightening up the atmosphere. Smiling sincerely, Dennis waves to her, his anxiety abated by a beautiful familiar face.

"So good to finally see you," Dennis greets her with a warm smile, offering a modest hug.

Her pleasing fragrance, balanced with lavender notes, evokes a warm sensation he can feel throughout his limbs.

"I know, it's been a minute," Christine jokes, removing her crossbody purse and wrapping it around her chair with a cordial smile.

Her ponytail drapes over her shoulder, pressing against her ruched blouse, a different look, more sophisticated.

It takes a few minutes before he can find the familiarity in her face, but he finally recognizes her eyes, her comforting gaze, soft, non-judgmental, like she's seeing him in the moment without prejudice.

"How're your parents?" she asks with an eager lilt, like she's been genuinely thinking about them.

"They're doing well. Still crazy, but healthy," Dennis smiles, thinking about how his mother called him earlier, voicing a concern about how his father is napping too much, how unintentionally hilarious she is.

"They're so lucky they have each other," Christine smiles warmly, as if she's envisioning them, recalling the last time she saw the two.

"How's school going?" she asks, unfolding her napkin, placing it on her lap.

"It's going," Dennis murmurs, fighting off recent imagery of Megan and her disturbed stalker Jonathan complicating his professional life.

"How about you? How is your family?" Dennis asks with an earnest tone, focusing the conversation back on her, ensuring reciprocal questions.

"Mom is doing okay, best she can do. But Jasmine is still dating losers," Christine laments, shaking her head before taking a sip of water.

Nodding uncomfortably, curling his lip as he listens, Dennis wonders if maybe he's a loser too, and if the family discussed how she also dated one.

"Are we ready to put some drinks in or order?" a friendly, mature waitress inquires with artificial but sufficient enthusiasm.

She holds an outstretched notepad, standing with her pen pressed against the pad, ready for recording.

"I'll have an old fashioned," Dennis blurts, before realizing he should have let Christine order first, a juvenile blunder.

"I'm sorry, you should order first."

"That's okay, I'm just going to have one glass of Chardonnay, since I have to get up early tomorrow morning for work."

"Okay, I'll put those drinks in for you," the amiable server says, flashing a smile; her contour poorly blended in the grooves of her cheeks, like translucent snow covering a tattered trail.

"So, an old fashioned, huh?" Christine chuckles, flashing crisp white teeth; her eyes sparkling, her face blushed, glowing beauty in the moody, lightly lit dining space.

"Yeah, I don't know where that came from. Guess I want to be old fashioned," Dennis concedes, forgetting Christine isn't like most dense girls he seeks; she doesn't have a pretentious bone in her body.

He thinks about how there aren't a lot of suitors around his age on the dating apps anymore and how almost all the women in their thirties are single mothers.

He's the furthest thing from old fashioned or traditional; he doesn't even have a retirement plan besides his inefficient 403B to which he contributes the bare minimum. He's been doing it all wrong; he probably should have explored sex trafficking or Bitcoin, but he'd have to find a madam to groom the girls or download an app to trade stocks, both equally cumbersome.

"Here are your drinks," the waitress announces, placing the mason jar and stemless wine glass down before darting off to welcome new diners.

"Thanks for coming tonight," Dennis says with sincerity, shifting from gaiety.

"I think this is good for both of us," Christine smiles, holding her glass up.

"Cheers."

The evening progresses with friendly dialogue, occasional laughs, and recalling times together; her inherent spark for life still flickers, despite Dennis's destruction of their relationship. She's friendly, but not flirty: no hair flips or exposed wrists, no grazing hands or leg brushing underneath the table, no accidental touching, just platonic mannerisms; the night is closure for her, Dennis speculates.

He can't tell if she's seeing anyone, and the topic never comes up, since he would be wrecked if he found out she is, still being selfish and territorial. Christine is still warmhearted, seemingly unaffected by the culmination of their romance a year ago, which elicits ambivalence in him, relieved that she's doing just fine yet sour that he doesn't seem to have any lingering effect on her. Maybe that's the biggest difference between Christine and Dennis, he deliberates; Renee breaking his heart made him bitter, him breaking Christine's made her better, and he doesn't want to ever jeopardize tarnishing her.

Walking to their cars, side by side and conversing, a deep-seated sadness washes over him, sending chills to his limbs and restricting his optimism. He realizes he really does love her and how bleak his world has been without her, but he doesn't deserve her. The starry skyline illuminates the parking lot, shining down on the two as they approach their vehicles; Christine's bewitching gaze captures Dennis, and the urge to kiss her pulls at his lips, a natural magnetism. But he knows if he really cares, if he truly loves her, the best thing he can do is leave her alone, let her burn as bright as the glorious sun without subjecting her to his toxic influence, a dark insidious cloud.

It would only be a matter of time before he became comfortable again, complacent, and then unsatisfied, trapped in his thoughts, perpetual discontent, a blight for any successful relationship, an extinguisher to even the most raging fires, and he couldn't bear to ever witness her flame doused. And pretty soon, his perceived trauma will be recycled, repurposed with the death of his parents, like a rubber band ball expanded with additional layers, burying his broken heart with tighter loops and rows of concealing elastic until the constriction becomes too much. He knows, too, he's completely cognizant that if it wasn't Renee, it'd be the ex-girlfriend before that and then the one before that, all the way back to his ninth-grade girlfriend Amanda, always identifying a scapegoat for his discontent.

And if it weren't for girls, the nucleus would revolve around how he got cut from the baseball team or how he had to wait twenty minutes in line at the bank once. It might even be as simple as the time a projectile pebble on the highway put a tiny crack in his windshield and he had to use his last half-day to pay Safelite $159 to come fill the chip.

It's always going to be there, that abyss, that existential vacuum with Dyson suction power. An endless, inescapable pit that feeds on manufactured suffering, feasting on even the most trivial inconveniences and disappointments. It's never satiated, no matter how many mindfulness techniques he practices or how many gratitude journals he completes; it's innate, it's incurable; it's endless.

"Thank you for treating me to dinner tonight, Dennis. I think it was a good idea for us to get together to talk," Christine comments, smiling with her arms crossed, leaning against the door of her white Elantra.

A swell of emotion builds, an itch in his sinuses, as if he's about to cry.

"I really did too, and I just want to say I'm sorry," he says, voice strained. "I wish that I had met you at a different time in my life. When it was easier to be happy."

A natural empath, Christine reaches out and hugs Dennis, pulling him close as they share an emotional embrace; he squeezes her tightly, unsure if he'll ever be able to let go.

"Even if we're no longer together, it doesn't mean I don't still care about you," Christine whispers, rubbing the back of his neck as they continue their clasp; her words soothing even his deepest turmoil, bringing a relief he feels he doesn't deserve.

"How did you do it, Christine? How did you not let losing your father destroy you?"

Breaking from their hug, Christine smiles, a caring gaze transfixed on a bleary-eyed Dennis. Her hair, loose now, no longer in a ponytail, her wavy locks wafting in the faint nighttime wind, free, beautiful, and unburdened. She's the best thing he ever lost.

"Life is too short, Dennis," she says gently.

"And you have to choose happiness. It's an active choice you have to make, every single day."

15. So it Goes

There were spiders in his applesauce before, crawling through the viscid puree; helpless critters drowning in the sweet, stewed creamy substance, like shipwrecked passengers engulfed by swallowing waves. It was a real existential tragedy as they curled their tiny legs into permanent positions like Pompeii victims, and he probably should have mixed the scraps of magic mushrooms into something more humane, something less tart and less hazardous to tiny crawlers. But he needed immediate sustenance, something to help digest the psychedelics quicker, a hearty breakfast.

It's a disaster, though. Not just the countless deaths of tiny arthropods that succumbed to the sugary relish. No, it's terrible because he doesn't actually have applesauce for lunch. He's eaten it all, so he'll have to spend money on the square doughy pizza from the school cafeteria. That's okay though. It kind of reminds him of being a kid again, both the pizza and the spiders. He remembers his mom letting him host Halloween pizza parties every year with his classmates. She'd set out a table with an orange and black tablecloth in the basement, adorned with spiders on the hems, little plastic ones on the top surface, and skinny, long pizza slices for everyone to enjoy. Real core memories.

The submarine teeters with the turn of the wheel, cutting off passerby fish, and Dennis is pretty sure he shouldn't be maneuvering anything, especially not his car, since he hasn't slept. His limbic system is haywire two hours after consuming his early morning snack, negating any negative emotions, even as he's dodging yellow bullets on the roadway, semi-aware he's going to have to give his father's eulogy one day; golden blocks fly at his car the faster he goes, evading visuals and hazardous visualizations. He's got his seatbelt on, so that's good; it makes him feel safe. Its taut resistance providing a reassuring sensation, like he's being hugged with protection by the Michelin Man as he melts into the seat, real snuggly throw blanket comfort.

He should probably call his mom to check on her, make sure she's eaten something instead of just drinking coffee all day, since if it weren't for her, he wouldn't have a perfect memory stored. It's a pleasant remembrance stashed away, a place to visit in his mind when he needs it most: a recollection of playing outside in the evening sunlight after school, verdant leaves of the tall trees swishing, susurrating with the passing wind as he and his friends lay on their backs, looking up at the lucid crystal sky from the neighbor's treehouse.

And if it weren't for her, John wouldn't have been home from college that Christmas wearing his New York Knick shorts, holding the WrestleMania 2000 box for N64 up in the air with two hands in the foyer after everyone had finished opening their presents; the rapturous joy oozing from Dennis's eyes as he goggled at the game, a deep sense of relief after thinking he didn't get it, a major childhood triumph.

"Robert's got a quick hand. He'll look around the room but won't tell you his plan," the processed voice sings against synthesized melodic sounds.

He really should call his parents, but it's that "Pumped Up Kicks" song on the radio again; it's all that ever plays on that indie station from Sirius. He's pretty sure they've been fucking with him since he only pays five dollars a month, way below the current advertised rate of fifteen. But it's not his fault he's diligent; he calls every three months and threatens to cancel, so they always renew his promo price. The song doesn't even bother him, really, it's just the fact that there's not enough variety anymore, everything feels the same; it's all repetitive music. He'd change the channel, but he fears it's not safe, like maybe twisting the dial on his center console might result in something dire, completely catastrophic and momentous. Maybe it'll do more damage than just lowering the volume, some butterfly effect bullshit, and he's not ready to risk it, especially since he'll have to decide on a positive or negative integer to stop on, something that takes commitment.

It's a daunting dial, the glossy black face and sleek silver encasing staring back at him, goading him into turning the wheel, gambling on other channels, possible outcomes. There's a good chance all the other stations are just as boring, so there's no point in trying, he reasons. The speakers echo, flanking Dennis with humming surfaces, bass chords and simple, energetic drumbeats, and he can't tell if the octave illusion, the instrumental alternating between his ears, is part of the song or he's just tripping balls.

"Yeah, he's coming home late, and he's bringing me a surprise," the autotuned voice recites over the indie techno tune.

It's doable though, even with all this sound; he thinks he can find his way, navigating through the relentless ocean, absorbing tumbling waves; it's just going to take some extra focus, a clearer mind to get to school, mental endurance. He can't remember what just happened or if the song is playing for the first or fiftieth time, but he's thinking it doesn't matter what's happened in the past; maybe right now is the only thing that matters as he grips the steering wheel, putting his hands at ten and two. Limbs adhered to cold leather, his torso, a mesh polyester seat as he presses his foot to the lightweight pedal: acceleration, movement against oncoming currents, absorbing energized tempests, a connection to his surroundings, a familiar street. It's a force that drives, operated by subconscious behavior, automaticity, turning down streets and flipping his blinker on, the quick clicking echo reminding him of a Nickelodeon show and to check his blind spots; it's a video game, like Mario Kart, it's fun, but crashing has major consequences.

He's making decisions, he has to, choosing streets and directions, guiding him to an ultimate terminus. It's been a series of these choices, over 12,000 days of selecting actually, that led him to the driver seat of his car a month before the end of school, dormant synapses firing as he hallucinates: fast memories of a peculiar drive to the parking lot, swirls of vibrant scenery captivating his altered state, interludes of time. But he's arrived at his destination as a pharmacologist savant, agnostic, his mind feeling at ease, even as he thinks about all the relationships and friendships he's lost over the span of his life.

Dennis collects himself in the driver's seat, moving the gear like a joystick from D to P, accessing the visor mirror to witness his dilated pupils and fuzzy face, a stoic expression. He's not a monster; no, not even a little bit, even if his face looks like a bunch of macaroni put together in a kindergarten class. There's something about the breeze, yeah, it's familiar, brushing through the open windows as he wiggles a hand outside, parked.

Or maybe it's the chirping, the tweeting of the vibrant robins perched on the roof of the cafeteria, not digital tweets either, real nature, sitting on the drain; he's got a great view too, and he's pretty sure there's some significant kinesis being communicated to him from the universe with the presence of the cheerful birds. There's probably some special meaning behind their attendance, but he can't think of the symbolism; the semiotics are fleeting. He should probably look it up, check his phone.

The possessive device pulls at his fingertips, a magnetism from the center console, an internal itching, a burning desire, like maybe something important is waiting for him, a follow request or someone liked an old photo of his. It's a heavy energy, a strong negativity that radiates from the square polycarbonate gadget, ever since James stopped answering his texts weeks ago. Maybe it's better if he doesn't indulge in the compulsions, the escape; he doesn't need the dopamine right now.

Scintillas of sage suffuse the air, an airy scent from the fresh environment, a botanical breeze that triggers a warm, settling memory of his grandmother; her room always smelled like pleasant herbs. The tingling of sunlight skimming his forearms delights his senses as he walks to the building, a promenade in the beautiful weather. Venturing off the pavement to the grass, he opts for the soft pile with incredible give instead of the hard, unforgiving terrain; its dewy fragrance, the earthy aroma of freshly cut grass pervades as he springs along.

It's the same scent he smelled while having sex with his eleventh-grade girlfriend on the football field late one summer night, the first girl he honestly thought he was in love with. And he thinks about the irony of the aroma, how it's such a relaxing redolence, one that pacifies his angst, even though it's a distress call from the grass, released in desperation after it's been sliced, trying to save itself.

He's careful though, not to make quick movements as he travels, watching for snakes in the grass, and he doesn't want to disturb the birds, they're stunning, a real pleasure to stare at. He passes with a smile, cognizant of the cracking pavement that runs alongside him, like a Tyrannosaurus rex is approaching, big thunderous footsteps, catastrophic damage on the horizon.

But it's the birds, really, the cute, majestic little creatures twittering, waving their wings in the magnificent sunlit morning, that make him forget the hurt, the natural splendor that surrounds him. And it's not that familiar breeze anymore, that mild wind that brushed against their backs on the rooftop bar that summer from almost a decade ago. No, it's a new zephyr, one that Renee can't take from him, a warm gust for this particular moment, connected with his environment, the ethereal elements of nature; a synergy of thought and feeling, an occupation of the now, without consideration of the past or future, it's a stillness of the mind, an elucidation, a reminder that he can't keep waiting until he's happy to start enjoying being alive.

"Come on, Dennis, you're a real trooper!" The smallest one coos, his breast a solid white hue of feathers.

"Don't you just love the scenery?" Dennis asks, smiling as he pulls the door handle with a giggle, waving at the creatures with a zealous hand.

"Poo-tee-weet! You wouldn't believe the view from up here," the taller bird replies, a deep raspy voice, a reincarnated chain smoker; its cartoonish wings folded like miniature elbows.

He's got his phone out, scrolling through his Instagram feed, but he doesn't think it matters because he doesn't recall opening the app or removing his phone from his pocket as he strolls down the hallway; it's out of his control. It's strange, his legs, long oversized appendages fused to his torso for transportation purposes, but everything has its purpose; he's thinking he's got everything he needs. Megan has sent him eight direct messages, his corner icon is highlighted red, talking about something involving jealousy, caution, and sex; the words make him uncomfortable, his chest tight, like paranoia is looming, so he looks away, watching the motion of his feet lead, supportive attachments for movement and stability.

A Tinker Bell chime sounds, a real magical noise; it's an email from some scammer with a strange address, or maybe it's a publisher, but "Fiction submission" could pertain to a variety of subject matters, Dennis thinks, since everyone is fake. Especially if there's no true objectivity, since bias serves as a major influence for everything perceived, rendering life truly fictional, just a simulated existence of stimuli created by 7.9 billion users behind smartphones.

It's an acceptance letter, he's 66.6% sure; it says his name, personalization, which most of his emails do with automation, but it says, "'Swimming' has been accepted for print this fall in the Paris Review."

And that's exhilarating, imagining standing at the edge, looking out from the top of the Eiffel Tower, the awareness of gravity's severity at such an alarming height but also his publication. He's going to be an author, officially published by the top magazine in the world. He's not going to France though, but he's feeling romantic, so he might visit Michael Fairchild to share the great news, maybe tongue kiss him too, but in a purely platonic, published author way, since his classroom is on the way. He doesn't have the munchkin donuts from Dunkin' or a reasonable explanation for his alarming interaction with Megan, let alone a hanging vocabulary to construct a sentence, so he prances past with a springy stride, an untethered disposition with no time for negativity.

He's over chasing notifications because everything is all right; it all makes sense now, how he needed Renee to destroy him so he could write with authentic pain, the inspiration for his short story; how he needed Christine to realize he was capable of loving and Megan to know he still had a conscience. And it's a coltish urge that compels Dennis to hop and skip down the corridor, imagining himself as a pirate, hoisting his phone like a sword in the air, just like he did when he was a kid. The publication wants a biography to include with his story, so now he's got to think about how to define himself, how to sum up his existence. He's lived most of his life in his mind, gathering thoughts and ruminating, revisiting moments and memorable instances, playing reruns of reels, a free streaming subscription. But that's probably not acceptable for a biography, so he'll have to come back to it, unsure of how his life should be depicted.

Opening the door to his classroom, Dennis pirouettes inside, an absurd ballerina.

"This one is mine," he announces in motion; his tie whirling with his rotation, sporting the same attire from last night's date with Christine.

Skirting down the row of desks, Dennis pries open the back awning windows of the classroom with a goofy grin, forcing the glass outwards, allowing the intoxicating air to enter. Summer is on the brink, just hiding on the other side, and he can't stop the seasons, he can't prevent change, and he's starting to think that's okay. The air is light, balmy, invigorating as it fills his airways.

Darting back to the front of the room, building momentum with his sprint, Dennis jumps into his chair, a superhero plunge with arms raised like wings. The chair scampers into the wall, thudding against the bulletin board as Dennis holds onto the armrests, laughing uncontrollably. He pushes the chair back out into the center of the classroom with his feet, spinning as he propels. Letting his legs dangle as he twirls, a Himalaya ride with distorted vision; he witnesses a gorgeous sight of golden beams peering through the open classroom windows, cascading from the open blinds to the vinyl floor, the same gilded rays from his childhood. He's having a great time as he plays, he really is, and it's not the mushrooms, no, it's not even the short story acceptance. It's his mind, the introspection, like maybe it's time to forgive himself for everything he's done wrong; it's been long enough. Maybe it's time to live; maybe it's time to finally let go.

The seat creaks as he moves, his whirl comes to a wheezing stop, so Dennis winds up and gives his chair another spin with an animated smile, a roulette whirl, a merry-go-round of memories play as his sight blurs, fading to a carousel of captured images; the faint barks of Cooper from outside echo along with the piano chords of Gymnopedie, a soft instrumental. The collage flips in his mind, brief glimpses into special occurrences in his life until his swivel slows again, coming to a stop as he realizes there's a visitor.

There's a silhouette of the devil standing in the doorway, the frozen familiar face of a youth. Jonathan, with a quick hand draw, raises a glistening barrel, fingers wrapped around the trigger. With a dead stare, he fires two shots, the sky thundering with gunpowder and deafening rounds. The air quakes with force as the slugs slam into Dennis's chest, sending him across the room on the rolling chair.

The impact bludgeons his senses, clouding his vision and rattling his ears as he sinks into the seat, sliding down the back support, his chest cavity throbbing as the chair crashes into the wall. With the ringing of impact, tinnitus stupefying his perception, Dennis clutches his chest; the taste of cold copper leaks into his mouth; the smell of burning sulfur infiltrates his nose. Dennis gasps, careful not to breathe too deeply for fear that he only has a few respirations left; his body tingles with nervous vigor, a weightiness ensues as he assesses the situation. Jonathan drops the pistol and dashes in his pumped-up kicks, a dress code violation and perpetuation of the white student school shooter stereotype, a contribution to the statistics.

The siren sounds, the alert of the fire alarm ringing, blinding caution lights flashing throughout the room and hall. He can't decide what's happened; he can't find the details to create an accurate description, but maybe it's okay to not always have the right words; maybe it's okay to not have control of it all. He's not sure if the wounds are fatal or not, but he thinks of his parents, possibly predeceased by their son, his short story published posthumously. And maybe he wasn't even really depressed, and that terrible sadness inside of him wasn't personal, no, it was just part of being human. Perhaps it's just how life goes on, whether you participate or not, even without closure; maybe it was balanced, but he was too shaky to realize. Maybe he needed to be comfortable living between the negative and the positive, an appreciation for both the light and darkness, because the stars can't be seen without the nighttime.

The siren squeals, piercing his inner ears as he hunches over, a chaotic scene, but he's tranquil, optimistic, reveling in the traveling sun rays sprawled on the floor. The anxiety subdues, and he's no longer fret with worry. No, he's relaxed, comfortably numb as the red ruddles his buttoned-down shirt, like maybe it's a dream after all, and he's nestled in his bed, covered in a cozy comforter. Yeah, that's it; tomorrow he'll wake up in his childhood bed, burrowed in colorblock linens. He's never felt better than right now, actually; he's not concerned about the blood stains or wiping down a countertop in his kitchen, vacuuming area rugs, checking his story for views or his profile for likes. It kinda feels like he's a kid again, being carried inside by his dad after falling asleep on the car ride home.

His thoughts slow for once; he's finally out of his head. And he's not even troubled by the damage that's broken his body, the cracked concrete, because now the light can get in, or so it goes. The water is warm, really, the depths welcoming, and nothing hurts anymore; he's swimming, fading in the glorious sunshine, grateful for having loved and lost.